Quantum Nonlinear Function Obfuscation Theory and Application

Tao Shang

Quantum Nonlinear Function Obfuscation Theory and Application

Springer

Tao Shang
School of Cyber Science and Technology
Beihang University
Beijing, China

ISBN 978-981-97-6721-2   ISBN 978-981-97-6722-9 (eBook)
https://doi.org/10.1007/978-981-97-6722-9

This Springer imprint is published by the registered company Springer Nature Singapore Pte Ltd.
The registered company address is: 152 Beach Road, #21-01/04 Gateway East, Singapore 189721, Singapore

Preface

In 2017, the author Tao Shang attended the 7th International Conference on Quantum Cryptography at the University of Cambridge, and first learned about quantum obfuscation from the conference reports. In fact, the concept of quantum obfuscation was first proposed in 2005 and has been always a hot topic of quantum cryptography field till now. At that time, the author became interested in quantum obfuscation and attracted by the great charm of quantum obfuscation. That is to say, functional encryption can be implemented by quantum approach instead of classical approach and greatly enhance the security of quantum computation, which will become a kind of overturning technology for quantum computation. Thus the author began to dedicate more efforts to quantum obfuscation from principle to application.

As far as I know, quantum obfuscation was first raised by Aaronson in the "Ten Semi-Grand Challenges for Quantum Computing Theory". Till 2016, Alagic and Fefferman wrote the paper "On Quantum Obfuscation". There were few achievements and only several schemes were proposed. However, it aroused the author's immense interest, he attempted to combine quantum mechanics theory with cryptography. From the viewpoint of quantum obfuscation, the author focused on nonlinear function obfuscation and designed a series of quantum obfuscation schemes by means of combining quantum obfuscation into quantum computation. During the process of research, many students showed great enthusiasm in quantum obfuscation and provided many valuable achievements.

Although many schemes have been proposed till now, theoretical knowledge on quantum obfuscation such as classification, security analysis and future direction is still not clear.

Since quantum obfuscation was proposed for quantum computation, the advent of quantum obfuscation gave a new dimension to the use of quantum cryptography. The advent in the last few years of this technology has given an added dimension to the classical obfuscation.

Persistent objective is to effectively combine cryptography into computation, or quantum communication, even if quantum communication is thought to be unconditionally secure in the case of two-party communication. The author believes that quantum obfuscation can facilitate the design of quantum cryptographic protocols.

The author expects the readers of this book to first learn about quantum obfuscation, its principle, classification, development and main problems. The author expects them to design quantum obfuscation schemes and finally develop the theory of quantum obfuscation.

What is the range of topics, innovative technologies for designing a quantum obfuscation scheme? This book will help readers understand these with ease. What is an effective design for quantum obfuscation? Exemplary schemes are shown such as quantum symmetric encryption, quantum asymmetric encryption, quantum homomorphic encryption, quantum one-way function, quantum access control, and quantum zero-knowledge proof.

The organization of the chapters is described as follows:

Chapter 1 gives a detailed introduction to quantum obfuscation. It emphasizes the basic concept of quantum obfuscation and introduce the development of quantum obfuscation.

Chapter 2 explains the preliminaries of quantum obfuscation, including main notions and key operations. Classification is provided for the existing schemes of quantum obfuscation. Also, main directions are discussed for the research.

Chapter 3 describes the paradigm schemes of quantum point obfuscation. To analyze the obfuscatability of quantum point functions, we introduce the strict definition of a quantum point function and discuss its variants of multiple points and multiple qubits.

Chapter 4 concentrates on quantum power obfuscation. To analyze the obfuscatability of quantum power functions, we introduce the strict definition of a quantum power function. Furthermore, we discuss the generalization of quantum power obfuscation.

Chapter 5 explains quantum symmetric encryption. We introduce a quantum symmetric encryption scheme by means of quantum obfuscator. We start with the basic requirement of indistinguishability security and point out that a quantum virtual black-box obfuscator satisfies this requirement unconditionally.

Chapter 6 explains quantum asymmetric encryption. We construct a quantum asymmetric encryption scheme based on quantum obfuscation. We combine the advantage of quantum obfuscation with asymmetric encryption to achieve indistinguishability security.

Chapter 7 is for quantum homomorphic encryption. Homomorphic encryption enables computation on encrypted data while maintaining secrecy. We construct the quantum homomorphic encryption scheme with quantum obfuscation, including quantum point obfuscation and quantum power obfuscation.

Chapter 8 covers quantum one-way function. We focus on the design of a full quantum one-way function which is 'quantum-to-quantum' and the application of the full quantum one-way function to quantum cryptography.

Chapter 9 describes quantum access control. We define the quantum access control problem using quantum point function and an abstract model of the graph-based access control problem. The obfuscatability of the quantum access control problem is demonstrated.

Chapter 10 describes quantum zero-knowledge proof. We discuss the application of quantum obfuscation in quantum zero-knowledge proof. As a start of study on quantum nonlinear function obfuscation, such work will be very useful in the future development of quantum obfuscation theory.

Beijing, China Tao Shang

Acknowledgements

The author Tao Shang is grateful to his advisor, Prof. ShuoYu Wang at the Kochi University of Technology in Japan, an eminent scientist and educationist. From this teacher, he learned about the great role of self-learning and interest arousing for understanding emerging technologies, and he developed passion and patience for knowledge acquirement.

The author Tao Shang is grateful to Prof. JianWei Liu at the Beihang University, a distinguished scientist in the field of network security and cryptography. Professor Liu guided him into the field of cryptography, gave him an opportunity to set up from scratch the quantum cryptography group, and supported on the writing of this book. The research group members include RanYiLiu Chen (2017–2020) at the Beihang University, Yao Tang (2019–2024) at the Beihang University, YuanJing Zhang and YaZhuo Jiang (2020–2024) at the Beihang University, ChuYue Pan (2020–2023) at the Beihang University, ChenYi Zhang and Kun Zhang (2022–2024) at the Beihang University, PengLin Hou and ShuoLin Wang (2021–2024) at the Beihang University, YuChen Liu and KeYu Xiong (2023–2024) at the Beihang University. All members proofreaded the manuscript, particularly Yao Tang, YuanJing Zhang, YaZhuo Jiang and YuChen Liu provided many services for the editing of the book, such as checking and minutely tracing the errors in the book.

The author Tao Shang is especially thankful to Prof. XiuBo Chen at the Beijing University of Posts and Telecommunications and Prof. Gang Xu at the North China University of Technology for the cooperation of quantum cryptography and Prof. QianHong Wu, Jian Mao, and ZhenYu Guan at the Beihang University for the support during this process.

Blessings of Prof. Cong Wang at the school of Integrated Circuit Science and Engineering of Beihang University, and his continuous support in theory and experiment are also unforgettable.

The book is supported by the National Natural Science Foundation of China (No. 61971021, No. 62471020 and No. 61571024), the Key Research and Development Program of Hebei Province (No. 22340701D), the Chinese Universities Industry-Education-Research Innovation Foundation of BII Education Grant

Program (No. 2021BCA0200), and the 2023 Monograph Construction Project of Beihang University.

Finally, the author Tao Shang is grateful to his understanding spouse, two lovely daughters and his kind parents.

Contents

1 Introduction 1
1.1 Classical Obfuscation 1
1.2 Quantum Computation 3
1.2.1 Quantum Circuit 3
1.2.2 Quantum Algorithm 4
1.3 Quantum Cryptography 5
1.3.1 Challenge to Classical Cryptography 5
1.3.2 Development of Quantum Cryptography 5
1.4 Quantum Obfuscation 6
1.4.1 Development of Quantum Obfuscation 6
1.4.2 Reduction for Quantum Obfuscation 8
1.4.3 Obfuscation of Combined Quantum Circuits 10
1.5 Summary 12
References 12

2 Preliminary 15
2.1 Quantum Information 15
2.1.1 Quantum Operator 15
2.1.2 Quantum Measurement 16
2.1.3 Quantum Teleportation 18
2.2 Security Analysis Methods Based on Random Oracle Model 19
2.2.1 Quantum-Accessible Random Oracle Model 19
2.2.2 Quantum Random Oracle Model 20
2.3 Definition of Quantum Obfuscation 21
2.4 Quantum Obfuscation for Quantum Nonlinear Functions 23
2.4.1 Quantum Point Obfuscation 23
2.4.2 Quantum Power Obfuscation 24
2.4.3 Construction of Quantum Obfuscation 24
2.4.4 Universality of Quantum Obfuscation 26

2.4.5 Application to Quantum Nonlinear Function ... 27
2.5 Summary ... 29
References ... 29

3 Quantum Point Obfuscation ... 31
3.1 Quantum Point Function ... 31
3.1.1 Quantum Point Function Family and Its Obfuscatability ... 31
3.1.2 Quantum Point Function with Multi-Qubit Output ... 33
3.1.3 Quantum Multi-point Function with Multi-qubit Output ... 34
3.2 Quantum Obfuscation for Quantum Point Function ... 35
3.3 Multi-valued Quantum Point Obfuscation ... 36
3.3.1 Multi-valued Quantum Random Oracle Model ... 36
3.3.2 Property of Multi-valued Quantum States ... 38
3.3.3 Multi-valued Quantum Single-Point Function ... 39
3.3.4 Multi-valued Quantum Multi-point Function ... 39
3.4 Instantiation of Quantum Point Obfuscation ... 40
3.4.1 Requirement of Instantiation ... 40
3.4.2 Instantiation Procedure: From Classic to Quantum ... 41
3.4.3 Definition of Instantiation of Quantum Point Obfuscation ... 43
3.4.4 Instantiation Scheme of Quantum Point Obfuscation ... 44
3.5 Summary ... 47
References ... 48

4 Quantum Power Obfuscation ... 51
4.1 Quantum Power Function ... 51
4.2 Quantum Obfuscation for Quantum Power Function ... 52
4.2.1 Construction of Obfuscator and Interpreter ... 52
4.2.2 Quantum Power Obfuscation Scheme ... 54
4.2.3 Obfuscatability of Quantum Nonlinear Function ... 55
4.3 Generalized Quantum Power Functions with Coefficients ... 56
4.3.1 Quantum Power Function with a Leading Coefficient ... 56
4.3.2 Quantum n-th Power Function ... 57
4.4 Quantum Obfuscation for Generalized Quantum Power Functions ... 59
4.4.1 Quantum Obfuscation Scheme for Quantum Power Function with a Leading Coefficient ... 59
4.4.2 Quantum Obfuscation Scheme for Quantum n-th Power Functions ... 63
4.4.3 Complex Factors to Quantum Power Obfuscation ... 66
4.5 Summary ... 67
References ... 68

5 Quantum Symmetric Encryption 69
5.1 Quantum Symmetric Encryption Based on Quantum Point Obfuscation 69
5.1.1 Indistinguishability for Quantum Encryption 69
5.1.2 Efficient Quantum Circuit and Quantum Computation 70
5.1.3 Quantum One-Time Pad 70
5.1.4 Security of Quantum Symmetric Encryption 71
5.1.5 Quantum Point Obfuscation and Combinability 73
5.1.6 IND-Secure Quantum Symmetric Encryption Scheme 74
5.1.7 Security Analysis 77
5.2 Quantum Symmetric Encryption with Quantum Point Obfuscation instantiated 79
5.2.1 Quantum Symmetric Encryption Scheme with Quantum Error-Correcting Code 79
5.2.2 Security Analysis 81
5.2.3 Simulation Analysis 83
5.3 Summary 83
References 84

6 Quantum Asymmetric Encryption 87
6.1 Quantum Asymmetric Encryption Based on Quantum Point Obfuscation 87
6.1.1 Requirement of Asymmetric Encryption 87
6.1.2 Indistinguishability Obfuscation and Single-Qubit Rotation 88
6.1.3 IND-Secure Quantum Asymmetric Encryption Scheme 89
6.1.4 Security Analysis 91
6.2 Quantum Asymmetric Encryption Based on Quantum Power Obfuscation 93
6.2.1 IND-Secure Quantum Asymmetric Encryption Scheme 93
6.2.2 Security Analysis 95
6.2.3 Simulation Analysis 97
6.3 Summary 98
References 99

7 Quantum Homomorphic Encryption 101
7.1 Quantum Homomorphic Encryption Based on Quantum Point Obfuscation 101
7.1.1 Requirement of Homomorphic Encryption 101
7.1.2 Basic QHE Scheme 103
7.1.3 QHE Scheme Based on Quantum Point Obfuscation 105

7.1.4 Security Analysis 108
7.1.5 Scheme Comparison 109
7.2 Quantum Fully Homomorphic Encryption Based on Multi-valued Quantum Point Obfuscation 110
7.2.1 Requirement of Fully Homomorphic Encryption 110
7.2.2 Multi-valued Quantum State 111
7.2.3 Quantum-Hash Random Oracle Model 113
7.2.4 Multi-valued Quantum Point Obfuscation 113
7.2.5 Quantum Fully Homomorphic Encryption Scheme 117
7.2.6 Security Analysis 124
7.2.7 Scheme Comparison 129
7.3 Quantum Homomorphic Encryption Based on Quantum Power Obfuscation 129
7.3.1 Requirement of Quantum Nonlinear Obfuscation 129
7.3.2 Construction of Quantum Power Obfuscation 130
7.3.3 QHE Scheme Based on Quantum Power Obfuscation 131
7.3.4 Security Analysis 134
7.4 Non-interactive Quantum Homomorphic Encryption Based on Rotation Operator 135
7.4.1 Requirement of Non-interactive Homomorphic Encryption 135
7.4.2 Quantum One-Time Pad 136
7.4.3 QHE Scheme for Clifford Circuit 136
7.4.4 Symmetric QHE Scheme Based on Rotation Operator 137
7.4.5 Non-interactive QHE Scheme Based on Rotation Operator 138
7.4.6 Security Analysis 142
7.5 Two-Round Quantum Homomorphic Encryption Based on Matrix Decomposition 143
7.5.1 Limitation of Decryption Efficiency 143
7.5.2 Quantum Computation and Circuit Synthesis 144
7.5.3 Key Update for T Gate Based on Matrix Decomposition 145
7.5.4 QHE Scheme Based on Matrix Decomposition 146
7.5.5 Security Analysis 149
7.5.6 Scheme Comparison 149
7.5.7 Application to Ciphertext Retrieval 150
7.6 Summary 155
References 155

8 Quantum One-Way Function 159
8.1 Full Quantum One-Way Function 159
8.1.1 Development of One-Way Function 159
8.1.2 Classical One-Way Function 161
8.1.3 Quantum One-Way Function 161
8.1.4 Identity Authentication 163
8.1.5 Full Quantum One-Way Function 164
8.1.6 One-Wayness 164
8.1.7 Application to Quantum Identity Authentication 165
8.2 Full Quantum One-Way Function Based on Quantum Point Obfuscation 172
8.2.1 Requirement of Universal Construction 172
8.2.2 Challenges in Quantum One-Way Function 173
8.2.3 Quantum Black-Box Obfuscation 174
8.2.4 Quantum Point Obfuscation 174
8.2.5 Obfuscation-Based Full Quantum One-Way Function 176
8.2.6 Application to Quantum Message Authentication 181
8.3 Dynamic Full Quantum One-Way Function Based on Quantum Circuit Mapping 183
8.3.1 Requirement of Dynamic Mapping 183
8.3.2 Quantum One-Way Function 184
8.3.3 Quantum Circuit Optimization 185
8.3.4 Quantum Money 186
8.3.5 Dynamic Full Quantum One-Way Function 187
8.3.6 Scheme Analysis 192
8.3.7 Full Quantum Trapdoor One-Way Function 195
8.3.8 Simulation Anlysis 196
8.3.9 Application to Quantum Currency Notes 200
8.4 Full Quantum One-Way Function Based on Quantum Hypergraph State 201
8.4.1 Advantage of Multipartite Entanglement 201
8.4.2 Quantum Hypergraph States 202
8.4.3 Full Quantum One-Way Function 203
8.4.4 Aggregate Signature 204
8.4.5 Hypergraph-Based Full Quantum One-Way Function 204
8.4.6 One-Wayness 207
8.4.7 Application to Quantum Aggregate Signature 208
8.5 Quantum Hash Function Based on Quantum Walks 211
8.5.1 From One-Way Function to Hash Function 211
8.5.2 Cryptographic Hash Function 212
8.5.3 Lively Quantum Walk on an N-Length Cycle 213
8.5.4 Periodic Quantum Walk on a Cycle 214

8.5.5 Quantum Hash Function Based on Controlled Alternate Lively Quantum Walks ... 216
8.5.6 Security Analysis ... 217
8.5.7 Performance Analysis ... 219
8.5.8 Computing Complexity ... 224
8.5.9 Advantage ... 227
8.6 Summary ... 229
References ... 230

9 Quantum Access Control ... 235
9.1 Access Control Problem ... 235
9.2 Quantum Obfuscation ... 236
9.3 Access Control Based on Graphs ... 237
9.4 Definition of Quantum Access Control Problem ... 238
9.5 Obfuscability of Quantum Point Function and Quantum Multi-qubit Point Function ... 239
9.6 Obfuscability of Auxiliary Problem for Quantum Access Control Problem ... 240
9.7 Obfuscability of Quantum Access Control Problem ... 241
9.8 Future Direction ... 242
9.9 Summary ... 243
References ... 243

10 Quantum Zero-Knowledge Proof ... 245
10.1 Zero-Knowledge Proof ... 245
10.2 Quantum Cryptographic Protocols Based on Zero-Knowledge Proof ... 247
10.2.1 Zero-Knowledge Proof Protocol Based on Quantum Teleportation ... 248
10.2.2 Non-interactive Zero-Knowledge Proof Protocol on Quantum State ... 248
10.2.3 Quantum Oblivious Transfer Protocol ... 249
10.3 Quantum Point Obfuscation ... 250
10.4 Quantum Zero-Knowledge Proof Based on Quantum Point Obfuscation ... 252
10.5 Summary ... 254
References ... 254

Index ... 257

Chapter 1
Introduction

Obfuscation is the concept of functionality encryption conceived from the concept of data encryption. As a derivative of classical obfuscation theory, quantum obfuscation theory combines classical obfuscation and quantum computation and is a powerful tool for information protection of quantum circuits in the quantum environment, and has been emphasized and developed rapidly in recent years. Quantum obfuscation can hide the information of quantum circuits without changing their functions, thus realizing function preservation, effectively resisting reverse engineering attacks, and solving the problems of secure outsourced computation and copyright protection in the quantum environment. In this chapter, we summarize the main research results of classical obfuscation and quantum obfuscation in recent years. Firstly, we briefly introduce the concept of obfuscation. Then we introduce the development of quantum computation, quantum cryptography and quantum obfuscation.

1.1 Classical Obfuscation

Promoted by the vigorous development of computer science, cryptology became a new discipline in the 1970s. The study of cryptography has made remarkable achievements over the past few decades, especially in secure protocols and encryption methods based on complexity theory. However, there are still some problems left unsolved. As a powerful means to protect information, obfuscation can obstruct malicious analysis effectively.

In software development, obfuscation is the deliberate act of creating obfuscated code, i.e., source or machine code that is difficult for humans to understand. Like obfuscation in natural language, it may use needlessly roundabout expressions to compose statements. As a concept in cryptography, obfuscation refers to the transformation of a Turing machine or circuit into a form that is functionally equivalent

T. Shang, *Quantum Nonlinear Function Obfuscation Theory and Application*,
https://doi.org/10.1007/978-981-97-6722-9_1

but difficult to read and comprehend. Obfuscation is derived from code obfuscation, which prevents users from decompiling programmes to obtain logic in order to safeguard intellectual property rights.

The first formal definition of program obfuscation was proposed by Hada [1], which we call a strong virtual black-box obfuscation. Hada's definition is modeled on a simulation paradigm and requires an attacker to learn information from the obfuscated code which can be learned by simply accessing the function with a black-box oracle. In 2001, Barak et al. [2] first introduced the concept of obfuscation into the field of cryptography and proposed its three features as follows:

1. (Functionality) The obfuscated program has the same computational function as the original one.
2. (Polynomial slowdown) The running time of the obfuscated program cannot exceed the polynomial-size of the original running time.
3. (Black-box property) Any valid message computed through the obfuscated program can be effectively computed with access to the oracle of the original program. This is a guarantee of security of the obfuscator program, which is based on the security of simulation.

They also pointed out that obfuscators have cryptographic applications such as constructing homomorphic encryption and replacing random oracles and that general virtual black-box obfuscators do not exist. Consequently, research on obfuscation is divided into two categories. One is not to target all circuits or functions but to construct an obfuscation scheme for a subset of functions and study its obfuscation; the other is to weaken the definition of virtual black-box and analyze the feasibility of weak obfuscation, such as virtual grey-box obfuscation.

In the next few years, some positive results of obfuscation were proposed. Lynn et al. [3] discussed point functions and the simple obfuscation of combined point functions, and gave the first positive result of obfuscation theory by means of access control problem based on regular expression. After that, point functions become one of focus problems of obfuscation theory. In 2005, Goldwasser and Kalai [4] denied the idea that functions with specific conditions and even auxiliary inputs can be obfuscated, and they also demonstrated that point function obfuscation can occur. In the same year, Wee [5] made a more detailed study on the obfuscation of point functions and drew some important conclusions. He proved that we can construct a valid obfuscator for point functions by weakening the concept of obfuscation, although an obfuscator has certain constrains. For example, a simulated adversary must output a single bit. For such constrains, Canetti et al. [6] proposed indistinguishable security for the multi-qubit output quantum point function, constrcuted an obfuscator for multi-bit output point functions, and discussed the possibility of its application in symmetric encryption [7]. In 2007, Goldwasser and Rothblum [8] proposed the concept of the best possible obfuscation and relaxed the obfuscation condition of the virtual black-box so that it leaks as little information as comparable programmes. In 2010, in connection with obfuscation of combined point functions, Bitansky et al. [9] presented a concept of virtual grey-box obfuscation, which is weaker than a virtual black-box obfuscator. and demonstrated that under certain strengthening conditions, virtual grey-box obfuscation is effective in achieving point obfuscation. The virtual grey-box obfuscation permits the simulator to query the oracle in multiple polynomial ranges in infinite computing time. In 2014, Boyle et al. [10] proposed extractable obfuscation for the first time, which is essentially equivalent to functional witness encryption, and described its cryptographic applications. In 2016, Zhang [11] proposed the construction of bilinear maps and multilinear maps, as well as their relationship, and described the cryptographic application of multilinear maps in the construction of indistinguishable obfuscation. In 2022, Hu et al. [12] provided efficiency analysis and simplified scheme of reusable garbling. Their convoluted scheme simplifies the underlying fully homomorphic encryption components from variable to fixed keys, which has significant applications in obfuscation. Also, some researches suggest that there is a certain connection between obfuscation theory and zero-knowledge proof [1].

1.2 Quantum Computation

Quantum supremacy means that a powerful quantum computer can accomplish a nearly impossible task for a classical computer at some point in the future. In quantum computation, such function can be regarded as a quantum algorithm which is usually described by quantum circuit. Quantum circuits consist of a series of quantum gates that directly interact with quantum states without destroying them.

1.2.1 Quantum Circuit

Similar to classical ones, quantum circuits consist of quantum gates, which are described by the individual behavior of state of microscopic particles, and evolve from one state to another. The unitarity is the only limitation of a quantum logic gate and each unitary matrix defines an effective quantum gate. Deutsch et al. [13] proved that we can construct a reversible quantum gate sequence for classical computable functions. Any classical function f that has m-bit inputs and k-bit outputs can be implemented on a quantum computer. Assuming that there is a quantum gate sequence U_f of $m + k$ qubits, the function f is implemented as $U_f : |x, y\rangle \mapsto |x, y \oplus f(x)\rangle$. The quantum gate sequence U_f represented above is unitary for any function f. To calculate $f(x)$, we can apply U_f to the state $|x, 0\rangle$. $f(x) \oplus f(x) = 0$, so $U_f U_f = I$.

We can combine quantum circuits together to construct a new quantum circuit. In this case, a control register is needed to decide which circuit is to be used. Formally, a combined quantum circuit denoted by

$$C_1\#C_2\#\ldots\#C_t$$

has a control register of most $\lceil \log t \rceil$ qubits and an input register of n qubits. Of course, to meet the request of unitarity, all component circuits have to be of the same input size of n.

Quantum polynomial time (QPT) algorithm A is a uniform set of quantum circuits. It can also include operations of measurement and tracing-out any qubit. Thus the input and output size can be verified according to the definition of QPT [14].

In the noisy intermediate-scale quantum (NISQ) era [15], there is a gap between physical devices and logical quantum circuits [16]. Because the coupling relationship between logical qubits might not exist in physical qubits, several gates of quantum circuits cannot be directly performed on real quantum systems. Quantum circuits need to be optimized to make the remapped quantum circuit meet the constraints of physical devices. Quantum circuit optimization maps a logical quantum circuit to another different quantum circuit which satisfies the coupling relationship between physical qubits. Recently, quantum circuit optimization employs the exact methods [17, 18] and the heuristic search algorithms to implement quantum circuit mapping. The heuristic search algorithms insert Bridge gate [19] or SWAP gate [16] into the original quantum circuit. These heuristic search algorithms can accelerate the execution of some quantum circuit tasks on IBM's physical quantum platform. Thus we can use quantum circuit optimization to construct a quantum function in which the average-case complexity of the inverting task is out of polynomial time.

1.2.2 Quantum Algorithm

With the continuous development of quantum computation technology, its threat to traditional cryptography has become increasingly apparent. It is foreseeable that the emergence of large-scale quantum computer and quantum algorithms will significantly impact traditional cryptography. Among them, Shor's algorithm [20] and Grover's algorithm [21] are the most representative. By applying Shor's algorithm, quantum adversaries can break any public key cryptography based on large integer factorization or discrete logarithm problems, which has been widely deployed at the present stage. Grover's algorithm provides quadratic speed-up for any exhaustive unstructured scheme. It reduces the brute-force cost of an n-bit key from 2^n to $2^{n/2}$, which makes the traditional encryption methods have to double the key length to achieve the same security as before. In addition to Shor's algorithm and Grover's algorithm, Simon's algorithm [22], Bernstein-Vazirani's algorithm [23], and other quantum algorithms also show solid quantum advantages. Every advance in quantum computation will affect the traditional security system. In 2016, the national institute of standards and technology (NIST) issued a notice to collect, evaluate and standardize public key cryptographic algorithms resistant to quantum attacks, marking the arrival of the post-quantum cryptography era. As NIST notes, it takes a long process for researchers to create new cryptographic schemes. While large-scale quantum computers have not yet been widely deployed, it is important to start moving towards quantum-resistant cryptography before then.

1.3 Quantum Cryptography

Quantum cryptography is a new type of cryptography, which is based on cryptography and quantum mechanics and uses quantum physical methods to realize the idea of cryptography. It is consistent with the goal of classical cryptography, which protects communication systems from being attacked illegally from inside or outside.

1.3.1 Challenge to Classical Cryptography

With the rapid development of quantum computation, the classical cryptographic system is facing severe security challenges. For example, the public-key cryptography represented by RSA algorithm based on the hard mathematical problem of large integer factorization and the symmetric cryptography represented by AES algorithm are under a great security threat. Shor's algorithm [20] can utilize the parallelism of quantum computation to efficiently factorize large integers. By transforming the RSA algorithm into the combinatorial optimization problem [24], Peng et al. [25] completed a 20-bit integer factorization based on the quantum annealing algorithm in the D-Wave quantum computer. By accelerating the key exhaustive attack, the Grover's algorithm [21] and the variational algorithm [26] can effectively attack the AES algorithm. So far, the scale of quantum circuits for attacking AES has been continuously optimized [27]. Kaplan et al. [28] also pointed out that the quantum cycle discovery algorithm Simon [22] can reduce the attack complexity of many classical symmetric cryptographic algorithms from the exponential level to the polynomial level. In 2023, Regev [29] showed that n-bit integers can be factorized by independently running a quantum circuit with $O(n^{\frac{3}{2}})$ gates for $\sqrt{n}+4$ times and then using polynomial-time classical post-processing. If such improvement was realized on a real quantum computer, the public-key cryptography has to face a great challenge in the near future.

1.3.2 Development of Quantum Cryptography

Quantum cryptography is based on quantum mechanics, and the security is guaranteed by physical principles such as the Heisenberg uncertainty principle and quantum no-cloning theorem, rather than the difficulty of mathematical problems. Quantum cryptography was revived in 1979 when Bennett and Brassard combined the concept of public-key cryptography with Wiesner's quantum approach. Moreover, quite a few effective defense strategies have been proposed, such as quantum image steganography algorithm [30]. Compared with the classical encryption scheme, the quantum encryption scheme is relatively simple and easy to implement in physics.

The origin of quantum cryptography is marked by the proposal of the BB84 protocol [31], which uses a single quantum state to transmit the keys required by a symmetric encryption algorithm. It can transfer classical keys securely between authenticated communicators. So far, quantum cryptography has made fruitful achievements in the fields of quantum secret sharing [32–34], quantum secure direct communication [35], quantum bit commitment [36, 37], quantum teleportation [38], quantum multi-party computation [39, 40], quantum message authentication [41], quantum signature [42–44] , quantum homomorphic encryption [45, 46] and secure quantum network coding [47]. These fields have enriched the theoretical system of quantum cryptography. Furthermore, quantum cryptography has developed some fundamental primitives such as quantum one-time pad and quantum IND (indistinguishability)-security. Compared with other terms in quantum cryptography, quantum obfuscation attracts less attention and is still in its infancy due to its difficulty in implementation and application.

1.4 Quantum Obfuscation

Quantum computation integrates concepts from quantum physics, computer science, and classical information theory. With the advent of quantum computation, the security of classical cryptography cannot be ensured. Quantum cryptography is a new form of cryptographic system that extends the definition of security in classical cryptography to the quantum field and employs quantum mechanics to achieve security goals. In quantum cryptography research, cryptographic primitives such as the quantum one-time pad and quantum currency have arisen successively. Quantum obfuscation is based on the principle of quantum mechanics and uses qubits to safeguard circuit information in order to encrypt circuits or functionalities and guarantee communication security.

1.4.1 Development of Quantum Obfuscation

In quantum cryptography, quantum obfuscation is one of the strongest forms of encryption. It is different from encrypting data, but encrypting quantum functionality. In 2016, Alagic et al. [14] initially gave the definition of quantum obfuscation. They introduced the concept of quantum obfuscation into quantum cryptography, because not only quantum obfuscation had a wide range of applications in quantum cryptography, but also quantum black-box obfuscation was first defined and had great potential.

Quantum obfuscation is based on the theory of quantum circuit and quantum computation. Since quantum computation theory is far from maturer than its classical counterpart, until 2014, no one had publicly published research on quantum obfuscation. At the 2014 quantum computing theory conference (TQC), Alagic et al.

[48] first proposed quantum obfuscation based on quantum topological calculations. They used the specific high-dimensional expression of the braid group to compile quantum circuits into braids, and then convert it into a normal form. In 2016, Alagic et al. [14] formally proposed the definition of quantum obfuscation. The quantum black-box obfuscator was first defined and proved more practicable than classical black-box obfuscator. Then they defined the quantum indistinguishable obfuscator and pointed out some possible application such as quantum-secure one-way function (qOWF) and public-key quantum money.

In 2016, Alagic et al. [14] proposed the very first model of quantum obfuscation. They discussed the prospect of quantum obfuscation in several cryptographic schemes, including quantum symmetric encryption, quantum asymmetric encryption, quantum homomorphic encryption, and the development of quantum currency. In 2019, Shang et al. [49–51] proposed a quantum point function obfuscation scheme and demonstrated its applications in symmetric encryption, zero-knowledge, and access control. In 2020, Alagic et al. [52] proved that quantum black-box obfuscation of classical circuits is generally impossible. Broadbent et al. [53, 54] proposed a method for constructing quantum indistinguishable obfuscation and an indistinguishable obfuscation scheme based on quantum T gate circuits in the same year. In 2021, Bartusek et al. [55] demonstrated a post-quantum indistinguishable obfuscation scheme for classical circuits under the quantum random oracle model. Balachandran et al. [56] proposed a method for utilizing entangled qubits to obfuscate classical control flow in hybrid quantum-classical systems. In 2022, Zhang et al. [57] clarified the definition of instantiation of quantum point obfuscation, gave the instantiation of quantum point obfuscation scheme with quantum error-correcting code and single-qubit rotation, respectively and discussed the security under the definition of instantiation. In 2023, Pan et al. [58] proposed quantum obfuscation for quantum nonlinear functions and applied it in quantum power function. The obfuscation illuminated the connection between quantum obfuscation and quantum teleportation. In particular, this work just suggested the idea of designing quantum obfuscation for quantum nonlinear functions, so the structure of quantum obfuscator and interpreter is variable according to the specific properties of quantum nonlinear functions to be obfuscated. Jiang et al. [59] defined two generalized quantum power functions. The generalized quantum power functions are created in order to better extend to larger quantum nonlinear functions. These functions illustrate the functional design of the generalized quantum functions and construct different circuits to obfuscate and interpret these functions using quantum techniques such as teleportation and quantum superdense coding.

In the current study of quantum obfuscation for particular quantum functions, the circuit of quantum linear functions is reversible, which cannot be applied to the implementation of cryptographic functions such as quantum one-way functions and has certain application limitations.

1.4.2 Reduction for Quantum Obfuscation

In this section, we will discuss reduction skills for quantum obfuscation and the obfuscator for combined quantum circuits. Many ideas of quantum obfuscation come from Lynns' work [3] on classical obfuscation theory, which helps extend obfuscation into quantum circumstances.

Definition 1.1 A quantum circuit family $\mathcal{C}$ is said to be obfuscatable if there is a quantum state family $\mathcal{S}$, for every $C \in \mathcal{C}$, there is a $|s\rangle \in \mathcal{S}$ such that $|s\rangle = O(C)$.

This definition is similar to its classical counterpart.

Definition 1.2 A n-qubit quantum circuit family $\mathcal{C}$ is said to be oracle implementable relative to a n-qubit quantum circuit family $\mathcal{D}$, if there exists n-qubit quantum circuits M and N, for every $C \in \mathcal{C}$, there exists a $D \in \mathcal{D}$ such that

$$\|\delta(M^{U_D}(|0\rangle^n) \otimes \rho) - U_C \rho U_C^\dagger\|_{tr} \leq negl(n)$$

$$\|\delta(N^{U_C}(|0\rangle^n) \otimes \rho) - U_D \rho U_D^\dagger\|_{tr} \leq negl(n)$$

for every valid input ρ. This relationship is called oracle implementable relationship. Here we denote such relationship of $\mathcal{C}$ and $\mathcal{D}$ by $\mathcal{C} \ll \mathcal{D}$.

In this definition, we follow the idea of Alagics' work that a quantum state achieves a specific function with an interpreter δ. This is consistent with the definition of a quantum obfuscator.

Since an interpreter is necessary in the application of an obfuscated quantum circuit, we denote $\delta(s \otimes \rho)$ by $\delta_s(\rho)$, for any quantum state s and ρ. Therefore $N^{\delta_{O(C)}}$ refers to a quantum circuit N with oracle access to the obfuscation of C. We note that in this circumstance, an oracle $\delta_{O(C)}$ receives a quantum state ρ, computes $\delta(O(C) \otimes \rho)$ and returns it to N. So, functionally, the interaction between N and $\delta_s(\rho)$ is exactly the same as N^{U_C}, due to the functional equivalence property defined by the reference [14]. And $N^{\delta_{O(C)}}$ is also effective so long as N^{U_C} is effective, since the definition of obfuscation guarantees the polynomial property of an interpreter δ.

Lemma 1.1 *if $\mathcal{C} \ll \mathcal{D}$, $\mathcal{D}$ is obfuscatable, then so is $\mathcal{C}$.*

Proof. The goal is to construct an obfuscation of $\mathcal{C}$. Since $\mathcal{D}$ is obfuscatable, we set $O'(D)$ to be an obfuscation result of any $D \in \mathcal{D}$. Given $\mathcal{C} \ll \mathcal{D}$, we have a quantum circuit M such that

$$\|\delta(M^{U_D}(|0\rangle^n) \otimes \rho) - U_C \rho U_C^\dagger\|_{tr} \leq negl(n).$$

Now we show that $M^{\delta'_O(D)}(|0^n\rangle)$ is an obfuscation of C. Here $M^{\delta'_O(D)}(|0^n\rangle)$ and $O(C)$ are both quantum states. According to previous discussion, $M^{\delta'_O(D)}$ works exactly the same as M^{U_D}, therefore $M^{\delta'_O(D)}(|0^n\rangle)$ satisfies polynomial slowdown and functionality.

Here we prove the black-box property. For any adversary $A(O(C)) = A(M^{\delta'_O(D)}(|0^n\rangle))$, consider QPT $A'(M'^{O'(D)})$, which runs A internally. A' works as follows.

1. With an input $O'(D)$ and a quantum circuit M, A' constructs a quantum circuit $M^{O(D)}$.
2. A' passes $M^{O(D)}(|0^n\rangle)$ to A.
3. A' outputs what A outputs.

So we have

$$Pr[A'(O'(D)) = 1] = Pr[A(M_{O(D)}) = 1]. \tag{1.1}$$

Due to the black-box property of $O'(D)$, there exists a simulator S' such that

$$\begin{aligned} &|Pr[A'(O'(D)) = 1]- \\ &Pr[S'^{U_D}(|0^n\rangle) = 1]| \le negl(n) \end{aligned}. \tag{1.2}$$

Then we construct a simulator S^{U_C} from S'^{U_D}. The key of this construction is to response the query which S' interacts with an oracle U_D. Note that $\mathcal{C} \ll \mathcal{D}$, we have a quantum circuit N such that

$$\|\delta(N^{U_C}(|0\rangle^n) \otimes \rho) - U_D \rho U_D^{\dagger}\|_{tr} \le negl(n). \tag{1.3}$$

It indicates that, with a quantum circuit N and oracle access to U_C, one can simulate an oracle access to U_D, with negligible Euclid distance. So S^{U_C} works as follows.

1. S^{U_C} obtains its input $|0^n\rangle$, then passes it to S'.
2. For every query by which S' interacts with U_D with state ρ, S^{U_C} computes $\delta_{N^{U_C}(|0^n\rangle)}(\rho)$ and returns the result to S'.
3. S^{U_C} outputs what S' outputs.

In this case, we have

$$\Pr[S^{U_C}(|0^n\rangle) = 1] = \Pr[S'^{U_D}(|0^n\rangle) = 1]. \tag{1.4}$$

Finally, according to Eqs. 1.1, 1.2 and 1.4, we have

$$\begin{aligned} &|\Pr[A(M'^{O(D)}) = 1]- \\ &\Pr[S^{U_C}(|0^n\rangle) = 1]| \le negl(n) \end{aligned}.$$

The structures of A' and S are shown in Figs. 1.1 and 1.2. So we finish the proof that $M'^{O(D)}(|0^n\rangle)$ is an obfuscation of C. □

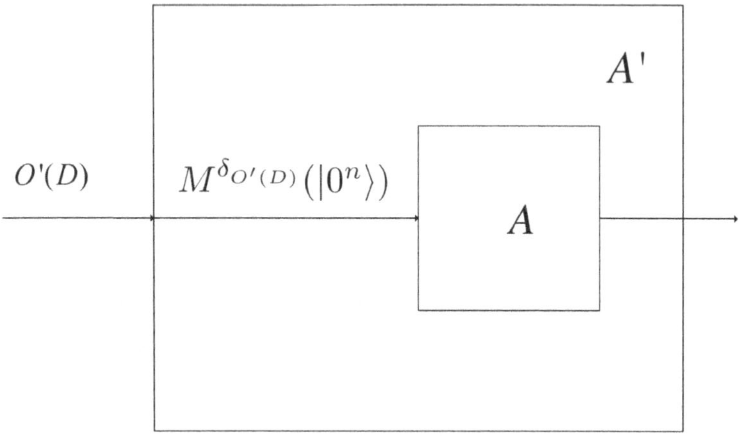

Fig. 1.1 Structure of A'

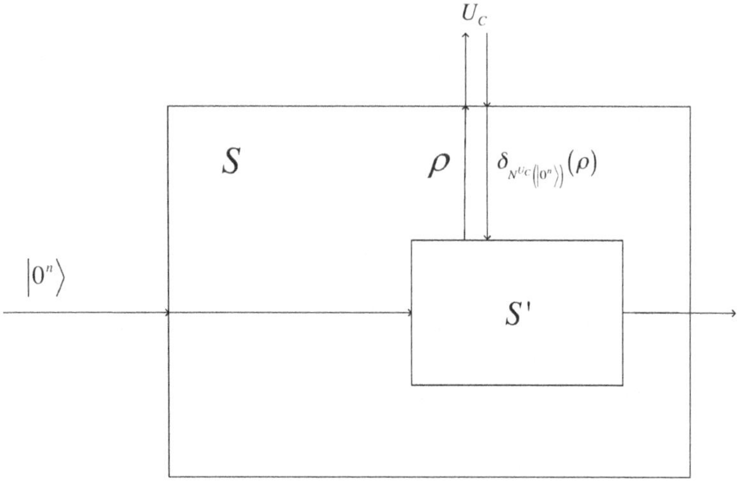

Fig. 1.2 Structure of S

1.4.3 Obfuscation of Combined Quantum Circuits

An obfuscated quantum circuit can be idealized as an oracle access to the original quantum circuit. Naturally, we want to combine different obfuscation results so as to compose a new obfuscation which also can be idealized as an oracle access to the original one. We then discuss the obfuscatability of combined quantum circuits.

The definition of a combined quantum circuit has been introduced in Sect. 1.2.1. Here we give out some intuitive obfuscations of combined quantum circuits.

Definition 1.3 Given an obfuscatable quantum circuit family $\mathcal{C}$. If

$$O^*(C_1\#\ldots\#C_k) = O(C_1)\#\ldots\#O(C_k)$$

is an effective obfuscation of $C_1\#\ldots\#C_k$ for any $C_i \in \mathcal{C}$, we say it is a simple obfuscation of combined quantum circuits $C_1\#\ldots\#C_k$.

Even in the classical setting, it is hard to construct a non-trivial simple obfuscation of combined circuits. However, we can define a simple obfuscation of any trivial combined quantum circuit.

Definition 1.4 A quantum circuit family $\mathcal{C}$ is learnable, if for any $C \in \mathcal{C}$ there exists a quantum circuit P such that

$$\|\delta(P^C(|0\rangle^{\otimes|C|}) \otimes \rho) - U_C\rho U_C^\dagger\|_{tr} \leq negl(n).$$

If a quantum circuit family $\mathcal{C}$ is learnable, it is easy to prove that $\mathcal{C}$ is also obfuscatable. To obtain $O(C)$, an obfuscator takes an input C, makes oracle access to C over P to obtain $P^C(|0\rangle^{\otimes|C|})$. Obviously, $P^C(|0\rangle^{\otimes|C|})$ is an effective obfuscation of $\mathcal{C}$, since for any adversary A, a simulator can have oracle access to $\mathcal{C}$, obtain $P^C(|0\rangle^{\otimes|C|})$ and pass it to A.

Definition 1.5 A learnable quantum circuit family is called trivial quantum obfuscatable family. Given a quantum-circuit learnable family, the obfuscation via learning is called trivial quantum obfuscation.

Lemma 1.2 *Given a learnable quantum circuit family $\mathcal{C}$, $\mathcal{D}$ is obfuscatable if and only if $\{C\#D|C \in \mathcal{C}, D \in \mathcal{D}\}$ is obfuscatable.*

Proof. Firstly, we prove that $\{C\#D\}$ is obfuscatable $\Rightarrow$ $\mathcal{D}$ is obfuscatable. We randomly choose $C \in \mathcal{C}$, $D \in \mathcal{D}$. With similar technique in the proof of Lemma 1.2, for any adversary A, we construct a QPT $A'(O(C\#D))$ which works as follows: A' sets the control register of $O(C\#D))$ to $|1\rangle$, then passes it to A, finally outputs what A outputs. Clearly, we have

$$\Pr[A'(O(C\#D)) = 1] = \Pr[A(O(C\#D)_{|1\rangle}) = 1].$$

Since $O(C\#D)$ is an obfuscation of $C\#D$, there exists a simulator S' such that

$$\begin{aligned} &|\Pr[A'(O(C\#D)) = 1] - \\ &\Pr[S'^{U_{C\#D}}(|0\rangle^{\otimes|C\#D|}) = 1]| \leq negl(n). \end{aligned} \tag{1.5}$$

Then we construct S^{U_D} from $S'^{U_{C\#D}}$. S^{U_D} works as follows: firstly S^{U_C} obtains input $|0\rangle^{\otimes|D|}$, adds $|0\rangle$ to it and passes $|0\rangle^{\otimes|C\#D|}$ to $S'^{U_{C\#D}}$. Every time $S'^{U_{C\#D}}$ queries $U_{C\#D}$ with ρ, S^{U_D} checks the control register of ρ. If it is $|0\rangle$, S^{U_D} returns $\delta(C(\rho)$, otherwise S^{U_D} has oracle access to U_D and returns it to $S'^{U_{C\#D}}$. Finally it outputs what $S'^{U_{C\#D}}$ outputs. Through the construction, we have

$$\begin{aligned}&\Pr[S'^{U_{C\#D}}(|0\rangle^{\otimes|C\#D|}) = 1]\\&= \Pr[S^{U_D}(|0\rangle^{\otimes|D|}) = 1].\end{aligned} \tag{1.6}$$

With Eqs. 1.5 and 1.6, we have

$$\begin{aligned}&|\Pr[A(O(D)_{|1\rangle}) = 1]-\\&\Pr[S^{U_D}(|0\rangle^{\otimes|D|}) = 1]| \leq negl(n).\end{aligned}$$

So we finish the proof that $\{C\#D\}$ is obfuscatable $\Rightarrow \mathcal{D}$ is obfuscatable. The proof of reverse direction is very similar and will not be described again. □

1.5 Summary

In order to clarify the meaning of obfuscation, we introduced the development from classical obfuscation to quantum obfuscation. Meanwhile, from the viewpoint of quantum computation, we introduced the quantum circuit and algorithm. From the viewpoint of quantum cryptography, we introduced many quantum cryptographical protocols. In this book, we introduce the strict definition of quantum obfuscation as well as the variants and provide some positive results of quantum obfuscation. Furthermore, we will design a series of quantum obfuscation schemes by means of combining obfuscation theory with quantum computation. These methods will provide effective tools for the research and application of quantum cryptography. As a start of study on quantum obfuscation, such work will be very useful in the future development of quantum cryptography.

References

1. Hada, S.: Zero-knowledge and code obfuscation. In: International Conference on the Theory and Application of Cryptology and Information Security (ASIACRYPT 2000), vol. 1976, pp. 443–457 (2000)
2. Barak, B., Goldreich, O., Impagliazzo, R., et al.: On the (IM) possibility of obfuscating programs. In: Annual International Cryptology Conference (CRYPTO 2001), vol. 2139(2), pp. 1–18 (2001)
3. Lynn, B., Prabhakaran, M., Sahai, A.: Positive results and techniques for obfuscation. In: International Conference on the Theory and Applications of Cryptographic Techniques (EUROCRYPT 2004), vol. 3027, pp. 20–39. Springer Berlin Heidelberg (2004)
4. Goldwasser, S., Kalai, Y.T.: On the impossibility of obfuscation with auxiliary input. In: IEEE Symposium on Foundations of Computer Science, pp. 553–562. IEEE (2014)
5. Wee, H.: On obfuscating point functions. In: ACM Symposium on Theory of Computing (STOC), pp. 523–532 (2005)
6. Canetti, R., Dakdouk, R.R.: Obfuscating point functions with multibit output. In: International Conference on the Theory and Applications of Cryptographic Techniques (EUROCRYPT 2008). Lecture Notes in Computer Science, vol. 4965, pp. 489–508 (2008)

7. Canetti, R., Kalai, Y.T., Varia, M., et al.: On symmetric encryption and point obfuscating. In: Theory of Cryptography Conference (TCC), vol. 5978, pp. 52–71 (2010)
8. Goldwasser, S., Rothblum, G.N.: On best-possible obfuscation. In: Conference on Theory of Cryptography, pp. 194–213. Springer (2007)
9. Bitansky, N., Canetti, R.: On strong simulation and composable point obfuscation. In: The 30th Annual Conference on Advances in Cryptology, pp. 520–537 (2010)
10. Boyle, E., Chung, K.M., Pass, R.: On extractability obfuscation. In: Theory of Cryptography (TCC). Lecture Notes in Computer Science, vol. 8349 (2014)
11. Zhang, F.G.: From bilinear pairings to multilinear maps. J. Cryptologic Res. **3**(3), 211–228 (2016)
12. Hu, Y.P., Liu, J., Wang, B.C.: Efficiency analysis and simplified scheme of reusable garbling. J. Cryptologic Res. **9**(1), 106–112 (2022)
13. Deutsch, D., Richard J.: Rapid solution of problems by quantum computation. In: Proceedings of the Royal Society of London. Series A: Mathematical and Physical Sciences, vol. 439(1907), pp. 553–558 (1992)
14. Alagic, G., Fefferman, B.: On quantum obfuscation (2016). arXiv:1602.01771
15. Preskill, J.: Quantum computing in the NISQ era and beyond. Quantum **2**, 79 (2018)
16. Li, G., Ding, Y., Xie, Y.: Tackling the qubit mapping problem for NISQ-era quantum devices. In: The 24th International Conference on Architectural Support for Programming Languages and Operating Systems (ASPLOS '19), pp. 1001–1014. Association for Computing Machinery (2019)
17. Wille, R., Aaron, L., Rolf, D.: Optimal SWAP gate insertion for nearest neighbor quantum circuits. In: The 19th Asia and South Pacific Design Automation Conference (ASP-DAC), pp. 489–494 (2014)
18. Siraichi, M., Santos, V., Collange, C., et al.: Qubit allocation. In: The International Symposium on Code Generation and Optimization (CGO 2018), pp. 113–125. Association for Computing Machinery (2018)
19. Itoko, T., Raymond, R., Imamichi, T., et al.: Optimization of quantum circuit mapping using gate transformation and commutation. Integration **70**, 43–50 (2020)
20. Shor, P.W.: Algorithms for quantum computation: discrete logarithms and factoring. In: The 35th Annual Symposium on Foundations of Computer Science, pp. 124–134 (1994)
21. Grover, L.K.: A fast quantum mechanical algorithm for database search. In: The Twenty-Eighth Annual ACM Symposium on Theory of Computing, pp. 212–219 (1996)
22. Simon, D.R.: On the power of quantum computation. SIAM J. Comput. **26**(5), 1474–1483 (1997)
23. Bernstein, E., Vazirani, U.: Quantum complexity theory. In: The Twenty-fifth Annual ACM Symposium on Theory of Computing, pp. 11–20 (1993)
24. Burges, C.J.C.: Factoring as optimization. Microsoft Res. **83**, 19 (2002)
25. Peng, W.C., Wang, B.N., Hu, F., et al.: Factoring larger integers with fewer qubits via quantum annealing with optimized parameters. Sci. China-Phys. Mech. Astron. **62**(6), 5–12 (2019)
26. Wang, Z.G., Wei, S.J., Long, G.L., et al.: Variational quantum attacks threaten advanced encryption standard based symmetric cryptography. Sci. China-Inf. Sci. **65**(10), 200503 (2022)
27. Li, Z.Q., Cai, B.B., Sun, H.W., et al.: Novel quantum circuit implementation of advanced encryption standard with low costs. Sci. China-Phys. Mech. Astron. **65**(9), 290311 (2022)
28. Kaplan, M., Leurent, G., Leverrier, A., et al.: Breaking symmetric cryptosystems using quantum period finding. In: CRYPTO 2016, pp. 207–237. Springer Berlin Heidelberg (2016)
29. Regev O.: An efficient quantum factoring algorithm (2023). arXiv:2308.06572
30. Qu, Z., Cheng, Z., Wang, X.: Matrix coding-based quantum image steganography algorithm. IEEE Access **7**, 35684–35698 (2019)
31. Bennett, C.H.: Quantum cryptography: public key distribution and coin tossing. In: IEEE International Conference on Computers Institute of Electrical and Electronics Engineers, pp. 157–179 (1984)
32. Gottesman, D.: On the theory of quantum secret sharing. Phys. Rev. A **61**(4), 042311 (1999)

33. Hillery, M., Nek, V., Berthiaume, A.: Quantum secret sharing. Phys. Rev. A **59**(3), 1829–1834 (1999)
34. Xiao, L., Long, G.L., Deng, F.G., et al.: Efficient multi-party quantum secret sharing schemes. Phys. Rev. A **69**(5), 521–524 (2004)
35. Wang, C., Deng, F.G., Long, G.L.: Multi-step quantum secure direct communication using multi-particle Green-Horne-Zeilinger state. Opt. Commun. **253**(1–3), 15–20 (2005)
36. Dominic, M.: Unconditionally secure quantum bit commitment is impossible. Phys. Rev. Lett. **78**(17), 3414–3417 (1997)
37. Lo, H.K., Chau, H.F.: Is quantum bit commitment really possible? Phys. Rev. Lett. **78**(17), 3410–3413 (1997)
38. Braunstein, S.L., Mann, A.: Measurement of the Bell operator and quantum teleportation. Phys. Rev. A **51**(3), 1727–1730 (1995)
39. Chau, H.F.: Quantum classical complexity-security tradeoff in secure multi-party computation. Phys. Rev. A **61**(3), 167–169 (2000)
40. Dominique, U.: Universally composable quantum multi-party computation. In: CRYPTO 2010, pp. 486–505. Springer Berlin Heidelberg (2010)
41. Boneh, D., Zhandry, M.: Quantum-secure message authentication codes. In: International Conference on the Theory & Applications of Cryptographic Techniques, pp. 592–608 (2013)
42. Haake, F.: Quantum Signatures of Chaos. Springer (2001)
43. Chuang, I., Gottesman, D.: Quantum digital signatures (2007). arXiv:quant-ph/0105032
44. Shang, T., Zhao, X.J., Wang, C., et al.: Quantum homomorphic signature. Quantum Inf. Process. **14**(1), 393–410 (2015)
45. Rohde, P.P., Fitzsimons, J.F., Gilchrist, A.: Quantum walks with encrypted data. Phys. Rev. Lett. **109**(15), 150501 (2012)
46. Liang, M.: Symmetric quantum fully homomorphic encryption with perfect security. Quantum Inf. Process. **12**(12), 3675–3687 (1999)
47. Shang, T., Liu, J.W.: Secure Quantum Network Coding Theory. Springer (2020)
48. Alagic, G., Jeffery, S., Jordan, S.: Circuit obfuscation using braids. In: Conference on the Theory of Quantum Computation, Communication and Cryptography (TQC), vol. 27, pp. 141–160 (2014)
49. Chen, R.Y.L., Shang, T., Liu, J.W.: Obfuscatability of quantum access control problem (in Chinese). J. Cryptologic Res. **6**(3), 362–369 (2019)
50. Shang, T., Chen, R.Y.L., Liu, J.W.: On the obfuscatability of quantum point functions. Quantum Inf. Process. **18**, 55 (2019)
51. Chen, R.Y.L., Shang, T., Liu, J.W.: IND-secure quantum symmetric encryption based on point obfuscation. Quantum Inf. Process. **18**, 161 (2019)
52. Alagic, G., et al.: Impossibility of quantum virtual black-box obfuscation of classical circuits (2020). arXiv:2005.06432
53. Broadbent, A., Kazmi, R.A.: Constructions for quantum indistinguishability obfuscation. In: The Seventh International Conference on Cryptology and Information Security in Latin America (LATINCRYPT 2021). Lecture Notes in Computer Science, vol. 12912 (2021)
54. Broadbent, A., Kazmi, R. A.: Indistinguishability obfuscation for quantum circuits of low T-count. In: The Seventh International Conference on Cryptology and Information Security in Latin America (LATRINCRYPT 2021). Lecture Notes in Computer Science, vol. 12912 (2021)
55. Bartusek, J., Malavolta G.: Indistinguishability obfuscation of null quantum circuits and applications (2021). arXiv:2106.06094
56. Balachandran, V.: Quantum obfuscation: quantum predicates with entangled qubits. In: Eleventh ACM Conference on Data and Application Security and Privacy (CODASPY 21), pp. 293–295. ACM (2021)
57. Zhang, Y.J., Shang, T., Chen, R.Y.L., et al.: Instantiation of quantum point obfuscation. Quantum Inf. Process. **21**(1), 1–16 (2022)
58. Pan, C.Y., Shang, T., Zhang, Y.J.: Universal quantum obfuscation for quantum non-linear functions. Front. Phys. **10**, 1342 (2023)
59. Jiang, Y.Z., Shang, T., Tang, Y., et al.: Quantum obfuscation of generalized quantum power functions with coefficient. Entropy **25**(11), 1524 (2023)

Chapter 2
Preliminary

Quantum obfuscation is an important and cross research topic between quantum cryptography and quantum computation. As an extension to classical obfuscation, quantum obfuscation is based on the theory of quantum computation. Usually, the handling of quantum information is harder than that of classical counterpart. The question is whether or not quantum obfuscation is feasible with the quantum counterpart of key operations. In this chapter, we introduce the preliminaries of quantum obfuscation, including quantum information technology and security analysis methods. Then we present the strict definition of quantum obfuscation and quantum nonlinear function and discuss the universality of quantum obfuscation.

2.1 Quantum Information

2.1.1 Quantum Operator

Let $\hat{A}$ be a linear quantum operator on a Hilbert space $\mathcal{E}_H$.

$$\hat{A} : \mathcal{E}_H \longrightarrow \mathcal{E}_H$$

The **hermitian conjugate** or **adjoint** of $\hat{A}$: $\hat{A}^\dagger : \mathcal{E}_H \longrightarrow \mathcal{E}_H$ is defined by

$$(|v\rangle\,,\hat{A}\,|w\rangle) = (\hat{A}^\dagger\,|v\rangle\,,|w\rangle)$$

where $|v\rangle$ and $|w\rangle$ belong to $\mathcal{E}_H$, $(\cdot,\cdot)$ is the inner product of quantum states.

T. Shang, *Quantum Nonlinear Function Obfuscation Theory and Application*,
https://doi.org/10.1007/978-981-97-6722-9_2

Once we defined the hermitian conjugation, we can classify the quantum operators.

1. **Normal operator**: $\hat{A}$ is a normal operator if $\hat{A}\hat{A}^{\dagger} = \hat{A}^{\dagger}\hat{A}$.
   - Normal operator $\Leftrightarrow$ diagonalizable operator.
   - If all eigenvalues of a normal operator $\hat{A}$ are real, $\hat{A}$ is Hermitian.
2. **Hermitian operator**: $\hat{A}$ is a hermitian operator if $\hat{A} = \hat{A}^{\dagger}$.
   - Hermitian operator $\Rightarrow$ normal operator.
   - All eigenvalues of hermitian operator are real.
3. **Positive operator**: Positive operators are a special subclass of hermitian operators. $\hat{A}$ is a positive operator if $(|v\rangle, \hat{A}|v\rangle)$ is a real and non-negative number for any vector $|v\rangle$.
   - If $(|v\rangle, \hat{A}|v\rangle)$ is strictly greater than zero for all $|v\rangle \neq \mathbf{0}$, $\hat{A}$ is positive definite.
4. **Unitary operator**: $\hat{A}$ is a unitary operator if $\hat{A}^{\dagger}\hat{A} = \hat{I}$.
   - $\hat{A}\hat{A}^{\dagger} = \hat{A}^{\dagger}\hat{A} = \hat{I}$, unitary operator $\Rightarrow$ normal operator.
   - Unitary operator preserves the inner product, i.e., $(U|v\rangle, U|w\rangle) = \langle v|w\rangle$.

Pauli matrix refers to four frequently used matrices which are of 2×2 size and own their names, respectively. Equation (2.1) shows these matrices and their symbols.

$$\sigma_I = \begin{bmatrix} 1 & 0 \\ 0 & 1 \end{bmatrix}, \sigma_X = \begin{bmatrix} 0 & 1 \\ 1 & 0 \end{bmatrix}, \sigma_Y = \begin{bmatrix} 0 & -i \\ i & 0 \end{bmatrix}, \sigma_Z = \begin{bmatrix} 1 & 0 \\ 0 & -1 \end{bmatrix}. \tag{2.1}$$

2.1.2 *Quantum Measurement*

Quantum measurement is the main way to observe the internal situation of a quantum system. The state of the system will collapse to a state when the measurement is completed. Quantum measurement is an irreversible operation which transforms quantum information into classical information. If quantum measurement was reversible, it would never reveal any information on quantum states.

Quantum measurement is described by a set of operations of measurement M_m, where m represents any possible measurement results for the subsystems measured. The measurement operation M_m satisfies the completeness equation.

$$\sum M_m^{\dagger} M_m = I. \tag{2.2}$$

The possible measurement result of a quantum system of the state $|\psi\rangle$ can be expressed as $p = \langle\psi|M_m^{\dagger}M_m|\psi\rangle$, which holds for all $|\psi\rangle$. After the measurement of a quantum system is finished, its state converts to be $\frac{M_m|\psi\rangle}{\sqrt{\langle\psi|M_m^{\dagger}M_m|\psi\rangle}}$.

1. **Projective measurement:** There exists a particular type of measurement in quantum mechanics, projective measurement. The projective measurement turns out to be equivalent to the general measurement defined in the postulate of the measurement if we can perform the unitary transformation as described in the postulate of the evolution. Firstly, let us look at the definition of the projective measurement according to Ref. [1].

A projective measurement is described by an observable $\hat{\mathcal{M}}$, a hermitian operator on the state space of the system being observed. The observable has a spectral decomposition:

$$\hat{\mathcal{M}} = \sum_m m\hat{P}_m,$$

where $\hat{P}_m$ is the projector onto the eigenspace of $\hat{\mathcal{M}}$ with eigenvalue m. The possible outcomes of the measurement correspond to the eigenvalues, m, of the observable. Upon measuring the state $|\psi\rangle$, the probability of obtaining result m is given by

$$\mathcal{P}(m) = \langle\psi| \hat{P}_m |\psi\rangle .$$

Given that the outcome m occurred, the state of the quantum system immediately after the measurement is

$$\frac{\hat{P}_m |\psi\rangle}{\sqrt{\langle\psi| \hat{P}_m |\psi\rangle}}.$$

The projective measurement is a special case of the general measurement with $\hat{P}_m = \hat{M}_m$, for all m. However, the projective measurement is equivalent to the general measurement if we perform the unitary transformation.

2. **Positive Operator-Valued Measure (POVM):** Projective measurement is important and useful in the quantum measurement, but sometimes it is complicated to use. To utilize these good properties of the projective measurement, we also have many restrictions on the choice of the operators. What's more, we usually have little interest in the quantum state after the measurement, but concern more about the probabilities of the respective measurement outcomes. The POVM formalism is a well-adapted tool to analyze the result of the measurement. Certainly, we will lose some good properties, such as the repeatability, but sometimes we cannot repeat the measurement, we can only measure a quantum state once. At the beginning, we put the definition of POVM here.

Conversely, suppose that we have a set of positive hermitian operators $\left\{\hat{E}_m\right\}$ such that $\sum_m \hat{E}_m = \hat{I}$. We can prove that there exists a set of measurement operators $\hat{M}_m$ defining a measurement described by POVM $\left\{\hat{E}_m\right\}$. By defining $\hat{M}_m \equiv \sqrt{\hat{E}_m}$, we obtain $\sum_m \hat{M}_m^{\dagger}\hat{M}_m = \sum_m \hat{E}_m = \hat{I}$, and therefore the set $\left\{\hat{M}_m\right\}$ describes a measurement with POVM $\left\{\hat{E}_m\right\}$.

For this reason, we can simply define a POVM to be a set of operators $\left\{\hat{E}_m\right\}$ satisfying

- $\hat{E}_m$ is hermitian and positive, for all m
- $\sum_m \hat{E}_m = \hat{I}$

2.1.3 Quantum Teleportation

Quantum teleportation is a quantum communication branch proposed by Bennett et al. [2]. It is used to transfer quantum states between sender Alice and receiver Bob without direct connection of a quantum communication channel. Alice and Bob share an EPR (Einstein-Podolsky-Rosen) pair to form a quantum entanglement channel, the initial state is $|\beta_{00}\rangle = \frac{1}{\sqrt{2}}(|00\rangle + |11\rangle)$.

The circuit of Fig. 2.1 gives an accurate description of quantum teleportation. The state ready to be teleported is $|\phi\rangle = \alpha|0\rangle + \beta|1\rangle$, in which α and β represent unknown amplitudes, and the input state is $|\phi_0\rangle$.

$$|\phi_0\rangle = |\phi\rangle|\beta_{00}\rangle = \frac{1}{\sqrt{2}}[\alpha|0\rangle(|00\rangle + |11\rangle) + \beta|1\rangle(|00\rangle + |11\rangle)]. \tag{2.3}$$

In Eq. (2.3), we define that the first two qubits belong to Alice while the third qubit belongs to Bob. The second qubit of Alice and the qubit of Bob derive from the same EPR pair. Alice sends her qubit to a CNOT (controlled NOT) gate to obtain the state $|\phi_1\rangle$.

$$|\phi_1\rangle = \frac{1}{\sqrt{2}}[\alpha|0\rangle(|00\rangle + |11\rangle) + \beta|1\rangle(|10\rangle + |01\rangle)]. \tag{2.4}$$

Then Alice has the first qubit implementated by a Hadamard gate to obtain the state $|\phi_2\rangle$.

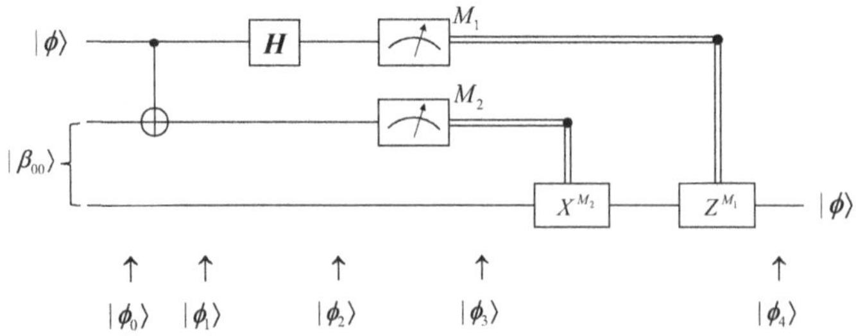

Fig. 2.1 Quantum teleportation circuit of a qubit

Table 2.1 Relationship of measurement results, collapsed states and unitary operations

Measurement results	Collapsed states	Unitary operations
$\|00\rangle$	$[\alpha\|0\rangle + \beta\|1\rangle]$	$Z^{M_1}X^{M_2}(M_1 = 0, M_2 = 0)$
$\|01\rangle$	$[\alpha\|1\rangle + \beta\|0\rangle]$	$Z^{M_1}X^{M_2}(M_1 = 0, M_2 = 1)$
$\|10\rangle$	$[\alpha\|0\rangle - \beta\|1\rangle]$	$Z^{M_1}X^{M_2}(M_1 = 1, M_2 = 0)$
$\|11\rangle$	$[\alpha\|1\rangle - \beta\|0\rangle]$	$Z^{M_1}X^{M_2}(M_1 = 1, M_2 = 1)$

$$|\phi_2\rangle = (\frac{1}{\sqrt{2}})^2[\alpha(|0\rangle + |1\rangle)(|00\rangle + |11\rangle) + \beta(|0\rangle - |1\rangle)(|10\rangle + |01\rangle)]. \tag{2.5}$$

After regrouping these items, the state can be rewritten as follows.

$$|\phi_3\rangle = (\frac{1}{\sqrt{2}})^2[|00\rangle(\alpha|0\rangle + \beta|1\rangle) + |01\rangle(\alpha|1\rangle + \beta|0\rangle) + |10\rangle(\alpha|0\rangle - \beta|1\rangle) + |11\rangle(\alpha|1\rangle - \beta|0\rangle)]. \tag{2.6}$$

As listed in Table 2.1, Alice may obtain four measurement results and send them to Bob via a classical channel. Bob needs to perform the transformation of $Z^{M_1}X^{M_2}$ on the qubit received.

In brief, quantum teleportation is a technique for transferring an unknown quantum state to a distant place by means of employing entangled states.

2.2 Security Analysis Methods Based on Random Oracle Model

As for quantum circumstance, security proof becomes complicated. Bennett et al. [3] discussed an oracle quantum Turing machine A, which responds intuitively a string in the entangled state $\sum_x a_x|x \circ A(x)\rangle$ when called with a query tape of superposition state $\sum_x a_x|x \circ 0\rangle$. It will also be useful to put the target bit b into a superposition, like $\beta = (|0\rangle - |1\rangle)/\sqrt{2}$. In this case, the whole input state will be left unchanged if $A(x) = 0$ and will be left unchanged while introducing a phase factor 1 if $A(x) = 1$. Such an oracle quantum Turing machine can also be assumed as a length-preserving one, and it can be achieved by interpreting the oracle answer on the pair (x, i) as the i-th bit of the function value. In this case, A is called a permutation oracle.

2.2.1 *Quantum-Accessible Random Oracle Model*

In 1993, Bellare and Rogaway [4] proposed the classical random oracle (RO) model, which provides a rigorous reduction method for cryptographic security proof. Under such a model, all parties, namely adversaries and legal ones, have access to the same oracle R, and get random yet consistent answers. An algorithm S is denoted by S^R, so long as queries to R have been made.

Intuitively, a query with a superposition state should also be allowed in the quantum-accessible random oracle (QRO) model. A QRO must simultaneously compute for the query at possibly exponentially many points. For post-quantum cryptography, Boneh et al. [5] gave out a key separation by presenting that a protocol is secure in the classical random oracle model while insecure in the quantum-accessible random oracle model.

In this work, a QRO, when no confusion may arise, will be interpreted as a length-preserving oracle, which means $R_q : |x, y\rangle \mapsto |x, y \oplus R(x)\rangle$, where $R : \{0, 1\}^* \mapsto \{0, 1\}^*$.

2.2.2 Quantum Random Oracle Model

Different from the classical RO model and the prior QRO model (precisely, quantum-accessible random oracle model), a new QRO (quantum random oracle) model was designed for the security analysis of quantum cryptographic protocols.

Considering the possible quantum collision problem resulted from quantum measurement, the quantum random oracle model assumes that there exists a collision-free quantum one-way function and different quantum states produced by QRO are distinguishable when QRO measures. Since an adversary may have access to all quantum states, all parties, including sender Alice, receiver Bob and adversary A, query QRO for classical random bits, quantum one-way function outputs and quantum states comparison results. For a quantum adversary, this QRO can respond consistently to quantum superposition queries like the quantum-accessible oracle [5]. It is also assumed that quantum states are transmitted without interference.

Definition 2.1 A quantum random oracle is a tuple of efficient algorithms $(\mathcal{G}, H_q, Measure)$ where $\mathcal{G}$: for any input of a classical bit-string m, it outputs a random bit-string $k = \{0, 1\}^k$.

H_ψ: for any input of a classical bit-string $k = \{0, 1\}^k$, it operates

$$\psi : \{0, 1\}^k \mapsto \mathcal{H}^{\otimes s},$$

to generate distinguishable quantum states $|\psi_{k^i}\rangle$, where

$$\mathcal{H}^{\otimes s} = \mathcal{H}_1 \otimes \ldots \otimes \mathcal{H}_s$$

is a 2^s-dimensional Hilbert space made up of s products of single-qubit spaces $\mathcal{H}_i^2$.

$Measure$: any qubits $|\psi_{k^i}\rangle, |\psi_{k^j}\rangle$ QRO generates are distinguishable when QRO measures, i.e.,

$$|\langle\psi_{k^i}\ |\psi_{k^j}\rangle|^2 = \varepsilon,$$

where ε is negligible for $i \neq j$.

Property 2.1 *Quantum random oracle can respond consistently to quantum queries* $\sum_m \psi_m |m\rangle$ *by mapping* $\mathcal{X} \rightarrow \mathcal{Y}$*:*

$$O(m, k) : \sum_m \psi_m |m\rangle \rightarrow \sum_m \psi_m |m, k\rangle,$$

where k is a random bit-string on m.

Then it samples r times from some distribution on $\mathcal{X}$ *such that, for every m and k,* $O(m, k)$ *is uniformly distributed on* $\mathcal{Y}$.

Proof Let r be some integer to be chosen later. Replace $\mathcal{X}$ with small-range distributions of r samples on $\mathcal{Y}$. An adversary can distinguish $\mathcal{X}$ from $\mathcal{Y}$ with a probability less than $C_0 q^3/r$. Thus, we use r samples of a small-range $\mathcal{Y}$ to replace r samples of an exponentially-large range $\mathcal{X}$ with distinguishable probability less than $C_0 q^3/r$, which facilitates the quantum random oracle to respond to a quantum query with suitable r. □

Property 2.2 *Quantum random oracle can accurately match classical secret keys with corresponding quantum public keys.*

Proof A quantum one-way function transforms an input of classical bit-string to an output of quantum states. A forgery of signature can be made when an adversary finds out a collision-error, i.e., different quantum states pass the test of equality by measurement. In case of possible quantum collision error, we use a quantum random oracle to generate collision-free quantum states $|\psi_{k^i}\rangle$ as Definition 2.1:

$$|\langle \psi_{k^i} | \psi_{k^j} \rangle|^2 = \varepsilon, \tag{2.7}$$

where ε is negligible for $i \neq j$. Equation 2.7 implies that all quantum states generated by QRO vary with different classical inputs and can be measured by QRO accurately, so this quantum random oracle can accurately match classical secret keys with corresponding quantum public keys. □

2.3 Definition of Quantum Obfuscation

Quantum obfuscation is derived from classical obfuscation and was first proposed by Alagic et al. [6].

Definition 2.2 A black-box quantum obfuscator is a quantum algorithm O and a QPT (quantum polynomial time) interpreter δ such that whenever C is an n-qubit quantum circuit, the output of O is an m-qubit state $O(C)$ satisfying the following three conditions:

1. *Polynomial expansion:*

$$m = poly(n). \tag{2.8}$$

where m means the scale of a quantum algorithm.

2. *Functional equivalence:* For any possible qubit ρ,

$$\left\| \delta(O(C) \otimes \rho) - U_C \rho U_C^{\dagger} \right\|_{tr} \leq negl(n). \tag{2.9}$$

where O is quantum obfuscator, δ is quantum interpreter, U_C represents a quantum circuit.

3. *Virtual black-box:* For any QPT adversary A who has the output of obfuscation, there exists S which can simulate A's behavior by virtual-black box access to the circuit C,

$$\left| \Pr[A(O(C)) = 1] - \Pr\left[S^{U_C}\left(|0^n\rangle\right) = 1\right] \right| \leq negl(n). \tag{2.10}$$

where S represents a quantum simulator.

When carrying obfuscation over to the quantum case, the "interpreter" algorithm δ must be well explained. Since an end user (and hence also any adversary) should be in possession of a quantum computer, it is conceivable that the obfuscation result may not just be another description of a quantum circuit. Instead, the obfuscator might output a quantum state, which is then to be employed by the end user to execute a desired function in some "well-specified" manner [6]. Now we no longer have any quantum circuit description in hand, therefore an interpreter algorithm δ must be used to execute a specific function.

How to understand such a QPT δ? One may think of δ as an algorithm which is fixed once and for all for a certain state class. It is also feasible to regard the obfuscation result as a quantum state $O(C)$ and an algorithm δ which inputs $O(C)$ and ρ and implements the function of U_C. Alagic et al. [6] pointed out that all of these variants are equivalent, in the sense that a black-box quantum obfuscator of each variant exists if and only if the other variants exist. Since the interpreter is used not only when obfuscating a quantum circuit but also in some reduction skills, we will set the interpreter δ to be universal, and it is conceivable to assume that we can always implement a function by producing a specific state and executing it with δ.

We note that the quantum obfuscation theory is so far a relatively rough one. Many critical concepts and theorems in classical case have not yet been well presented in quantum behavior.

2.4 Quantum Obfuscation for Quantum Nonlinear Functions

In the current research on quantum obfuscation for specific quantum functions, the circuit of quantum linear functions is reversible, which cannot be applied to the realization of cryptographic functions such as quantum one-way function, and has certain application restrictions. In terms of quantum nonlinear functions, although quantum point function obfuscation has achieved a series of positive results, its application in cryptography has certain limitations due to the single form of functions. The important application of nonlinear functions in classical cryptography has promoted the construction and research of quantum nonlinear functions. In 2023, Pan et al. [7] proposed quantum obfuscation for quantum nonlinear functions and applied it to quantum power function. In particular, this work just suggested the idea of designing quantum obfuscation for quantum nonlinear functions, so the structure of quantum obfuscator and interpreter is variable according to the specific properties of quantum nonlinear functions to be obfuscated. On the premise of quantum obfuscation theory, the definition and obfuscation of quantum nonlinear functions need further research. Therefore, quantum obfuscation schemes based on quantum nonlinear functions and their applications in cryptography will become the focus of this book.

A nonlinear function indicates that the relationship between the independent variable and the dependent variable of a function is not linear. The square relationship, logarithmic relationship, power exponential relationship, trigonometric relationship, point function relationship, and so on. are all examples of nonlinear relationships. The input and output of quantum nonlinear functions are quantum states with nonlinear relationship, and distinct categories of quantum nonlinear functions correspond to distinct definitions. In this book, we define typical quantum nonlinear functions.

2.4.1 Quantum Point Obfuscation

Definition 2.3 A quantum point function $U_{\alpha,\beta}$ with a general output is

$$U_{\alpha,\beta} : |x, 0^n\rangle \mapsto |x, P_{\alpha,\beta}(x)\rangle, \tag{2.11}$$

where $\alpha \in \{0, 1\}^n$, $\beta \in \{0, 1\}^n \backslash 0^n$, and $P_{\alpha,\beta}$ is a classical point function with a multi-bit output working as

$$P_{\alpha,\beta}(x) = \begin{cases} \beta & \text{if } x = \alpha \\ 0^n & \text{otherwise} \end{cases}. \tag{2.12}$$

By means of constructive proof, Shang et al. [8] demonstrated the obfuscatability of the quantum point function with a general output.

2.4.2 Quantum Power Obfuscation

Definition 2.4 A quantum power function is derived from the classical power function $y = x^a$, defined as U_a.

$$U_a : |x, y\rangle \mapsto |x\rangle \otimes P_a(|x\rangle). \tag{2.13}$$

Here, $a \in \{0, 1\}$, and P_a is a function expressed as

$$P_a(|x\rangle) = |x\rangle^{|a\rangle} = \begin{cases} |1\rangle \text{ if } a = 0 \\ |x\rangle \text{ if } a = 1 \end{cases}. \tag{2.14}$$

In 2023, Pan et al. [7, 9] illustrated the functional design of the generalized quantum power functions and constructed different circuits to obfuscate and interpret these functions using quantum techniques.

2.4.3 Construction of Quantum Obfuscation

In this section, we introduce the construction of quantum obfuscation based on quantum teleportation to obfuscate quantum nonlinear functions. Quantum nonlinear functions derive from classical nonlinear functions which mean nonlinear relationship between independent variables and dependent variables. The property of quantum functions can be extracted to a quantum state or some quantum states which we name as parameter states. Here we obfuscate one quantum state for example.

For the quantum obfuscation based on quantum teleportation, an obfuscator is used to obfuscate a quantum function and output an obfuscated state, while an interpreter can transform the obfuscated state back to its original state.

The parameter of quantum function is expressed as an m-qubit state $C_q(|\phi\rangle)$. $C_q(|\phi\rangle)$ is extracted from the n-qubit circuit C of the quantum nonlinear function. It can be obtained by inputting an auxiliary state into the circuit of quantum function. For example, we obtain the parameter $|a\rangle$ of quantum exponential function $|y\rangle = |a\rangle^{|x\rangle}$ with $|\ x\rangle = |0\rangle$ input. So $C_q(|\phi\rangle)$ is another representation of the function's functionality.

The state $|\psi\rangle$ is measured so that we can obtain a classical bit string. According to the classical bit string measured, we use corresponding Pauli matrix to restore the quantum state $C'_q(|\phi\rangle)$. Both $C_q(|\phi\rangle)$ and $C'_q(|\phi\rangle)$ represent the functionality of the quantum function. We input a quantum state $|x\rangle$ into an interpreter. With the input quantum state $|x\rangle$ and the circuit C restored from the parameter $C_q(|\phi\rangle)$, we obtain the output value $C_q(|x\rangle)$. In this way, we achieve the objective of quantum obfuscation, which utilizes the functionality of quantum functions to calculate some values without divulging any information.

Theorem 2.1 *Quantum nonlinear functions are obfuscatable by means of quantum teleportation. It satisfies the three conditions of quantum obfuscation.*

Proof To prove the correctness of quantum obfuscation based on quantum teleportation, we prove its polynomial expansion, functional equivalence, and virtual black-box property as follows.

For the quantum polynomial functions of quantum nonlinear functions, the input and output size of quantum obfuscator are certainly of polynomial size. While for other quantum nonlinear functions, the state $C_q(|\phi\rangle)$ is transformed into an obfuscated state $|\psi\rangle$ with a Bell state through quantum teleportation. Obviously, the obfuscator O computes $H(C_q(|\phi\rangle) \oplus |\beta\rangle)$ and generates $|\psi\rangle$ which is also of polynomial size. Supposing $C_q(|\phi\rangle) = |\phi_0\rangle$, the output of O, i.e., the obfuscation of C, is

$$O(C) = H|\phi_0 \oplus \beta\rangle, \tag{2.15}$$

where C is an n-qubit quantum circuit, β is varable according to the size of C, ϕ_0 is m-qubit. The total size of the output of quantum obfuscator O is $m + n$.

In the obfuscator, the state $C_q(|\phi\rangle)$ is obfuscated by the kernel operation KO. In the interpreter (take one-qubit $C_q(|\phi\rangle)$ as an example), the first two qubits of the obfuscated quantum state $|\psi\rangle$ are measured into a classical bit string so that we can perform the operation of Pauli matrix to obtain the state $C'_q(|\phi\rangle)$. According to the principle of quantum teleportation, we know $C'_q(|\phi\rangle)$ is equal to $C_q(|\phi\rangle)$, and they both present the functionality of the quantum function to be obfuscated. Then we implement the kernel operation KI equivalent to the functionality of the quantum function on the input state $|x\rangle$ to obtain $C_q(|x\rangle)$. Thus the interpreter makes $C'_q(|\phi\rangle)$ correspond to the function correctly with the probability 1. For specific quantum nonlinear functions, the construction of interpreter and its property are elaborated in Sect. 2.4.5.

The size of $O(C)$ is $m + n$. So the polynomial expansion property holds when $m = ploy(n)$. Through the above explanation and the overall construction of δ in Fig. 2.2 (Figs. 2.5 and 2.6 for specific quantum functions), the functionality equivalence property is demonstrated. Since the oracle is truly random to any adversary, the obfuscation $O(C)$ leaks no information about $C_q(|\phi\rangle)$. Therefore, quantum nonlinear functions are obfuscatable. □

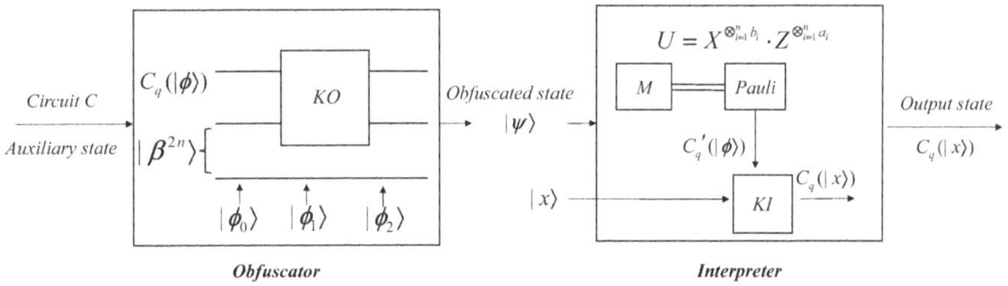

Fig. 2.2 Overall construction of quantum obfuscation for quantum nonlinear functions

2.4.4 Universality of Quantum Obfuscation

Quantum obfuscation based on quantum teleportation is universal to quantum non-linear functions. The specific explanation is described as follows.

Theorem 2.2 *Quantum obfuscation based on quantum teleportation is universal to quantum nonlinear functions whose parameter can be represented as a quantum state* $|a\rangle$. *That is*

$$|x, O(C)\rangle \mapsto |x, a\rangle. \tag{2.16}$$

Proof For quantum nonlinear functions, we can transform its parameter into a corresponding quantum state and input it into quantum obfuscator. KO operation in the obfuscator contains a set of quantum gates. It depends on what the input quantum state of parameter is. If we input a single-qubit state, the KO operation can be represented as the circuit shown in Fig. 2.3. If we input a multi-qubit state, the circuit can be altered by other forms of quantum gates. According to the function we want to obfuscate, we can design KI operation in the interpreter to restore its functionality respectively. Significantly for KI operation, we just introduce the idea of constructing the interpreter for quantum nonlinear functions, so the basic circuit of KI operation cannot be described as a unified form, but adaptive to the type of a function to be obfuscated. Hence we achieve the universality of quantum obfuscation based on quantum teleportation.

For example, if we want to obfuscate a quantum point function in Definition 2.3 to determine whether the input quantum state is equal to $|a\rangle$, we can obfuscate its parameter $|a\rangle$. In the same way, if we would like to obfuscate a quantum power function $|y\rangle = |x\rangle^{|a\rangle}$, we can obfuscate $|a\rangle$. The exact KO operation of qunatum teleportation in the obfuscator in Fig. 2.2 depends on whether the parameter is a single-qubit state or multi-qubit state. To utilize the functionality of the original function, we just need to design the corresponding KI operation of the interpreter. Through the proof above, these functions are obfuscatable and satisfy the three properties of quantum obfuscation. □

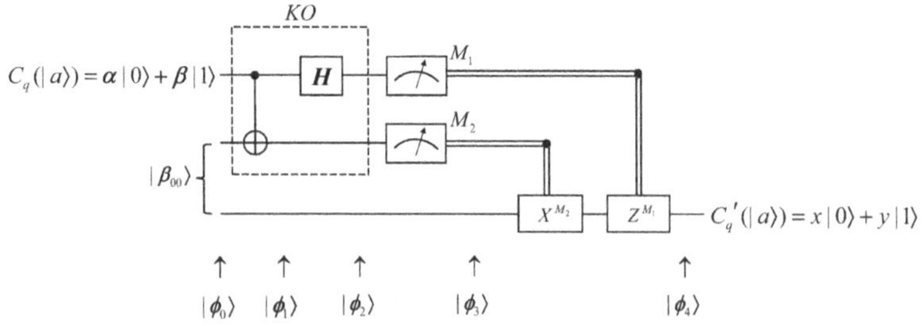

Fig. 2.3 Obfuscation for quantum nonlinear functions

2.4.5 *Application to Quantum Nonlinear Function*

Quantum obfuscation based on quantum teleportation is universal to various types of quantum nonlinear functions. Universal phase of quantum obfuscation is listed in Table 2.2. The obfuscator keeps the functionality secret, while the interpreter is designed to interpret the functionality to implement it on the input state. Figure 2.4 shows the construction of an interpreter of quantum nonlinear function. In this section, we take two quantum nonlinear functions which have only one parameter for example. One is a quantum point function which is an easy form of quantum nonlinear functions to implement the functionality of judgement. The other is a quantum power function which is the component of quantum polynomial functions.

2.4.5.1 A. Quantum Point Function Obfuscation

The concept of quantum point function is presented in Definition 2.3. We transform the property of a point function into a single-qubit quantum state $|a\rangle$. Then for every

Table 2.2 Universal steps of quantum obfuscation

Step	Operation
Step 1	Input the auxiliary state acted on point function to obtain the parameter of quantum state $|a\rangle = \alpha|0\rangle + \beta|1\rangle$
Step 2	Obfuscate the quantum state via quantum teleportation to obtain one state of the four possible states
Step 3	Measure the obfuscated state and transform it back to the initial parameter to obtain $C_q'(|a\rangle)$
Step 4	Input $|x\rangle$ and implement the equivalent functionality of the quantum nonlinear function to calculate and output $|0\rangle$ or $|1\rangle$

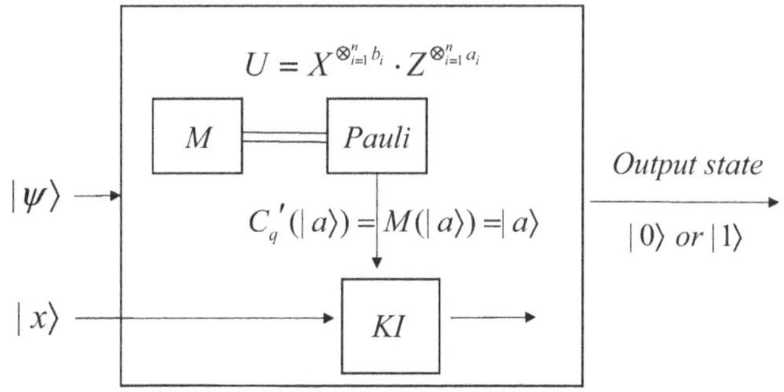

Fig. 2.4 Interpreter of quantum nonlinear function

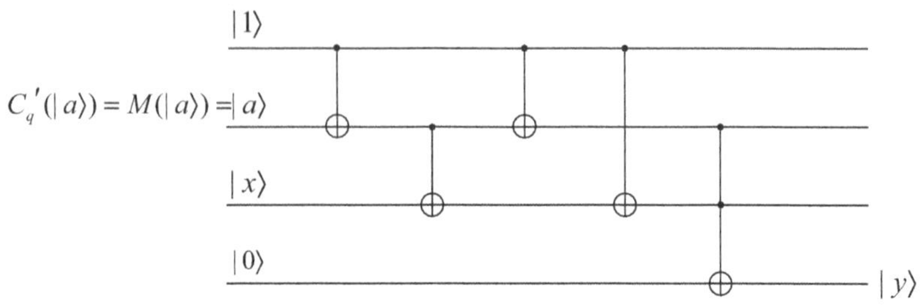

Fig. 2.5 Equivalent circuit of a quantum power function in the KI operation of an interpreter

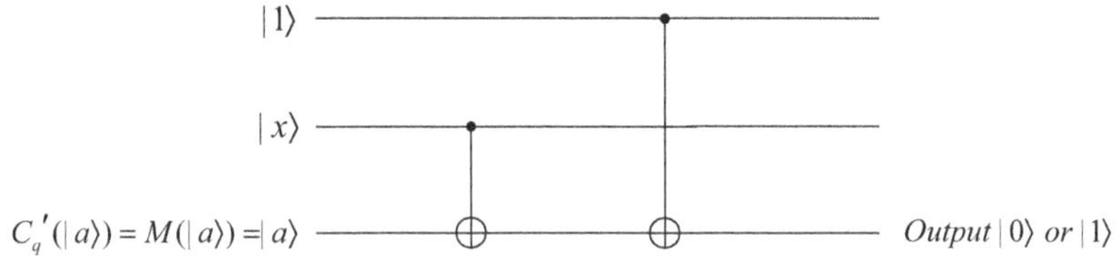

Fig. 2.6 Equivalent circuit of a single-qubit quantum point function in the KI operation of an interpreter

qubit, we measure its first two qubits to obtain a classical bit string. According to the classical bit string obtained, the corresponding Pauli matrix is performed to restore each qubit and the result is represented as the quantum state $M(|a\rangle)$. Here $M(|a\rangle) = |a\rangle$ holds. In this way, we design the quantum circuit in Fig. 2.6 and provide an implementable way to determine the equivalence of two quantum states to represent a quantum point function. We use it to judge whether $|x\rangle$ is equal to $|a\rangle$ or not and finally output $|0\rangle$ or $|1\rangle$.

2.4.5.2 B. Quantum Power Function Obfuscation

The concept of quantum power function is presented in Definition 2.4. The parameter of the quantum power function is represented as $|a\rangle$. We then obfuscate it by quantum teleportation to obtain an obfuscated state $|\psi\rangle$ which is one of the possible states $\alpha|0\rangle + \beta|1\rangle$, $\alpha|\ 0\rangle - \beta|1\rangle$, $\alpha|1\rangle + \beta|0\rangle$, or $\alpha|1\rangle - \beta|0\rangle$. For every qubit, we measure its first two qubits to obtain a classical bit string. According to classical bit string obtained, we perform the corresponding Pauli matrix to restore each qubit making up the state $M(|a\rangle)$. Hence we know what exactly $|a\rangle$ is. Apparently, with the superposition state $\alpha|0\rangle + \beta|1\rangle$ input, we can give the overall construction of the quantum power function interpreter in Fig. 2.5. The 'OR' operation can be achieved by NAND relation. Thus we reach the goal of outputting $|1\rangle$ when $|a\rangle = |0\rangle$ and outputting $|x\rangle$ when $|a\rangle = |1\rangle$, which satisfies the functionality of a quantum power function.

2.5 Summary

Quantum obfuscation is based on the theory of quantum computation. Since quantum computation is far from mature than its classical counterpart, we gave a further introduction on the preliminaries of quantum obfuscation. To precisely define quantum nonlinear functions and analyze its obfuscatability, we introduced essential security analysis methods such as quantum-accessible random oracle model and quantum random oracle model. For the construction of quantum obfuscation schemes for quantum nonlinear functions, quantum teleportation is utilized to obfuscate two quantum states. We can construct different quantum circuits to obfuscate and interpret each function, and extend various properties of an obfuscator and corresponding security. Further work lies in the routine similar to classical obfuscation theory on nonlinear functions such as obfuscatability under the security model, or how to construct obfuscators by cryptographic schemes.

References

1. Nielson, M.A., Chuang, I.L.: Quantum Computation and Quantum Information. Cambridge University Press (2002)
2. Bennett, C.H., Brassard, G., Crepeau, C., Jozsa, R., Peres, A., Wootters, W.K.: Teleporting an unknown quantum state via dual classical and Einstein-Podolsky-Rosen channels. Phys. Rev. Lett. **70**, 1895–1899 (1993)
3. Bennett, C.H., Brassard, G.: Strengths and weaknesses of quantum computing. SIAM J. Comput. **26**(5), 1510–1523 (1997)
4. Bellare, M., Rogaway, P.: Random oracles are practical: a paradigm for designing efficient protocols. In: ACM Conference on Computer and Communications Security (CCS), pp. 62–73 (1993)
5. Boneh, D., Dagdelen, O., Fischlin, M., et al.: Random oracles in a quantum world. Comput. Sci. **7073**(1), 41–69 (2010)
6. Alagic, G., Fefferman, B.: On quantum obfuscation (2016). arXiv:1602.01771
7. Pan, C.Y., Shang, T., Zhang, Y.J.: Universal quantum obfuscation for quantum non-linear functions. Front. Phys. **10**, 1342 (2023)
8. Shang, T., Chen, R.Y.L., Liu, J.W.: On the obfuscatability of quantum point functions. Quantum Inf. Process. **18**, 55 (2019)
9. Jiang, Y.Z., Shang, T., Tang, Y., et al.: Quantum obfuscation of generalized quantum power functions with coefficient. Entropy **25**(11), 1524 (2023)

Chapter 3
Quantum Point Obfuscation

We take two typical quantum nonlinear functions for example. One is a quantum point function which is an easy form of quantum nonlinear functions to implement the functionality of judgement. The other is a quantum power function which is the component of quantum polynomial functions. Quantum point obfuscation is fundamental and practical in quantum obfuscation. It is necessary for us to give rigorous proof and derive the extended property of quantum cryptography by fulfilling elementary primitives in quantum point obfuscation. In this chapter, to analyze the obfuscatability of quantum point functions, we introduce the strict definition of a quantum point function and discuss its variants of multiple points and multiple qubits. Furthermore, we discuss the instantiation procedure of quantum point obfuscation.

3.1 Quantum Point Function

In this section, we will give a precise definition of quantum point functions, especially the ones with an input of quantum superposition.

3.1.1 Quantum Point Function Family and Its Obfuscatability

In the classical case, a point function is defined by

$$P_\alpha(x) = \begin{cases} 1 \; if \; x = \alpha \\ 0 \; otherwise \end{cases}. \tag{3.1}$$

T. Shang, *Quantum Nonlinear Function Obfuscation Theory and Application*,
https://doi.org/10.1007/978-981-97-6722-9_3

According to quantum computation theory, any classical function f can be implemented by a quantum circuit. To implement such a function, a quantum circuit maps input register x and target register b, $|x \circ b\rangle$, to $|x \circ b \oplus f(x)\rangle$, where $\circ$ denotes concatenation. For convenience, the target register b can be set to zero. From this premise, we can define a quantum point function as follows:

Definition 3.1 A quantum point function U_α is defined as

$$U_\alpha : |x, 0\rangle \mapsto |x, P_\alpha(x)\rangle, \tag{3.2}$$

where $\alpha \in \{0, 1\}^n$.

Obviously, with an input in superposition $\sum_x a_x |x \circ 0\rangle$, the point function will also return a result of superposition $\sum_x a_x |x \circ P_\alpha(x)\rangle$, where a_x is a complex coefficient. After defining $\mathcal{U}_n = \{U_\alpha : \alpha \in \{0, 1\}^n\}$ and $\mathcal{U} = \bigcup_n \mathcal{U}_n$, we can construct the obfuscation of $\mathcal{U}$ and prove the following lemma.

Lemma 3.1 *A quantum point function family $\mathcal{U}$ is obfuscatable, under the quantum-accessible random oracle model.*

Proof Note that the quantum-accessible random oracle R_q is interpreted as a length-preserving permutation oracle, $R_q : |x, y\rangle \mapsto |x, y \oplus R(x)\rangle$, where $R : \{0, 1\}^n \mapsto \{0, 1\}^n$ and $x, y \in \{0, 1\}^n$. The obfuscator for quantum point function U_α works as follows: $O^R(U_\alpha)$ firstly makes a query to oracle R_q with a classical bit string α to obtain $R(\alpha)$, then removes any information about α except $R(\alpha)$. When it receives an input $|x, 0\rangle$, $O^R(U_\alpha)$ accesses to quantum-accessible random oracle R_q with $|x, 0^n\rangle$ to obtain $|x, R(x)\rangle$. Finally, $O^R(U_\alpha)$ implements the checking function

$$Ch(x) = \begin{cases} 1 \; if \; x = R(\alpha) \\ 0 \; otherwise \end{cases} \tag{3.3}$$

by quantum gate $Ch_q : |x, y\rangle \mapsto |x, y \oplus Ch(x)\rangle$ and uses it on both the second register of return result of the oracle and the target register of input of the quantum circuit. The whole quantum circuit is implemented as Fig. 3.1. □

Firstly, we prove the functional equivalence property of U_α. We point out that the quantum-accessible random oracle is implemented as a permutation oracle $\{0, 1\}^n \mapsto \{0, 1\}^n$. In this sense R is a bijective, hence $R(x) = R(\alpha)$ if and only if $x = \alpha$. Therefore $O^R(U_\alpha)$ correctly maps $\sum_x a_x |x \circ 0\rangle$ to $\sum_x a_x |x \circ P_\alpha(x)\rangle$.

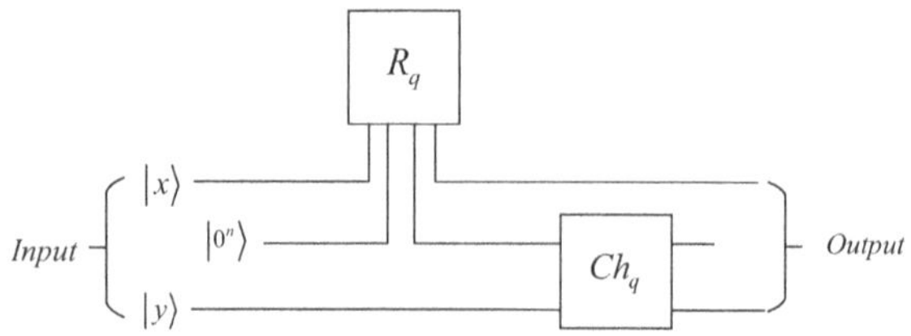

Fig. 3.1 Quantum circuit for $O(U_\alpha)$

Since quantum random query is made once for any input, the polynomial slowdown property holds. Now we prove the black-box property. For any adversary A, a simulator S^{U_α} can be constructed as follows: S sets a copy of A internally (denoted by A'), then S randomly chooses $a \in \{0,1\}^n$ and constructs a quantum state $|\alpha, 0^m\rangle$, then queries the random oracle R_q with it twice to obtain two same quantum states $|r_1\rangle, |r_2\rangle$. Then it constructs a circuit C like this: for an input $|x, y\rangle$, C queries random oracle with $|x, 0^m\rangle$, keeps the return value $|r'\rangle$, and checks if $r_1 = r'$. If so, it reverses register $|y\rangle$. Next, S puts C into A', every time A' queries R_q with $|x, y\rangle$, S queries U_α with $|x, 0\rangle$. If S obtains $|1\rangle$, it returns $|x, y \oplus r_2\rangle$, otherwise S randomly chooses a number in $\{0,1\}^n$, queries R with it and returns to A'. Finally, S outputs what A' outputs. Obviously, A' performs exactly the same as A.

$$|\Pr[A = 1] - \Pr[S^{U_\alpha} = 1]| = 0 \tag{3.4}$$

So the black-box property holds.

3.1.2 Quantum Point Function with Multi-Qubit Output

In the context of multi-qubit output, $|0^n\rangle$ becomes a possibly valid output. In classical case, the invalid output $\perp$ is introduced and a classical point function with multi-qubit output is defined by

$$P_{\alpha,\beta}(x) = \begin{cases} \beta \ if \ x = \alpha \\ \perp \ otherwise \end{cases}, \tag{3.5}$$

where $\alpha, \beta \in \{0,1\}^n$. As the quantum circuits are required to be invertible and unitary, concession must be made to keep consistence with well-formed QPT. Concretely, to avoid the use of $\perp$, we manually set $|0^n\rangle$ to represent an invalid input, therefore β is restricted in any bit-string in $\{0,1\}^n$ except 0^n. In this sense, $P_{\alpha,\beta}$ will be modified as $P'_{\alpha,\beta}$ to output 0^n when $x \neq \alpha$.

Definition 3.2 A quantum point function with a multi-qubit output is defined as follows.

$$U_{\alpha,\beta} : |x, 0^n\rangle \mapsto |x, P'_{\alpha,\beta}\rangle, \tag{3.6}$$

where $\alpha \in \{0,1\}^n$, and $\beta \in \{0,1\}^n \backslash 0^n$.

Let $C_{\alpha,\beta}$ be a quantum circuit which implements $U_{\alpha,\beta}$. Define $\mathcal{C}_n = \{C_{\alpha,\beta} : \alpha, \beta \in \{0,1\}^n\}$.

Lemma 3.2 *A quantum point function family $\mathcal{C}$ with multi-qubit output is obfuscatable, under the quantum-accessible random oracle model.*

Proof A QRO R_q is used in the proof. Firstly, we randomly choose $r \in \{0,1\}^n$, query R_q with $|r, \alpha, 0^{2n}\rangle$ and obtain $|r, \alpha, 0^{2n} \oplus R(r, \alpha)\rangle = |r, \alpha, a \circ b\rangle$, where a and b is the first n bits and the last n bits of $R(r, \alpha)$. Note that R is a length-preserving oracle.

Then we calculate $c = b \oplus \beta$. Now we can remove any information on α and β, and just keep r, a and c. Next, for every input $|x, 0\rangle$, $O^R(U_{\alpha,\beta})$ makes query to R_q with $|r, x\rangle|0^{2n}\rangle$, obtains $|r, x\rangle|R(r, x)\rangle = |r, x\rangle|R_1(r, x), R_2(r, x)\rangle$ in return. Finally, $O^R(U_{\alpha,\beta})$ implements the checking function

$$Ch(x) = \begin{cases} c \oplus R_2 \; if \; x = a \\ 0^n \qquad otherwise \end{cases} \tag{3.7}$$

by a quantum gate $Ch_q : |x, y\rangle \mapsto |x, y \oplus Ch(x)\rangle$ and implies it on both the second register of return result of the oracle and the target register of input of the quantum circuit.

It is obvious that this obfuscation is valid, with the similar method used in the proof of Lemma 3.1.

We can see that $\mathcal{C}$ can be simply obfuscated. Note that we have only polynomial-many obfuscations, the probability that two of them happen to pick up the same r is negligible. Under this condition, the simulator will be able to simulate any adversary. □

3.1.3 Quantum Multi-point Function with Multi-qubit Output

Definition 3.3 A quantum multi-point function with multi-qubit output is defined as

$$U_{(\alpha_1,\beta_1),\dots,(\alpha_t,\beta_t)} : |x, y\rangle \mapsto |x, y \oplus P_{(\alpha_1,\beta_1),\dots,(\alpha_t,\beta_t)}\rangle, \tag{3.8}$$

where $\alpha_i \in \{0, 1\}^n$, $\beta_i \in \{0, 1\}^n \backslash 0^n$ and $P_{(\alpha_1,\beta_1),\dots,(\alpha_t,\beta_t)}$ is a classical function that maps $\{0, 1\}^n$ to $\{0, 1\}^{tn}$:

$$P_{(\alpha_1,\beta_1),\dots,(\alpha_t,\beta_t)}(x)|_i = \begin{cases} \beta_i \; if \; x = \alpha_i \\ 0^n \; otherwise \end{cases} \tag{3.9}$$

and $P_{(\alpha_1,\beta_1),\dots,(\alpha_t,\beta_t)}(x) = P_{(\alpha_1,\beta_1),\dots,(\alpha_t,\beta_t)}(x)|_1 \circ \cdots \circ P_{(\alpha_1,\beta_1),\dots,(\alpha_t,\beta_t)}(x)|_t$.

Let $C_{(\alpha_1,\beta_1),\dots,(\alpha_t,\beta_t)}$ be a quantum circuit which implements $U_{(\alpha_1,\beta_1),\dots,(\alpha_t,\beta_t)}$, define $\mathcal{C}_n^t = \{C_{(\alpha_1,\beta_1),\dots,(\alpha_t,\beta_t)} : \alpha_i, \beta_i \in \{0, 1\}^n\}$, define $\mathcal{C}^* = \bigcup_{poly \; t} \mathcal{C}_n^t$

Lemma 3.3 *A quantum circuit family $\mathcal{C}^*$ is obfuscatable.*

Proof We will show that $\mathcal{C}_n^t \ll \{C_{n1}\# \dots \#C_{nt} : C_{ni} \in \mathcal{C}_n\}$. Since $\mathcal{C}$ can be simply obfuscated, $\{C_1\# \dots \#C_t : C_i \in \mathcal{C}\}$ is obfuscatable. If $\mathcal{C}^t$ is obfuscatable, so is $\mathcal{C}^*$.

To construct a QPT M that $M^{U_{C_{n1}\#\dots\#C_{nt}}}$ computes $\mathcal{C}_n^t$, M has access to each oracle successively and simply concatenates all return values. To construct a QPT N that $N^{U_{\mathcal{C}_n^t}}$ computes $C_{n1}\# \dots \#C_{nt}$, N queries the oracle of $\mathcal{C}_n^t$ with the input register once and discards the unwanted part of output according to the control register. Since the control register is fixed to be a basic state, the measurement will not cause any information loss of the input register. □

3.2 Quantum Obfuscation for Quantum Point Function

A point function returns an internal value m when the input equals a specific k, and 0 elsewise. According to the theory of quantum computation, such a function can be described as

$$U_{k,m} : |x, y\rangle \mapsto \begin{cases} |x, y \oplus m\rangle & if\ x = k \\ |x, y\rangle & otherwise \end{cases}. \tag{3.10}$$

Since an obfuscator for all functions does not exist, we consider a quantum obfuscator only for quantum point functions, then we assume that the input of an obfuscator is delineated by m and k. Therefore, n equals $|m| + |k|$, and we have $|O(U_{m,k})| = poly(|m| + |k|)$.

We then define a stronger version of the quantum point obfuscator, which preserves security even when an adversary has a combination of different point functions. With respect to quantum encryption, we are interested in the case where the point functions are of the same k. In this case, we call it self-combinable.

Definition 3.4 A quantum point obfuscator is self-combinable, if for any $t = poly(n)$ the combination of t's obfuscators is still secure, i.e., we have a simulator S such that

$$\begin{aligned} &|\Pr[A(O(U_{k,r_1}), O(U_{k,r_2}), \ldots, O(U_{k,r_t})) = 1] \\ &-\Pr[S^{U_{k,r_1}, U_{k,r_2}, \ldots, U_{k,r_t}}(0^n) = 1]| \leq negl(n). \end{aligned} \tag{3.11}$$

In quantum encryption, we are also interested in the case where A is provided with some auxiliary inputs (always some information on k). In this case, we define a quantum-secure obfuscator with auxiliary inputs.

Definition 3.5 A quantum point obfuscator with auxiliary inputs f is secure, if we have a simulator S such that

$$\begin{aligned} &|\Pr[A(O(U_{k,r}), f(k)) = 1] \\ &-\Pr[S^{U_{k,r}}(f(k)) = 1]| \leq negl(n). \end{aligned} \tag{3.12}$$

A quantum circuit family is obfuscatable if there exists a quantum state family that is the obfuscation of the quantum circuit family. The work of Alagic and Fefferman [1] gives the impossible result of universal quantum obfuscation as follows.

Theorem 3.1 *There exists a quantum circuit family C such that no state family is a reusable-black-box quantum obfuscation of C.*

Due to this negative conclusion, quantum obfuscation is possible only for limited quantum functions. A positive technique of quantum obfuscation is to obfuscate a quantum point function [2], namely quantum point obfuscation.

Theorem 3.2 *Let $C_{\alpha,\beta}$ be a quantum circuit which implements $U_{\alpha,\beta}$, define $C_n = \{C_{\alpha,\beta} : \alpha \in \{0,1\}^n, \beta \in \{0,1\}^n\}$. A quantum function family C is obfuscatable under the quantum-accessible random oracle model.*

The obfuscator and interpreter of $\mathcal{C}$ can be roughly described as follows.

The obfuscator $O^{R_q}(U_{\alpha,\beta})$ queries the quantum random oracle with $|\alpha\rangle$ and obtains $|R(\alpha)\rangle$. Then the obfuscation of $U_{\alpha,\beta}$ is

$$O^{R_q}(U_{\alpha,\beta}) = |R(\alpha), \alpha \oplus \beta\rangle. \tag{3.13}$$

The interpreter δ firstly performs the exclusive OR (XOR) operation on the oracle response to an input $|R(x)\rangle$ and the first n qubits of $O^{R_q}(U_{\alpha,\beta})$, i.e., $R(\alpha)$. Then, δ reverses the XOR result. Next, δ bit-wise ANDs the reversed qubits. So far, the interpreter has achieved the function of 'comparing' $|\alpha\rangle$ and $|x\rangle$. In the last step, δ outputs the XOR result of $|x\rangle$ and the last n qubits of $O^{R_q}(U_{\alpha,\beta})$, i.e., $\alpha \oplus \beta$, if $x = \alpha$, otherwise, δ outputs $|0^n\rangle$. This can be achieved by a Toffoli gate with the inputs of bit-wise AND result, namely $|x \oplus \alpha \oplus \beta\rangle$ and $|0^n\rangle$.

It is easy to see the functionality of a quantum point function with a multi-qubit output preserved. The size of $O^{R_q}(U_{\alpha,\beta})$ is $m = 2n = poly(n)$. Similarly, the black-box property can be proved. Thus this obfuscation is valid.

We can see that combined $\mathcal{C}$ can be simply obfuscated, i.e., $O(C_1)\#\cdots\#O(C_k)$ is an obfuscation of $C_1\#\cdots\#C_k$. This is because k is polynomial in n. Any adversary having $O(C_1)\#\cdots\#O(C_k)$ can be simulated with oracle access to $C_1\#\cdots\#C_k$.

3.3 Multi-valued Quantum Point Obfuscation

Since quantum cryptographic scheme is expected to be applicable to multi-valued quantum states, Zhang et al. [3] defined a multi-valued quantum random oracle model for analyzing the obfuscatability of multi-valued quantum point functions, and gave the structure and properties of the multi-valued quantum random oracle model. Then two kinds of multi-valued quantum point functions are defined and their obfuscation schemes are designed under the multi-valued quantum random oracle model.

3.3.1 Multi-valued Quantum Random Oracle Model

In this section, the 'quantum-hash' random oracle model is extended to make it possible to analyze multi-valued quantum obfuscation.

Firstly, the generation range of the key k is modified. It is no longer a random classical bit string, but is closely related to the dimension d.

Secondly, a binary converter B is added, and the dimension d will be a large decimal number. In order to enhance security, the decimal number is converted into a corresponding binary string $\{0, 1\}^m$.

Finally, the range limit of the constant c for the number of quantum random oracles is added. When the challenger accesses the quantum random oracle, the quantum random oracle produces at most c copies of the output to the adversary, and the number of c is related to d. This limitation reflects that under the constraint of the quantum non-cloning theorem, an adversary can only obtain a limited number of unknown qubits.

Based on the above analysis, the multi-valued quantum random oracle machine is defined as follows:

Definition 3.6 The multi-valued quantum random oracle machine is a quantum polynomial time algorithm R_q that satisfies the following properties:

1. When any party (adversary or challenger) accesses with the classical constant $k \in N$, the binary converter B will convert k into a classical bit string $\{0, 1\}^m$.
2. R_q randomly and uniformly generates the quantum state $\left|R_q\left(B(k)\right)\right\rangle \in \left(\mathcal{H}^2\right)^{\otimes s}$ of s-qubits, where $s = ploy\,(m)$.
3. The output of the different inputs of any pair of multi-valued quantum random oracles R_q is nearly orthogonal

$$\left|\left\langle R_q\left(B(k)\right) \middle| R_q\left(B(k')\right)\right\rangle\right|^2 < \varepsilon, \tag{3.14}$$

where $B(k) \neq B(k')$, ε is negligible for the parameter m.
4. If R_q is accessed by the challenger as the input k, the multi-valued quantum random oracle machine R_q produces c copies of the output for the adversary.

Similar to the classical random oracle model, the adversary-challenger game is required to analyze the security of quantum obfuscation in the multi-valued quantum random oracle model.

Definition 3.7 The quantum obfuscated adversary-challenger game consists of the following three phases:

Phase 1. For the quantum circuit family C, the challenger selects the quantum circuit $C_i \in C, i = 1, \ldots, t$, and the challenger uses the multi-valued quantum random oracle to generate the corresponding obfuscation result $O^{R_q}\left(C_i\right)$. In this phase, for each input of R_q, the multi-valued quantum random oracle machine produces at most c copies of the output to the adversary. So, for each quantum circuit C, the adversary produces at most c copies of the obfuscation result $O^{R_q}\left(C_i\right)^{\otimes C}$.

Phase 2. In this phase, the adversary uses any input to access the multi-valued quantum random oracle. If the times the adversary visits the random oracle machine is q_{ro}, then for any $k = k_1, \ldots, k_{q_{ro}}$, the multi-valued quantum random oracle machine returns $\left|R_q\left(B(k)\right)\right\rangle$ to the adversary.

Phase 3. The challenger selects a quantum circuit $C \in C$ different from C_i from the quantum circuit family C, and uses a multi-valued quantum random oracle to generate the corresponding obfuscation result $O^{R_q}(C)$. The adversary outputs the quantum state $A^{R_q}\left(O(C)\right)$. In this phase, the multi-valued quantum random oracle produces at most c copies of the output to the adversary. So, for the quantum circuit C, the adversary can directly generate c obfuscation results $O^{R_q}(C)$.

When the output of the adversary is described as follows:

$$A^{R_q}(O(C)) = O^{R_q}(C)^{\otimes(c+1)}, \tag{3.15}$$

the adversary wins the adversary-challenger game. The adversary's advantage is

$$\mathrm{Adv}(adversary) = \Pr[A^{R_q}(O(C)) = O^{R_q}(C)^{\otimes(c+1)}]. \tag{3.16}$$

When the adversary's advantage is negligible relative to the input size m, the challenger is said to have won the game. At this time, the quantum obfuscator O is considered to be secure under the multi-valued quantum random oracle model.

3.3.2 Property of Multi-valued Quantum States

For any prime number d, multi-valued quantum states have $d+1$ groups of mutually unbiased bases. Any vector in $d+1$ groups of mutually unbiased bases can be denoted by

$$G_{l,j} = \left|g_l^{(j)}\right\rangle, \tag{3.17}$$

where j represents the basis of the vector, and l represents the value of the vector. j and l meet $j = 0, \ldots, d$ and $l = 0, \ldots, d-1$, respectively. $g_l^{(j)}$ corresponds to the states from 0 to $d-1$ for the d-dimensional Hilbert space. $G_{l,j}$ is an arbitrary multi-valued unitary operator. The $d+1$ groups of mutually unbiased bases are used as quantum measurement bases. When $j = d$, a set of bases are called computational bases and denoted by $\left\{\left|g_l^{(d)}\right\rangle\right\}$. The quantum measurement bases of group $j\ (0 \leq j \leq d-1)$ are denoted by $\left\{\left|g_l^{(j)}\right\rangle\right\}$. Through the computational bases, any vector in the remaining d groups of unbiased bases can be expressed in Equation (3.18).

$$G_{l,j} = \left|g_l^{(j)}\right\rangle = \frac{1}{\sqrt{d}} \sum_{x=0}^{d-1} \omega^{x(l+jx)} |x\rangle, \tag{3.18}$$

where $\omega = e^{2\pi i/d}$.

When the vector $G_{l,j}$ is measured by using the correct quantum measurement basis $\left\{\left|g_l^{(j)}\right\rangle\right\}$, the measurement result will be the only confirmed α. When the vector $G_{l,j}$ is measured by using an incorrect quantum measurement basis, a value between 0 and $d-1$ is obtained with the same probability $(1/d)$.

3.3.3 Multi-valued Quantum Single-Point Function

Definition 3.8 The multi-valued quantum single-point function is defined as follows:

$$U_{a,b} : \left|x, y, G_{l,j}\right\rangle \to \left|x, y, G_{l+P_a(x),j+P_b(y)}\right\rangle, \tag{3.19}$$

where $x, y \in G_{l,j}$, $j = 1, \ldots, d$, $l = 0, \ldots, d-1$, $P_a(x)$ and $P_b(y)$ are the following classical functions:

$$P_a(x) = \begin{cases} a & x = a \\ d-a & x \neq a \end{cases} \tag{3.20}$$

$$P_b(y) = \begin{cases} b & y = b \\ d-b & y \neq b \end{cases} \tag{3.21}$$

where $a, b \in \{1, \ldots, d-1\}$.

We define $C_{a,b} = \left\{C_{a,b} : a, b \in \{0, \ldots, d\}\right\}$, where $C_{a,b}$ is a quantum circuit that implements the corresponding function of the unitary matrix $U_{a,b}$. The structure of the multi-valued quantum single-point function obfuscator $O^{R_q}\left(U_{a,b}\right)$ can be given as follows:

Scheme 3.1 (Multi-valued quantum single-point obfuscation scheme). *The obfuscator $O^{R_q}\left(U_{a,b}\right)$ asks the multi-valued quantum random oracle machine R_q with a, b to obtain the quantum states $R_q\left(B\left(a\right)\right), R_q\left(B\left(b\right)\right)$, and the obfuscator $O^{R_q}\left(U_{a,b}\right)$ stores the obtained quantum state $r_a = R_q\left(B\left(a\right)\right), r_b = R_q\left(B\left(b\right)\right)$, when inputting $x, y \in G_{l,j}$, will output $G_{l+a,j}$ if $R_q\left(B(x)\right) = r_a$, $G_{l,j+b}$ if $R_q\left(B(y)\right) = r_b$, $G_{l+a,j+b}$ if $R_q\left(B(x)\right) = r_a$, $R_q\left(B(y)\right) = r_b$, otherwise $G_{l+d-a,j+d-b}$.*

3.3.4 Multi-valued Quantum Multi-point Function

Definition 3.9 The multi-valued quantum multi-point function is defined as follows:

$$U_{(a_1,b_1),\ldots,(a_i,b_i)} : \left|x, y, G_{l,j}\right\rangle \to \left|x, y, G_{l+P_{a_1,\ldots,a_i}(x),j+P_{b_1,\ldots,b_i}(y)}\right\rangle, \tag{3.22}$$

where $x, y \in G_{l,j}$, $j = 1, \ldots, d$, $l = 0, \ldots, d-1$. $P_{a_1,\ldots,a_i}(x)$ and $P_{b_1,\ldots,b_i}(y)$ are the following classical functions:

$$P_{a_1,\ldots,a_n}(x) = \begin{cases} a_i & x = a_i \\ d-a_i & x \neq a_i \end{cases} \tag{3.23}$$

$$P_{b_1,\ldots,b_n}(y) = \begin{cases} b_i & y = b_i \\ d-b_i & y \neq b_i \end{cases} \tag{3.24}$$

where $a_i, b_i \in \{1, \ldots, d-1\}$, $i \in 1, \ldots, n$.

We define $C_{(a_1,b_1),\ldots,(a_i,b_i)} = \{C_{(a_1,b_1),\ldots,(a_i,b_i)} : a_i, b_i \in \{0, \ldots, d\}\}$, where $C_{(a_1,b_1),\ldots,(a_i,b_i)}$ is a quantum circuit that implements the corresponding function of the unitary matrix $U_{(a_1,b_1),\ldots,(a_i,b_i)}$. We define $\mathcal{C}_n^t = \{C_{(a_1,b_1),\ldots,(a_t,b_t)} : a_i, b_i \in \{0, 1\}^n\}$ and define $\mathcal{C}^* = \cup_{poly\, t} \mathcal{C}_n^t$. The structure of the multi-valued quantum single-point function obfuscator $O^{R_q}\left(U_{(a_1,b_1),\ldots,(a_i,b_i)}\right)$ can be given as follows:

Scheme 3.2 (Multi-valued quantum multi-point obfuscation scheme). *The obfuscator* $O^{R_q}\left(U_{(a_1,b_1),\ldots,(a_i,b_i)}\right)$ *asks the multi-valued quantum random oracle machine* R_q *with* $(a_1, b_1), \ldots, (a_i, b_i)$ *to obtain the quantum states* $R_q(B(a_1)), \ldots, R_q(B(a_i)), R_q(B(b_1)), \ldots, R_q(B(b_i))$, *and the obfuscator* $O^{R_q}\left(U_{(a_1,b_1)}, \ldots, (a_i, b_i)\right)$ *stores the obtained quantum states* $r_{a_1,\ldots,a_i} = R_q(B(a_1)), \ldots, R_q(B(a_i)), r_{b_1,\ldots,b_i} = R_q(B(b_1)), \ldots, R_q(B(b_i))$, *when inputting* $x, y \in G_{l,j}$, *will output* $G_{l+a_i,j}$ *if* $R_q(B(x)) = r_{a_1,\ldots,a_i}$, $G_{l,j+b_i}$ *if* $R_q(B(y)) = r_{b_1,\ldots,b_i}$, $G_{l+a_i,j+b_i}$ *if* $R_q(B(x)) = r_{a_1,\ldots,a_i}, R_q(B(y)) = r_{b_1,\ldots,b_i}$, *otherwise* $G_{l+d-a_i,j+d-b_i}$.

3.4 Instantiation of Quantum Point Obfuscation

There is a question whether the security of quantum point obfuscation can continue to be maintained after instantiation with a quantum function or not. So how to instantiate quantum point obfuscation under the premise of security deserves to be discussed further.

3.4.1 Requirement of Instantiation

Obfuscation of point functions is a branch of obfuscation theory. Since the point function is an abstraction of many commonly used functions, such as access control, low-entropy password protection, the obfuscation of point functions can effectively enhance the security of application scenarios of these functions. The obfuscation regarding point functions is also named point obfuscation. Research works on point obfuscation focus on how to construct an obfuscation scheme. Lynn et al. [4] summarized the impossible results of obfuscation in the past and gave positive results for obfuscation for the first time. They used the combination of point obfuscation to construct an access control function model under the random oracle model, and proposed the obfuscation of finite automata and regular expressions, which was not in the study "On the (im)possibility of obfuscating programs" by Barak et al. [5]. In 2005, Wee et al. [6] did a more detailed study on point obfuscation and drew some important conclusions. In view of the limitation of the obfuscator in Wee's work, Ran *et al.* [7] proposed the obfuscation of multi-bit output point functions and verified the obfuscation in the work of Lynn et al. [4] was not secure. Ran et al. [8]

gave a new definition of secure obfuscation combinations, but there were no effective obfuscators that met this requirement. So Bitansky and Ran [9] proposed the concept of virtual grey-box (VGB) which is weaker than virtual black-box (VBB). It has been proved that using the new virtual grey-box definition can construct an effective obfuscator to implement the obfuscation combinations in the reference [8]. The above indicates that there is indeed an effective obfuscator to implement obfuscation, but these studies are still on the way.

Although point functions have been widely discussed in classical obfuscation, they have not yet drawn much attention in the quantum circumstance. Shang et al. [2, 10] first set forth practical primitives in quantum point obfuscation, together with defining a quantum point function as well as presenting its obfuscatability. They proved that quantum point obfuscation is secure under the quantum-accessible random oracle model and adopted quantum point obfuscation for strictly constructing an indistinguishability-secure quantum symmetric encryption scheme. In order to make the scheme efficient, it is necessary to replace the random oracle model with the standard model, which is called instantiation.

According to the quantum instantiation procedure and the unique instantiation characteristics of quantum point obfuscation, we attempt to clarify the definition of instantiation of quantum point obfuscation from a general perspective and instantiate quantum point obfuscation by means of feasible construction of quantum hash functions. Consequently, we will choose a suitable instantiation scheme to guarantee the security of a quantum cryptographic scheme [11].

3.4.2 Instantiation Procedure: From Classic to Quantum

So far, many protocols rely on the use of a hash function. The hash function is originally designed in computer science to map a string of arbitrary length to a hash value of fixed length. In cryptography, additional properties, such as one-wayness and collision-resistance, are required for hash functions to be secure against various attacks [12, 13]. Such properties make hash functions resemble random oracles. A random oracle O from a domain $\mathcal{D}$ to a codomain $\mathcal{R}$ is a uniformly random function taken from the universe of all functions from $\mathcal{D}$ to $\mathcal{R}$. As $\mathcal{D}$ generally has fully exponential size, and often is infinite in size, it is impossible to describe or even generate a complete random oracle when $\mathcal{D}$ is large. This is why hash functions are used instead, as a sort of efficiently computable and manageable random oracle that anyone can implement or use. Generally, security models in which a real hash function is used are called standard models, and security models in which a random oracle is used in place of a hash function are called random oracle models [14, 15]. The random oracle model is immensely popular in establishing security reductions, but it has yet to result in any significant lack of security in practice. Specifically, there has yet to be a protocol that was proved to have a reduction in the random oracle model and was later shown to be insecure in the standard model. Thus the instantiation procedure is an effective solution to providing the guarantee of security from the random oracle model to the standard model.

With reference to the classical instantiation procedure, the quantum instantiation procedure is realized with a quantum hash function. The quantum hash function takes a classical bit string as an input and produces quantum states of fixed length. In contrast to classical approach, the security of a quantum hash function is guaranteed by quantum physical laws. Ablayev et al. [16, 17] discussed the one-wayness and collision-resistance properties of a quantum hash function. Similar to the classical case, the one-wayness of a quantum hash function requires that the input classical bit string cannot be deduced from the output quantum state. The quantum no-cloning theorem avoids an adversary obtaining unlimited copies of unknown hash values. The one-wayness can be guaranteed by Holevo bound [18], no more than $O(s)$ classical bits of information can be extracted from s qubits. According to the Holevo bound, the one-wayness property holds when the length of the input is much larger than that of the output.

As for collision resistance, quantum circumstance is more complex and very different from its classical counterpart. Since the Hilbert space is an infinite field (while $\{0, 1\}^*$ is a finite one), we can easily design a quantum hash function that is mathematically an injective function, i.e., there is no collision according to its definition. However, when comparing two quantum states or recovering classical information from a quantum state, one will introduce measurement operations, which can lead to collision-type errors. Now the 'collision' refers to the case where quantum hash values are measured to be the same while they are actually different. The probability of this collision is closely related to the inner product of the two quantum states. Quantum collision attack means that an adversary fails to obtain any information on the access of a challenger to the quantum random oracle during the attack. The adversary's input to the quantum random oracle can only rely on random guesses, so that the correct output of the quantum random oracle can be obtained with a negligible probability. For the instantiation of quantum point obfuscation, only when the output of the quantum function is non-orthogonal, can a quantum collision attack occur.

Based on the above considerations, the quantum instantiation procedure must follow two conditions:

1. *One-wayness*: For any quantum algorithm A, the probability of finding preimage of ψ is bounded by
$$\Pr[A(\psi(x)) = x] < \epsilon. \tag{3.25}$$

2. *Collision-resistance*: For any pair (w, w'), the norm of the inner product of their hash values is bounded by $\sqrt{\delta}$, and the probability of the two different hash values are measured to be the same is bounded by
$$\Pr[Measure(|\psi(w)\rangle) = Measure(|\psi(w')\rangle)] = |\langle\psi(w)|\psi(w')\rangle|^2 < \delta, \tag{3.26}$$

where $\epsilon > 0, \delta > 0, \psi : \{0,1\}^n \mapsto (\mathcal{H}^2)^{\otimes s}$ and $w, w' \in \{0,1\}^n$.

However, it is not enough to instantiate quantum point obfuscation by considering the properties of one-wayness and collision-resistance. It is necessary to ensure that the instantiation of quantum point obfuscation is obfuscatable. So we will give the definition of instantiation of quantum point obfuscation.

3.4.3 Definition of Instantiation of Quantum Point Obfuscation

Definition 3.10 According to the quantum instantiation procedure and the unique instantiation characteristics of quantum point obfuscation, the instantiation of quantum point obfuscation should meet the following three conditions:

1. (One-wayness) Let X be a random variable over bit strings which are encoded as mixed states over m qubits and let $P(X, d)$ denote the probability of the d most likely strings in the sample space of X. If Y is any random variable obtained by making some measurement of the encoding of X, then for any decoding function $\mathcal{D}$, there exists
$$\Pr[\mathcal{D}(Y) = X] \leq P(X, 2^m). \tag{3.27}$$
In particular, this implies that when X is distributed uniformly, the mutual information $I(X : Y)$ of X and Y is at most m. The bound obviates the need for a translation of in-probability statements into statements about mutual information. According to the reference [19], it also gives better bounds than Holevo's theorem [18].
2. (Security under quantum collision attacks) If the outputs of different inputs (w, w') of the quantum function f_q are nearly orthogonal:
$$\left|\left\langle f_q(w) \mid f_q\left(w'\right)\right\rangle\right| = \epsilon, \tag{3.28}$$
where ϵ can be negligible, the quantum obfuscator is secure under quantum collision attacks.
The input of the challenger to the quantum function is w, and the input of the adversary to the quantum function is w'. Since the operation of the quantum obfuscator on the quantum state is a unitary operation, the unitary matrix of the output operation on the quantum function is set as U, i.e., the output of the quantum function is $U\left|f_q(w)\right\rangle$, then the inner product is
$$\left\langle f_q\left(w'\right)\left|U^{\dagger}U\right| f_q(w)\right\rangle = \left\langle f_q\left(w'\right) \mid f_q(w)\right\rangle = \epsilon. \tag{3.29}$$
Set $|\phi\rangle = U\left|f_q(w)\right\rangle$. The challenger measures $\left\{M_{1,2}\right\} = \{|\phi\rangle\langle\phi|, I - |\phi\rangle\langle\phi|\}$. Then the probability that $U\left|f_q\left(w'\right)\right\rangle$ is 1 by measuring $\left\{M_{1,2}\right\}$ is

$$\begin{aligned}\Pr[m=1] &= \left\langle f_q\left(w'\right)\left|U^{\dagger}M_1^{\dagger}M_1U\right|f_q\left(w'\right)\right\rangle \\ &= \left\langle f_q\left(w'\right)\left|U^{\dagger}U\right|f_q(w)\right\rangle\left\langle f_q(w)\left|U^{\dagger}U\right|f_q\left(w'\right)\right\rangle \\ &= \left\langle f_q\left(w'\right)\mid f_q(w)\right\rangle^2 \\ &= \epsilon^2\end{aligned}. \tag{3.30}$$

That is, the adversary's advantage $\mathrm{Adv}(adversary)=\epsilon^2$ can be negligible, and the quantum obfuscator is secure under quantum collision attacks.

3. (Quantum point obfuscation instantiated is still obfuscatable) The definition of a quantum obfuscator, proposed by Alagic et al. [1], is similar to its classical counterpart.
   A quantum point obfuscator after instantiation contains quantum algorithm O and QPT δ, for any $n-$qubit quantum circuit C, the output of O is an $m-$qubit state $O(C)$ and the following three conditions hold.
   Polynomial expansion:

$$m = poly(n) \tag{3.31}$$

   Functional equivalence: for any possible ρ

$$\|\delta(O(C)\otimes\rho) - U_C\rho U_C^{\dagger}\|_{tr} \le negl(n) \tag{3.32}$$

   Virtual black-box: for every QPT A, there exists a QPT S^{U_C} such that for any QPT distinguisher D

$$|Pr[D(A(O(C)))=1] - Pr[D(S^{U_C}(|0^n\rangle))=1]| \le negl(n) \tag{3.33}$$

   An interpreter δ can be regarded as a device for 'interpreting' the function of C from $O(C)$. Detailed discussions can be found in the references [1, 2].

3.4.4 Instantiation Scheme of Quantum Point Obfuscation

In this section, we give the definition of instantiation of quantum point obfuscation. Quantum error-correcting code and quantum single-qubit rotation are two optional approaches to instantiating quantum point obfuscation. It can be seen that the case of quantum error-correcting code can satisfy the three conditions defined by instantiation of quantum point obfuscation, whereas the case of quantum single-qubit rotation cannot satisfy the conditions.

A. Quantum Point Obfuscation with Quantum Error-Correcting Code
Quantum error-correcting code can be used to construct balanced quantum hash functions [16]. It is defined by

$$|E(x)\rangle = \frac{1}{\sqrt{d}} \sum_{i=1}^{d} |i\rangle \cdot \left(\cos\left(\frac{2\pi k_i x}{2^n}\right) |0\rangle + \sin\left(\frac{2\pi k_i x}{2^n}\right) |1\rangle \right). \tag{3.34}$$

Because of the orthogonality between codes, quantum error-correcting code can be used to instantiate quantum point obfuscator against quantum collision attacks. The quantum point obfuscation obtained by replacing the quantum random oracle with the quantum error-correcting code is described as follows.

Scheme 3.3 (Instantiation of quantum point obfuscation with quantum error-correcting code). *Let O be a quantum point obfuscator, and U_α is a quantum point function, $\alpha \in \{0, 1\}^n$. The obfuscator randomly generates d parameters $K = \{k_1, \ldots, k_d\}$, $k_i \in Z_{2^n}$, and makes the parameter K public. Then the output of the quantum obfuscator is*

$$|O(U_\alpha)\rangle = \frac{1}{\sqrt{d}} \sum_{i=1}^{d} |i\rangle \cdot \left(\cos\left(\frac{2\pi k_i \alpha}{2^n}\right) |0\rangle + \sin\left(\frac{2\pi k_i \alpha}{2^n}\right) |1\rangle \right). \tag{3.35}$$

The interpreter δ is constructed as follows: δ firstly returns the results of $|E(x)\rangle$ and $O(U_\alpha)$ through n CNOT gates to perform bit-by-bit XOR operation, then the interpreter δ reverses n qubits through n Pauli-X gates. After that, the interpreter δ performs the AND operation of all qubits through $n-1$ Toffoli gates. The auxiliary qubit introduced in the Toffoli gate will be released through the reverse operation after the operation is completed to avoid entanglement between the auxiliary qubit and the output result. Finally, the interpreter δ outputs all qubits and calculation results.

Lemma 3.4 *For quantum functions [16], there is*

$$|E(\alpha)\rangle = \frac{1}{\sqrt{d}} \sum_{i=1}^{d} |i\rangle \cdot \left(\cos\left(\frac{2\pi k_i \alpha}{2^n}\right) |0\rangle + \sin\left(\frac{2\pi k_i \alpha}{2^n}\right) |1\rangle \right). \tag{3.36}$$

And any $\epsilon > 0$, for any pair (α, α'), there are parameters $K = \{k_i\}$ satisfying

$$\left|\langle E(\alpha) \mid E(\alpha')\rangle\right| < \epsilon. \tag{3.37}$$

Proof According to the reference [16] that for a reasonably chosen parameter K, the output of the quantum obfuscator corresponding to any pair (α, α') is almost orthogonal. Since the quantum obfuscation results are not entangled with each other, the inner product of any two quantum obfuscation output results is $|\langle O(U_\alpha) \mid O(U'_\alpha)\rangle| = |\langle E(\alpha) \mid E(\alpha')\rangle| < \epsilon$. □

Theorem 3.3 *Quantum point obfuscation with quantum error-correcting code can be instantiated.*

Proof Firstly, quantum point obfuscation instantiated is one-wayness. In Scheme 3.3, the security of the point information α is implemented by the Holevo bound. According to Definition 3.10, the probability that the adversary obtains α through c quantum obfuscation results $|O(U_\alpha)\rangle^{\otimes c} = \left(\cos\left(\frac{2\pi k_i \alpha}{2^n}\right)|0\rangle + \sin\left(\frac{2\pi k_i \alpha}{2^n}\right)|1\rangle\right)^{\otimes c}$ is

$$\Pr\left[A\left(|O(U_\alpha)\rangle^{\otimes C}\right) = \alpha\right] < \frac{2^c}{2^n}. \tag{3.38}$$

It can be seen that the point information α is secure.

Secondly, quantum point obfuscation instantiated is secure under quantum collision attacks. By reasonably choosing the parameter K, the instantiation scheme is resistant to quantum collision attacks. For any quantum point information pair (α, α'), it can be proved that the outputs $|E(\alpha)\rangle$, $|E(\alpha')\rangle$ are almost orthogonal.

According to Lemma 3.4, the advantage $\Pr(adversary) = |\langle O(U_\alpha) \mid O(U'_\alpha)\rangle|^2 < \epsilon^2$ obtained by the adversary performing the quantum collision attack in the adversary-challenger game is negligible. The quantum point obfuscation instantiation scheme with quantum error-correcting code is secure under quantum collision attacks.

Thirdly, quantum point obfuscation instantiated is still obfuscatable. In order to prove that $|E(\alpha)\rangle$ is a correct obfuscation of multi-valued quantum single-point function U_α, we firstly prove the functional equivalence. Since $|E(\alpha)\rangle$ is an ideal random function without collision, $|E(\alpha)\rangle$ is a bijective, i.e., $|E(x)\rangle = |E(\alpha)\rangle$ if and only if $x = \alpha$. So when $x = \alpha$, the interpreter δ correctly maps $\sum_x a_x |x, 0\rangle$ to $\sum_x a_x |x, \alpha\rangle$ with the probability 1. Then $x = \alpha$ can be obtained by measurement and the functional equivalence is established. Then $|E(\alpha)\rangle$ is a s-qubit and polynomial expansion is established. Under the quantum standard model, any party of the security game has access to R_q. For any adversary A, the simulator S is constructed as follows: the simulator S retains a copy of the adversary A internally (denoted as A'), and then randomly selects $\omega \in N$ and prepares the quantum state $|\omega\rangle$. S passes $|\omega\rangle$ to the internal A' as input, and whenever A' queries $E(\alpha)$ with quantum state $|\phi\rangle = \sum_{x=\alpha} a_x |x, y\rangle + \sum_{x\neq\alpha} a_x |x, y\rangle$, S queries U_α with $|\phi\rangle$ and obtains $|\psi\rangle = \sum_{x=\alpha} a_x |x, y \oplus 1\rangle + \sum_{x\neq\alpha} a_x |x, y\rangle$. So the simulator S can answer the correct guess of α with $|\omega\rangle$ and the wrong guess of α with the randomly chosen result $|r\rangle$. Finally, S outputs what A' outputs. The simulator S successfully simulates the external environment of the internal adversary A', and we have

$$\left|\Pr[A = 1] - \Pr\left[S^{U_{a,b}} = 1\right]\right| = 0. \tag{3.39}$$

The virtual black-box condition is satisfied. Thus Scheme 3.3 is a correct instantiation of quantum point obfuscation. □

B. Optional Instantiation with Single-Qubit Rotation

For a given pair of integers n, s, quantum hash function $s \mapsto |\psi_s(\theta_n)\rangle$ is easy to compute since it involves single-qubit rotation only [20]. Then we compare quantum point obfuscation with single-qubit rotation with the instantiation Scheme 3.3. The single-qubit rotation operation is mathematically embodied as the rotation operator $\hat{R}(\theta)$. Note that the initial state $|0\rangle$ rotates around the Y axis of the Bloch sphere by an angle of θ.

When quantum point obfuscation is instantiated with the single-qubit rotation, for the input $k \in \{0, 1\}^n$, $|0\rangle$ is rotated around the Y axis of the Bloch sphere by an angle of $\theta = \frac{2xk}{2^n}$, and the rotated qubit is used as the output. So the instantiated quantum point obfuscation is described as follows:

$$O\left(U_\alpha\right) = \hat{R}\left(\frac{2\pi\alpha}{2^n}\right)|0\rangle = \cos\left(\frac{\pi\alpha}{2^n}\right)|0\rangle + \sin\left(\frac{\pi\alpha}{2^n}\right)|1\rangle. \tag{3.40}$$

The structure of the interpreter δ is similar to the instantiation Scheme 3.3.

However, under the premise that the point information α is secure, quantum point obfuscation with single-qubit rotation is insecure under quantum collision attacks. The output of the quantum obfuscator is not in an orthogonal state. For an adversary performing the quantum collision attack, the inner product of the colliding quantum state and the quantum state output by the obfuscator is

$$\begin{aligned} &|\left(\cos\left(\frac{\pi\alpha}{2^n}\right)|\,0\rangle\right) + \sin\left(\frac{\pi\alpha}{2^{n/s}}\right)|1\rangle\bigg), \left(\cos\left(\frac{\pi\alpha'}{2^n}\right)|\,0\rangle\right) + \sin\left(\frac{\pi\alpha'}{2^n}\right)|1\rangle\bigg)| \\ &= |\cos\left(\frac{\pi\left(a-\alpha'\right)}{2^n}\right)|\,. \end{aligned} \tag{3.41}$$

It cannot be negligible. The adversary performing quantum collision attacks can win the adversary-challenger game with an advantage of $\mathrm{Adv} = \left|\cos\left(\frac{\pi\left(\alpha-\alpha'\right)}{2^n}\right)\right|^2$. Under random collisions, this advantage is 1/6 greater than 10%. Therefore, quantum point obfuscation instantiated with single-qubit rotation is insecure.

3.5 Summary

In this chapter, to precisely define quantum point function family and analyze its obfuscatability, we introduced essential reduction and combination skills, proved that a quantum multi-point function family with multi-qubit output was obfuscatable under the quantum-accessible random oracle model. Furthermore, we proposed multi-valued quantum point obfuscation schemes and proved that there is indeed an effective obfuscator that can achieve quantum point obfuscation. We clarified the definition of instantiation of quantum point obfuscation, gave the instantiation of quantum point obfuscation scheme with quantum error-correcting code and single-qubit rotation respectively and discussed the security under the definition of instantiation. We can know that the instantiation of the quantum point obfuscation with quantum error-correcting code is more secure under the definition of instantiation. Of course, the instantiation scheme provides guidance for the application of quantum obfuscation through the definition of instantiation and more attempts at quantum hash function are still needed.

References

1. Alagic, G., Fefferman, B.: On quantum obfuscation (2016). arXiv:1602.01771
2. Shang, T., Chen, R.Y., Liu, J.W.: On the obfuscatability of quantum point functions. Quantum Inf. Process. **18**(2), 55 (2019)
3. Zhang, Y.J., Shang, T., Liu, J.W.: A multi-valued quantum fully homomorphic encryption scheme. Quantum Inf. Process. **20**(3), 101 (2021)
4. Lynn, B., Prabhakaran, M., Sahai A.: Positive results and techniques for obfuscation. In: International Conference on Advances in Cryptology-Eurocrypt, pp. 20–39. Springer, Berlin, Heidelberg (2004)
5. Barak, B., Goldreich, O., Impagliazzo, R., et al.: On the (im)possibility of obfuscating programs (extended abstract). J. ACM **59**(2), 1–18 (2001)
6. Wee, H.: On obfuscating point functions. In: The 37th Annual ACM Symposium on Theory of Computing, pp. 523–532 (2005)
7. Ran, C., Dakdouk, R.R.: Obfuscating point functions with multibit output. In: Proceedings of Theory and Applications of Cryptographic Techniques, International Conference on Advances in Cryptology, pp. 489–508. Springer (2008)
8. Hada, S.: Secure obfuscation for encrypted signatures. In: International Conference on Theory and Applications of Cryptographic Techniques, pp. 92–112, Springer (2010)
9. Bitansky, N., Ran, C.: On strong simulation and composable point obfuscation. J. Cryptol. **27**(2), 317–357 (2010)
10. Chen, R.Y.L., Shang, T., Liu, J.W.: IND-secure quantum symmetric encryption based on point obfuscation. Quantum Inf. Process. **18**(6), 16 (2019)
11. Zhang, Y.J., Shang, T., Chen, R.Y.L., et al.: Instantiation of quantum point obfuscation. Quantum Inf. Process. **21**(1), 1–16 (2022)
12. Moni, N., Moti, Y.: Universal one-way hash functions and their cryptographic applications. In: The 21th ACM Symposium on Theory of Computing, pp. 33–43 (1989)
13. Merkle, R.C.: One Way Hash Functions and DES. Lecture Notes in Computer Science Vol. 435, pp. 428–446 (1990)
14. Canetti, R., Goldreich, O., Halevi, S.: The random oracle methodology. J. ACM **51**(4), 557–594 (2004)
15. Eaton, E.: Signature Schemes in the Quantum Random-oracle Model. University of Waterloo, Waterloo, Ontario, Canada (2017)
16. Ablayev, F., Vasiliev, A.: Cryptographic quantum hashing. Laser Phys. Lett. **11**(2), 25202 (2014)
17. Ablayev, F., Ablayev, M., Vasiliev, A.: On the balanced quantum hashing. In: Journal of Physics Conference, vol. 681(1), p. 012019 (2016)
18. Holevo, A.S.: Bounds for the quantity of information transmitted by a quantum communication channel. Probl. Inf. Transm. **9**(3), 3–11 (1973)

19. Nayak, A.: Optimal lower bounds for quantum automata and random access codes. In: The 40th Annual Symposium on Foundations of Computer Science, pp. 369–377 (1999)
20. Nikolopoulos, G.M.: Applications of single-qubit rotations in quantum public-key cryptography. Phys. Rev. A **77**(78), 032348 (2008)

Chapter 4
Quantum Power Obfuscation

As a fundamental component of nonlinear functions and composite functions, quantum power function is less well-defined at present. So it is essential to define quantum power functions. In this chapter, to analyze the obfuscatability of quantum power functions, we introduce the obfuscation scheme of a basic quantum power function. Furthermore, we provide a formal definition of two more quantum power functions called generalized quantum power functions with coefficient and discuss the obfuscation scheme for generalized quantum power functions. This work establishes the fundamental basis for constructing more quantum functions that can be utilized for quantum obfuscation, thereby contributing to the theory of quantum obfuscation.

4.1 Quantum Power Function

Quantum power function derives from classical power function. In the classical case, a power function is defined as

$$y = x^a. \tag{4.1}$$

According to the theory of quantum computation, any classical function f can be implemented by a quantum circuit. To implement such a function, a quantum circuit maps input register and target register $|x, b\rangle$ to $|x, b \oplus f(x)\rangle$. On this premise, we define a quantum power function.

Definition 4.1 A quantum power function U_a is defined as

$$U_a : |x, y\rangle \mapsto |x\rangle \otimes P_a(|x\rangle), \tag{4.2}$$

T. Shang, *Quantum Nonlinear Function Obfuscation Theory and Application*,
https://doi.org/10.1007/978-981-97-6722-9_4

where $a \in \{0, 1\}$, and P_a is a function working as

$$P_a(|x\rangle) = |x\rangle^{|a\rangle} = \begin{cases} |1\rangle \text{ if } a = 0 \\ |x\rangle \text{ if } a = 1 \end{cases}. \tag{4.3}$$

4.2 Quantum Obfuscation for Quantum Power Function

Chapter 2 establishes an effective relationship between quantum teleportation and quantum obfuscation and simplifies the obfuscation of functions into the obfuscation of parameters and the design of linear quantum circuits.

The parameter of a quantum power function is represented as $|a\rangle$. We obfuscate it by quantum teleportation to obtain the obfuscated state $|\psi\rangle$ which is one of the possible states $\alpha|0\rangle + \beta|1\rangle$, $\alpha|0\rangle - \beta|1\rangle$, $\alpha|1\rangle + \beta|0\rangle$, or $\alpha|1\rangle - \beta|0\rangle$. For every qubit, we measure its first two qubits to obtain a classical bit string. According to the classical bit string obtained, we perform the corresponding Pauli matrix to restore each qubit making up the state $M(|a\rangle)$. Hence we know what exactly $|a\rangle$ is. The 'OR' operation can be achieved by the NAND relationship. Thus we reach the goal of outputting $|1\rangle$ when $|a\rangle = |0\rangle$ and outputting $|x\rangle$ when $|a\rangle = |1\rangle$, which satisfies the functionality of a quantum power function.

4.2.1 *Construction of Obfuscator and Interpreter*

In 2023, Pan et al. [1] proposed quantum obfuscation for quantum nonlinear functions and applied it to quantum power function. Quantum nonlinear function obfuscation focuses on the construction of quantum obfuscator and quantum interpreter. By selecting the parameters (such as the exponential quantum states of quantum power functions) of quantum nonlinear functions other than the inputs and outputs and combining them with quantum teleportation, the quantum obfuscator employs different obfuscation circuits according to the number of qubits of the parameter to be obfuscated in order to obfuscate the parameter of quantum nonlinear functions. After the receiver measures the obfuscation result, the parameter is restored according to the obtained classical bits, and the restored parameter, along with the input, is put into the quantum interpreter and outputs the result after performing the quantum interpreter.

A. Quantum Obfuscator

We construct a quantum nonlinear function obfuscator based on quantum teleportation. To obfuscate a parameter in the form of a single qubit, for instance, $|y\rangle = |x\rangle^{|a\rangle}$, in addition to the input and output quantum states, $|a\rangle$ serves as the parameter that is put into the quantum nonlinear function obfuscator. As is shown in Fig. 4.1, the parameter $|a\rangle$ and the Bell state $|\beta_{00}\rangle = \frac{1}{\sqrt{2}}(|00\rangle + |11\rangle)$ under the CNOT gate, the

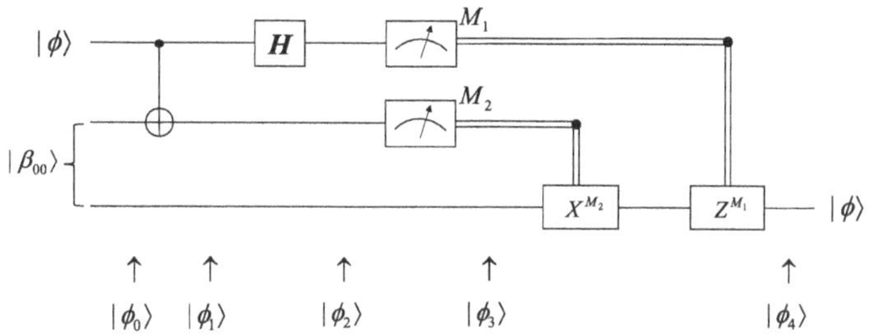

Fig. 4.1 Quantum teleportation circuit of one qubit

first qubit of the result is put into the Hadamard gate, and the terms are recombined under the quantum gate $H = \frac{1}{\sqrt{2}}\begin{bmatrix} 1 & 1 \\ 1 & -1 \end{bmatrix}$.

The recombination result is subjected to a joint quantum measurement, the classical result is transmitted to the receiver via a channel, and the parameter before obfuscation is restored by applying the unitary transformation to the corresponding quantum state of the collapsed states. The restored parameter and the input of the function are simultaneously transmitted into the quantum interpreter circuit to realize the quantum power function.

We obfuscate the quantum states and input them into the interpreter for quantum nonlinear functions with multi-parameter quantum states. For multi-qubit parameters, we extend the basic quantum teleportation circuit into a multi-qubit quantum teleportation circuit and obfuscate the parameter quantum states.

B. Quantum Interpreter

We design a circuit of quantum nonlinear function interpreter based on the functions and properties of quantum nonlinear functions. Firstly, the quantum interpreter performs quantum measurements on the obfuscated quantum states in order to obtain the classical two-bit measurements. On the basis of measurement results, the Pauli matrix is transformed to restore the quantum states of the obfuscated parameters. The quantum interpreter not only utilizes the functionality of a quantum nonlinear function but also encrypts the circuit of a quantum nonlinear function, thereby guaranteeing the security of the quantum communication system. Considering the quantum power function interpreter, shown in Fig. 4.2, we design the specific circuit of the equivalent quantum power function functionality in the quantum interpreter and obtain the output of the quantum power function.

According to the definition of the quantum power function, when the parameter $|a\rangle$ is $|0\rangle$, the output is $|1\rangle$ regardless of the input. When the parameter $|a\rangle$ is quantum state $|1\rangle$, the output is $|x\rangle$. Thus, we construct a quantum interpreter of the quantum power function based on its functionality. In order to reverse the quantum state $|\, a\rangle$, we firstly utilize the quantum state $|1\rangle$ to perform a quantum XOR operation with the parameter $|a\rangle$. Then, we perform a quantum XOR operation between $|\bar{a}\rangle$ and the input quantum state $|x\rangle$, which utilizes quantum XOR to realize the logical relationship between the

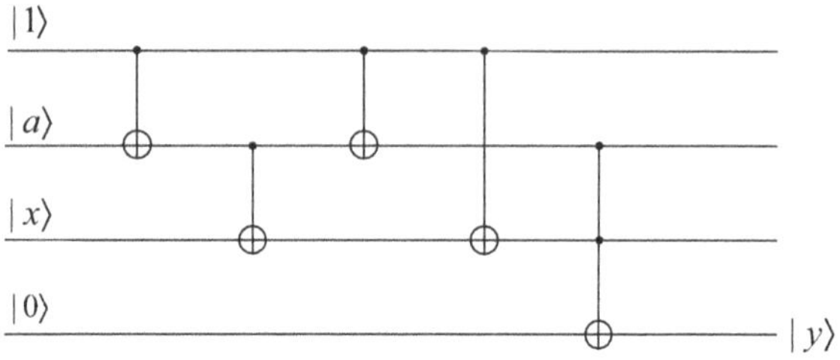

Fig. 4.2 Circuit of a quantum power function interpreter

base of the power function and the exponential operation. Quantum OR operation implementation is required to simultaneously output $|1\rangle \oplus |a\rangle$ and $|\bar{a}\rangle \oplus |x\rangle$. Since there is no quantum OR gate, we realize quantum OR gate through quantum NAND relationship, i.e., let the above two results be inverted with $|1\rangle$ respectively, and then add the two inverted results to generate the final output.

4.2.2 Quantum Power Obfuscation Scheme

A quantum obfuscator obfuscates a quantum nonlinear function by taking the parameter of the quantum nonlinear function as input and outputting the obfuscated quantum state as output. When restoring the quantum nonlinear function, the obfuscated quantum state is inputted into the quantum interpreter, and the circuits in the quantum interpreter are utilized to restore the quantum nonlinear function. Here we use the quantum power function as an example and introduce an obfuscation scheme for quantum nonlinear functions based on the construction schemes of quantum obfuscator and quantum interpreter, and prove the obfuscability of quantum nonlinear functions based on the three properties of virtual black-box obfuscation. The quantum obfuscation scheme is described as follows:

1. *Both sender Alice and receiver Bob construct quantum communication environments.*
   Assuming that Alice is the sender in quantum communication environments and Bob is the receiver. Alice uses the public key *pk* to encrypt the plaintext message $|m\rangle$, and Bob uses the private key to decrypt the ciphertext message $|\mu\rangle$ in the quantum communication environment, so as to realize quantum encryption for secure communication.
2. *Sender Alice constructs a quantum obfuscator O for a quantum power function.*
   A quantum power function can be denoted by $|y\rangle = |x\rangle^{|a\rangle}$, taking the exponential quantum state $|a\rangle$ as the parameter to be obfuscated. The quantum state $|a\rangle$ to be obfuscated with a single qubit, is put into the quantum obfuscator alongside the Bell state $|\beta_{00}\rangle = \frac{1}{\sqrt{2}}(|00\rangle + |11\rangle)$ in order to execute the tensor product operation. The exponential quantum state $|a\rangle$ and the first qubit of the Bell state $|\beta_{00}\rangle = \frac{1}{\sqrt{2}}(|00\rangle + |11\rangle)$ jointly perform a CNOT operation, taking $|a\rangle$ and

$|\beta_{00}\rangle = \frac{1}{\sqrt{2}}(|00\rangle + |11\rangle)$ as inputs, and perform a Hadamard gate operation on the first qubit of the inputs.

3. *Receiver Bob constructs a quantum interpreter δ for a quantum power function.* We design a quantum interpreter to restore the functionality of a quantum power function. Initially, a quantum measurement is used to restore the exponential quantum state $|a\rangle$. We perform a Bell measurement on the obfuscated output. Upon the completion of the measurement, we obtain a classical outcome of two bits, namely 00, 01, 10, or 11.
4. *Receiver Bob puts the qubit $|1\rangle$, the restored exponential parameter $|a\rangle$, the base $|x\rangle$ and the qubit $|0\rangle$ into the circuit of the interpreter.* We perform the XOR operation on $|1\rangle$ and $|a\rangle$. The output is $|1\rangle \oplus |a\rangle$ which is the same as inverting $|a\rangle$ to be $|\bar{a}\rangle$. It guarantees that when $|a\rangle = |0\rangle$ and the input state is $|x\rangle$, the output is all $|y\rangle = |x\rangle^{|a\rangle} = |x\rangle^{|0\rangle} = |1\rangle$. Subsequently, we perform the XOR operation on $|\bar{a}\rangle$ and the base $|x\rangle$ to obtain $|\bar{a}\rangle \oplus |x\rangle$. When the exponential quantum state $|a\rangle$ is $|1\rangle$, the output is $|\bar{a}\rangle \oplus |x\rangle = |0\rangle \oplus |x\rangle = |x\rangle$. It guarantees that when $|a\rangle = |1\rangle$ and the input state is $|x\rangle$, the output is $|y\rangle = |x\rangle^{|a\rangle} = |x\rangle^{|1\rangle} = |x\rangle$. Finally, we realize the quantum OR gate by the quantum NAND relationship and output two cases $|1\rangle \oplus |a\rangle$ and $|\bar{a}\rangle \oplus |x\rangle$ simultaneously: (1) Preform the quantum XOR operation on $|1\rangle$ and $|1\rangle \oplus |a\rangle$ to invert the output state when $|a\rangle = |0\rangle$ and the input state is $|x\rangle$, (2) Perform the quantum XOR operation on $|1\rangle$ and $|\bar{a}\rangle \oplus |x\rangle$ to invert the output state when $|a\rangle = |1\rangle$ and the input state is $|x\rangle$. Then, we take the outcomes of (1) and (2) to a quantum AND operation, and then perform an XOR operation on the result state and the qubit $|0\rangle$ to produce the output quantum state $|y\rangle$.

4.2.3 Obfuscatability of Quantum Nonlinear Function

Theorem 4.1 *A quantum nonlinear function is obfuscatable and satisfies the three properties for quantum obfuscation based on quantum teleportation.*

Proof To prove the correctness of quantum obfuscation based on quantum teleportation, we prove its polynomial expansion, functional equivalence, and virtual black-box property as follows.

For the quantum polynomial functions of quantum nonlinear functions, the input size and output size of the quantum obfuscator are certainly of polynomial size. For a quantum nonlinear function, the state $C_q(|\phi\rangle)$ is transformed into an obfuscated state $|\psi\rangle$ through quantum teleportation. Obviously, the obfuscator O computes $H(C_q(|\phi\rangle) \oplus |\beta\rangle)$ and generates $|\psi\rangle$, which is also of polynomial size. Supposing $C_q(|\phi\rangle) = |\phi_0\rangle$, the output of O, i.e., the obfuscation of C, is

$$O(C) = H|\phi_0 \oplus \beta\rangle. \tag{4.4}$$

Here, C is an n-qubit quantum circuit, β is a Bell state that conforms to the quantum circuit C, and ϕ_0 is m-qubit. The total size of the output of the quantum obfuscator O is $m+n$ and thus satisfies the property of polynomial expansion. In the quantum obfuscator, after the quantum state $C_q(|\phi\rangle)$ is obfuscated into $|\psi\rangle$, it is measured in the interpreter, and based on the classical result of the measurement, a unitary transformation is performed by means of utilizing the Pauli matrices to restore the parameter. Then, the transformed quantum state, under the influence of the quantum interpreter, restores the functionality of the quantum power function and outputs the corresponding quantum state, satisfying the requirement for functional equivalence. Since the quantum-accessible random oracle model is truly random for any adversary, the quantum obfuscation $O(C)$ leaks no information about the quantum circuits, thereby satisfying the virtual black-box property. Therefore, quantum nonlinear functions are obfuscatable. □

4.3 Generalized Quantum Power Functions with Coefficients

Quantum power functions are originally defined without coefficients and are restricted to quantum states. In 2023, Jiang et al. [2] defined two generalized quantum power functions. The generalized quantum power functions are created in order to better extend to larger quantum nonlinear functions. These functions illustrate the functional design of the generalized quantum functions and construct different circuits to obfuscate and interpret these functions using quantum techniques such as teleportation and quantum superdense coding. Here we provide a formal definition of two quantum power functions, referred to as generalized quantum power functions with coefficients. Each function is characterized by an exponent that corresponds to either a quantum or classical state, together with a leading coefficient. It is more straightforward to extend quantum power functions with a coefficient into other quantum functions. The first function, which combines the fundamental quantum power function with a leading coefficient in quantum states, is referred to as the quantum power function with a leading coefficient. The second function, which combines both quantum coefficient and classical exponent, is referred to as the quantum n-th power function.

4.3.1 Quantum Power Function with a Leading Coefficient

According to the theory of quantum computation, classical functions can be mapped to quantum functions by means of quantum circuits. A classical polynomial function is a function that can be written as

$$f(x) = a_n x^n + \cdots + a_2 x^2 + a_1 x^1 + a_0. \tag{4.5}$$

Table 4.1 Relationship between parameter and output

$\|\mathbf{ab}\rangle$	$\|\mathbf{y}\rangle$
$\|00\rangle$	$\|0\rangle$
$\|01\rangle$	$\|0\rangle$
$\|10\rangle$	$\|1\rangle$
$\|11\rangle$	$\|x\rangle$

Each a_i is a coefficient, and each product $a_i x^i$ is an independent term in the form of a power function with a leading coefficient. To further the development of a quantum polynomial function, we define a quantum power function with a leading coefficient as

$$|y\rangle = |ax^b\rangle, \tag{4.6}$$

where parameters $|a\rangle$ and $|b\rangle$ are quantum states, $|a\rangle$ is the leading coefficient and $|b\rangle$ is the exponent of quantum power function. Equation (4.7) explains the functionality of a quantum power function with a leading coefficient.

$$|y\rangle = |ax^b\rangle = \begin{cases} |0\rangle, \text{ if } a = 0 \\ |1\rangle, \text{ if } a = 1, b = 0 \\ |x\rangle, \text{ if } a = 1, b = 1 \end{cases} \tag{4.7}$$

The relationship between quantum coefficient $|a\rangle$, quantum exponent $|b\rangle$, and the output $|y\rangle$ is listed in Table 4.1.

4.3.2 *Quantum n-th Power Function*

A. Bloch Sphere and Qubit Rotation

In quantum computation, the Bloch sphere is a geometrical representation of a universal qubit. The north and south poles of the Bloch sphere correspond to the computational basis vectors $|0\rangle$ and $|1\rangle$. A universal qubit represented by the Bloch sphere can be written as

$$|q\rangle = \cos\left(\frac{\theta}{2}\right)|0\rangle + \sin\left(\frac{\theta}{2}\right)e^{i\varphi}|1\rangle, \tag{4.8}$$

where $0 \le \theta \le \pi$ and $0 \le \varphi \le 2\pi$, and it is shown in Fig. 4.3.

Each quantum state vector can also be written in $\mathbb{R}^3$ as

$$\overline{q} = (\sin\theta\cos\varphi, \sin\theta\sin\varphi, \cos\theta). \tag{4.9}$$

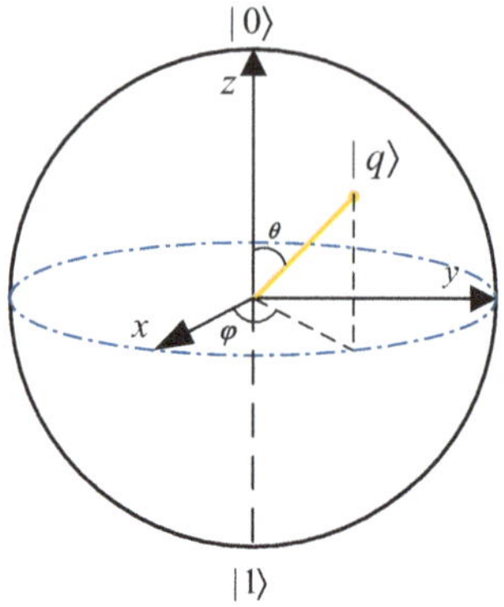

Fig. 4.3 A universal qubit represented by the Bloch sphere

RX, RY, and RZ gates are rotation operators, indicating the rotation of a qubit through the angle α around each axis, and the associated transformation equations for these rotational gates are given by

$$RX(\alpha) = e^{\frac{-i\alpha X}{2}} = \cos\left(\frac{\alpha}{2}\right) I - i\sin\left(\frac{\alpha}{2}\right) X = \begin{bmatrix} \cos\left(\frac{\alpha}{2}\right) & -i\sin\left(\frac{\alpha}{2}\right) \\ -i\sin\left(\frac{\alpha}{2}\right) & \cos\left(\frac{\alpha}{2}\right) \end{bmatrix} \quad (4.10)$$

$$RY(\alpha) = e^{\frac{-i\alpha Y}{2}} = \cos\left(\frac{\alpha}{2}\right) I - i\sin\left(\frac{\alpha}{2}\right) Y = \begin{bmatrix} \cos\left(\frac{\alpha}{2}\right) & -\sin\left(\frac{\alpha}{2}\right) \\ \sin\left(\frac{\alpha}{2}\right) & \cos\left(\frac{\alpha}{2}\right) \end{bmatrix} \quad (4.11)$$

$$RZ(\alpha) = e^{\frac{-i\alpha Z}{2}} = \cos\left(\frac{\alpha}{2}\right) I - i\sin\left(\frac{\alpha}{2}\right) Z = \begin{bmatrix} e^{\frac{-i\alpha}{2}} & 0 \\ 0 & e^{\frac{i\alpha}{2}} \end{bmatrix} = \begin{bmatrix} 1 & 0 \\ 0 & e^{i\alpha} \end{bmatrix} \quad (4.12)$$

By combining these operations, qubits can rotate freely on the Bloch sphere.

B. Functionality of Quantum *n*-th Power Function

According to the classical n-th power function, the n-th power of a number x is the result of multiplying x to itself n times $(x * x * x \ldots * x)$ when n is an integer. It can be written as x^n.

Since every qubit can be expressed as (θ, φ), we consider $|x\rangle^1$ as the final state of rotating $|0\rangle$ by angles θ and φ around the Y and Z axes, respectively. According to Eq. (4.13), quantum n-th power function can be described as the result of several rotations.

$$|x\rangle^n = \cos\left(\frac{n\theta}{2}\right)|0\rangle + \sin\left(\frac{n\theta}{2}\right) e^{ni\varphi}|1\rangle \quad (4.13)$$

Equation (4.14) describes the functionality of quantum n-th power function. The transformation of $|0\rangle$ can be expressed as $RZ(n\varphi)RY(n\theta)|0\rangle$, which means the $n\theta$

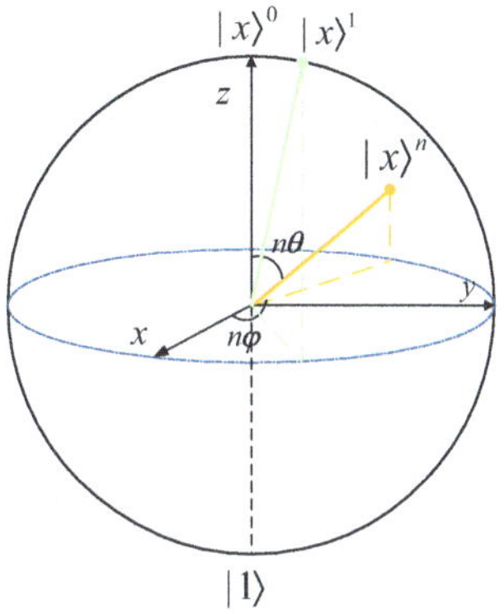

Fig. 4.4 Functionality of quantum n-th power function represented by the Bloch sphere

angle is rotated around the Y axis, followed by the $n\varphi$ angle around the Z axis when $|a\rangle = |1\rangle$. $|a\rangle$ is the leading coefficient in quantum n-th power functions.

$$|y\rangle = |a\rangle|x\rangle^n = \begin{cases} \cos\left(\frac{n\theta}{2}\right)|0\rangle + \sin\left(\frac{n\theta}{2}\right)e^{ni\varphi}|1\rangle, \text{ if } |a\rangle = |1\rangle \\ |0\rangle, \text{ if } |a\rangle = |0\rangle \end{cases} \tag{4.14}$$

The functionality of quantum n-th power functions can be visualized in Fig. 4.4.

4.4 Quantum Obfuscation for Generalized Quantum Power Functions

We introduce the quantum obfuscation scheme for generalized quantum power functions by combining quantum teleportation and enhanced quantum superdense coding. Quantum teleportation is used to obfuscate quantum parameters, while enhanced quantum superdense coding is used to obfuscate classical parameters. We construct a specific quantum obfuscator to obfuscate each quantum generalized power function and quantum interpreter to restore their original functionality.

4.4.1 Quantum Obfuscation Scheme for Quantum Power Function with a Leading Coefficient

A. Construction of Quantum Obfuscator

Quantum power function with a leading coefficient has the form $|y\rangle = |ax^b\rangle$, where $|a\rangle$ and $|b\rangle$ are both quantum states. To obfuscate two quantum states, we construct the obfuscator by quantum teleportation for multiple qubits [3]. We can teleport

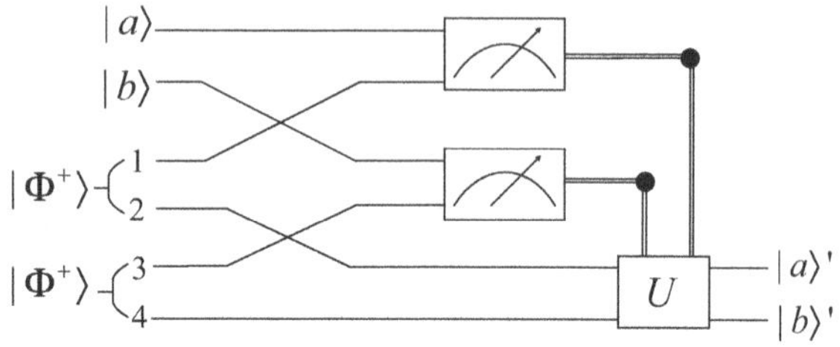

Fig. 4.5 Circuit of quantum teleportation for multiple qubits

Table 4.2 Unitary operations corresponding to the measurement result of Alice

Measurement result	Unitary operation	Measurement result	Unitary operation
$\|\Phi^+\rangle_{A1}\|\Phi^+\rangle_{B3}$	$Z^0X^0 \otimes Z^0X^0$	$\|\Psi^+\rangle_{A1}\|\Phi^+\rangle_{B3}$	$Z^0X^1 \otimes Z^0X^0$
$\|\Phi^+\rangle_{A1}\|\Phi^-\rangle_{B3}$	$Z^0X^0 \otimes Z^1X^0$	$\|\Psi^+\rangle_{A1}\|\Phi^-\rangle_{B3}$	$Z^0X^1 \otimes Z^1X^0$
$\|\Phi^-\rangle_{A1}\|\Phi^+\rangle_{B3}$	$Z^1X^0 \otimes Z^0X^0$	$\|\Psi^-\rangle_{A1}\|\Phi^+\rangle_{B3}$	$Z^1X^1 \otimes Z^0X^0$
$\|\Phi^-\rangle_{A1}\|\Phi^-\rangle_{B3}$	$Z^1X^0 \otimes Z^1X^0$	$\|\Psi^-\rangle_{A1}\|\Phi^-\rangle_{B3}$	$Z^1X^1 \otimes Z^0X^0$
$\|\Phi^+\rangle_{A1}\|\Psi^+\rangle_{B3}$	$Z^0X^0 \otimes Z^0X^1$	$\|\Psi^+\rangle_{A1}\|\Psi^+\rangle_{B3}$	$Z^0X^1 \otimes Z^0X^1$
$\|\Phi^+\rangle_{A1}\|\Psi^-\rangle_{B3}$	$Z^0X^0 \otimes Z^1X^1$	$\|\Psi^+\rangle_{A1}\|\Psi^-\rangle_{B3}$	$Z^0X^1 \otimes Z^1X^1$
$\|\Phi^-\rangle_{A1}\|\Psi^+\rangle_{B3}$	$Z^1X^0 \otimes Z^0X^1$	$\|\Psi^-\rangle_{A1}\|\Psi^+\rangle_{B3}$	$Z^1X^1 \otimes Z^0X^1$
$\|\Phi^-\rangle_{A1}\|\Psi^-\rangle_{B3}$	$Z^1X^0 \otimes Z^1X^1$	$\|\Psi^-\rangle_{A1}\|\Psi^-\rangle_{B3}$	$Z^1X^1 \otimes Z^1X^1$

the product states of two arbitrary particles independently. We consider the tensor product of two quantum states is $|\Phi\rangle = |a\rangle \otimes |b\rangle$. The quantum circuit receives two particles as input, namely $|a\rangle = \alpha|0\rangle + \beta|1\rangle$ and $|b\rangle = \gamma|0\rangle + \delta|1\rangle$. Particles $|a\rangle, |b\rangle$, 1, 3 belong to the sender Alice, and particles 2, 4 belong to the receiver Bob. The circuit is shown in Fig. 4.5.

Alice measures the particles ($|a\rangle$, 1) and ($|b\rangle$, 3) by Bell basis. The measurement result of Alice and the unitary operations corresponding to the result are listed in Table 4.2.

Thus we can construct an obfuscator for the quantum power function with a leading coefficient by obfuscating the leading coefficient and the exponent. The obfuscation scheme is described as follows.

1. *Alice inputs the leading coefficient $|a\rangle$, the exponent $|b\rangle$ into the obfuscator.*
2. *Alice measures the particles ($|a\rangle$, 1) and ($|b\rangle$, 3) by Bell basis and obtains the measurement result.*
3. *Alice sends the measurement result to Bob through a classical channel.*
4. *Bob performs corresponding unitary operations to restore the initial leading coefficient and the exponent of the function.*

B. Construction of Quantum Interpreter

The original quantum circuits, which realize the functionality of a quantum power function with a leading coefficient, are obfuscated into qubits through the obfuscator. Consequently, we should design a specific interpreter to explain the obfuscated quantum states and restore the original functionality.

The interpreter is used to restore the functionality of a quantum power function with a leading coefficient. We can derive a logical expression among the output $|y\rangle$, the leading coefficient $|a\rangle$, the exponent $|b\rangle$ and the input variable $|x\rangle$ in Equation (4.15).

$$|y\rangle = (|a\rangle \wedge |\neg b\rangle) \vee (|a\rangle \wedge |\neg b \oplus x\rangle) \tag{4.15}$$

There are no corresponding quantum 'AND' and quantum 'OR' gates in quantum circuits, so we utilize Toffoli gates to implement quantum 'AND' and quantum 'OR' gates instead. The circuits are shown in Fig. 4.6.

Consequently, we can construct the interpreter by means of corresponding quantum gates to realize the functionality of a quantum power function with a leading coefficient according to the logical expression. Figure 4.7 shows the quantum circuit of the interpreter.

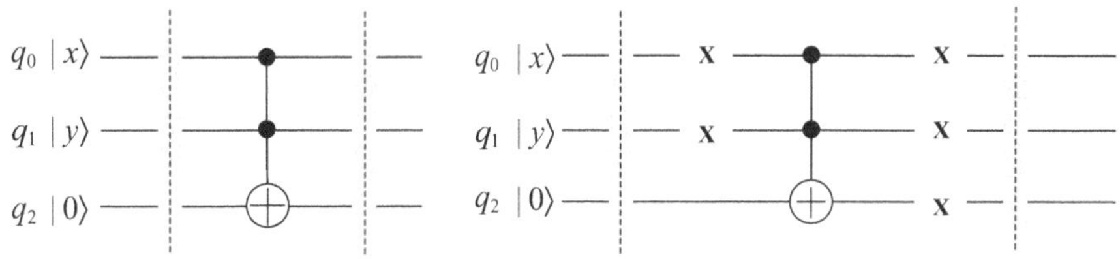

Fig. 4.6 Circuits of quantum 'AND' and quantum 'OR' gates

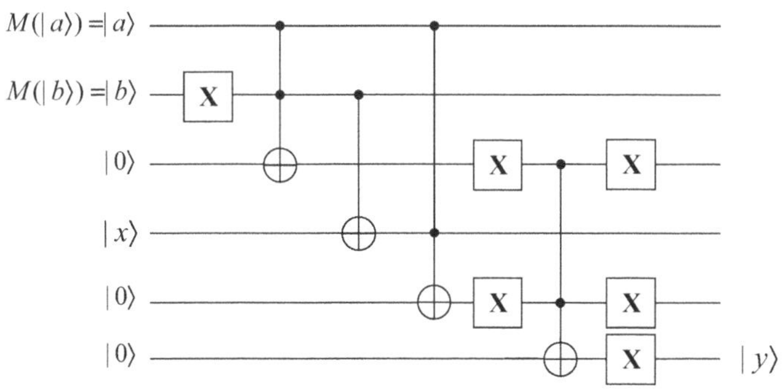

Fig. 4.7 Interpreter of a quantum power function with a leading coefficient

Initially, the receiver Bob performs quantum measurement on the obfuscated results to restore the leading coefficient $|a\rangle$ and the exponent $|b\rangle$. Then, Bob puts the restored leading coefficient $|a\rangle$, the restored exponent $|b\rangle$, the base $|x\rangle$, and three auxiliary qubits $|0\rangle$ into the circuit. The details of the interpreter are described as follows.

1. Perform an X gate on the restored exponent $|b\rangle$, then obtain $|\neg b\rangle$.
2. Perform a Toffoli gate on $|a\rangle$, $|b\rangle$, and the first auxiliary qubit $|0\rangle$, in which $|a\rangle$ and $|b\rangle$ are control qubits and $|0\rangle$ is the target qubit. Consequently, obtain $|a\rangle \wedge |\neg b\rangle$.
3. Perform a CNOT gate on $|b\rangle$ and $|x\rangle$, in which $|b\rangle$ is the control qubit and $|x\rangle$ is the target qubit. Consequently, obtain $\neg|b\rangle \oplus |x\rangle$.
4. Perform a Toffoli gate on $|a\rangle$,$|x\rangle$ and the second auxiliary qubit $|0\rangle$, in which $|a\rangle$ and $|x\rangle$ are the control qubits and $|0\rangle$ is the target qubit.
5. Perform a quantum 'OR' gate on $|a\rangle \wedge |\neg b\rangle$ and $|a\rangle \wedge |\neg b \oplus x\rangle$. Then we can obtain $(|a\rangle \wedge |\neg b\rangle) \vee (|a\rangle \wedge |\neg b \oplus x\rangle)$ which satisfies the functionality of a quantum power function with a leading coefficient.

Theorem 4.2 *A quantum power function with a leading coefficient is obfuscatable by quantum teleportation for multiple qubits. It satisfies all properties of quantum obfuscation.*

Proof To demonstrate the obfuscatability of a quantum power function with a leading coefficient, we prove the properties of polynomial expansion, functional equivalence, and virtual black-box property as follows.

Assume that a quantum power function with a leading coefficient is denoted by $|y\rangle = |a\rangle|x\rangle^{|b\rangle}$, the parameters extracted from it are denoted by $C_q(|a\rangle \otimes |b\rangle)$, which is another representation of the functionality. These parameters are transformed into the obfuscated states $O(C_q(|a\rangle \otimes |b\rangle))$ through the obfuscator.

Suppose the original circuit C is n-qubit, the obfuscated leading coefficient $O(|a\rangle)$ is m_1-qubit and the obfuscated power $O(|b\rangle)$ is m_2-qubit. Since all quantum gates contained in the obfuscator operate linearly, the size of m_1 and m_2 are certainly of polynomial size. Consequently, the total size of the output is $m_1 + m_2 + n$, which is also of polynomial size, satisfying the property of polynomial expansion.

The quantum power function with a leading coefficient must satisfy the preservation of functionality by the interpreter. In this construction, the two obfuscated parameters can be restored by performing the corresponding unitary operations, which satisfies the property of functional equivalence.

Since the oracle is truly random to any adversary, the obfuscation $O(C)$ leaks no information on the parameters. Thus, it satisfies the virtual black-box property.

Therefore, a quantum power function with a leading coefficient is obfuscatable. □

4.4.2 *Quantum Obfuscation Scheme for Quantum n-th Power Functions*

A. Construction of Quantum Obfuscator

The parameters that need to be obfuscated for quantum n-th power functions include both classical and quantum states. So we utilize quantum teleportation and enhanced quantum superdense coding [4] to obfuscate the quantum and classical states simultaneously.

Equation (4.14) explains the functionality of quantum n-th power functions, and Fig. 4.8 shows the obfuscator for quantum n-th power functions, assuming the exponent n of the function contains two classical bits denoted by ij.

This quantum circuit can be divided into two parts, used to obfuscate quantum parameters and classical parameters, respectively. To obfuscate the leading coefficient $|a\rangle$, we use quantum teleportation to obfuscate the qubit $|a\rangle$. Depending on different measurements, we perform corresponding unitary operations to restore the initial state according to Table 4.3.

The classical exponent n of quantum n-th power function is obfuscated by enhanced quantum superdense coding. Firstly, Alice and Bob generate a pair of Bell

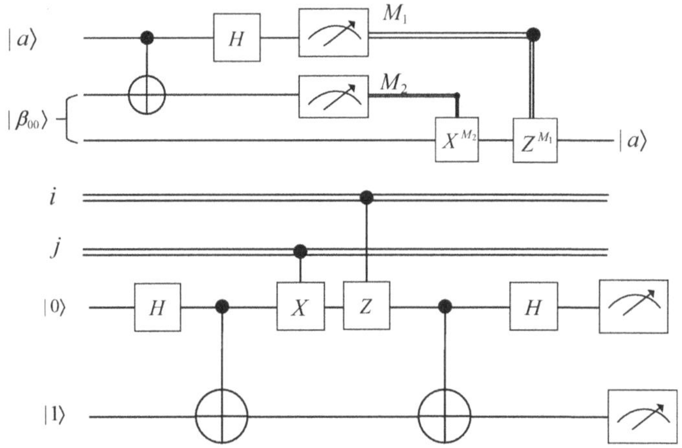

Fig. 4.8 Construction of the obfuscator for quantum n-th power functions

Table 4.3 Unitary operation for specific measurement

Measurement	Collapsed state	Unitary operation
$\|00\rangle$	$\alpha\|0\rangle + \beta\|1\rangle$	Z^0X^0
$\|01\rangle$	$\alpha\|1\rangle + \beta\|0\rangle$	Z^0X^1
$\|10\rangle$	$\alpha\|0\rangle - \beta\|1\rangle$	Z^1X^0
$\|11\rangle$	$\alpha\|1\rangle - \beta\|0\rangle$	Z^1X^1

Table 4.4 Obfuscation for two-bit exponent

Classical exponent	Operation	States after operation
00	Z^0X^0	$\|\Phi^+\rangle_{AB}$
01	Z^0X^1	$\|\Psi^+\rangle_{AB}$
10	Z^1X^0	$\|\Phi^-\rangle_{AB}$
11	Z^1X^1	$\|\Psi^-\rangle_{AB}$

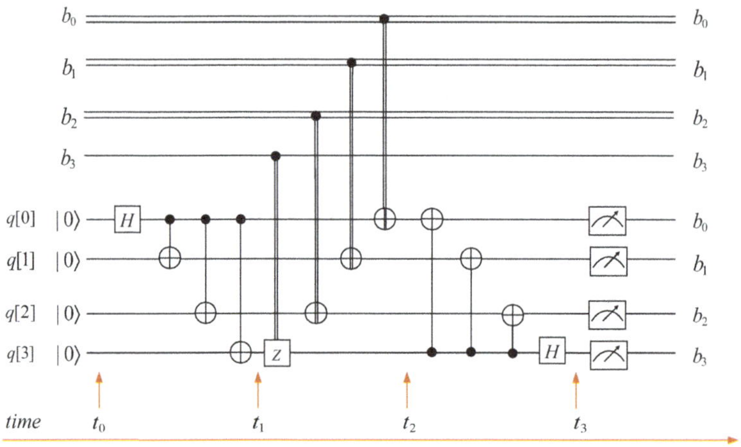

Fig. 4.9 Quantum circuit of the enhanced superdense coding for four classical bits

states $|\Phi^+\rangle_{AB} = \frac{1}{\sqrt{2}}(|00\rangle + |11\rangle)$ by means of the Hadamard and CNOT gates, each of which holds a qubit. To obfuscate the two-bit parameter n, Alice performs the corresponding operation listed in Table 4.4.

If the exponent of the quantum n-th power function is 11, then Alice performs Z^1X^1 to obtain a specific entangled state. Equation (4.16) demonstrates the specific transformation of the entangled state $|\Phi^+\rangle_{AB}$.

$$|\Phi^+\rangle_{AB} \xrightarrow{X} \frac{1}{\sqrt{2}}(|10\rangle + |01\rangle) \xrightarrow{Z} \frac{1}{\sqrt{2}}(|01\rangle - |10\rangle) = |\Psi^-\rangle_{AB} \tag{4.16}$$

Then, Alice sends the transformed qubit to Bob via a quantum channel, and Bob obtains the whole entangled state. Bob performs the CNOT gate on the entangled state, where the received qubit is the control bit, and the qubit he originally owned is the target bit, then performs the Hadamard gate to the received qubit. The last step is to perform the measurement operation under the computational basis, which restores the exponent b of the quantum n-th power function.

If the exponent n contains multiple bits, it can be obfuscated by means of enhanced superdense coding. This is implemented by constructing the GHZ state, and the circuit for transmitting four bits is shown in Fig. 4.9.

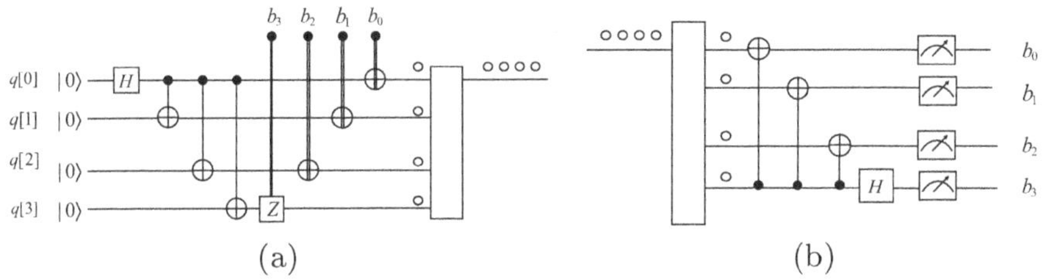

Fig. 4.10 Construction of the obfuscator and the interpreter for four classical bits: (**a**) Quantum circuit for obfuscating classical parameters (**b**) Quantum circuit for restoring classical parameters

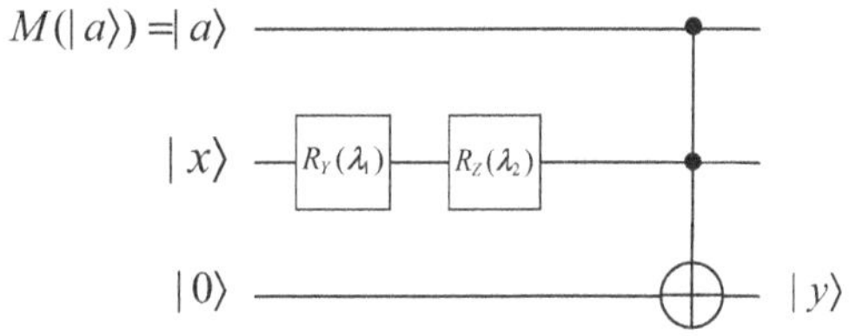

Fig. 4.11 Interpreter of quantum n-th power function, where $\lambda_1 = (n-1)\theta$ and $\lambda_2 = (n-1)\varphi$

By means of this kind of structure, the number of classical bits to be teleported cannot be restricted any more. This makes it possible to obfuscate any classical parameters. We split the quantum circuit into two parts to construct the obfuscator and interpreter for classical parameters in Fig. 4.10.

B. Construction of Quantum Interpreter

The obfuscator has obfuscated the functionality of the quantum n-th power function, so we design an interpreter for the quantum n-th power function to restore the parameters and realize the original functionality. The circuit for interpreting the quantum n-th power function is shown in Fig. 4.11.

According to the functionality of the quantum n-th power function, the parameters to be obfuscated are the hybrid state of quantum and classical states.

The quantum n-th power function is characterized by the parameters $|a\rangle$ and n. When $|a\rangle = |1\rangle$, the rotation on auxiliary qubit $|0\rangle$ is $RZ(n\varphi)RY(n\theta)|0\rangle$, this occurs by rotation around the Y axis by $n\theta$ angles and rotation around the Z axis by $n\varphi$ angles. If $|a\rangle = |0\rangle$, the output is $|0\rangle$.

Consequently, we construct a quantum circuit to implement the functionality. Initially, the receiver Bob performs a quantum measurement on the obfuscated results to restore the leading coefficient $|a\rangle$ and the exponent n. Then, Bob puts the restored leading coefficient $|a\rangle$, the base $|x\rangle$, and an auxiliary qubit $|0\rangle$ into the circuit. The classical exponent, b, is reflected in the rotation angle.

The details of the interpreter are described as follows.

1. Perform a RY gate on the base $|x\rangle$ with the angle λ_1 where $\lambda_1 = (b-1)\theta$. Thus, obtain $RY(n\theta)|0\rangle$.
2. Perform a RZ gate on $RY(n\theta)|0\rangle$ with the angle λ_2 where $\lambda_2 = (n-1)\varphi$. Thus, obtain $RZ(n\varphi)RY(n\theta)|0\rangle$.

3. Perform a Toffoli gate on $|a\rangle$, $RZ(n\varphi)RY(n\theta)|0\rangle$ and the auxiliary qubit $|0\rangle$, where $|0\rangle$ is the target qubit. Thus, obtain the result $|y\rangle = (|a\rangle \wedge |x\rangle) \oplus |0\rangle$. When $|a\rangle = |0\rangle$, $|y\rangle = |0\rangle$. When $|a\rangle = |1\rangle$, $|y\rangle = RZ(n\varphi)RY(n\theta)|0\rangle$.

Theorem 4.3 *A quantum n-th power function is obfuscatable by quantum teleportation and quantum superdense coding. It satisfies all properties of quantum obfuscation.*

Proof To prove a quantum n-th power function is obfuscatable, we prove its polynomial expansion, functional equivalence, and virtual black-box property as follows.

Assume that quantum n-th power function with a leading coefficient is denoted by $|y\rangle = |a\rangle|x\rangle^n$, the parameters extracted from it are denoted by $C_q(|a\rangle \otimes n)$, which is another representation of the functionality. These parameters are transformed into the obfuscated states $O(C_q(|a\rangle \otimes n))$ through the obfuscator.

Suppose the original circuit C is n-qubit, the obfuscated leading coefficient $O(|a\rangle)$ is m_1-qubit and the obfuscated power $O(n)$ is m_2-qubit. Since all quantum gates contained in the obfuscator operate linearly, the size of m_1 and m_2 are certainly of polynomial size. Consequently, the total size of the output is $m_1 + m_2 + n$, which is also of polynomial size, satisfying the property of polynomial expansion.

The quantum n-th power function must satisfy the preservation of its original functionality by the interpreter. In this construction, the two obfuscated parameters can be restored by performing the corresponding unitary operation, which satisfies the property of functional equivalence.

Since the oracle is truly random to any adversary, the obfuscation $O(C)$ leaks no information about the parameters. Thus it satisfies the virtual black-box property.

Therefore, a quantum n-th power function is obfuscatable. □

4.4.3 Complex Factors to Quantum Power Obfuscation

A. Impossibility and Possibility

Alagic et al. [5] proposed an impossibility result of quantum obfuscation of classical circuits under the assumption that learning-with-errors (LWE) is hard for quantum computers. Their work is based on the work of Barak [6], who demonstrated that a universal obfuscator that obfuscates classical circuits into other classical circuits is impossible. Alagic made a quantum generalization of this obfuscation and extended the impossible result of Barak to quantum settings, proving the impossibility of universal quantum black-box obfuscation.

Following the demonstration by Barak that a universal black-box obfuscation does not exist, two categories of research were established for classical obfuscation. The first objective is to develop and analyze the obfuscation strategy for particular functions, the second is to weaken the definition of black-box obfuscation. Similarly, Alagic et al. demonstrated the impossibility of universal virtual black-box obfuscation in quantum settings, but quantum obfuscation can still be achieved by particular obfuscation methods for specific functions or circuits. In 2023, Bartusek et al. [7] implemented a quantum obfuscation scheme for polynomial-sized pseudo-deterministic quantum circuits. In particular, this scheme can obfuscate the circuit implementing Shor's algorithm. This work provides a new method to achieve efficient quantum communication. Thus, the feasibility of quantum obfuscation as a tool for quantum software protection remains widely open, and the obfuscation scheme for a specific generalized quantum power function with coefficients does not conflict with the impossibility result proposed by Alagic.

B. Obfuscation Circuits in a Noisy Channel

Quantum teleportation and quantum superdense coding are utilized in the construction of the obfuscator and the interpreter. Quantum teleportation requires a noiseless quantum channel to transmit a purely entangled state. However, in practice, the shared entanglement usually becomes degraded because of various decoherence mechanisms, and the noise and decoherence are unavoidable. When applying the obfuscation circuits to realistic channels, we can implement the idealized quantum teleportation circuit and quantum superdense coding circuit through correspondingly improved protocols to enhance the fidelity of each protocol and overcome the effects of severe noise and loss.

There are several methods to overcome the impact of severe noise and loss. Zhao et al. [8] utilized a noiseless amplifier as a pre-device for quantum teleportation and achieved a high fidelity of 92% for teleporting coherent states, which also presented a new way of applying teleportation to purify quantum systems from thermal noise. Islam et al. [9] demonstrated that the decoherence noise can enhance the quantum correlation between two qubits and restore the entanglement lost in the environment, therefore improving the fidelity of quantum teleportation and the capacity of quantum superdense coding and contributing to efficient quantum communication.

4.5 Summary

The construction and application of quantum power obfuscation are important to the development of quantum computation. In this chapter, we introduced quantum obfuscation for quantum power functions. The obfuscation illuminated the connection between quantum obfuscation and quantum teleportation. In particular, this work just suggested the idea of designing quantum obfuscation for quantum nonlinear functions, so the structure of quantum obfuscator and interpreter is variable according to the n-th specific properties of quantum nonlinear functions to be obfuscated. For a more general manner, we have defined a generalized quantum power function with coefficients and applied quantum mechanics to construct circuits for quantum obfuscator and interpreter. Quantum and classical parameters are obfuscated by quantum teleportation for multi-qubit and enhanced quantum superdense coding, respectively. Other types of quantum functions, such as quantum polynomial functions and quantum composite functions, have not yet been defined, and corresponding obfuscation schemes have not yet been developed either. Also, it remains unexplored how to use the quantum circuit to restore the functionality of an obfuscated quantum function and how to construct a simple and efficient quantum interpreter.

References

1. Pan, C.Y., Shang, T., Zhang, Y.J.: Universal quantum obfuscation for quantum non-linear functions. Front. Phys. **10**, 1342 (2023)
2. Jiang, Y.Z., Shang, T., Tang, Y., et al.: Quantum obfuscation of generalized quantum power functions with coefficient. Entropy **25**(11), 1524 (2023)
3. Tan, X., Li, X., Yang, P.: Perfect quantum teleportation via Bell states. Comput. Mater. Continua **57**, 495–503 (2018)
4. Mastriani, M.: Quantum key secure communication protocol via enhanced superdense coding. Opt. Quant. Electron. **55**, 10 (2023)
5. Alagic, G., Brakerski, Z., Dulek, Y., et al.: Impossibility of quantum virtual black-box obfuscation of classical circuits. In: Advances in Cryptology-CRYPTO 2021: 41st Annual International Cryptology Conference, pp. 497–525. Springer, Berlin/Heidelberg, Germany (2021)
6. Barak, B., Goldreich, O., Impagliazzo, R., et al.: On the (im)possibility of obfuscating programs. In: The Annual International Cryptology Conference, pp. 1–18. Springer, Berlin/Heidelberg, Germany (2001)
7. Bartusek, J., Kitagawa, F., Nishimaki, R., et al.: Obfuscation of Pseudo-Deterministic Quantum Circuits (2023). arXiv preprint arXiv:2302.11083
8. Zhao, J., Jeng, H., Conlon, L.O., et al.: Enhancing quantum teleportation efficacy with noiseless linear amplification. Nat. Commun. **14**, 4745 (2023)
9. Islam, A., Wang, A.M., Abliz, A.: Optimizing quantum teleportation and dense coding via mixed noise under non-Markovian approximation. Int. J. Theor. Phys. **60**, 1225–1236 (2021)

Chapter 5
Quantum Symmetric Encryption

Quantum symmetric encryption can be based on the obfuscation of a specific kind of function, which will not be ruled out by the impossible result. Also, quantum point obfuscation is practical in the quantum random oracle model. These facts derive the extended properties of quantum symmetric encryption. In this chapter, we introduce quantum symmetric encryption schemes based on quantum point obfuscation. We start with the basic requirement of indistinguishability security and point out that a quantum virtual black-box obfuscator satisfies this requirement unconditionally. Such work formally demonstrates the implementation and application of quantum obfuscation.

5.1 Quantum Symmetric Encryption Based on Quantum Point Obfuscation

5.1.1 Indistinguishability for Quantum Encryption

One branch of quantum cryptography, beyond quantum key distribution (QKD) and post-quantum cryptography, is to carry classical cryptographic primitives over to quantum circumstances. Quantum one-time pad (QOTP) [1] is a representative example, but for so long there have been lacking even the most basic cryptographic concepts. Scattered primitives such as quantum homomorphic encryption [2], quantum homomorphic signature [3], and quantum random oracle (QRO) [4, 5], have been discussed. In 2016, Alagic et al. [6] proposed the concept of semantic security, IND-CPA (indistinguishability under chosen plaintext attack) and IND-CCA1 (indistinguishability under non-adaptive chosen ciphertext attack) for quantum situation. More recent work includes quantum non-malleability [7], quantum IND-

T. Shang, *Quantum Nonlinear Function Obfuscation Theory and Application*,
https://doi.org/10.1007/978-981-97-6722-9_5

CCA2 (indistinguishability under adaptive chosen ciphertext attack) and authenticated encryption [8]. As for the notion of obfuscation, the research is relatively immature. The first idea of "protecting software by a quantum state" originated in Scott Aaronson's ten semi-grand challenges for quantum computation. In 2016, the definition of quantum VBB obfuscation and quantum indistinguishable obfuscation (iO) was proposed [9], although many basic concepts in this area are yet to be set.

In this chapter, we rigorously construct a quantum symmetric encryption scheme by means of a quantum obfuscator [10]. We start with the basic requirement of IND-secure and point out that a quantum VBB obfuscator satisfies this requirement unconditionally. Then we prove that a quantum obfuscator with combinable property or auxiliary input property corresponds to encryptions with IND-CPA security or leakage resilience. Note that the absence of the usefulness of quantum obfuscation may eliminate the positivity of related research. We hope that such work will be inspiring in the field of quantum obfuscation.

5.1.2 *Efficient Quantum Circuit and Quantum Computation*

Due to the strong Church-Turing thesis [11], the deterministic polynomial-time (PT) algorithm and probabilistic polynomial-time (PPT) algorithm are the most representative computing models in classical complexity theory. In quantum circumstance, the first model formalized by Deutsch [12] was realized by quantum circuits consisting of unitary quantum gates. An improved solution takes measurements in the middle of computation and decoherence into account [13]. Here, a quantum polynomial-time (QPT) algorithm is defined as a family of quantum circuits, each composed of polynomial-many admissible (rather than unitary) quantum gates. Oracle gates are feasible only under such model of QPT, which is crucial in IND-CPA security.

5.1.3 *Quantum One-Time Pad*

The single-qubit Pauli operators are defined as

$$\sigma_X = \begin{bmatrix} 0 & 1 \\ 1 & 0 \end{bmatrix}, \sigma_Y = \begin{bmatrix} 0 & -\mathrm{i} \\ \mathrm{i} & 0 \end{bmatrix}, \sigma_Z = \begin{bmatrix} 1 & 0 \\ 0 & -1 \end{bmatrix}.$$

Here we take an identity matrix I_2 into account. So the Pauli operation set consists of four Pauli matrices $P = \{I_2, \sigma_X, \sigma_Y, \sigma_Z\}$.

The definition of quantum one-time pad is quite simple: for each qubit ρ, randomly choose one operator from the Pauli operation set P and apply it on ρ. It is evident that such operation is information-theoretically indistinguishable, since the output state is maximally mixed as follows:

$$\frac{1}{4}(\rho + \sigma_X \rho \sigma_X^\dagger + \sigma_Y \rho \sigma_Y^\dagger + \sigma_Z \rho \sigma_Z^\dagger) = \frac{I_2}{2}$$

Since the Pauli operators are self-adjoint, the above operation can be achieved by choosing two single bits $\alpha, \beta \in \{0, 1\}$, and applying the mapping

$$\rho \mapsto \sigma_X^\alpha \sigma_Z^\beta \rho \sigma_Z^\beta \sigma_X^\alpha$$

In the case of n-qubit message $\rho, \alpha, \beta \in \{0, 1\}^n$. We define $X^\alpha = \otimes \sigma_X^{\alpha_i}$ and $Z^\beta = \otimes \sigma_Z^{\beta_i}$. The quantum one-time pad [1] for n-qubit goes

$$\rho \mapsto X^\alpha Z^\beta \rho Z^\beta X^\alpha$$

Through analysis, the output is still maximally mixed as follows:

$$\begin{aligned}
\frac{1}{2^{2n}} \Sigma U_n \rho U_n^\dagger &= \frac{1}{2^{2n}} \Sigma_{\alpha,\beta} X^\alpha Z^\beta \rho Z^\beta X^\alpha \\
&= \Sigma_{\alpha,\beta} Tr(\rho Z^\beta X^\alpha) \delta_{\alpha,0} \delta_{\beta,0} X^\alpha Z^\beta \\
&= \frac{Tr(\rho)}{2^n} I_{2n} \\
&= \frac{I_{2n}}{2^n}
\end{aligned}$$

5.1.4 Security of Quantum Symmetric Encryption

Following the idea of quantum one-time pad, we are interested in the circumstances where the message space and cypher-text space are the set of density operators on Hilbert space $\mathcal{H}_M$, $\mathcal{H}_C$, and the key space $\mathcal{K} = \{0, 1\}^n$ [6]. The set of density operators, i.e., all physically possible quantum states on Hilbert space $\mathcal{H}$ is denoted by $\mathcal{D}(\mathcal{H})$. Then a quantum symmetric encryption scheme is defined as follows:

Definition 5.1 A quantum symmetric encryption scheme is a triple QPTs of (key generation)$Gen : 1^n \mapsto k \in \mathcal{K}_n$, (encryption)$Enc_k : \mathcal{K} \times \mathcal{D}(\mathcal{H}_\mathcal{M}) \mapsto \mathcal{D}(\mathcal{H}_\mathcal{C})$ and (decryption)$Dec_k : \mathcal{K} \times \mathcal{D}(\mathcal{H}_\mathcal{C}) \mapsto \mathcal{D}(\mathcal{H}_\mathcal{M})$, satisfying correctness property:

$$\|Enc_k \circ Dec_k - I_M\|_\diamond \leq negl(n)$$

for all $k \in \mathcal{K}_n$, where $\|\cdot\|_\diamond$ denote the diamond norm.

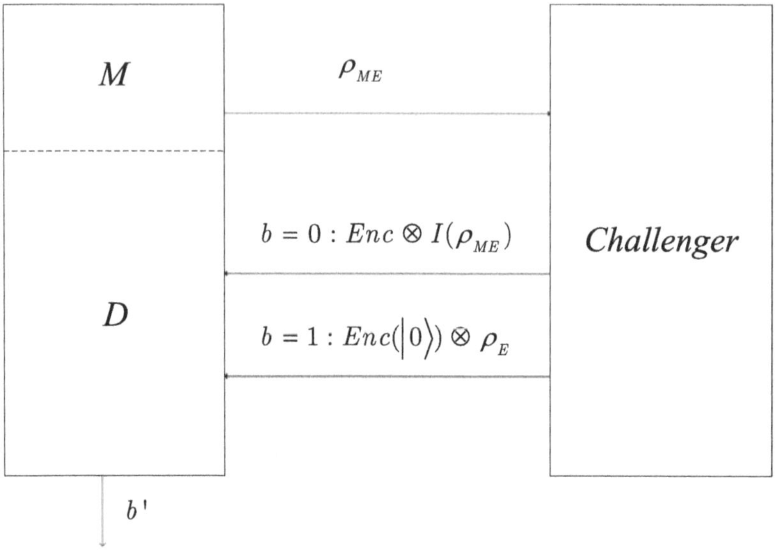

Fig. 5.1 IND-security game

To analyze the security of a quantum encryption scheme, we introduce Alagic's work [6] on indistinguishability of encryption.

Definition 5.2 A quantum symmetric encryption scheme is indistinguishable (or IND-secure), if for any QPT adversary A with message generator M and distinguisher D we have

$$|\Pr\{D[(Enc_k \otimes I_E)\rho_{ME}] = 1]\}$$
$$-\Pr\{D[(Enc_k \otimes I_E)(|0\rangle\langle 0|_M \otimes \rho_E)] = 1]\}| < negl(n),$$

where $\rho_{ME} \leftarrow M(1^n)$, $\rho_E = tr_M(\rho_{ME})$.

Figure 5.1 shows the IND-security game.

Definition 5.3 An IND-secure quantum symmetric encryption scheme is IND-CPA, if A has oracle access to Enc_k.

We denote again that A runs in polynomial time. If we assume that an oracle gate runs in a unit of time $O(1)$, then A has only polynomial many of oracle queries sent to Enc_k.

5.1.5 Quantum Point Obfuscation and Combinability

The definition of a quantum obfuscator, proposed by Alagic et al. [9], is similar to its classical counterpart.

Definition 5.4 A quantum black-box obfuscator is a quantum algorithm O and QPT δ, for any n-qubit quantum circuit C, the output of O is an m-qubit state $O(C)$ and the following three conditions hold.

1. (Polynomial expansion)

$$m = poly(n)$$

2. (Functional equivalence) for any possible ρ

$$\|\delta(O(C) \otimes \rho) - U_C \rho U_C^{\dagger}\|_{tr} \leq negl(n)$$

3. (Virtual black-box) for every QPT A, there exists a QPT S^{U_C} such that

$$|\Pr[A(O(C)) = 1] - \Pr[S^{U_C}(|0^n\rangle) = 1]| \leq negl(n)$$

A point function returns an internal value m when the input equals a specific k, and 0 elsewise. According to the theory of quantum computation, such a function can be described as

$$U_{k,m} : |x, y\rangle \mapsto \begin{cases} |x, y \oplus m\rangle & if\ x = k \\ |x, y\rangle & otherwise \end{cases}$$

Since an obfuscator for all functions does not exist, we consider a quantum obfuscator only for quantum point functions, then we assume that the input of an obfuscator is delineated by m and k. Therefore, n in Definition 5.4 equals $|m| + |k|$, and we have $|O(U_{m,k})| = poly(|m| + |k|)$.

We then define a stronger version of quantum point obfuscator, which preserves security even when an adversary has combination of different point functions. With respect to quantum encryption, we are interested in the case where the point functions are of the same k. In this case, we call it self-combinable.

Definition 5.5 A quantum point obfuscator is self-combinable, if for any $t = poly(n)$ the combination of t's obfuscators is still secure, i.e., we have a simulator S such that

$$|Pr[A(O(U_{k,r_1}), O(U_{k,r_2}), \ldots, O(U_{k,r_t}))) = 1]$$
$$-Pr[S^{U_{k,r_1}, U_{k,r_2}, \ldots, U_{k,r_t}}(0^n) = 1]| \leq negl(n)$$

In quantum encryption, we are also interested in the case where A is provided some auxiliary inputs (always some information on k). In this case, we define a quantum secure obfuscator with auxiliary inputs.

Definition 5.6 A quantum point obfuscator with auxiliary inputs f is secure, if we have a simulator S such that

$$
\begin{aligned}
&|\Pr[A(O(U_{k,r}), f(k)) = 1] \\
&- \Pr[S^{U_{k,r}}(f(k)) = 1]| \leq negl(n)
\end{aligned}
$$

5.1.6 IND-Secure Quantum Symmetric Encryption Scheme

In this section, we give the construction of quantum symmetric encryption scheme based on quantum point obfuscation. Then we prove its IND security, which comes from the VBB property of the quantum obfuscator.

Scheme 1 *Let O be a quantum point obfuscator and $U_{k,r}$ be a quantum point function. A quantum symmetric encryption scheme is a triple QPTs of following algorithms:*

1. (key generation)$Gen(1^n) = k \in \mathcal{K}_n$,

2. (encryption)$Enc_k(\rho) = P_r \rho P_r \otimes O(U_{r,k}) = c \otimes \Omega$, where r is randomly chosen from $\{0, 1\}^{2n}$,

3. (decryption)$Dec_k(c \otimes \Omega) = P_{r'} c P_{r'}$, where r' is the measurement result of $Tr_1[\delta(\Omega \otimes |k, 0^{2n}\rangle\langle k, 0^{2n}|)]$.

The encryption and decryption algorithms are shown in Figs. 5.2 and 5.3.

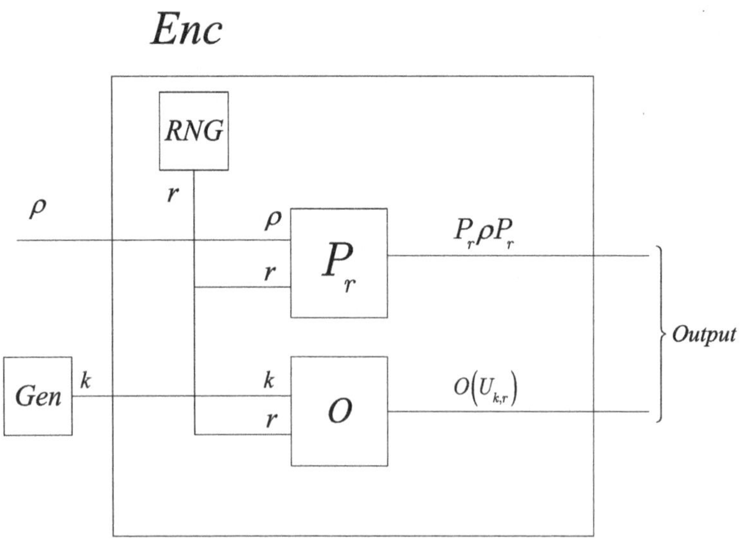

Fig. 5.2 Encryption algorithm

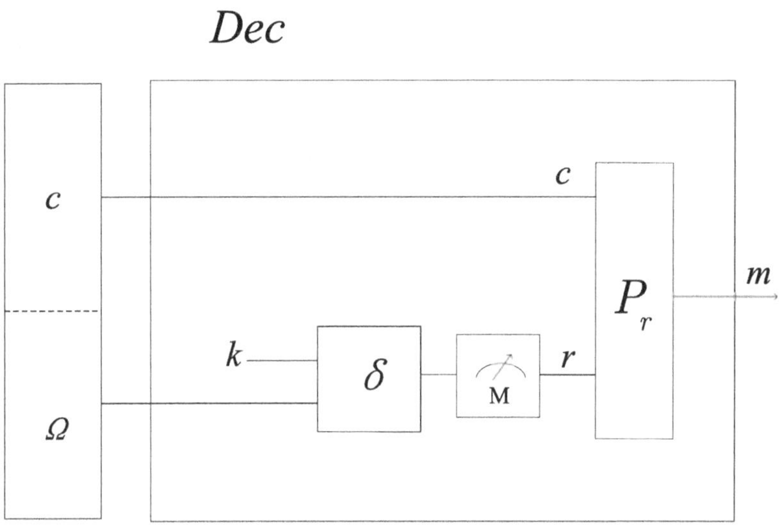

Fig. 5.3 Decryption algorithm

To prove the correctness of Scheme 1, we apply $|k_{right}, 0^{2n}\rangle$ with the right key $k_{right} = k$ to the obfuscated point function. According to the functional equivalence property, we obtain

$$\begin{aligned}\delta(\Omega \otimes |k, 0^{2n}\rangle\langle k, 0^{2n}|) &= \delta(O(U_{k,r}) \otimes |k, 0^{2n}\rangle\langle k, 0^{2n}|) \\ &\approx_p U_{k,r}(|k, 0^{2n}\rangle) = |k, r\rangle\end{aligned}$$

After tracing out the first register of $|k|$ qubits and measurement, we obtain $r' = r$, with which we can correctly recover ρ from $P_r \rho P_r$.

While with the wrong key $k_{wrong} \neq k$, the measurement gives $r' = 0$, and the message is kept secret.

Now we indicate the security of the quantum encryption scheme. Specifically, we have the following theorem.

Theorem 5.1 *If a quantum point obfuscator exists, then the quantum symmetric encryption scheme in Scheme 1 is IND-secure.*

Proof For any adversary $A = (M, D)$, set $s = (P_r \otimes I_E)\rho_{ME}$, and $t = (Enc_k \otimes I_E)(|0\rangle\langle 0|_M \otimes \rho_E)$, we have

$$\begin{aligned}
&|\Pr\{D[(Enc_k \otimes I_E)\rho_{ME}] = 1\} \\
&- \Pr\{D[(Enc_k \otimes I_E)(|0\rangle\langle 0|_M \otimes \rho_E)] = 1\}| \\
&= |\Pr\{D[s \otimes O(U_{k,r})] = 1\} - \Pr\{D[t \otimes O(U_{k,r})] = 1\}| \\
&= |\Pr\{D[s, O(U_{k,r})] = 1\} - \Pr\{D[t, O(U_{k,r})] = 1\}| \\
&\leq \Sigma_{g(r)} |\Pr\{D[s, g(r)] = 1\} - \Pr\{D[t, g(r)] = 1\}| \\
&\cdot \Pr[D'(O(U_{k,r})) = g(r)]
\end{aligned} \tag{5.1}$$

In Eq. 5.1, the sum symbol is for all possible $g(r)$, and D' is a subroutine of D dealing with O. By the VBB property, we have a simulator S satisfying

$$|\Pr[D(O(U_{k,r})) = f(r)] - \Pr[S^{U_{k,r}}(0^n) = f(r)]| \leq negl(n) \tag{5.2}$$

Note that S has oracle access to $U_{k,r}$, then $g(r)$ can only be r (when S successfully accesses the oracle with k), or 0 (when not). So we can rewrite Eq. 5.1 as

$$\begin{aligned}
&\Sigma_{g(r)} |\Pr\{D[s, g(r)] = 1\} - \Pr\{D[t, g(r)] = 1\}| \\
&\cdot \Pr[D(O(U_{k,r})) = g(r)] \\
&\leq \Sigma_{g(r)} |\Pr\{D[s, g(r)] = 1\} - \Pr\{D[t, g(r)] = 1\}| \\
&\cdot |\Pr[S^{U_{k,r}}(0^n) = g(r)] + negl(n)| \\
&= |\Pr\{D(s, r) = 1\} - \Pr\{D(t, r) = 1\}| \\
&\cdot |\Pr[S^{U_{k,r}}(0^n) = r] + negl(n)| \\
&+ |\Pr\{D(s, 0) = 1\} - \Pr\{D(t, 0) = 1\}| \\
&\cdot |\Pr[S^{U_{k,r}}(0^n) = 0] + negl(n)|.
\end{aligned} \tag{5.3}$$

For the first item to the right side of the inequality, we consider the QPT S with polynomial many queries. While the key space $\mathcal{K}$ is uniformly random $\{0, 1\}^n$, the probability $Pr[S^{U_{k,r}}(0^n) = r] = poly(n)/2^n \leq negl(n)$. For the second item to the right of inequality, we have

$$\begin{aligned}
&|\Pr\{D(s, 0) = 1\} - \Pr\{D(t, 0) = 1\}| \\
&= |\Pr\{D[(P_r \otimes I_E)\rho_{ME}] = 1\} \\
&- \Pr\{D[(Enc_k \otimes I_E)(|0\rangle\langle 0|_M \otimes \rho_E)] = 1\}|
\end{aligned} \tag{5.4}$$

According to the indistinguishableness of quantum one-time pad, this difference is negligible.

Finally, we have

$$\begin{aligned}
&|\Pr\{D[(Enc_k \otimes I_E)\rho_{ME}] = 1\} \\
&- \Pr\{D[(Enc_k \otimes I_E)(|0\rangle\langle 0|_M \otimes \rho_E)] = 1\}| \\
&\le |\Pr\{D(s, r) = 1\} - \Pr\{D(t, r) = 1\}| \\
&\cdot |\Pr[S^{U_{k,r}}(0^n) = r] + negl(n)| \\
&+ |\Pr\{D(s, 0) = 1\} - \Pr\{D(t, 0) = 1\}| \\
&\cdot |\Pr[S^{U_{k,r}}(0^n) = 0] + negl(n)| \\
&\le |\Pr\{D(s, r) = 1\} - \Pr\{D(t, r) = 1\}| \cdot negl(n) \\
&+ negl(n) \cdot |\Pr[S^{U_{k,r}}(0^n) = 0] + negl(n)| \\
&\le negl(n)
\end{aligned} \tag{5.5}$$

This is exactly what we need for IND security.

5.1.7 Security Analysis

In this section, we provide the extension of an obfuscator and a quantum symmetric encryption scheme. Specifically, a self-combinable obfuscator implements IND-CPA-secure encryption and an auxiliary-input obfuscator implements leakage-resilient encryption.

A. Self-Combinable Obfuscator and IND-CPA-Secure Encryption

Here we point out that the self-combinable property in obfuscation corresponds to the IND-CPA security in quantum encryption.

We continue to use the construction of Scheme 1, requiring that the obfuscator O is self-combinable. We prove the following theorem.

Theorem 5.2 *If a quantum point obfuscator O is self-combinable, then the quantum symmetric encryption scheme in Scheme 1 is IND-CPA-secure.*

Proof The correctness holds obviously. Assume that any adversary $A = (M, D)$ queries encryption oracle for $t = poly(n)$ times. Then there are $r_1, \ldots, r_t$ (used by the encryption oracle) and r (used by the challenger) that maximize the difference

$$\begin{aligned}
&|\Pr\{D^{Enc}[(Enc_k \otimes I_E)\rho_{ME}] = 1\} \\
&- \Pr\{D^{Enc}[(Enc_k \otimes I_E)(|0\rangle\langle 0|_M \otimes \rho_E)] = 1\}|.
\end{aligned} \tag{5.6}$$

From A we construct an adversary A' attacking the obfuscator. Specifically, when A queries the encryption oracle for the ith time, A' responds with $P_{r_i}\rho P_{r_i} \otimes O(U_{k,r_i})$.

During the distinguishing challenge game, A' responds either $P_r \rho P_r \otimes O(U_{k,r})$ or $P_r|0\rangle\langle 0|P_r \otimes O(U_{k,r})$. Therefore, when A' outputs the same as A,

$$\begin{aligned}
&|\Pr\{D^{Enc}[(Enc_k \otimes I_E)\rho_{ME}] = 1\} \\
&- \Pr\{D^{Enc}[(Enc_k \otimes I_E)(|0\rangle\langle 0|_M \otimes \rho_E)] = 1\}| \\
&\leq |\Pr\{A'[O(U_{k,r_1}), \ldots, O(U_{k,r_t}); Enc_k(\rho)] = 1|\} \\
&- \Pr\{A'[O(U_{k,r_1}), \ldots, O(U_{k,r_t}); Enc_k(|0\rangle)] = 1\}| \\
&\leq |\Pr\{S^{O(U_{k,r_1}),\ldots,O(U_{k,r_t})}[Enc_k(\rho)] = 1|\} \\
&- \Pr\{S^{O(U_{k,r_1}),\ldots,O(U_{k,r_t})}[Enc_k(|0\rangle)] = 1\}| + negl(n) \\
&\leq negl(n),
\end{aligned} \tag{5.7}$$

where the last inequality comes from self-combinability.

B. Auxiliary Input and Leakage Resilience

Here we prove that auxiliary input corresponds to the quantum leakage resilience. We firstly define a quantum leakage-resilient encryption scheme, which is similar to its classical counterpart just like many other quantum cryptographic terminologies.

Definition 5.7 An IND-secure quantum symmetric encryption scheme is leakage-resilient, if any adversary A submits a quantum-secure one-way function (qOWF) f and gets $f(k)$ after $Gen(1^n)$ generates a key k.

We now show that a quantum point obfuscator with auxiliary inputs implements quantum leakage-resilient encryption.

Theorem 5.3 *If (O, δ) is a quantum point obfuscator with auxiliary input f, then Scheme 1 is leakage-resilient against key information $f(k)$.*

Proof The correctness holds obviously. For any adversary $A = (M, D)$, we set $s = (P_r \otimes I_E)\rho_{ME}$, and $t = (Enc_k \otimes I_E)(|0\rangle\langle 0|_M \otimes \rho_E)$, we have

$$\begin{aligned}
&|\Pr\{D[(Enc_k \otimes I_E)\rho_{ME}, f(k)] = 1\} \\
&- \Pr\{D[(Enc_k \otimes I_E)(|0\rangle\langle 0|_M \otimes \rho_E), f(k)] = 1\}| \\
&= |\Pr\{D[s, O(U_{k,r}), f(k)] = 1\} \\
&- \Pr\{D[t, O(U_{k,r}), f(k)] = 1\}| \\
&\leq \Sigma_{g(r)}|\Pr\{D[s, g(r)] = 1\} - \Pr\{D[t, g(r)] = 1\}| \\
&\cdot \Pr[D'[O(U_{k,r}), f(k)] = g(r)].
\end{aligned} \tag{5.8}$$

Similarly, we have

$$\begin{aligned}
&\Sigma_{g(r)}|\Pr\{D[s, g(r)] = 1\} - \Pr\{D[t, g(r)] = 1\}| \\
&\cdot \Pr[D'[O(U_{k,r}), f(k)] = g(r)] \\
&\leq |\Pr\{D(s, r) = 1\} - \Pr\{D(t, r) = 1\}| \\
&\cdot |\Pr[S^{U_{k,r}}(f(k)) = r]| \\
&+ |\Pr\{D(s, 0) = 1\} - \Pr\{D(t, 0) = 1\}| \\
&\cdot |\Pr[S^{U_{k,r}}(f(k)) = 0]| \\
&+ negl(n).
\end{aligned} \tag{5.9}$$

For the first item to the right side of the inequality, $\Pr[S^{U_{k,r}}(f(k)) = r] \leq negl(n)$ due to the irreversibility of f and uniformity of k. For the second item to the right side of the inequality, it is negligible according to indistinguishableness of quantum one-time pad. Therefore, the whole difference is negligible and Scheme 1 is leakage-resilient against f.

5.2 Quantum Symmetric Encryption with Quantum Point Obfuscation instantiated

5.2.1 Quantum Symmetric Encryption Scheme with Quantum Error-Correcting Code

In this section, we apply quantum point obfuscation with quantum error-correcting code to quantum symmetric encryption [14]. So we need to instantiate quantum point obfuscation with a multi-qubit output.

Scheme 2 *(Quantum point obfuscation instantiated with a multi-qubit output) Let O be a quantum point obfuscator, and $U_{\alpha,\beta}$ is a quantum point function, $\alpha, \beta \in \{0, 1\}^n$. Then the output of the quantum obfuscator is*

$$O\left(U_{\alpha,\beta}\right) = |E(\alpha), \alpha \oplus \beta\rangle. \tag{5.10}$$

The interpreter δ is constructed as follows: δ firstly returns the results of $|E(x)\rangle$ and $O(U_\alpha)$ through n CNOT gates to perform bit-by-bit XOR operation, then the interpreter δ reverses n qubits through n Pauli-X gates. When $x = \alpha$, all $|y_1\rangle, |y_2\rangle, \ldots, |y_n\rangle$ are $|1\rangle$. When $x \neq \alpha$, $|y_1\rangle, |y_2\rangle, \ldots, |y_n\rangle$ are the results of $|E(x) \oplus E(\alpha)\rangle$ after Pauli-X operation. After that, the interpreter δ performs the AND operation on all qubits through $n-1$ Toffoli gates. Finally, if $x = \alpha$, the interpreter δ outputs the bit-by-bit XOR result of the last n qubits ($|\alpha \oplus \beta\rangle$) of $O(U_\alpha)$ and $|x\rangle$, otherwise, the interpreter δ outputs $|0^n\rangle$.

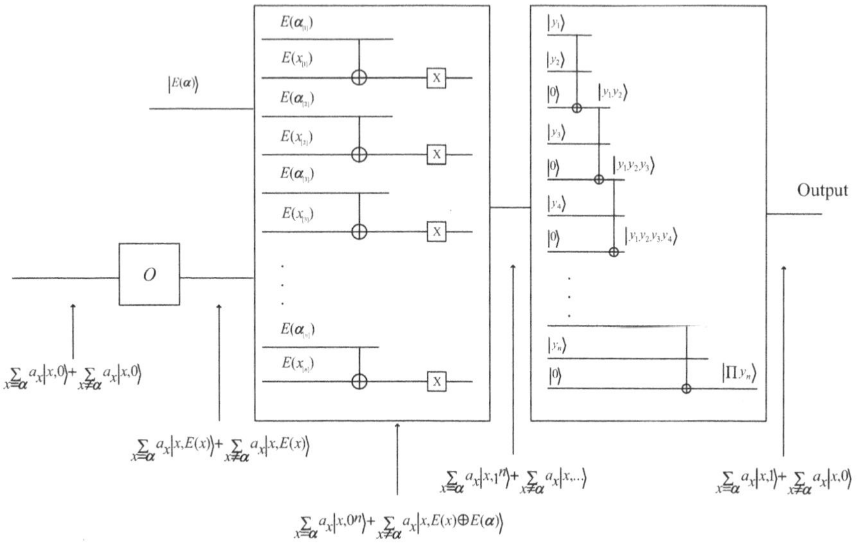

Fig. 5.4 Interpreter δ

The interpreter δ is shown in Fig. 5.4. The auxiliary qubit introduced in the Toffoli gate will be released through the reverse operation after the operation is completed to avoid entanglement between the auxiliary qubit and the output result.

We give the construction of a quantum symmetric encryption scheme with quantum error-correcting code and prove its indistinguishable security.

Scheme 3 *Let O be a quantum point obfuscator and $U_{k,r}$ be a quantum point function with a multi-qubit output. A quantum symmetric encryption scheme with quantum point obfuscation is a four-tuple QPT algorithm as follows:*

1. (Key generation) $Gen(1^n) = k \in \mathcal{K}_n$, where $\mathcal{K}_n$ is the uniform key-space $\{0, 1\}^n$, and Gen randomly chooses k from $\mathcal{K}_n$.

2. (Encryption) $Enc_k(\rho) = X^\alpha Z^\beta \rho Z^\beta X^\alpha$, where r is randomly chosen from $\{0, 1\}^n$, α is the first $n/2$ bits of r, and β is the last $n/2$ bits of r.

3. (Obfuscation) $O(U_{k,r}) = |E(k), k \oplus r\rangle$, where $|E(k)\rangle$ is the first n qubits of $O(U_{k,r})$, and $|k \oplus r\rangle$ is the last n qubits of $O(U_{k,r})$.

4. (Decryption) $Dec_k(c) = Z^{\beta'} X^{\alpha'} c X^{\alpha'} Z^{\beta'}$, where r' is the measurement result of $Tr_1[\delta(O(U_{k,r}) \otimes |k, 0^n\rangle\langle k, 0^n|)]$, α' is the first $n/2$ bits of r', and β' is the last $n/2$ bits of r'.

The quantum circuits of encryption and decryption are shown in Fig. 5.5.

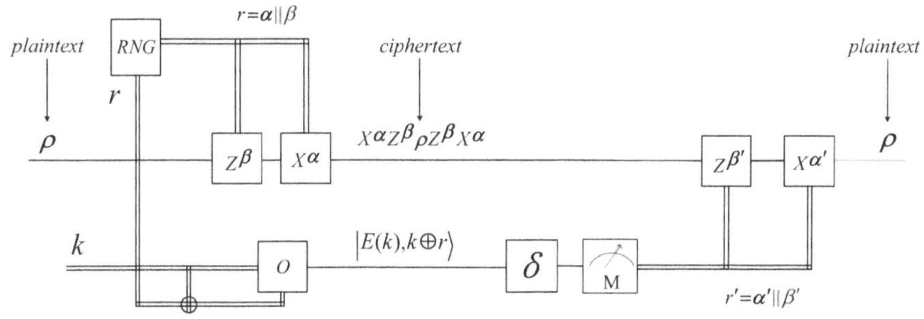

Fig. 5.5 Quantum circuits of encryption and decryption

5.2.2 Security Analysis

To prove the correctness of the quantum symmetric encryption scheme, we apply $|k_{right}, 0^n\rangle$ with the correct key $k_{right} = k$ to the obfuscated quantum point function. By functional equivalence property, we obtain

$$\begin{aligned}\delta(|E(k), k \oplus r\rangle \otimes |k, 0^n\rangle\langle k, 0^n|) &= \delta(O(U_{k,r}) \otimes |k, 0^n\rangle\langle k, 0^n|) \\ &\approx_p U_{k,r}(|k, 0^n\rangle) = |k, r\rangle.\end{aligned} \tag{5.11}$$

After tracing out the first register of $|k|$ qubits and measurement, we obtain $r' = r$, with which we can correctly recover ρ from $P_r \rho P_r$.

With the wrong key $k_{wrong} \neq k$, the measurement gives $r' = 0$ and the message is kept secret.

Then we indicate the security of the quantum symmetric encryption scheme.

Theorem 5.4 *If a quantum point obfuscator is instantiated, then the quantum symmetric encryption scheme with quantum point obfuscation instantiated is indistinguishably secure.*

Proof For any adversary $A = (M, D)$, we set $s = (P_r \otimes I_E)\rho_{ME}$, and $t = (P_r \otimes I_E)(|0\rangle\langle 0|_M \otimes \rho_E)$. Here P_r refers to the corresponding operation of $X^\alpha Z^\beta$, and α is the first $n/2$ bits of r, β is the last $n/2$ bits of r. We have

$$\begin{aligned}&|\Pr\{D[(Enc_k \otimes I_E)\rho_{ME}] = 1\} \\ &\quad - \Pr\{D[(Enc_k \otimes I_E)(|0\rangle\langle 0|_M \otimes \rho_E)] = 1\}| \\ &= |\Pr\{D[s \otimes O(U_{k,r})] = 1\} - \Pr\{D[t \otimes O(U_{k,r})] = 1\}| \\ &= |\Pr\{D[s, O(U_{k,r})] = 1\} - \Pr\{D[t, O(U_{k,r})] = 1\}| \\ &\leq \Sigma_{g(r)}|\Pr\{D[s, g(r)] = 1\} - \Pr\{D[t, g(r)] = 1\}| \\ &\cdot \Pr[D'(O(U_{k,r})) = g(r)].\end{aligned} \tag{5.12}$$

In the last inequality, the sum symbol is for all possible $g(r)$, and D' is a subroutine of D dealing with O. According to the VBB property, we have a simulator S satisfying

$$|\Pr[D(O(U_{k,r})) = f(r)] - \Pr[S^{U_{k,r}}(0^n) = f(r)]| \leq negl(n). \tag{5.13}$$

Note that S has oracle access to $U_{k,r}$, then $g(r)$ can only be r if S successfully accesses the oracle with k, otherwise 0. So we can rewrite Eq. 5.12 as

$$\begin{aligned}
&\Sigma_{g(r)}|\Pr\{D[s, g(r)] = 1\} - \Pr\{D[t, g(r)] = 1\}| \\
&\cdot \Pr[D(O(U_{k,r})) = g(r)] \\
&\leq \Sigma_{g(r)}|\Pr\{D[s, g(r)] = 1\} - \Pr\{D[t, g(r)] = 1\}| \\
&\cdot |\Pr[S^{U_{k,r}}(0^n) = g(r)] + negl(n)| \\
&= |\Pr\{D(s, r) = 1\} - \Pr\{D(t, r) = 1\}| \\
&\cdot |\Pr[S^{U_{k,r}}(0^n) = r] + negl(n)| \\
&+ |\Pr\{D(s, 0) = 1\} - \Pr\{D(t, 0) = 1\}| \\
&\cdot |\Pr[S^{U_{k,r}}(0^n) = 0] + negl(n)|.
\end{aligned} \tag{5.14}$$

For the first item to the right side of the inequality, we consider the QPT S with polynomial many queries. While the key space $\mathcal{K}$ is uniformly random $\{0, 1\}^n$, the probability $\Pr[S^{U_{k,r}}(0^n) = r] = poly(n)/2^n \leq negl(n)$. For the second item to the right of inequality, we have

$$\begin{aligned}
&|\Pr\{D(s, 0) = 1\} - \Pr\{D(t, 0) = 1\}| \\
&= |\Pr\{D[(Enc_k \otimes I_E)\rho_{ME}] = 1\} \\
&- \Pr\{D[(Enc_k \otimes I_E)(|0\rangle\langle 0|_M \otimes \rho_E)] = 1\}|.
\end{aligned} \tag{5.15}$$

According to indistinguishability of quantum one-time pad, this difference is negligible.

Finally, we have

$$\begin{aligned}
&|\Pr\{D[(Enc_k \otimes I_E)\rho_{ME}] = 1\} \\
&- \Pr\{D[(Enc_k \otimes I_E)(|0\rangle\langle 0|_M \otimes \rho_E)] = 1\}| \\
&\leq |\Pr\{D(s, r) = 1\} - \Pr\{D(t, r) = 1\}| \\
&\cdot |\Pr[S^{U_{k,r}}(0^n) = r] + negl(n)| \\
&+ |\Pr\{D(s, 0) = 1\} - \Pr\{D(t, 0) = 1\}| \\
&\cdot |\Pr[S^{U_{k,r}}(0^n) = 0] + negl(n)| \\
&\leq |\Pr\{D(s, r) = 1\} - \Pr\{D(t, r) = 1\}| \cdot negl(n) \\
&+ negl(n) \cdot |\Pr[S^{U_{k,r}}(0^n) = 0] + negl(n)| \\
&\leq negl(n).
\end{aligned} \tag{5.16}$$

This is exactly what we need for indistinguishable security.

5.2.3 Simulation Analysis

Since various implementation schemes of quantum computer have limitations on the number of qubits and the logic gate operation accuracy, the cost of actual quantum computation is relatively high. In addition, the operating laws and mathematical principles of quantum computers with quantum circuit models are actually known, so small-scale quantum computation can be simulated under ideal conditions on classical computers.

Here we use QLib quantum computing simulation tool to simulate the quantum symmetric encryption scheme to verify the correctness of Scheme 1 and the ciphertext is secure. The partial circuits of interpreter δ are shown in Fig. 5.6. We set k and r to 4 qubits, x is the key input by the decryptor. In the circuit, q_0, q_2, q_5, q_8 is the 4 qubits of $E(k)$. q_1, q_3, q_6, q_9 is the first 4 qubits of $O(U_{x,r})$ and $q_{11}, q_{13}, q_{15}, q_{17}$ is the last 4 qubits of $O(U_{x,r})$. q_4, q_7, q_{10} are all $|0\rangle$ and $q_{12}, q_{14}, q_{16}, q_{18}$ are $|x\rangle$. The measurement result is r'. In the simulation, we suppose the transmitted quantum plaintext $\rho = [0.077873, -0.92719 - 0.36641i]$, the classical key is k=0111. When the random number generator RNG outputs $r = 10$, $X^\alpha Z^\beta \rho Z^\beta X^\alpha = [0.99696, -0.072423 + 0.028621i]$, the obfuscated result $O(U) = [0.19509, 0, 0, 0, 0.98079, 0, 0, 0]$. If decrypted with the correct key, we can obtain the correct plaintext $\rho = [0.077873, -0.92719 - 0.36641i]$ with the fidelity $F = 1$. If decrypted with the wrong key $x = 0011$, the decryption result $\rho = [0.99696, -0.072423 + 0.028621i]$, the fidelity is only $F = 0.14441$. As the length of the key increases, the fidelity of the plaintext obtained by the wrong key is further reduced and the fidelity is less than 0.1 at $|k| = 128$. So the quantum symmetric encryption scheme can guarantee the security of ciphertext.

5.3 Summary

In this chapter, we demonstrated the usability of quantum obfuscation in quantum symmetric encryption. We introduced an IND-secure quantum symmetric encryption scheme based on point obfuscation and proved the corresponding relationship between IND security and the obfuscator for quantum symmetric encryption. Especially, different encryption security can be implemented according to the properties of an obfuscator. We can know that the instantiation of quantum point obfuscation with quantum error-correcting code is more secure under the definition of instantiation. By applying quantum point obfuscation to quantum symmetric encryption, we can verify that the instantiation of quantum point obfuscation is useful to realize the security of ciphertext. Meanwhile, it is challenging to construct more suitable quantum encryption schemes by means of quantum point obfuscator instantiated. Of course, the instantiation scheme can provide guidance to the application of quantum obfuscation through the definition of instantiation and more attempts of quantum hash function are still needed.

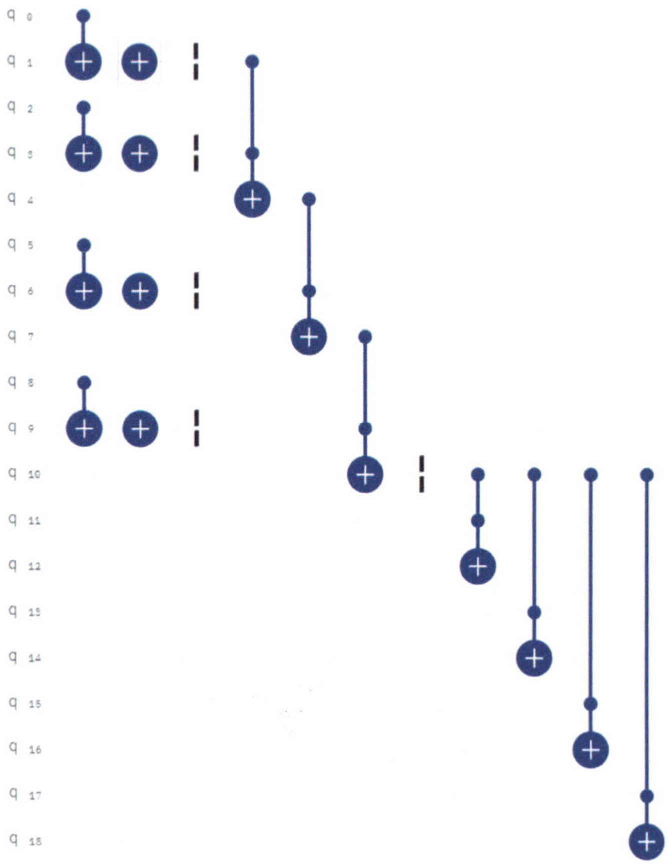

Fig. 5.6 Quantum circuit of interpreter δ

References

1. Ambainis, A., Mosca, M., Tapp, A., et al.: Private quantum channels. In: Annual IEEE Symposium on Foundations of Computer Science (FOCS), pp. 547–553 (2000)
2. Broadbent, A., Jeffery, S.: Quantum homomorphic encryption for circuits of low T-gate complexity. In: Annual International Cryptology Conference (CRYPTO 2015), vol. 9216, pp. 609–629 (2015)
3. Shang, T., Zhao, X.J., Liu, J.W.: Quantum homomorphic signature. Quant. Inform. Process. **14**(1), 393–410 (2015)
4. Boneh, D., Dagdelen, O., Fischlin, M., et al.: Random oracles in a quantum world. Comput. Sci. **7073**(1), 41–69 (2010)
5. Shang, T., Lei, Q., Liu, J.W.: Quantum random oracle model for quantum digital signature. Phys. Rev. A **94**(4), 042314 (2016)
6. Alagic, G., Broadbent, A., Fefferman, B., et al.: Computational security of quantum encryption. In: International Conference on Information Theoretic Security (ICITS), vol. 10015, pp. 47–71 (2016)

7. Alagic, G., Majenz, C.: Quantum non-malleability and authentication. In: International Conference on Information Theoretic Security (ICITS), pp. 310–341 (2017)
8. Alagic, G., Gagliardoni, T., Majenz, C.: Unforgeable Quantum Encryption (2017). arXiv preprint arXiv:1709.06539
9. Alagic, G., Fefferman, B.: On Quantum Obfuscation (2016). arXiv preprint arXiv:1602.01771
10. Chen, R.Y.L., Shang, T., Liu, J.W.: Quantum symmetric encryption based on quantum obfuscation. Quant. Inform. Process. **18**(6), 161 (2019)
11. Slot, C., Boas, P.: On tape versus core an application of space efficient perfect hash functions to the invariance of space. In: ACM Symposium on Theory of Computing (STOC), pp. 391–400 (1984)
12. Deutsch, D.: Quantum theory, the Church-Turing principle and the universal quantum computer. SIAM J. Comput. **400**(1818), 97–117 (1985)
13. Dorit A., Alexei Y.K., Noam N.: Quantum circuits with mixed states. In: ACM Symposium on Theory of Computing (STOC), pp. 20–30 (1998)
14. Zhang, Y.J., Shang, T., Chen, R.Y.L., et al.: Instantiation of quantum point obfuscation. Quant. Inform. Process. **21**(1), 1–16 (2022)

Chapter 6
Quantum Asymmetric Encryption

Quantum cryptography has developed some fundamental primitives such as quantum one-time pad and quantum indistinguishability security. Compared with symmetric encryption in quantum cryptography, quantum asymmetric encryption based on quantum obfuscation attracts less attention and is still in its infancy due to its difficulty in implementation and application. In this chapter, we provide two quantum asymmetric encryption schemes based on quantum obfuscation. These schemes not only achieve indistinguishability security without classical cryptography, but also solve the problem of key management in symmetric encryption.

6.1 Quantum Asymmetric Encryption Based on Quantum Point Obfuscation

6.1.1 Requirement of Asymmetric Encryption

Quantum computation combines the ideas of classical information theory, computer science, and quantum physics [1]. It introduces some quantum concepts including quantum information, quantum algorithm and quantum error correction, and so on. Among the existing quantum algorithms, quantum obfuscation, which means encrypting the functionality of circuits or functions by quantum mechanics, is an emergent branch to improve the security and confidentiality of quantum information.

In 2016, Alagic et al. [2] formally put forward the definition of quantum obfuscation which is a form of quantum computation to protect quantum circuits. In 2019, Shang et al. [3, 4] initiated the obfuscatibility of quantum point function and proposed the IND-secure quantum symmetric encryption scheme based on point obfus-

T. Shang, *Quantum Nonlinear Function Obfuscation Theory and Application*,
https://doi.org/10.1007/978-981-97-6722-9_6

cation. Since quantum obfuscation promotes the research on quantum computation and provides a more secure method to achieve the confidentiality of cryptography, it is natural to consider to attach quantum obfusacation to asymmetric encryption schemes to improve security.

In order to construct an asymmetric encryption scheme based on quantum point obfuscation, we need to combine the advantage of quantum obfuscation with asymmetric encryption to achieve indistinguishability security. Here, quantum point function is just an instantiation of quantum obfuscation [5]. Asymmetric encryption schemes of other quantum functions remain widely open.

6.1.2 Indistinguishability Obfuscation and Single-Qubit Rotation

Definition 6.1 If there exists (O, δ) in a QPT algorithm of indistinguishability obfuscation, then the following three conditions hold:

1. *Functional equivalence:* the obfuscation result $O(C)$ is interpreted as $\delta_{O(C)}$, which holds the same functionality as the input circuit C:

$$\|\delta_{O(C)} - C\| \le negl(n). \tag{6.1}$$

2. *Polynomial slowdown:* the length of the obfuscator $O(C)$ must be limited to polynomial qubits, which refers to

$$\|O(C)\| = poly(n). \tag{6.2}$$

3. *Indistinguishability:* for any $\rho_n \in R_n$, $\sigma_n \in S_n$, there are three types of indistinguishability:

   - Perfect indistinguishability: $\rho_n = \sigma_n$.
   - Statistical indistinguishability: $\|\rho_n - \sigma_n\| \le negl(n)$.
   - Computational indistinguishability: for any QPT interpreter δ, $\|\delta_{\rho_n} - \delta_{\sigma_n}\| \le negl(n)$.

Here the interpreter $\delta(C)$ refers to a compiler interpreting the functionality of the circuit C from $O(C)$.

Definition 6.2 Single-qubit rotation is a one-way function with a quantum trapdoor. The qubit is located in the $X - Z$ plane of three-dimensional Bloch sphere. The eigenstate $|0\rangle$ is located in the positive half axis of Z axis and the eigenstate $|1\rangle$ in the negative half. Single-qubit rotation is actually a rotation transformation around Y axis. That is

$$\hat{\gamma} = i(|1\rangle\langle 0| - |0\rangle\langle 1|). \tag{6.3}$$

The eigenstates are transformed into quantum superposition states on $X - Z$ plane, and the sum probabilities of eigenstates $|0\rangle$ and $|1\rangle$ is 1 which can be written as trigonometric function:

$$|\varphi\rangle = \cos\frac{\alpha}{2}|0\rangle + \sin\frac{\alpha}{2}|1\rangle. \tag{6.4}$$

Supposing $\hat{\gamma} = i(|1\rangle\langle 0| - |0\rangle\langle 1|)$, we have

$$|\varphi_b(\alpha_k)\rangle = \cos\frac{b\alpha_k}{2}|0\rangle + \sin\frac{b\alpha_k}{2}|1\rangle = e^{\frac{ib\alpha_k\hat{\gamma}}{2}}|0\rangle = R(b\alpha_k)|0\rangle. \tag{6.5}$$

The first result $\left|\varphi_{b_i,m_i}(\alpha_k)\right\rangle_i$ is transformed by the second rotation on the basis of superposition state. When the output state $|m_i\rangle$ of quantum point obfuscation is $|0\rangle$, the rotation about angle 0 is performed in Hilbert space. When $|m_i\rangle$ is $|1\rangle$, the rotation about angle π is performed. We can show the process with the equation

$$\left|\varphi_{b_i,m_i}(\alpha_k)\right\rangle_i = R(m_i\pi)\left|\varphi_{b_i}(\alpha_k)\right\rangle_i. \tag{6.6}$$

The previous result is inversely processed by qubit rotation shown in Fig. 6.1 and is subsequently measured after decryption. That is, if the information to be encrypted is $|0\rangle$, it will approach the positive half axis of Z axis with high probability after rotation. If it is $|1\rangle$, it will approach the negative half with high probability. After measurement, we can obtain specific plaintext m_i.

6.1.3 IND-Secure Quantum Asymmetric Encryption Scheme

Quantum asymmetric encryption scheme based on quantum obfuscation can be constructed as follows. Firstly, we implement the operations of qubit rotation and measurement before we obtain a quantum state. Then we interact the quantum state with the obfuscated quantum point function to obtain the qubit $|0\rangle$ or $|1\rangle$. Consequently, we encrypt the coefficients of the quantum state of point obfuscation by the asymmetric encryption algorithm. So the quantum asymmetric encryption scheme can be described as the following algorithms.

A. Key Generation

Firstly, we randomly select an integer string $b = (b_1, b_2, \ldots, b_K)$ of length K, a rotation angle $\alpha_k = \frac{2\pi}{2^k} = \frac{\pi}{2^{k-1}}$ where k is a positive integer, and the eigenstate $|0\rangle^{\otimes d}$ of d qubits to generate the corresponding public and private keys. Here we introduce a randomly generated $2(d+1)$-bit string $s = \{0, 1\}^{2d+2}$ and another random string $t = \{0, 1\}^{2d+2}$ of the same length which is only known by the sender (the public key

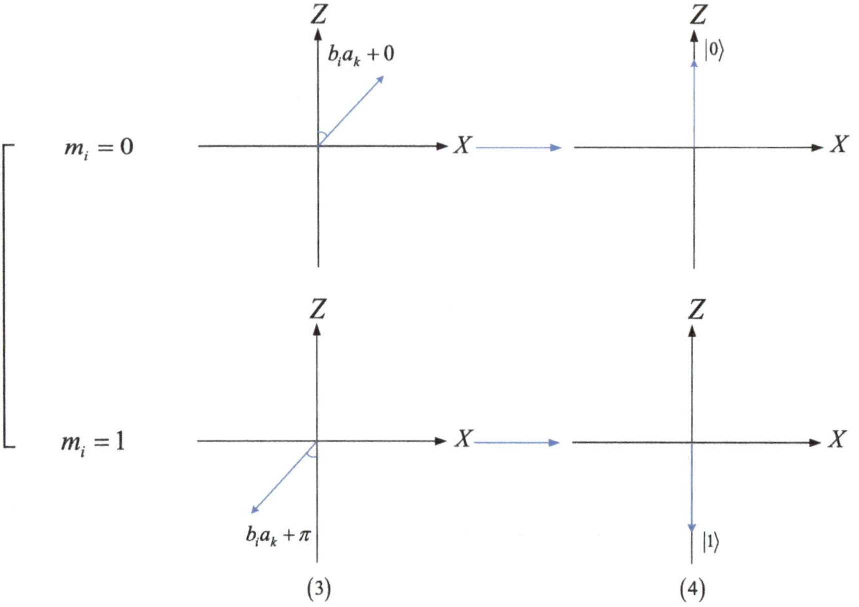

Fig. 6.1 Two dimensional planes of second qubit rotation

holder). We define $C_{a,b}$ as a classical one-way trapdoor function and its trapdoor is $u = (C_{0,0}^{-1}, C_{0,1}^{-1}, \ldots, C_{K,0}^{-1}, C_{K,1}^{-1})$, where $C_{a,b}^{-1}$ represents the inverse function of $C_{a,b}$. The algorithm based on function $C_{a,b}$ is easy to generate but difficult to inverse unless trapdoor u is used. Supposing $a = 0, 1, \ldots, K$, the sender chooses $C_{a,0}$ or $C_{a,1}$ to encrypt the coefficients x or y of the superposition quantum state output from quantum obfuscation.

The private key of the encryption scheme is divided into two parts: $\{k, b\}$ and $u = (C_{0,0}^{-1}, C_{0,1}^{-1}, \ldots, C_{K,0}^{-1}, C_{K,1}^{-1})$. The former is used to decrypt the quantum obfuscated state so as to obtain the specific angle of the inverse rotation operation while the latter is used to decrypt the quantum state after the second rotation.

B. Encryption

Alice wants to send Bob a multi-qubit string $|m\rangle = |(m_1, m_2, \ldots, m_d)\rangle$. Firstly, we need to compare d and K, if $d > K$, we need to extend the length of K in the public key. For the ith qubit $|m_i\rangle$, we interact it with a quantum point function and obtain $|0\rangle$ or $|1\rangle$ after obfuscation. Then we implement qubit rotation operation to obtain $\left|\varphi_{b_i}(\alpha_k)\right\rangle_i = R(b_i\alpha_k)|0\rangle_i$ and consequently implement qubit rotation operation for the second time to obtain $q_i = \left|\varphi_{b_i,m_i}(\alpha_k)\right\rangle_i = R(m_i\pi)\left|\varphi_{b_i}(\alpha_k)\right\rangle_i$. Finally, we encrypt the quantum superposition state result $q_i = x|0\rangle + y|1\rangle$. The specific encryption steps are described as follows.

The plaintext information to be encrypted is the coefficients of the superposition state $q = q_d q_{d-1} \ldots q_0$ of $(d+1)$ qubits. For example, the coefficients of the first qubit are encrypted by the sender as $C_{0,t_0}(x_0)$, $C_{0,t_1}(y_0)$. In addition, Alice also sends a function of string $t = \{0, 1\}^{2d+2}$. For any $a = 0, 1, \ldots, d$, the use of $C_{a,0}(t_a)$ or $C_{a,1}(t_a)$ depends on the fact that whether s_a is $|0\rangle$ or $|1\rangle$. Thus we have

$$En(q) = \left\{C_{0,t_0}(x_0), C_{0,t_1}(y_0), \ldots, C_{d,t_{2d}}(x_d), C_{d,t_{2d+1}}(y_d), F(t)\right\}, \tag{6.7}$$

$$F(t) = \{C_{0,s_0}(t_0), \ldots, C_{d,s_d}(t_d), C_{0,s_{d+1}}(t_{d+1}), \ldots, C_{d,s_{2d+1}}(t_{2d+1})\}. \tag{6.8}$$

In this way, Alice sends Bob the result $\left\{\left|\varphi_{b(PK)}(\alpha_k)\right\rangle, En(q)\right\}$.

C. Decryption

Bob receives the ciphertext from Alice. Firstly, we obtain the quantum state $\left|\varphi_{b_i}(\alpha_k)\right\rangle_i$ corresponding to each qubit $|m_i\rangle$ with the private key $sk = \{k, b\}$. Thus we obtain the angle of the first qubit rotation operation. As we have defined above, the trapdoor of the abstract function is $u = (C_{0,0}^{-1}, C_{0,1}^{-1}, \ldots, C_{k,0}^{-1}, C_{k,0}^{-1})$. Next, we utilize the trapdoor in the public key to obtain the coefficients of $q = q_d q_{d-1} \ldots q_0$. We know $q_i = \left|\varphi_{b_i,m_i}(\alpha_k)\right\rangle_i = R(m_i\pi)\left|\varphi_{b_i}(\alpha_k)\right\rangle_i$, so we have

$$F^{-1}(t) = \{C_{0,s_0}^{-1}(t_0), \ldots, C_{d,s_d}^{-1}(t_d), C_{1,s+2}^{-1}(t_{d+2}), \ldots, C_{d,s_{2d+1}}^{-1}(t_{2d+1})\}, \tag{6.9}$$

$$Dn(q) = \{C_{0,t_0}^{-1}(x_0), C_{0,t_1}^{-1}(y_1), \ldots, C_{d,t_{2d}}^{-1}(x_d), C_{d,t_{2d+1}}^{-1}(y_d), F^{-1}(t)\}. \tag{6.10}$$

At this time, we measure $R(b_i\alpha_k)_i^{-1}\left|\varphi_{b_i,m_i}(\alpha_k)\right\rangle_i$ on the X-Z plane of the Bloch sphere. If the qubit is on the positive half axis of the Z axis, the output of quantum point function is $|0\rangle$. If it is on the negative half, the output is $|1\rangle$. At this time, Alice replaces s with t and publishes the new private key sk.

6.1.4 Security Analysis

This scheme updates the randomly generated bit string s in the public key with the classical bit string $t = \{0, 1\}^{2d+2}$ generated randomly each time. Alice generates t randomly, and Bob needs to use the private key $(C_{0,0}^{-1}, C_{0,1}^{-1}, \ldots, C_{K,0}^{-1}, C_{K,1}^{-1})$ to calculate t, and then obtain the coefficients of the quantum state $q_i = \left|\varphi_{b_i,m_i}(\alpha_k)\right\rangle_i = R(m_i\pi)\left|\varphi_{b_i}(\alpha_k)\right\rangle_i$.

Because t is not published to the public, Bob can verify the identity information of the encrypting party while using the private key. The encryption and decryption scheme can be circularly carried out in two directions.

A. Indistinguishablility Security

The quantum asymmetric encryption scheme based on quantum point obfuscation satisfies IND security which can be described as follows.

Theorem 6.1 *If there exist quantum black-box obfuscation and secure quantum one-way trapdoor function, there also exists a quantum asymmetric encryption scheme which satisfies indistinguishability chosen-plaintext attack (IND-CPA) security.*

Proof A quantum polynomial time interpreter δ with only black-box access to En_{sk} can be used to simulate the access of any QPT adversary. Because of the access to the quantum encryption circuit, the interpreter can select a random number to be used for encryption.

For any QPT adversary, $A = \left(R, R^{-1}\right)$, $u = \left|\varphi_{b(PK)}\left(\alpha_k\right)\right\rangle \otimes R\left(m_j\right)$, $v = \left|\varphi_{b(PK)}\left(\alpha_k\right)\right\rangle \left(\left|0^d\right\rangle\left\langle 0^d\right| \otimes m_i\right)$, we have

$$\begin{aligned} &|\Pr\left\{R^{-1}\left[PK \otimes R\left(m_i\right)\right] = 1\right\} \\ &- \Pr\left\{R^{-1}\left[PK\left(\left|0^d\right\rangle\left\langle 0^d\right| \otimes m_i\right)\right] = 1\right\}| \\ &= \left|\Pr\left\{R^{-1}\left[u, O\left(U_{b,k}\right)\right] = 1\right\} - \Pr\left\{R^{-1}\left[v, O\left(U_{b,k}\right)\right] = 1\right\}\right| \\ &\le \sum_k \left|\Pr\left\{R^{-1}[u, \beta(b)] = 1\right\} - \Pr\left\{R^{-1}[v, \beta(b)] = 1\right\}\right| \\ &\cdot \Pr\left\{R_1^{-1}\left[u, O\left(U_{b,k}\right) = \beta(b)\right]\right\}. \end{aligned} \tag{6.11}$$

Here R_1^{-1} is the subline of R^{-1}. Owing to the virtual black-box property, there is

$$\left|\Pr\left[R^{-1}\left(O\left(U_{b,k}\right)\right) = 1\right] - \Pr\left[S^{U_{b,k}}\left(\left|0^d\right\rangle\right) = 1\right]\right| \le negl(n). \tag{6.12}$$

And we have

$$\begin{aligned} &\sum_k \left|\Pr\left\{R^{-1}[u, \beta(b)] = 1\right\} - \Pr\left\{R^{-1}[v, \beta(b)] = 1\right\}\right| \\ &\cdot \Pr\left\{R_1^{-1}\left[u, O\left(U_{b,k}\right) = \beta(b)\right]\right\} \\ &\le \sum_k \left|\Pr\left\{R^{-1}[u, \beta(b)] = 1\right\} - \Pr\left\{R^{-1}[v, \beta(b)] = 1\right\}\right| \\ &\cdot \left|\Pr\left\{S^{U_{b,k}}\left(\left|0^d\right\rangle\right) = b\right\} + negl(n)\right|. \end{aligned} \tag{6.13}$$

When S under the quantum-accessible random oracle accesses $U_{b,k}$ successfully, $\beta(b) = b_k$, otherwise $\beta(b) = 0$. So

$$\begin{aligned} &\sum_k \left|\Pr\left\{R^{-1}[u, \beta(b)] = 1\right\} - \Pr\left\{R^{-1}[v, \beta(b)] = 1\right\}\right| \\ &\cdot \left|\Pr\left\{S^{U_{b,k}}\left(\left|0^d\right\rangle\right) = b\right\} + negl(n)\right| \\ &= \left|\Pr\left\{R^{-1}\left[u, b_k\right] = 1\right\} - \Pr\left\{R^{-1}\left[v, b_k\right] = 1\right\}\right| \\ &\cdot \left|\Pr\left\{S^{U_{b,k}}\left(\left|0^d\right\rangle\right) = b\right\} + negl(n)\right| \\ &+ \left|\Pr\left\{R^{-1}[u, 0] = 1\right\} - \Pr\left\{R^{-1}[v, 0] = 1\right\}\right| \\ &\cdot \left|\Pr\left\{S^{U_{b,k}}\left(\left|0^d\right\rangle\right) = 0\right\} + negl(n)\right|. \end{aligned} \tag{6.14}$$

Owing to $\Pr\left\{S^{U_{bk}}\left(\left|0^K\right\rangle\right)=b_k\right\}=\text{poly}(n)/2^n\leq negl(n)$ and IND security of one-time pad, we have

$$\begin{aligned}
&\left|\Pr\left\{R^{-1}[u,0]=1\right\}-\Pr\left\{R^{-1}[v,0]=1\right\}\right| \\
&=\Bigg|\Pr\left\{R^{-1}\left[\left|\varphi_{b(PK)}\left(\alpha_k\right)\right\rangle\otimes R\left(m_i\right)\right]=1\right\} \\
&\quad-\Pr\left\{R^{-1}\left[\left|\varphi_{b(PK)}\left(\alpha_k\right)\right\rangle\left(\left|0^d\right\rangle\left\langle 0^d\right|\otimes m_i\right)\right]=1\right\}\Bigg| \\
&=negl(n).
\end{aligned} \tag{6.15}$$

Thus we have

$$\begin{aligned}
&\left|\Pr\left\{R^{-1}\left[PK\otimes R\left(m_i\right)\right]=1\right\}-\Pr\left\{R^{-1}\left[PK\left(\left|0^d\right\rangle\left\langle 0^d\right|\otimes m_i\right)\right]=1\right\}\right| \\
&\leq\left|\Pr\left\{R^{-1}\left[u,b_k\right]=1\right\}-\Pr\left\{R^{-1}\left[v,b_k\right]=1\right\}\right|\cdot\left|negl(n)+negl(n)\right| \\
&+negl(n)\cdot\left|\Pr\left\{S^{U_{b,k}}\left(\left|0^d\right\rangle\right)=0\right\}+negl(n)\right|=negl(n).
\end{aligned} \tag{6.16}$$

In conclusion, the asymmetric encryption scheme based on quantum obfuscation satisfies indistinguishability security.

6.2 Quantum Asymmetric Encryption Based on Quantum Power Obfuscation

In this section, we introduce a quantum asymmetric encryption scheme based on quantum power obfuscation [6]. We prove the IND security of the obfuscation scheme according to the VBB property of quantum obfuscation.

6.2.1 IND-Secure Quantum Asymmetric Encryption Scheme

Let O be a quantum obfuscator for quantum power functions and $U_{k,r}$ be a quantum power function. The quantum asymmetric encryption scheme based on quantum power obfuscation is shown in Fig. 6.2 (consisting of Figs. 6.3 and 6.4) and can be described as the following algorithms.

A. Key Generation

Output $sk=|k\rangle, k\in\{0,1\}^n$, $pk=X_\alpha Y_\beta Z_\gamma|k\rangle Z_\gamma^\dagger Y_\beta^\dagger X_\alpha^\dagger\otimes O(U_{k,r'})$, where sk is the secret key generated randomly from the uniform key space $\{0,1\}^n$. Thus the public key $pk=\text{Enc}'_{sk}=\text{Enc}'_k=X_\alpha Y_\beta Z_\gamma|k\rangle Z_\gamma^\dagger Y_\beta^\dagger X_\alpha^\dagger\otimes O(U_{k,r'})$, where r' is chosen from $\{0,1\}^{3n}$ randomly and α,β,γ is the first, second and last n bits of r', respec-

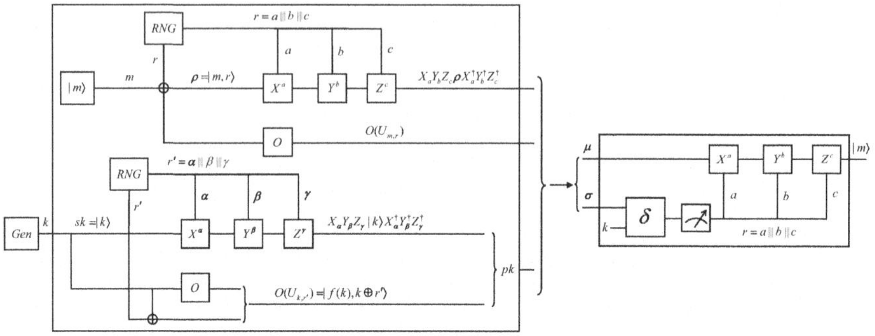

Fig. 6.2 Quantum encryption scheme

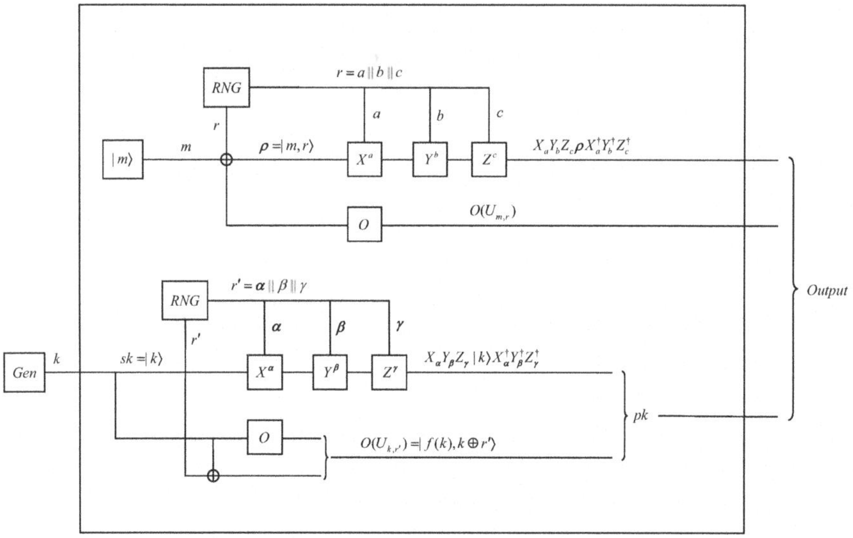

Fig. 6.3 Quantum circuit of encryption

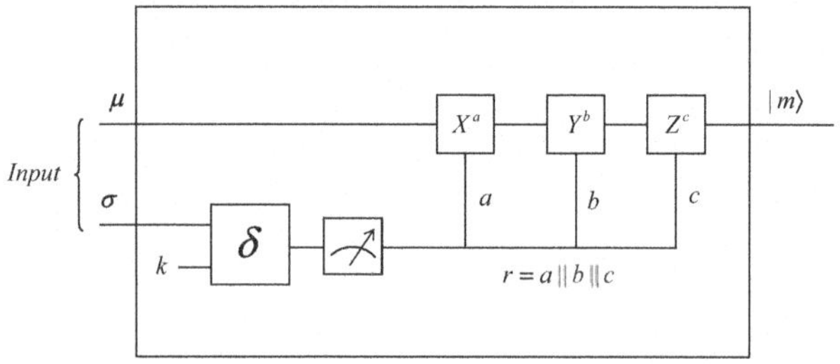

Fig. 6.4 Quantum circuit of decryption

tively. Here the quantum obfuscation is implemented to achieve the goal of generating the public key of quantum asymmetric encryption scheme.

B. Encryption

Output $\mathrm{Enc}_{pk}(\rho) = pk(|m, r\rangle) = [X_\alpha Y_\beta Z_\gamma |k\rangle Z_\gamma^\dagger Y_\beta^\dagger X_\alpha^\dagger \otimes O(U_{k,r'})] \otimes [X_a Y_b Z_c (|r\rangle\langle r| \otimes |m\rangle) Z_c^\dagger Y_b^\dagger X_a^\dagger]$, where $|m\rangle$ refers to the information to be encrypted, $r \in \{0, 1\}^{3n}$, and a, b, c represent the first, second and last n bits of the random bit r, respectively. $\mathrm{Enc}_{pk}(\rho)$ means utilizing the public key pk to encrypt the integration of random qubit $|r\rangle$ and the message $|m\rangle$.

C. Decryption

Output $\mathrm{Dec}_{sk}(\mu \otimes \sigma) = \delta(\sigma \otimes |k\rangle\langle k| \otimes \mu)$, where σ is the measurement result of $O(U_{k,r'})$ and μ is the measurement result of $X_a Y_b Z_c (|r\rangle\langle r| \otimes |m\rangle) Z_c^\dagger Y_b^\dagger X_a^\dagger$.

To demonstrate the correctness of the obfuscation scheme for quantum power functions, we suppose the information $|m, r\rangle$ is to be encrypted and thus have

$$\begin{aligned}
&\mathrm{Dec}_{sk}(\mathrm{Enc}_{pk}(|m, r\rangle)) \\
&= \mathrm{Tr}(\delta(\sigma \otimes |k\rangle\langle k| \otimes \mu)) \\
&= \mathrm{Tr}(O(U_{k,r'}) \otimes |k\rangle\langle k| \otimes X_a Y_b Z_c |m, 0^n\rangle Z_c^\dagger Y_b^\dagger X_a^\dagger) \\
&= \mathrm{Tr}(U_{k,r'}(|k\rangle\langle k| \otimes X_a Y_b Z_c |m, 0^n\rangle Z_c^\dagger Y_b^\dagger X_a^\dagger) U_{k,r'}^\dagger) \\
&= \mathrm{Tr}(|k\rangle\langle k| \otimes U_{m,r} |m, 0^n\rangle U_{m,r}^\dagger) \\
&= \mathrm{Tr}(|k\rangle\langle k| \otimes |m, 0^n\rangle) \\
&= \rho.
\end{aligned} \tag{6.17}$$

According to the properties of quantum obfuscation and density operator, we explain the correctness of the quantum asymmetric encryption scheme above. We calculate the trace of quantum state to obtain the value ρ which is the system density operator of quantum state $|m, r\rangle$. Here $\rho = \sum_i p_i |m_i, r\rangle\langle m_i, r|$ holds. In this way, the quantum state $|m, r\rangle$ is represented by ρ and the information to be encrypted is restored. Thus we prove the correctness of quantum asymmetric encryption scheme.

6.2.2 Security Analysis

The quantum asymmetric encryption scheme based on quantum power obfuscation satisfies IND security which can be described as follows.

Theorem 6.2 *If there exists a secure quantum one-way trapdoor function and quantum black-box obfuscation, then the quantum asymmetric encryption scheme based on quantum power obfuscation satisfies IND-CPA security.*

Proof A quantum polynomial time interpreter δ with only black-box access to Enc_{sk} can be used to simulate the access of any QPT adversary A and simulator S. Here for any QPT adversary, $A = (\Gamma, \Delta)$, $w = (P_u \rho P_u^\dagger \otimes I)_{\rho_\Gamma}$, $v = (P_u \rho P_u^\dagger \otimes I)(|0\rangle\langle 0| \otimes \rho)$, P_u represents unitary matrix transformation of $X_a Y_b Z_c$. So there is

$$\begin{aligned}
&\left| \Pr\left\{ \Delta\left[\mathrm{Enc}_{pk} \otimes I \right]_{\rho_\Gamma} = 1 \right\} - \Pr\left\{ \Delta\left[\left(\mathrm{Enc}_{pk} \otimes I \right) (|0\rangle\langle 0| \otimes \rho) \right] = 1 \right\} \right| \\
&= \left| \Pr\left\{ \Delta\left[w \otimes O\left(U_{k,r'} \right) \right] = 1 \right\} - \Pr\left\{ \Delta\left[v \otimes O\left(U_{k,r'} \right) \right] = 1 \right\} \right| \\
&= \left| \Pr\left\{ \Delta\left[w, O\left(U_{k,r'} \right) \right] = 1 \right\} - \Pr\left\{ \Delta\left[v, O\left(U_{k,r'} \right) \right] = 1 \right\} \right|.
\end{aligned} \tag{6.18}$$

After decomposing the above formula with probability theory,

$$\begin{aligned}
&\left| \Pr\left\{ \Delta[w, O(U_{k,r'})] - 1 \right\} - \Pr\left\{ \Delta[v, O(U_{k,r'})] = 1 \right\} \right| \\
&\leq \sum\nolimits_{p(r')} \left| \Pr\{\Delta[w, p(\rho)] = 1\} - \Pr\{\Delta[v, p(\rho)] = 1\} \right| \\
&\cdot \Pr\left\{ \Delta'(O(U_{k,r'})) = p(\rho) \right\}.
\end{aligned} \tag{6.19}$$

According to the properties of virtual black box, there is

$$|\Pr[\Delta(O(U_{k,r'})) = 1] - \Pr[S^{U_{k,r'}}(0^n) = 1]| \leq negl(n). \tag{6.20}$$

Under the quantum-accessible random oracle model, the simulator S successfully accesses the quantum power function $U_{k,r'}$, there is $p(\rho) = \rho$, otherwise there is $p(\rho) = 0$.

$$\begin{aligned}
&\sum_{p(\rho)} |\Pr\{\Delta[w, p(\rho)] = 1\} - \Pr\{\Delta[v, p(\rho)] = 1\}| \\
&\cdot \Pr\left\{ \Delta'(O(U_{k,r'})) = p(\rho) \right\} \\
&\leq \sum_{p(\rho)} |\Pr\{\Delta[w, p(\rho)] = 1\} - \Pr\{\Delta[v, p(\rho)] = 1\}| \\
&\cdot \left| \Pr[S^{U_{k,r'}}(0^n) = p(\rho)] + negl(n) \right| \\
&= |\Pr\{\Delta(w, \rho) = 1\} - \Pr\{\Delta(v, \rho) = 1\}| \cdot \left| \Pr[S^{U_{k,r'}}(0^n) = \rho] + negl(n) \right| \\
&+ |\Pr\{\Delta(w, 0) = 1\} - \Pr\{\Delta(v, 0) = 1\}| \cdot \left| \Pr[S^{U_{k,r'}}(0^n) = 0] + negl(n) \right|.
\end{aligned} \tag{6.21}$$

As $\Pr[S^{U_{k,r'}}(0^n) = \rho] \leq \frac{1}{2}\mathrm{poly}(n) \leq negl(n)$, there is

$$\begin{aligned}
&|\Pr\{\Delta(w, 0) = 1\} - \Pr\{\Delta(v, 0) = 1\}| \\
&= \left| \Pr\left\{ \Delta\left(P_u \rho P_u^\dagger \otimes I \right)_{\rho_\Gamma} = 1 \right\} - \Pr\left\{ \left(P_u \rho P_u^\dagger \otimes I \right) (|0\rangle\langle 0| \otimes \rho) = 1 \right\} \right|.
\end{aligned} \tag{6.22}$$

The above error can be ignored, so

$$\begin{aligned}
&|\Pr\left\{\Delta[\mathrm{Enc}_{pk}\otimes I]_{\rho_{\mathrm{r}}}=1\right\}-\Pr\left\{\Delta[(\mathrm{Enc}_{pk}\otimes I)(|0\rangle\langle 0|\otimes\rho)]=1\right\}| \\
&\le |\Pr\{\Delta(w,\rho)=1\}-\Pr\{\Delta(v,\rho)=1\}|\cdot\left|\Pr[S^{U_{k,r'}}(0^n)=\rho]+negl(n)\right| \\
&+|\Pr\{\Delta(w,0)=1\}-\Pr\{\Delta(v,0)=1\}|\cdot\left|\Pr[S^{U_{k,r'}}(0^n)=0]+negl(n)\right| \\
&\le |\Pr\{\Delta(w,\rho)=1\}-\Pr\{\Delta(v,\rho)=1\}|\cdot negl(n)+negl(n) \\
&\cdot\left|\Pr[S^{U_{k,r'}}(0^n)=0]+negl(n)\right| \\
&= negl(n).
\end{aligned} \tag{6.23}$$

In conclusion, the asymmetric encryption scheme based on quantum power obfuscation satisfies IND security.

6.2.3 Simulation Analysis

In this section, we use quantum computing simulation tool QLib [7] to simulate the quantum asymmetric encryption scheme above and prove the correctness of the scheme. The simulation results of average fidelity and bit error rate are shown in Fig. 6.5.

We simulate the circumstance of using different secret keys of eight bits to decrypt ciphertext and draw the curve below with average fidelity. For example, supposing the quantum plaintext to be transmitted $|m\rangle=[0.93614, -0.14736+0.31925i]$, random number $r=111$, $r'=000$, secret key $sk=11100010$, thus we have $pk=10000111$, $X_aY_bZ_c|m\rangle X_aY_bZ_c=[0.35161, 0.39234+0.84996i]$, the obfuscated result $O=[0,0,-0.93299,0,0,0,0.3599,0]$, ciphertext $c=[0,0,-0.32805,0,0,0,-36605-79301i,0]$. If correct secret key $sk=11100010$ is used to decrypt the ciphertext, we can obtain the original quantum plaintext $|m'\rangle=[0.93614, -0.14736+0.31925i]$ with the fidelity $F=1$. When wrong secret key $sk'=01101000$ is used, the fidelity is as low as 0.2759 and we cannot obtain the original quantum plaintext information. As the length of the erroneous bits of secret key increases, the fidelity of the information decrypted with the wrong secret key decreases further.

Although the problem of applying quantum obfuscation to quantum encryption scheme is solved, the real difficulty exists in the construction of the quantum circuits in the interpreter to restore the functionality of quantum functions. In the construction of quantum interpreter of a quantum power function, Definition 6.2 is achieved by quantum circuit which uses $|1\rangle$ and XOR gate to reverse quantum state $|a\rangle$. In this way, when $|a\rangle=|0\rangle$, $|x\rangle^{|a\rangle}=|1\rangle$ is output from the circuit. When $|a\rangle=|1\rangle$, quantum state $|0\rangle$ is obtained after reversal. The final result is $|x\rangle$ by operating XOR gate on $|0\rangle$ and $|x\rangle$. Now the key to the problem comes to the output of the whole interpreter. The OR result of the outputs under two cases should be output, but there is no quantum OR gate. Because just the functionality of the quantum power function

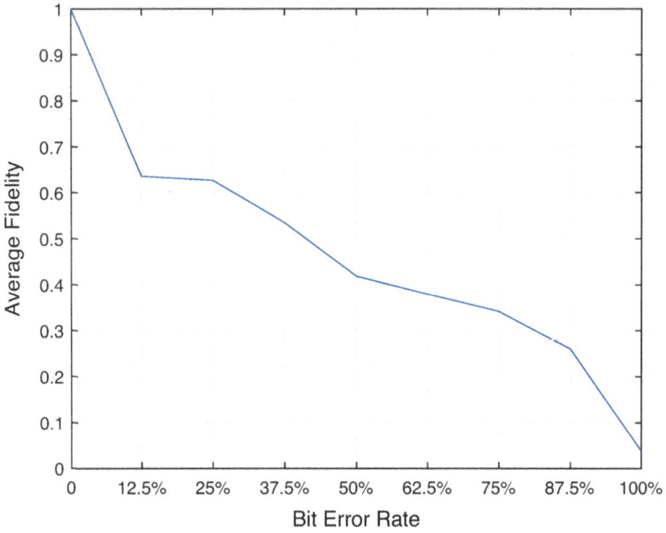

Fig. 6.5 Average fidelity—bit error rate curve for eight-qubit keys

needs to be achieved, NAND gate constructed by XOR gate will be used to achieve the functionality of quantum OR gate in the future implementation.

6.3 Summary

In this chapter, we introduced the asymmetric encryption schemes based on quantum point obfuscation and quantum power obfuscation, respectively. We implemented the operations of qubit rotation and measurement before obtaining a quantum state. Then we interacted the quantum state with the obfuscated quantum point function and consequently encrypted the coefficients of the quantum state of point obfuscation by the asymmetric encryption algorithm. Also, we demonstrated the usability of quantum power obfuscation in quantum asymmetric encryption and gave the construction of IND-secure encryption scheme and extended various properties of an obfuscator and corresponding encryption security. such work promotes the research on quantum computation and provides quantum obfuscation as a secure method to achieve confidentiality of cryptography.

References

1. Steane, A.: Quantum computing. Rep. Progress Phys. **61**(2), 117 (1997)
2. Alagic, G., Fefferman, B.: On Quantum Obfuscation (2016). arXiv preprint arXiv: 1602.01771
3. Shang, T., Chen, R., Liu, J.: On the obfuscatability of quantum point functions. Quant. Inform. Process. **18**, 55 (2019)
4. Chen, R., Shang, T., Liu, J.: IND-secure quantum symmetric encryption based on point obfuscation. Quant. Inform. Process. **18**(6), 161 (2019)
5. Pan, C.Y., Shang, T., Liu, J.W.: Quantum asymmetric encryption based on quantum point obfuscation. In: International Conference on Computational Science (ICCS 2021), LNCS 12747, pp. 142–148 (2021)
6. Pan, C.Y., Shang, T., Zhang, Y.J.: Universal quantum obfuscation for quantum non-linear functions. Front. Phys. **10**, 1342 (2023)
7. Machnes, S.: QLib—A Matlab Package for Quantum Information Theory Calculations with Applications (2007). arXiv preprint arXiv:0708.0478

Chapter 7
Quantum Homomorphic Encryption

In the era of cloud computing, homomorphic encryption, as a crucial technology for safeguarding data privacy, has garnered widespread attention. With the rapid advancement of quantum computation, an important open question arises: whether quantum computation can be delegated and verified in a non-interactive manner. In this chapter, we first affirmatively answer this question by means of constructing quantum homomorphic encryption schemes with quantum obfuscation. These schemes can exploit the interchangeability of unitary operators and achieve homomorphic encryption by exchanging the evaluation operator and the encryption operator through equivalent multiplication. Furthermore, two efficient non-interactive quantum homomorphic encryption schemes are introduced for general circuits.

7.1 Quantum Homomorphic Encryption Based on Quantum Point Obfuscation

7.1.1 Requirement of Homomorphic Encryption

Recent progress on quantum computers has led to theoretical research on cloud-based quantum computation. In such a setting, it is natural to ask whether users can keep their data secret from a server that performs quantum computation. Privacy-preserving database query is proposed to allow a user to retrieve a data item from the cloud database without revealing the information of the queried data item [1]. Limited to user's computing capabilities (for example, quantum computers are expensive), can users securely entrust their computing tasks to third parties? The answer is yes. The demand can be achieved through quantum homomorphic encryption (QHE) [2] or blind quantum computation (BQC) [3].

Classical homomorphic encryption was initiated by Rivest et al. [4]. Since then, many homomorphic encryption algorithms have been proposed [2, 5]. In addition,

T. Shang, *Quantum Nonlinear Function Obfuscation Theory and Application*,
https://doi.org/10.1007/978-981-97-6722-9_7

some of them have been widely used in the field of cryptography, such as electronic voting systems [6], confidential information retrieval protocols [7], and so on. However, with the development of quantum technology and the exponentially increasing computing power of quantum computers, these mathematically difficult homomorphic encryption algorithms are insufficient to ensure the confidentiality of calculated data in computing platforms.

A large number of QHE schemes are proposed based on the basic principles of quantum mechanics to break the limitations of classical homomorphic encryption schemes. Rohde et al. [5] proposed the first restricted QHE scheme based on quantum walks. Liang [8] first provided the definitions of QHE and quantum fully homomorphic encryption (QFHE), and constructed a symmetric QHE scheme for information-theoretic security based on the quantum one-time pad (QOTP). The evaluation function of this scheme is independent of the key, but the scheme implements homomorphic transformation with the help of universal quantum circuits instead of defining its own evaluation unit. Subsequently, based on universal quantum circuits (UQC), Liang [9] proposed another QFHE scheme. In this scheme, the evaluation function is independent of the encryption key, and the encryption key is decrypted through an iterative process. Then they [10] proposed two QFHE schemes based on a quantum fault-tolerant construction. In the symmetric QFHE scheme, the quantum error-correcting code is used as the private key, and a user also needs to provide some auxiliary quantum states. The other is the asymmetric QFHE, which requires a regular interaction between a server and a user. Ouyang et al. [11] proposed a QHE scheme based on arbitrary classical and quantum circuits, but their quantum circuits cannot exceed a fixed number of non-Clifford gates. Broadbent et al. [12] proposed two QHE schemes based on low-complexity T gates. In 2017, Sun et al. [13] proposed a symmetrical three-valued QHE scheme based on three-valued quantum gates and combination of three-valued quantum gates, but it was limited to three-dimensional Hilbert Space. As described in Ref. [14], an exponential price could be paid to obtain perfect security (unconditional security or information-theoretic security) by the determined QFHE scheme. It mainly refers to the high execution cost of the evaluation function which requires an interactive process and complex quantum line fitting.

As we can see, the design of QHE schemes focuses on the construction of homomorphic operators and the design of encryption schemes. The former is related to whether the QHE scheme can be designed and implemented efficiently, and the latter involves the security of a protocol and the scope of use, because in the symmetric scheme, the evaluator knows the decryption key, while in the asymmetric scheme, the evaluator requires a regular interaction with the user. It is desired to design a suitable QHE scheme to solve these problems.

Obfuscation derives from the study of delegated computation and is thought to be one of the most profound problems in cryptology. Researches in the field of quantum obfuscation are relatively immature. The obfuscation of point functions is also called the 'point obfuscation'. Especially, the point obfuscation was proved to be able to support symmetric function. If the symmetric QHE scheme was based on quantum point obfuscation, the evaluator will not know the decryption key and will not require a regular interaction with a user.

In this section, we will introduce the homomorphic operators and the QHE scheme based on quantum point obfuscation [15]. This scheme takes advantage of the interchangeability of the unitary operator, and exchanges the evaluation operator and the encryption operator by means of equivalent multiplication to complete homomorphic encryption. The evaluator does not know the decryption key and does not require a regular interaction with a user.

7.1.2 Basic QHE Scheme

In order to explain the QHE scheme clearly, we introduce the basic QHE scheme and the definition of d-dimensional unitary operator in this section.

Definition 7.1 A quantum homomorphic encryption scheme includes the following four algorithms.

1. **Key generation**: a key is randomly generated by the key generation algorithm $KeyGen_{\Delta}$.
2. **Encryption**: according to the key generated by the key generation algorithm, the encryption algorithm $Encrypt_{\Delta}$ encrypts the quantum plaintext state σ to generate the quantum ciphertext state $\rho = Encrypt_{\Delta}(key, \sigma)$
3. **Evaluation**: the evaluation algorithm $Evaluate_{\Delta}$ performs the corresponding evaluation calculation $\rho' = Evaluate_{\Delta}(C, \rho)$ on the quantum state ciphertext, where $C \in F_{\Delta}$, and F_{Δ} represents the set of allowed quantum operations.
4. **Decryption**: the decryption algorithm $Decrypt_{\Delta}$ decrypts ρ', thereby obtaining the direct calculation result $\sigma' = Decrypt_{\Delta}\left(key, \rho'\right)$ of the quantum plaintext state.

Definition 7.2 In a d-dimensional quantum system, a d-dimensional unitary operator is defined as follows:

$$U_{\alpha,\beta} = \sum_{x=0}^{d-1} \omega^{x(\alpha+\beta x)} |x\rangle \langle x| , \tag{7.1}$$

where $\alpha, \beta \in \{0, 1, \ldots, d-1\}, \omega = e^{2\pi i/d}$, '+' denotes modulo-d addition.

In the d-dimensional quantum system, the d-dimensional encryption-decryption unit operator gates V_d, W_d are defined as follows:

$$V_d = U_{1,0} = \sum_{x=0}^{d-1} \omega^{x} |x\rangle \langle x| \tag{7.2}$$

$$W_d = U_{0,1} = \sum_{x=0}^{d-1} \omega^{x^2} |x\rangle \langle x| \tag{7.3}$$

The security definition of a scheme is given for security analysis. The fully mixed state guarantees the security of the proposed QHE scheme [8, 13].

Definition 7.3 (*Security*) If all input state φ and output state φ_c are completely mixed, then the algorithm is secure. The relationship between the input state φ and the completely mixed state φ_c is described as follows:

$$\varphi_c = \sum_{a,b\in\{0,\ldots,d-1\}} \frac{1}{d} U_{a,b} \varphi \left(U_{a,b}\right)^{\dagger} = \frac{1}{d} I_d, \tag{7.4}$$

where φ denotes the density algorithm for all possible input state and $U_{a,b} = (a, b \in (0, \ldots, d-1))$ denotes the unitary transformations between the input and output states.

According to Definition 7.1 for QHE, we construct a QHE scheme based on quantum obfuscation, as shown in Fig. 7.1. The key generation algorithm generates an encryption key and the key of the encryption key. The encrypting party uses the encryption algorithm to encrypt a quantum state plaintext to generate a quantum state ciphertext, and then sends the quantum state ciphertext and the obfuscated key to the evaluator via the quantum-secure channel. After receiving the quantum state ciphertext, the evaluator executes the evaluation algorithm and sends the calculation result to the decrypting party. The decrypting party decrypts the evaluation calculation result sent back by the evaluator, and it is the calculation result expected by the decrypting party.

In Fig. 7.1, the encrypting party generates a *key* by a key generation algorithm $KeyGen_{\Delta}$, and then uses the encryption algorithm $Encrypt_{\Delta}$ to encrypt the quantum plaintext state σ to generate a ciphertext state ρ. The encrypting party sends the encrypted quantum state ciphertext and the quantum-obfuscated encryption key $O\left(U_{m,r}\right)$ to the homomorphic computing side. After the evaluator obtains the data sent by the encrypting party, it performs the evaluation algorithm $Evaluate_{\Delta}$ on the data, and sends the output result ρ' and the obfuscation result Ω to the decrypting party. Finally, the decrypting party performs decryption to obtain the encryption key by means of the obfuscation interpreter δ, and decrypts the quantum state ciphertext data calculated by homomorphism to obtain the direct calculation result $C(\sigma)$ of the quantum state plaintext by the evaluation operator.

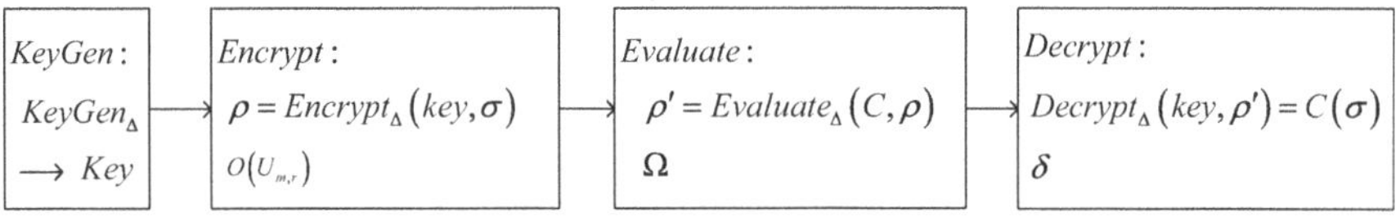

Fig. 7.1 QHE based on quantum obfuscation

7.1.3 QHE Scheme Based on Quantum Point Obfuscation

According to Definition 7.1, we introduce a QHE scheme based on point obfuscation, including the following four algorithms:

1. ***Key generation***: In this algorithm, the encrypting party encodes the classical plaintext information into quantum state plaintext σ as required, and then uses the key generation algorithm $KeyGen_\Delta$ to randomly generate three keys $k, j, m \in \{0, 1, \ldots, d-1\}$ and save them.
2. ***Encryption***: The encryption algorithm $Encrypt_\Delta$ performs encryption on the plaintext of quantum state according to the encryption key k, j to generate the quantum state ciphertext $\rho = Encrypt_\Delta(k, j, \sigma) = V_d^k W_d^j \sigma$. The encrypting party sends $\rho \otimes O(U_{m,r})$ to the evaluator, where k is the first bit of r and j is the last bit of r, m is a key generated by the $KeyGen_\Delta$, and its length is equal to r. The encrypting party must be fully quantum plaintext state and classical key information.
3. ***Evaluation***: After the evaluator receives the quantum state ciphertext ρ from the encrypting party, it generates the evaluation parameters α, β according to its computing requirements. It performs the evaluation $\rho' = Evaluate_\Delta(\alpha, \beta, \rho) = U_{\alpha,\beta} \cdot \rho$ on the received quantum state ciphertext, and sends the result $\rho' \otimes \Omega$ to the decrypting party via the quantum-secure channel.
4. ***Decryption***: After the evaluator receives the calculation result of the evaluation, it uses the interpreter δ to measure Ω to obtain k, j, and adopts the decryption algorithm $Decrypt_\Delta$ to perform the decryption $\sigma' = Decrypt_\Delta(k, j, \rho') = V_d^{-k} W_d^{-j} \rho' = U_{\alpha,\beta}\sigma$ based on the key k, j.

Figure 7.2 indicates that in the encryption algorithm, the encrypting party encrypts the input quantum state plaintext σ by using the key k, j generated by the key generation algorithm, and sends the encryption result $\rho \otimes O(U_{m,r})$ to the evaluator for evaluation calculation $U_{\alpha,\beta}$. The result $\rho' \otimes \Omega$ is sent to the decrypting party to perform the decryption to obtain a direct calculation result $U_{\alpha,\beta}$ of the plaintext σ of the quantum state.

This scheme takes advantage of the interchangeability of the d-dimensional unitary operator, and exchanges the evaluation operator and the encryption operator by means of equivalent multiplication to complete homomorphic encryption. The commutativity of d-dimensional unitary operators is proved before the correctness of this scheme is proved.

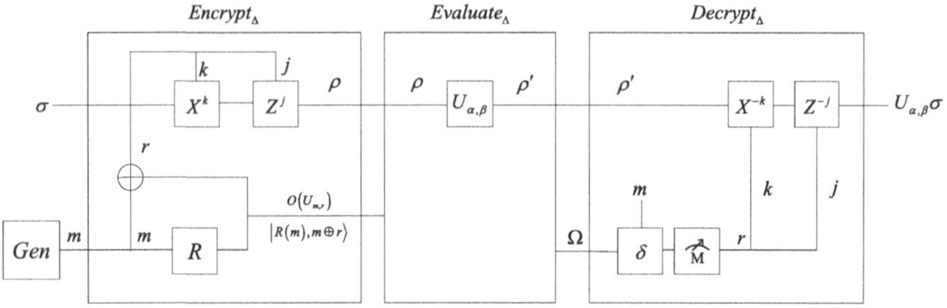

Fig. 7.2 Quantum circuit diagram of the QHE scheme with quantum point obfuscation

Theorem 7.1 *Let $U_{\alpha,\beta}$, $U_{p,q}$ be two arbitrary d-dimensional unitary operators, where $\alpha, \beta, p, q \in \{0, 1, \ldots, d-1\}$, which are commutative.*

Proof The product of two operators is expressed as

$$\begin{aligned}
&U_{\alpha,\beta} \cdot U_{p,q} \\
&= \sum_{i=0}^{d-1} \omega^{i\cdot(\alpha+\beta\cdot i)} |i\rangle\langle i| \cdot \sum_{j=0}^{d-1} \omega^{j\cdot(\alpha+\beta\cdot j)} |j\rangle\langle j| \\
&= \Big(\omega^{0\cdot(\alpha+\beta\cdot 0)} |0\rangle\langle 0| + \ldots \\
&\quad + \omega^{(d-1)\cdot(\alpha+\beta\cdot(d-1))} |d-1\rangle\langle d-1|\Big) \\
&\quad \cdot \Big(\omega^{0\cdot(p+q\cdot 0)} |0\rangle\langle 0| + \ldots \\
&\quad + \omega^{(d-1)\cdot(p+q\cdot(d-1))} |d-1\rangle\langle d-1|\Big) \\
&= \Big(\omega^{0\cdot(\alpha+\beta\cdot 0)+0\cdot(p+q\cdot 0)} |0\rangle\langle 0| + \ldots \\
&\quad + \omega^{(d-1)\cdot(\alpha+\beta\cdot(d-1))+(d-1)\cdot(p+q\cdot(d-1))} |d-1\rangle\langle d-1|\Big) \\
&= \sum_{x=0}^{d-1} \omega^{x\cdot(\alpha+p+(\beta+q)\cdot x)} |x\rangle\langle x| \\
&= U_{\alpha+p,\beta+q}
\end{aligned} \tag{7.5}$$

From Eq. (7.5), we can obtain $U_{\alpha,\beta} \cdot U_{p,q} = U_{\alpha+p,\beta+q}$ that the commutativity between $U_{\alpha,\beta}$ and $U_{p,q}$ is more intuitively expressed as

$$U_{\alpha,\beta} \cdot U_{p,q} = U_{\alpha+p,\beta+q} = U_{p,q} \cdot U_{\alpha,\beta} \tag{7.6}$$

Since $U_{\alpha,\beta}$, $U_{p,q}$ is randomly selected from Eq. (7.1), any two d-dimensional unitary operators are commutative.

According to Theorem 7.1, the correctness of the evaluator and the decrypting party of the QHE scheme with point function obfuscation will be further proved as follows.

Theorem 7.2 *When the evaluation operator acts on the ciphertext ρ of the quantum state, Eq. (7.7) is obtained.*

$$\rho' = U_{\alpha,\beta} \cdot \rho = V_d^k W_d^j U_{\alpha,\beta}\sigma \tag{7.7}$$

Proof According to the interchangeability between any two d-dimensional unitary operators in Theorem 7.1, we have

$$\begin{aligned} U_{\alpha,\beta} \cdot \rho &= U_{\alpha,\beta} \cdot \left(V_d^k W_d^j \sigma\right) \\ &= U_{\alpha,\beta} \left(U_{1,0}\right)^k \left(U_{0,1}\right)^j \sigma \\ &= U_{\alpha,\beta} U_{k,0} U_{0,j} \sigma \\ &= U_{\alpha+k,\beta+j} \sigma \\ &= U_{k,j} U_{\alpha,\beta} \sigma \\ &= U_{k,0} U_{0,j} U_{\alpha,\beta} \sigma \\ &= V_d^k W_d^j U_{\alpha,\beta} \sigma \end{aligned} \tag{7.8}$$

Therefore, when the evaluation operator acts on the ciphertext ρ of the quantum state, it is equivalent to directly encrypting the evaluation operator on the plaintext of the quantum state for following encryption. So far, the correctness of the evaluation algorithm is proved.

Theorem 7.3 *The decryption algorithm $\sigma' = Decrypt_{\Delta}(k, j, \rho') = U_{\alpha,\beta}\sigma$ is correct.*

Proof According to the interchangeability and correctness of any d-dimensional unitary operator of Theorem 7.1, we evaluate the homomorphic transformation result of the algorithm. When the decryption algorithm $Decrypt_{\Delta}$ performs decryption on the quantum state ρ' calculated by the algorithm, the following Eq. (7.9) is obtained:

$$\begin{aligned} \sigma' &= Decrypt_{\Delta}\left(k, j, \rho'\right) \\ &= V_d^{-k} W_d^{-j} \cdot \rho' \\ &= V_d^{-k} W_d^{-j} U_{\alpha,\beta} \cdot \rho \\ &= V_d^{-k} W_d^{-j} V_d^k W_d^j U_{\alpha,\beta} \sigma \\ &= U_{\alpha,\beta} \sigma \end{aligned} \tag{7.9}$$

It is known from Eq. (7.9) that the decryption algorithm is correct.

Theorem 7.1 describes the interchangeability of any d-dimensional unitary operator. Theorem 7.2 describes the evaluation of homomorphic transformation results and

Theorem 7.3 describes the decryption results. According to the above theorem and correctness proof, we fully prove that the QHE scheme based on point obfuscation is correct.

7.1.4 Security Analysis

According to the definition of security in Definition 7.3, the QHE scheme is secure and can be proved as follows. $\varphi = \sum_{m=0}^{d-1} p_m |m\rangle \langle m|$ is the density matrix of all possible plaintexts of the quantum state. It is assumed that an attacker cannot know the probability distribution related to quantum data transmission via other channels in advance, so the plaintext of the quantum state in front of the attacker has the same probability $p_m = \frac{1}{d}, m \in \{0, \ldots, d-1\}$. $k, j \in \{0, \ldots, d-1\}$ is the key chosen by the encrypting party, which is only held by a user. When an attacker tries to intercept the information sent by the encrypting party, the output of the encryption algorithm according to Eq. (7.7) is in a fully mixed state $\frac{1}{d^2} \sum_{k,j \in \{0,\ldots,d-1\}} V_d^k W_d^j \varphi \left(V_d^k W_d^j\right)^\dagger$. Because the result that an attacker can intercept or detect is only a fully mixed quantum state, the attacker cannot obtain any valuable information on the plaintext of the encrypting party from it.

$$
\begin{aligned}
&\frac{1}{d^2} \sum_{k,j \in \{0,\ldots,d-1\}} V_d^k W_d^j \varphi \left(V_d^k W_d^j\right)^\dagger \\
&= \frac{1}{d^2} \sum_{k,j \in \{0,\ldots,d-1\}} V_d^k W_d^j \varphi \left(W_d^j\right)^\dagger \left(V_d^k\right)^\dagger \\
&= \frac{1}{d^2} \sum_{k,j \in \{0,\ldots,d-1\}} U_{k,j} \varphi \left(U_{k,j}\right)^\dagger \\
&= \frac{1}{d^2} \sum_{k,j \in \{0,\ldots,d-1\}} \left(\sum_{x=0}^{d-1} \omega^{x(k+jx)} |x\rangle \langle x| \right. \\
&\quad \left. \cdot \sum_{m=0}^{d-1} p_m |m\rangle \langle m| \sum_{x=0}^{d-1} \omega^{-x(k+jx)} |x\rangle \langle x| \right) \\
&= \frac{1}{d^2} \sum_{k,j \in \{0,\ldots,d-1\}} \left(\sum_{x=0}^{d-1} p_m \omega^{m(k+jm)} |m\rangle \langle m| \right. \\
&\quad \left. \cdot \sum_{x=0}^{d-1} \omega^{-x(k+jx)} |x\rangle \langle x| \right) \\
&= \frac{1}{d^2} \sum_{k,j \in \{0,\ldots,d-1\}} \left(\sum_{x=0}^{d-1} p_m \omega^{m(k+jm)} \omega^{-m(k+jm)} |m\rangle \langle m| \right)
\end{aligned}
$$

$$
\begin{aligned}
&= \frac{1}{d^2} \sum_{k,j \in \{0,\ldots,d-1\}} p_m I_d \\
&= \frac{1}{d} I_d
\end{aligned} \tag{7.10}
$$

According to Eq. (7.10), the output of the evaluation algorithm is also completely mixed in front of the attacker, as shown in Eq. (7.11):

$$
\begin{aligned}
&\frac{1}{d^2} \sum_{k,j \in \{0,\ldots,d-1\}} U_{\alpha,\beta} V_d^k W_d^j \varphi \left(V_d^k W_d^j\right)^{\dagger} \left(U_{\alpha,\beta}\right)^{\dagger} \\
&= \frac{1}{d^2} \sum_{k,j \in \{0,\ldots,d-1\}} p_m U_{\alpha,\beta} I_d \left(U_{\alpha,\beta}\right)^{\dagger} \\
&= \frac{1}{d} I_d
\end{aligned} \tag{7.11}
$$

The above proof fully illustrates that the output quantum states of all possible information exposure points in the process of the QHE scheme have the property of complete mixture state, which makes it impossible for an attacker to obtain any useful information on the plaintext through analysis, even if the encrypted message is intercepted or detected by the attacker during transmission. Therefore, the QHE scheme based on point obfuscation is secure.

7.1.5 Scheme Comparison

We compare the QHE schemes in terms of four aspects such as multi-user, whether the evaluator knows the decryption key, a regular interaction between the evaluator and the user and complete mixture. The multi-user means that the encrypting party and the decrypting party can be different users. The multi-user is not equal to multi-party computing.

Table 7.1 lists the comparison of the QHE schemes. The evaluator does not know the decryption key and does not require a regular interaction with a user. Because of key transmission after quantum obfuscation, the encrypting party and the decrypting party can be different users. The output state has the property of complete mixture. Of course, there is still an exponential price for obtaining perfect security to multiple users, which should be paid more attention to solution.

Table 7.1 Scheme comparison

Scheme	Multi-user	The evaluator knows the key	Regular interaction	Exponential price	Information-theoretic security
Our scheme	Yes	No	No	Yes	Yes
Liang's QHE [8]	No	No	No	No	Yes
Liang's QFHE [9]	No	No	Yes	Yes	Yes
Liang's QFHE [10]	No	No	Yes	No	No
Ouyang's QHE [11]	No	Yes	No	No	Yes
Broadbent's QHE [12]	Yes	No	Yes	Yes	No
Sun's QHE [13]	Yes	Yes	No	No	No

7.2 Quantum Fully Homomorphic Encryption Based on Multi-valued Quantum Point Obfuscation

7.2.1 Requirement of Fully Homomorphic Encryption

As quantum technology develops and the computing power possessed by quantum computers presents an exponential increase, the homomorphic encryption algorithms with mathematical difficulties cannot ensure that the data calculated on computing platforms is confidential. Many quantum fully homomorphic encryption schemes have been set forth on the basis of the basic quantum mechanics principles, aiming at breaking the limitations of conventional homomorphic encryption schemes. In general, it is an FHE scheme that can be achieved by virtue of quantum computation technology. A QFHE scheme contains four algorithms, namely key generation algorithm, encryption algorithm, decryption algorithm and evaluation algorithm, which is similar to the conventional FHE scheme.

Rohde et al. [5] set forth a symmetric quantum homomorphic encryption scheme in 2012, relying on which quantum random walk is allowed on the encrypted quantum data. Nevertheless, the scheme does not achieve full homomorphism. Subsequently, Liang [8] formalized QFHE and constructed a scheme with weak symmetry. The scheme enables the direct application of encrypted quantum data in quantum computation, with no need to decrypt them in advance. In spite of this, it has some differences from the FHE scheme, because it needs secret key when computing the encrypted data. Then another QFHE scheme was proposed by Liang [9] on the basis of the universal quantum circuits, where the evaluation function has nothing to do with the encryption key and an iterative process can assist in decrypting the encryption key. The symmetric QFHE scheme adopts the quantum error-correcting code as private key, which requires users to offer certain auxiliary quantum states. The totally different scheme is the asymmetric QFHE scheme, where a server is required to regularly interact with a user.

As proved in the study by Yu et al. [14], under the requirement of the perfect security (information-theoretic security), the QHE scheme is capable of storing the encrypted results with $\log 2|S|$ qubits, thereinto, S is the size of the set S (of permitted computation). So the QFHE scheme which exhibits the perfect security will inevitably lead to exponential storage overhead. The QFHE scheme that was proposed by Tan et al. [16] fails to offer the security regarding cryptographic sense, because the scheme can only hide the $n/\log n$ bits (n denotes the size of a message), and with n moving toward infinite, the proportion of the hidden amount in the total amount verges to zero ($1/\log n - 0$). Broadbent and Jeffery [12] combined the quantum one-time pad with the conventional FHE scheme, thereby constructing three public-key QHE (not fully homomorphic) schemes, which can be restricted by the conventional FHE scheme with regard to the security and efficiency. Wang et al. [17] put forward a symmetrical three-valued QHE scheme combining three-valued quantum gates, while the scheme is only applicable to three-dimensional Hilbert space.

As we can see, the design of QFHE schemes focuses on the construction of homomorphic operators and the design of encryption schemes. The former is related to whether the QFHE scheme can be designed and implemented efficiently, and the latter involves the security of a protocol and the scope of use, because in the previous symmetric schemes, the evaluator knows the decryption key, while in the asymmetric scheme, the evaluator requires a regular interaction with a user. In addition, these schemes only focus on two-dimensional or three-dimensional Hilbert space, which is difficult to meet the need for quantum state expansion in free space. In order to solve these limitations, we hope to design a n-dimensional Hilbert space QFHE symmetric scheme in which the evaluator does not know the decryption key, and can achieve perfect security.

In the case that the symmetric QFHE scheme takes into account quantum point obfuscation, it is largely possible that the evaluator does not know the decryption key and does not need to regularly interact with a user. We aim at designing multi-valued quantum point obfuscation and different QFHE schemes based on multi-valued quantum point obfuscation [18].

7.2.2 *Multi-valued Quantum State*

In classical computers, in addition to using binary to store information, ternary has been used to store information. Quantum logic systems can be divided into two-valued quantum system and multi-valued quantum system. Three-valued or more is called multi-valued. At present, there is little research on multi-valued quantum systems. Multi-valued quantum systems are superior to two-valued quantum systems in terms of information security, coding qubits, and so on. So the development of multi-valued quantum logic is an indispensable trend.

For the multi-valued quantum state, a special set of quantum measurement bases can also be given, which are the computational bases of the multi-valued quantum state. The specific form is shown in Eq. (7.12).

$$|0\rangle = \begin{pmatrix} 1 \\ 0 \\ \cdots \\ 0 \end{pmatrix}, |1\rangle = \begin{pmatrix} 0 \\ 1 \\ \cdots \\ 0 \end{pmatrix}, \ldots, |d-1\rangle = \begin{pmatrix} 0 \\ 0 \\ \cdots \\ 1 \end{pmatrix} \tag{7.12}$$

Any multi-valued quantum state can be represented by computational bases, and the specific representation is shown in Eq. (7.13). The coefficients $a_0, a_1, \ldots, a_{d-1}$ in Eq. (7.13) are all complex numbers, and all coefficients satisfy Eq. (7.14)

$$\begin{aligned} |\varphi\rangle &= a_0 |0\rangle + a_1 |1\rangle + \cdots + a_{d-1} |d-1\rangle \\ &= a_0 \begin{pmatrix} 1 \\ 0 \\ \cdots \\ 0 \end{pmatrix} + a_1 \begin{pmatrix} 0 \\ 1 \\ \cdots \\ 0 \end{pmatrix} + \cdots + a_{d-1} \begin{pmatrix} 0 \\ 0 \\ \cdots \\ 1 \end{pmatrix} = \begin{pmatrix} a_0 \\ a_1 \\ \cdots \\ a_{d-1} \end{pmatrix} \end{aligned} \tag{7.13}$$

$$\sum_{i=0}^{d-1} |a_i|^2 = |a_0|^2 + |a_1|^2 + \cdots + |a_{d-1}|^2 = 1 \tag{7.14}$$

For the multi-valued particles, there will be their own unique quantum gates. Here two kinds of quantum gates for multi-valued particles are used, which are named V_d and W_d, respectively. It can be expressed in Eq. (7.15).

$$V_d = \sum_{x=0}^{d-1} \omega^x |x\rangle \langle x|, W_d = \sum_{x=0}^{d-1} \omega^{x^2} |x\rangle \langle x|, \tag{7.15}$$

where $\omega = e^{2\pi i/d}$.

We focus on the influence of the selection of quantum measurement basis on the results of quantum measurement, and the influence of quantum measurement on quantum states. So the specific process of quantum measurement is not introduced. Before quantum measurement, we need to select a set of quantum measurement bases, which are composed of a set of mutually orthogonal vectors. For two-dimensional quantum states, two orthogonal vectors can be used to form a group of quantum measurement bases. For example, $|0\rangle$ state and $|1\rangle$ state can form a group of quantum measurement bases, and $|+\rangle$ state and $|-\rangle$ state can also form a group of quantum measurement bases. For multi-valued quantum states, we can use d mutually orthogonal vectors to form a set of orthogonal bases. For the computational bases of multi-valued quantum state (a special set of quantum measurement bases), it can be expressed in the form shown in Eq. (7.12). After selecting a set of quantum measurement bases to measure the quantum state, the quantum state will collapse into a state of the selected quantum measurement bases, and the probability of collapse into each state is related to the quantum state. For the multi-valued particle $|\varphi\rangle = a_0 |0\rangle + a_1 |1\rangle + \cdots + a_{d-1} |d-1\rangle$, when it is measured using the computational bases, it will collapse to one of the computational basis states $|0\rangle, |1\rangle, \ldots, |d-1\rangle$, and the probability of collapse to the computational basis state $|i\rangle$ $(0 \le i \le d-1)$ is $|a_i|^2$.

7.2.3 Quantum-Hash Random Oracle Model

Quantum-accessible random oracle model [19] was proposed to help analyze security under the attack of quantum adversaries. In this model, all parties including an adversary can query a classical random number generator for classical random bits, a quantum random oracle for random qubits and a measurement device for the comparison result of quantum states. Unlike the quantum-accessible random oracle model designed for post-quantum cryptography, the quantum random oracle model was defined by Shang et al. [20] to analyze the provable security of quantum digital signature. Furthermore, Shang et al. [21] proposed the 'quantum-hash' random oracle model to extend the quantum random oracle model so that it can be used to analyze the security of quantum obfuscation. The quantum random oracle model is defined as follows.

Definition 7.4 (*Quantum-hash random oracle*) A quantum-hash random oracle is an efficient algorithm H_q that satisfies the following properties:

1. When queried with a classical bit string $k \in \{0,1\}^n$, H_q randomly and consistently generates s-qubit quantum state $|H_q(k)\rangle \in (\mathcal{H}^2)^{\otimes s}$, where $\mathcal{H}^2$ is a two-dimensional Hilbert space.
2. Any pair of the outputs of H_q with different inputs is nearly orthogonal:

$$\left|\langle H_q(\omega) \mid H_q(\omega')\rangle\right|^2 < \delta, \tag{7.16}$$

   where δ is negligible in n.
3. If H_q is invoked by the challenger with any input, it responds for at most C times for the same input.

7.2.4 Multi-valued Quantum Point Obfuscation

Since the QFHE scheme is expected to be applicable to multi-valued quantum states, we define a multi-valued quantum random oracle model for analyzing the obfuscatability of multi-valued quantum point functions, and give the structure and properties of the multi-valued quantum random oracle model. Then two kinds of multi-valued quantum point functions are defined and their obfuscation schemes are designed under the multi-valued quantum random oracle model.

7.2.4.1 A. Multi-valued Quantum Random Oracle Model

In this section, the 'quantum-hash' random oracle model is extended to make it possible to analyze multi-valued quantum obfuscation.

Firstly, the generation range of the key k is modified. It is no longer a random classical bit string, but is closely related to the dimension d.

Secondly, a binary converter B is added, and the dimension d will be a large decimal number. In order to enhance security, the decimal number is converted into a corresponding binary string $\{0, 1\}^m$.

Finally, the range limit of the constant c for the number of quantum random oracles is added. When the challenger accesses the quantum random oracle, the quantum random oracle produces at most c copies of the output to the adversary, and the number of c is related to d. This limitation reflects that under the constraint of the no-cloning theorem, adversary can only obtain a limited number of unknown qubits.

Based on the above analysis, the multi-valued quantum random oracle machine is defined as follows:

Definition 7.5 The multi-valued quantum random oracle machine is a quantum polynomial-time algorithm R_q that satisfies the following properties:

1. When any party (adversary or challenger) accesses with the classical constant $k \in N$, the binary converter B will convert k into a classical bit string $\{0, 1\}^m$.
2. R_q randomly and uniformly generates the quantum state $\left|R_q\left(B(k)\right)\right\rangle \in \left(\mathcal{H}^2\right)^{\otimes s}$ of s-qubits, where $s = ploy\,(m)$.
3. The output of the different inputs of any pair of multi-valued quantum random oracles R_q is nearly orthogonal

$$\left|\left\langle R_q\left(B(k)\right) \middle| R_q\left(B(k')\right)\right\rangle\right|^2 < \varepsilon, \tag{7.17}$$

   where $B(k) \neq B(k')$, ε is negligible for the parameter m.
4. If R_q is accessed by the challenger as input k, the multi-valued quantum random oracle machine R_q produces c copies of the output to the adversary.

Similar to the classical random oracle model, adversary-challenger game is required to analyze the security of quantum obfuscation in the multi-valued quantum random oracle model.

Definition 7.6 The quantum obfuscated adversary-challenger game consists of the following three phases:

Phase 1. For the quantum circuit family $\mathcal{C}$, the challenger selects the quantum circuit $C_i \in \mathcal{C}, i = 1, \ldots, t$, and the challenger uses the multi-valued quantum random oracle to generate the corresponding obfuscation result $O^{R_q}(C_i)$. In this phase, for each input of R_q, the multi-valued quantum random oracle machine produces at most c copies of the output to the adversary. So, for each quantum circuit C, the adversary produces at most c copies of the obfuscation result $O^{R_q}(C_i)^{\otimes \mathcal{C}}$.

Phase 2. In this phase, the adversary uses any input to access the multi-valued quantum random oracle. If the times the adversary visits the random oracle machine is q_{ro}, then for any $k = k_1, \ldots, k_{q_{ro}}$, the multi-valued quantum random oracle machine returns $|R_q(B(k))\rangle$ to the adversary.

Phase 3. The challenger selects a quantum circuit $C \in \mathcal{C}$ different from C_i from the quantum circuit family C, and uses a multi-valued quantum random oracle to generate the corresponding obfuscation result $O^{R_q}(C)$. The adversary outputs the quantum state $A^{R_q}(O(C))$. In this phase, the multi-valued quantum random oracle produces at most c copies of the output to the adversary. So, for the quantum circuit C, the adversary can directly generate c obfuscation results $O^{R_q}(C)$.

When the output of the adversary is described as follows:

$$A^{R_q}(O(C)) = O^{R_q}(C)^{\otimes(c+1)} \tag{7.18}$$

the adversary wins the adversary-challenger game. The adversary's advantage is

$$\mathrm{Adv}(adversary) = \Pr[A^{R_q}(O(C)) = O^{R_q}(C)^{\otimes(c+1)}] \tag{7.19}$$

When the opponent's advantage is negligible relative to the input size m, the challenger is said to have won the game. At this time, the quantum obfuscator O is considered to be secure under the multi-valued quantum random oracle model.

7.2.4.2 B. Property of Multi-valued Quantum States

For any prime number d, multi-valued quantum states have $d + 1$ groups of mutually unbiased bases. Any vector in $d + 1$ groups of mutually unbiased bases can be denoted by

$$G_{l,j} = \left|g_l^{(j)}\right\rangle, \tag{7.20}$$

where j represents the basis of the vector, and l represents the value of the vector. j and l meet $j = 0, \ldots, d$ and $l = 0, \ldots, d - 1$, respectively. $g_l^{(j)}$ corresponds to the states from 0 to $d - 1$ for the d-dimensional Hilbert space. $G_{l,j}$ is an arbitrary multi-valued unitary operator. The $d + 1$ groups of mutually unbiased bases are used as quantum measurement bases. When $j = d$, a set of bases are called computational bases and are denoted by $\left\{\left|g_l^{(d)}\right\rangle\right\}$. The vector expression of computational bases is shown in Eq. (7.12). The quantum measurement bases of group j $(0 \le j \le d - 1)$ are denoted by $\left\{\left|g_l^{(j)}\right\rangle\right\}$. Through the computational bases, any vector in the remaining d groups of unbiased bases can be expressed in Eq. (7.21).

$$G_{l,j} = \left|g_l^{(j)}\right\rangle = \frac{1}{\sqrt{d}} \sum_{x=0}^{d-1} \omega^{x(l+jx)} |x\rangle , \tag{7.21}$$

where $\omega = e^{2\pi i/d}$.

When the vector $G_{l,j}$ is measured by using the correct quantum measurement basis $\left\{\left|g_l^{(j)}\right\rangle\right\}$, the measurement result will be the only confirmed α. When the vector $G_{l,j}$ is measured by using an incorrect quantum measurement basis, a value between 0 and $d-1$ is obtained with the same probability $(1/d)$.

7.2.4.3 C. Multi-valued Quantum Single-Point Function

Definition 7.7 The multi-valued quantum single-point function is defined as follows:

$$U_{a,b} : \left|x, y, G_{l,j}\right\rangle \to \left|x, y, G_{l+P_a(x), j+P_b(y)}\right\rangle \tag{7.22}$$

where $x, y \in G_{l,j}$, $j = 1, \ldots, d$, $l = 0, \ldots, d-1$, $P_a(x)$ and $P_b(y)$ are the following classical functions:

$$P_a(x) = \begin{cases} a & x = a \\ d - a & x \neq a \end{cases} \tag{7.23}$$

$$P_b(y) = \begin{cases} b & y = b \\ d - b & y \neq b \end{cases} \tag{7.24}$$

where $a, b \in \{1, \ldots, d-1\}$.

We define $C_{a,b} = \left\{C_{a,b} : a, b \in \{0, \ldots, d\}\right\}$, where $C_{a,b}$ is a quantum circuit that implements the corresponding function of the unitary matrix $U_{a,b}$. The structure of the multi-valued quantum single-point function obfuscator $O^{R_q}\left(U_{a,b}\right)$ can be given as follows:

Scheme 1 (Multi-valued quantum single-point obfuscation scheme). *The obfuscator $O^{R_q}\left(U_{a,b}\right)$ asks the multi-valued quantum random oracle machine R_q with a, b to obtain the quantum states $R_q\left(B\left(a\right)\right), R_q\left(B\left(b\right)\right)$, and the obfuscator $O^{R_q}\left(U_{a,b}\right)$ stores the obtained quantum state $r_a = R_q\left(B\left(a\right)\right), r_b = R_q\left(B\left(b\right)\right)$, when inputting $x, y \in G_{l,j}$, will output $G_{l+a,j}$ if $R_q\left(B(x)\right) = r_a$, $G_{l,j+b}$ if $R_q\left(B(y)\right) = r_b$, $G_{l+a,j+b}$ if $R_q\left(B(x)\right) = r_a$, $R_q\left(B(y)\right) = r_b$, otherwise $G_{l+d-a,j+d-b}$.*

7.2.4.4 D. Multi-valued Quantum Multi-point Function

Definition 7.8 The multi-valued quantum multi-point function is defined as follows:

$$U_{(a_1,b_1),\ldots,(a_i,b_i)} : |x, y, G_{l,j}\rangle \to |x, y, G_{l+P_{a_1,\ldots,a_i}(x),j+P_{b_1,\ldots,b_i}(y)}\rangle \quad (7.25)$$

where $x, y \in G_{l,j}$, $j = 1, \ldots, d$, $l = 0, \ldots, d-1$ $P_{a_1,\ldots,a_i}(x)$ and $P_{b_1,\ldots,b_i}(y)$ are the following classical functions:

$$P_{a_1,\ldots,a_n}(x) = \begin{cases} a_i & x = a_i \\ d - a_i & x \neq a_i \end{cases} \quad (7.26)$$

$$P_{b_1,\ldots,b_n}(y) = \begin{cases} b_i & y = b_i \\ d - b_i & y \neq b_i \end{cases} \quad (7.27)$$

where $a_i, b_i \in \{1, \ldots, d-1\}, i \in 1, \ldots, n$.

We define $C_{(a_1,b_1),\ldots,(a_i,b_i)} = \{C_{(a_1,b_1),\ldots,(a_i,b_i)} : a_i, b_i \in \{0, \ldots, d\}\}$, where $C_{(a_1,b_1),\ldots,(a_i,b_i)}$ is a quantum circuit that implements the corresponding function of the unitary matrix $U_{(a_1,b_1),\ldots,(a_i,b_i)}$. We define $\mathcal{C}_n^t = \{C_{(a_1,b_1),\ldots,(a_t,b_t(n))} : a_i, b_i \in \{0,1\}^n\}$ and $\mathcal{C}^* = \cup_{polynomials\ t}\mathcal{C}_n^t$. The structure of the multi-valued quantum single-point function obfuscator $O^{R_q}(U_{(a_1,b_1),\ldots,(a_i,b_i)})$ can be given as follows:

Scheme 2 (Multi-valued quantum multi-point obfuscation scheme). *The obfuscator* $O^{R_q}(U_{(a_1,b_1),\ldots,(a_i,b_i)})$ *asks the multi-valued quantum random oracle machine* R_q *with* $(a_1, b_1), \ldots, (a_i, b_i)$ *to obtain the quantum states* $R_q(B(a_1)), \ldots, R_q(B(a_i)), R_q(B(b_1)), \ldots, R_q(B(b_i))$, *and the obfuscator* $O^{R_q}(U_{(a_1,b_1)}, \ldots, (a_i, b_i))$ *stores the obtained quantum states* $r_{a_1,\ldots,a_i} = R_q(B(a_1)), \ldots, R_q(B(a_i)), r_{b_1,\ldots,b_i} = R_q(B(b_1)), \ldots, R_q(B(b_i))$, *when inputting* $x, y \in G_{l,j}$, *will output* $G_{l+a_i,j}$ *if* $R_q(B(x)) = r_{a_1,\ldots,a_i}$, $G_{l,j+b_i}$ *if* $R_q(B(y)) = r_{b_1,\ldots,b_i}$, $G_{l+a_i,j+b_i}$ *if* $R_q(B(x)) = r_{a_1,\ldots,a_i}, R_q(B(y)) = r_{b_1,\ldots,b_i}$, *otherwise* $G_{l+d-a_i,j+d-b_i}$.

7.2.5 *Quantum Fully Homomorphic Encryption Scheme*

We introduce two QFHE schemes based on two kinds of multi-valued quantum point obfuscation. One is based on multi-valued quantum single-point obfuscation and the other is based on multi-valued quantum multi-point obfuscation.

A QFHE scheme is a quaternion of quantum algorithms (*Key generation, Encryption, Homomorphic evaluation, Decryption*) [12]. The key generation algorithm generates an encryption key. The encrypting party uses the encryption algorithm to encrypt a quantum state plaintext to generate a quantum state ciphertext, and then sends the quantum state ciphertext to the evaluator via the quantum-secure channel. After receiving the quantum state ciphertext, the evaluator executes the evaluation algorithm and sends the calculation result to the decrypting party. The decrypting party decrypts the calculation result sent back by the evaluator, and it is the calculation result expected by the decrypting party.

Here we use quantum gates to encrypt or decrypt. There are two kinds of quantum gates, one is used to change the value of a vector, which is denoted by V_d, the other is used to change the basis of a vector, which is denoted by W_d. V_d and W_d can be expressed in Eq. (7.28).

$$V_d = \sum_{x=0}^{d-1} \omega^x |x\rangle \langle x|,\ W_d = \sum_{x=0}^{d-1} \omega^{x^2} |x\rangle \langle x| \tag{7.28}$$

When the operation V_d is performed on any vector $G_{l,j}$, the value of $G_{l,j}$ will be changed so that the vector is converted to $G_{l+1,j}$. The specific process is shown in Eq. (7.29).

$$\begin{aligned} V_d G_{l,j} &= V_d \left|g_l^{(j)}\right\rangle = \frac{1}{\sqrt{d}} \sum_{x=0}^{d-1} \omega^x |x\rangle \langle x| \sum_{x=0}^{d-1} \omega^{x(l+jx)} |x\rangle \\ &= \frac{1}{\sqrt{d}} \sum_{x=0}^{d-1} \omega^{x((l+1)+jx)} |x\rangle = \left|g_{l+1}^{(j)}\right\rangle = G_{l+1,j^*} \end{aligned} \tag{7.29}$$

Similarly, when the operation W_d is performed on any vector $G_{l,j}$, the quantum measurement basis of $G_{l,j}$ will be changed so that the vector $G_{l,j}$ can be converted into $G_{l,j+1}$. The specific process is shown in Eq. (7.30).

$$\begin{aligned} W_d G_{l,j} &= W_d \left|g_l^{(j)}\right\rangle = \frac{1}{\sqrt{d}} \sum_{x=0}^{d-1} \omega^{x^2} |x\rangle \langle x| \sum_{x=0}^{d-1} \omega^{x(l+jx)} |x\rangle \\ &= \frac{1}{\sqrt{d}} \sum_{x=0}^{d-1} \omega^{x(l+(j+1)x)} |x\rangle = \left|g_l^{(j+1)}\right\rangle = G_{l,j+1^*} \end{aligned} \tag{7.30}$$

By using the combination of V_d and W_d, we can convert the vector $G_{l,j}$ to any desired vector $G_{l',j'}$. For example, if you want to change $G_{l,j}$ to $G_{l+x,j+y}$, you can perform V_d operations x times on the vector $G_{l,j}$, and then W_d operations y times. Thus the scheme has the property of full homomorphism.

7.2.5.1 A. QFHE Scheme Based on Multi-valued Quantum Single-Point Obfuscation

According to the obfuscator $O^{R_q}\left(U_{a,b}\right) = O$ and the quaternion of QFHE algorithms, the scheme based on multi-valued quantum single-point obfuscation is described as follows:

Scheme 3 (QFHE scheme based on multi-valued quantum single-point obfuscation). *The scheme is a quaternion of quantum algorithms* ($KeyGen_\Delta$, $Encrypt_\Delta$, $Evaluate_\Delta$, $Decrypt_\Delta$)*:*

1. ***Key generation**: $KeyGen_\Delta$: $(a, b, G_{l,j}) \to O$. The key generation algorithm $KeyGen_\Delta$ randomly generates two classical keys, namely $a, b \in \{1, \ldots, d-1\}$. Then the obfuscator O asks the multi-valued quantum random oracle machine R_q with a, b to obtain the quantum state $R_q\,(B\,(a))\,,\; R_q\,(B\,(b))$, and the obfuscator O stores the obtained quantum state $r_a = R_q\,(B\,(a))\,, r_b = R_q\,(B\,(b))$, $G_{l,j}$ is the multi-valued quantum state randomly generated by the encrypting party and the decrypting party.*
2. ***Encryption**: $Encrypt_\Delta$:$\sigma \to \rho$. The encryption algorithm $Encrypt_\Delta$ performs encryption on the plaintext σ of quantum state with the keys a, b to generate the quantum state ciphertext $\rho = Encrypt_\Delta\,(a, b, \sigma))$. Then the encrypting party sends ρ to the evaluator via the quantum-secure channel and sends the result $G_{l+P_a(x), j+P_b(y)}$ of obfuscator O to the decrypting party.*
3. ***Homomorphic evaluation**: $Evaluate_\Delta$: $\rho \to \rho'$. After the evaluator receives the quantum state ciphertext ρ from the encrypting party, it generates the evaluation parameters α, β according to its computing requirements. It performs the evaluation $\rho' = Evaluate_\Delta(\alpha, \beta, \rho) = V_d^\alpha W_d^\beta \rho$ on the received quantum state ciphertext, and sends the result ρ' to the decrypting party via the quantum-secure channel.*
4. ***Decryption**: $Decrypt_\Delta$: $\rho' \to \sigma'$. After the decrypting party receives the calculation result of the evaluator, it adopts the decryption algorithm $Decrypt_\Delta$ to perform the decryption $\sigma' = Decrypt_\Delta\left(a, b, \rho'\right) = V_d^\alpha W_d^\beta \sigma$ based on the keys a, b.*

Figure 7.3 indicates that the encrypting party encrypts the input quantum state plaintext σ by using the keys a, b, and sends the encryption result ρ to the evaluator for evaluation calculation $V_d^\alpha W_d^\beta \rho$. $G_{l,j}$ and a, b are input into the obfuscator O, and then the encrypting party sends the result $G_{l+P_a(x), j+P_b(y)}$ to the decrypting party. Because the selected basic multi-valued quantum state is $G_{l,j}$, $G_{l+P_a(x), j+P_b(y)}$ can obtain $G_{P_a(x), P_b(y)}$ by the operation of $V_d^{-l} W_d^{-j}$, and then the keys a, b can be obtained after measurement. The result ρ' is sent to the decrypting party to perform decryption to obtain a direct calculation result $V_d^\alpha W_d^\beta$ of the plaintext σ of the quantum state.

This scheme takes advantage of the interchangeability of the multi-valued unitary operator, and exchanges the evaluation operator and the encryption operator by

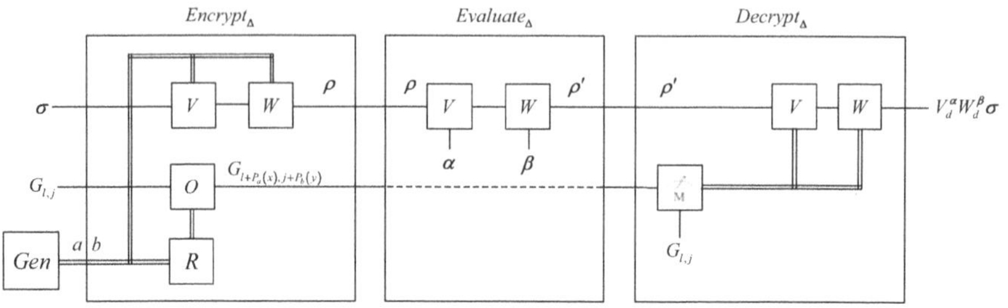

Fig. 7.3 Quantum circuit diagram of the QFHE scheme with single qubit

means of equivalent multiplication to complete homomorphic encryption. The commutativity of multi-valued unitary operators is firstly proved before the correctness of this scheme is proved.

Theorem 7.4 *Let* $G_{\alpha,\beta}$, $G_{p,q}$ *be two arbitrary multi-valued unitary operators, where* $\alpha, \beta, p, q \in \{0, 1, \ldots, d-1\}$, *which are commutative.*

Proof The product of two operators is expressed as

$$\begin{aligned} G_{\alpha,\beta} \cdot G_{p,q} &= \sum_{i=0}^{d-1} \omega^{i\cdot(\alpha+\beta\cdot i)} |i\rangle\langle i| \cdot \sum_{j=0}^{d-1} \omega^{j\cdot(\alpha+\beta\cdot j)} |j\rangle\langle j| \\ &= \Big(\omega^{0\cdot(\alpha+\beta\cdot 0)} |0\rangle\langle 0| + \ldots \\ &\quad + \omega^{(d-1)\cdot(\alpha+\beta\cdot(d-1))} |d-1\rangle\langle d-1|\Big) \\ &\quad \cdot \Big(\omega^{0\cdot(p+q\cdot 0)} |0\rangle\langle 0| + \ldots \\ &\quad + \omega^{(d-1)\cdot(p+q\cdot(d-1))} |d-1\rangle\langle d-1|\Big) \\ &= \Big(\omega^{0\cdot(\alpha+\beta\cdot 0)+0\cdot(p+q\cdot 0)} |0\rangle\langle 0| + \ldots \\ &\quad + \omega^{(d-1)\cdot(\alpha+\beta\cdot(d-1))+(d-1)\cdot(p+q\cdot(d-1))} |d-1\rangle\langle d-1|\Big) \\ &= \sum_{x=0}^{d-1} \omega^{x\cdot(\alpha+p+(\beta+q)\cdot x)} |x\rangle\langle x| \\ &= G_{\alpha+p,\beta+q} \end{aligned} \tag{7.31}$$

From Eq. (7.31), we can obtain $G_{\alpha,\beta} \cdot G_{p,q} = G_{\alpha+p,\beta+q}$ that the commutativity between $G_{\alpha,\beta}$ and $G_{p,q}$ is more intuitively expressed as

$$G_{\alpha,\beta} \cdot G_{p,q} = G_{\alpha+p,\beta+q} = G_{p,q} \cdot G_{\alpha,\beta} \tag{7.32}$$

Since $G_{\alpha,\beta}$, $G_{p,q}$ are randomly selected from Eq. (7.21), any two multi-valued unitary operators are commutative.

According to Theorem 7.4, the correctness of the evaluator and the decrypting party of the QFHE scheme with single qubit will be further proved as follows.

According to the interchangeability of any multi-valued unitary operator in Theorem 7.4, the correctness of the evaluation algorithm is proved as follows.

Lemma 7.1 *When the evaluation operator acts on the ciphertext ρ of the quantum state, the following Eq. (7.33) is obtained.*

$$\rho' = G_{\alpha,\beta} \cdot \rho = V_d^{P_a(x)} W_d^{P_b(x)} G_{\alpha,\beta}\sigma \tag{7.33}$$

Proof According to the interchangeability between any two multi-valued unitary operators in Theorem 7.4, we have

$$\begin{aligned} G_{\alpha,\beta} \cdot \rho &= G_{\alpha,\beta} \cdot \left(V_d^{P_a(x)} W_d^{P_b(x)} \sigma\right) \\ &= G_{\alpha,\beta} \left(G_{1,0}\right)^{P_a(x)} \left(G_{0,1}\right)^{P_b(x)} \sigma \\ &= G_{\alpha,\beta} G_{P_a(x),0} G_{0,P_b(x)} \sigma \\ &= G_{\alpha+P_a(x),\beta+P_b(x)} \sigma \\ &= G_{P_a(x),P_b(x)} G_{\alpha,\beta} \sigma \\ &= G_{P_a(x),0} G_{0,P_b(x)} G_{\alpha,\beta} \sigma \\ &= V_d^{P_a(x)} W_d^{P_b(x)} G_{\alpha,\beta} \sigma \end{aligned} \tag{7.34}$$

Therefore, when the evaluation operator acts on the ciphertext ρ of the quantum state, it is equivalent to directly encrypting the evaluation operator on the plaintext of the quantum state for following encryption. So the correctness of the evaluation algorithm is proved.

Theorem 7.5 *The decryption algorithm $\sigma' = Decrypt_{\Delta}(a, b, \rho') = G_{\alpha,\beta}\sigma$ is correct.*

Proof According to the interchangeability and correctness of any multi-valued unitary operator of Lemma 7.1, we evaluate the homomorphic transformation result of the algorithm. When the decryption algorithm $Decrypt_{\Delta}$ performs decryption on the quantum state ρ' calculated by the algorithm, the following Eq. (7.35) is obtained:

$$\begin{aligned} \sigma' &= Decrypt_{\Delta}\left(P_a(x), P_b(x), \rho'\right) \\ &= V_d^{-P_a(x)} W_d^{-P_b(x)} \cdot \rho' \\ &= V_d^{-P_a(x)} W_d^{-P_b(x)} G_{\alpha,\beta} \cdot \rho \\ &= V_d^{-P_a(x)} W_d^{-P_b(x)} V_d^{P_a(x)} W_d^{P_b(x)} G_{\alpha,\beta} \sigma \\ &= G_{\alpha,\beta} \sigma \end{aligned} \tag{7.35}$$

It is known from Eq. (7.35) that the decryption algorithm is correct.

Theorem 7.4 describes the interchangeability of any multi-valued unitary operator. The correctness describes the evaluation of homomorphic transformation results and the decryption results. According to the above theorem and lemma proof, we fully prove that the QFHE scheme based on multi-valued quantum single-point obfuscation is correct.

7.2.5.2 B. QFHE Scheme Based on Multi-valued Quantum Multi-point Obfuscation

In the previous section, the QFHE scheme with single qubit was introduced to handle homomorphic calculations on a qubit. When multiple qubits need to be processed simultaneously, a multi-qubit QFHE scheme is required. We will construct a QFHE scheme with multiple qubits.

According to the obfuscator $O^{R_q}\left(U_{(a_1,b_1),\ldots,(a_i,b_i)}\right)$ and the quaternion of QFHE algorithms, the scheme based on multi-valued quantum multi-point obfuscation is described as follows:

Scheme 4 (QFHE scheme with multi-valued quantum multi-point obfuscation). The scheme is a quaternion of quantum algorithms ($KeyGen_\Delta$, $Encrypt_\Delta$, $Evaluate_\Delta$, $Decrypt_\Delta$):

1. ***Key generation***: *$KeyGen_\Delta$: $(a_i, b_i, G_{l,j}) \to O$. The key generation algorithm $KeyGen_\Delta$ randomly generates two classical keys, $a_i, b_i \in \{1, \ldots, d-1\}$, where $i = 1, \ldots, n$. Then the obfuscator O asks the multi-valued quantum random oracle machine R_q with a_i, b_i to obtain the quantum state $R_q\left(B\left(a_i\right)\right), R_q\left(B\left(b_i\right)\right)$, and the obfuscator O stores the obtained quantum state $r_{a_i} = R_q\left(B\left(a_i\right)\right), r_{b_i} = R_q\left(B\left(b_i\right)\right)$, $G_{l,j}$ is the multi-valued quantum state randomly generated by the encrypting party and the decrypting party.*
2. ***Encryption***: *$Encrypt_\Delta$:$\sigma_i \to \rho_i$. The encryption algorithm $Encrypt_\Delta$ performs encryption on the plaintext $\sigma_1 \otimes \sigma_2 \otimes \ldots \otimes \sigma_n$ of quantum state with the keys a_i, b_i to generate the quantum state ciphertext $\rho_i = Encrypt_\Delta\left(a_i, b_i, \sigma_i\right)$. Then the encrypting party sends ρ_i to the evaluator via the quantum-secure channel and sends the result $G_{l+P_{a_1,\ldots,a_n}(x),\,j+P_{b_1,\ldots,b_n}(y)}$ of obfuscator O to the decrypting party.*
3. ***Homomorphic evaluation***: *$Evaluate_\Delta$: $\rho_i \to \rho_i{}'$. After the evaluator receives the quantum state ciphertext ρ_i from the encrypting party, it generates the evaluation parameters α_i, β_i according to its computing requirements. It performs the evaluation $\rho_i' = Evaluate_\Delta(\alpha_i, \beta_i, \rho_i) = \otimes_{i=1}^n V_d^{\alpha_i} W_d^{\beta_i} \rho_i$ on the received quantum state ciphertext, and sends the result ρ_i' to the decrypting party via the quantum-secure channel.*
4. ***Decryption***: *$Decrypt_\Delta$: $\rho_i' \to \sigma_i'$. After the decrypting party receives the calculation result of the evaluator, it adopts the decryption algorithm $Decrypt_\Delta$ to perform the decryption $\sigma_i' = Decrypt_\Delta\left(a_i, b_i, \rho_i'\right) = \otimes_{i=1}^n V_d^{\alpha_i} W_d^{\beta_i} \sigma_i$ based on the keys a_i, b_i.*

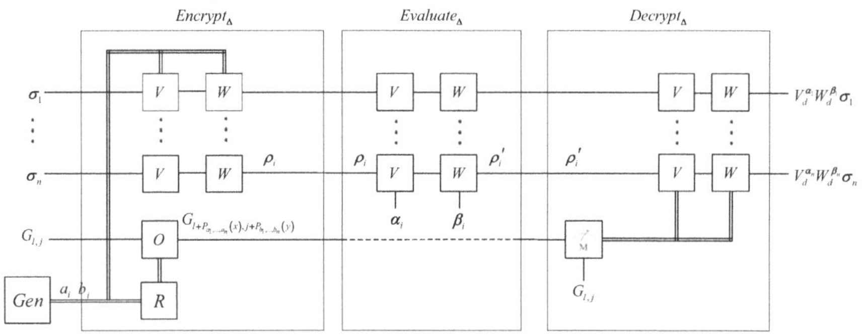

Fig. 7.4 Quantum circuit diagram of the QFHE scheme with multiple qubits

The quantum circuit diagram of the above scheme is shown in Fig. 7.4. The encrypting party uses n pairs of keys $a_i, b_i (i = 1, \ldots, n)$ generated by key generation algorithm to encrypt n quantum state plaintexts $\sigma_1 \otimes \ldots \otimes \sigma_n$ and sends the encryption result ρ_i to the evaluator. The evaluator performs evaluation calculations $V_d^{\alpha_i} W_d^{\beta_i} \rho_i$ separately. Finally, the corresponding result ρ' is sent to the decrypting party to perform decryption, and a direct calculation result $V_d^{\alpha_1} W_d^{\beta_1} \sigma_1 \otimes \ldots \otimes V_d^{\alpha_n} W_d^{\beta_n} \sigma_n$ of n quantum text plaintexts is obtained.

The correctness of the evaluation algorithm and the decryption algorithm of the QFHE scheme with multiple qubits is proved as follows.

Lemma 7.2 *The evaluation process* $\rho' = Evaluate_\Delta(\alpha_i, \beta_i, \rho) = \otimes_{i=1}^n G_{\alpha_i,\beta_i} \cdot \rho = \otimes_{i=1}^n V_d^{P_{a_i}(x_i)} W_d^{P_{b_i}(x_i)} G_{\alpha_i,\beta_i} \sigma_i$ *is correct.*

Proof According to Theorem 7.4 and Lemma 7.1, when the evaluation operator $\otimes_{i=1}^n G_{\alpha_i,\beta_i}$ acts on the quantum ciphertext ρ, we have

$$\begin{aligned} \otimes_{i=1}^n G_{\alpha_i,\beta_i} \cdot \rho &= \otimes_{i=1}^n G_{\alpha_i,\beta_i} \cdot \otimes_{i=1}^n V_d^{P_{a_i}(x_i)} W_d^{P_{b_i}(x_i)} \sigma_i \\ &= G_{\alpha_1+a_1,\beta_1+b_1} \sigma_1 \otimes \ldots \otimes G_{\alpha_n+a_n,\beta_n+b_n} \sigma_n \\ &= V_d^{a_1} W_d^{b_1} G_{\alpha_1,\beta_1} \sigma_1 \otimes \ldots \otimes V_d^{a_n} W_d^{b_n} G_{\alpha_n,\beta_n} \sigma_n \end{aligned} \quad (7.36)$$

The result is equivalent to directly encrypting the evaluation operator in the plaintext of the quantum state, so the process of evaluation is correct.

Theorem 7.6 *The process* $\sigma' = Decrypt_\Delta\left(P_{a_i}(x_i), P_{b_i}(x_i), \rho'\right) = \otimes_{i=1}^n V_d^{-P_{a_i}(x_i)} W_d^{-P_{b_i}(x_i)}, \rho' = \otimes_{i=1}^n G_{\alpha_i,\beta_i} \sigma_i$ *to decrypt the algorithm* $Decrypt_\Delta$ *is correct.*

Proof According to Theorem 7.4 and Lemma 7.2, when the decryption algorithm performs the decryption on the result of the evaluation:

$$\begin{aligned}\sigma' &= \otimes_{i=1}^{n} V_d^{-P_{a_i}(x_i)} W_d^{-P_{b_i}(x_i)} \cdot \rho' \\ &= \otimes_{i=1}^{n} V_d^{-P_{a_i}(x_i)} W_d^{-P_{b_i}(x_i)} \cdot \otimes_{i=1}^{n} V_d^{P_{a_i}(x_i)} W_d^{P_{b_i}(x_i)} G_{\alpha_i,\beta_i}\sigma_i \\ &= \otimes_{i=1}^{n} V_d^{-P_{a_i}(x_i)} W_d^{-P_{b_i}(x_i)} V_d^{P_{a_i}(x_i)} W_d^{P_{b_i}(x_i)} G_{\alpha_i,\beta_i}\sigma_i \\ &= \otimes_{i=1}^{n} G_{\alpha_i,\beta_i}\sigma_i \end{aligned} \tag{7.37}$$

The decryption result is the calculation of the plaintext of the quantum state by the evaluation operator, so the decryption process is also correct according to Eq. (7.37).

As a result, the above proof fully illustrates the correctness of the QFHE scheme with multiple qubits.

7.2.6 Security Analysis

The security of multi-valued quantum point obfuscation and two QFHE schemes will be analyzed in this section. The security definition is given for security analysis. The fully mixed state guarantees the security of the QHE scheme [8, 13, 24].

Definition 7.9 (*Information-theoretic security of quantum full homomorphic encryption*) If all input state φ and output state φ_c are completely mixed, then the algorithm is secure. The relationship between the input state φ and the completely mixed state φ_c is described as follows:

$$\varphi_c = \sum_{a,b\in\{0,\ldots,d-1\}} \frac{1}{d} V_d^a W_d^b \varphi \left(V_d^a W_d^b\right)^\dagger = \frac{1}{d} I_d, \tag{7.38}$$

where φ denotes the density algorithm for all possible input states and $U_{a,b} = (a, b \in (0, \ldots, d-1))$ denotes the unitary transformation between input state and output state.

7.2.6.1 A. Multi-valued Quantum Point Obfuscation

The definition of a quantum obfuscator, proposed by Alagic et al. [25], is similar to its classical counterpart and the three conditions (polynomial expansion, functional equivalence, virtual black-box) hold. The security of multi-valued quantum point obfuscation under the quantum random oracle model has the following theorem.

Theorem 7.7 *Under the multi-valued quantum random oracle model R_q, the multi-valued quantum point function circuit family $C_{a,b}$ is obfuscatable.*

Proof The obfuscator O of the multi-valued quantum single-point function $U_{a,b}$ is described in Definition 7.7.

In order to prove that $\left|R_q(B(a)), R_q(B(b))\right\rangle$ is a correct obfuscation of multi-valued quantum single-point function $U_{a,b}$, we firstly prove the functional equivalence. Since the multi-valued quantum random oracle machine R_q is an ideal random function without collision, so R_q is a bijective, i.e., $R_q(B(x)) = R_q(B(a))$, $R_q(B(y)) = R_q(B(b))$ if and only if $x = a$, $y = b$. Because the selected basic multi-valued quantum state is $G_{l,j}$, $G_{l+P_a(x),j+P_b(y)}$ can obtain $G_{P_a(x),P_b(y)}$ by the operation of $V_d^{-l}W_d^{-j}$, and then $P_a(x)$, $P_b(y)$ can be obtained after measurement, and the functional equivalence is established.

Secondly, $\left|R_q(B(a)), R_q(B(b))\right\rangle$ is a $2s$-qubits, here $s = ploy(m)$, and polynomial expansion is established.

Finally, under the multi-valued quantum random oracle model, any party of the security game has access to R_q. For any adversary A, the simulator S is constructed as follows: the simulator S retains a copy of the adversary A internally (denoted by A'), and then randomly selects $\omega \in N$ and prepares the quantum state $|\omega\rangle$. S passes $|\omega\rangle$ to the internal A' as input, and whenever A' queries R_q with quantum state $|\phi\rangle = \left|x, y, G_{l,j}\right\rangle$, S queries the oracle R_q with ϕ and obtains $|\psi\rangle = \left|x, y, G_{l+P_a(x),j+P_b(y)}\right\rangle$. So the simulator S can answer the correct guess of a, b with $|\omega\rangle$ and the wrong guess of a, b with the randomly chosen result $|r\rangle$. Finally, S outputs what A' outputs. So the simulator S successfully simulates the external environment of the internal adversary A', and we have

$$\left|\Pr[A = 1] - \Pr\left[S^{U_{a,b}} = 1\right]\right| = 0 \tag{7.39}$$

The virtual black-box condition is satisfied. So $\left|R_q(B(a)), R_q(B(b))\right\rangle$ is the correct obfuscation of the multi-valued quantum single-point function $U_{a,b}$.

Theorem 7.8 *The family of multi-valued quantum multi-point function $\mathcal{C}^*$ is obfuscatable under the quantum random oracle model.*

Proof We prove that $\mathcal{C}_n^t \ll \{C_{n_1}\#\ldots\#C_{n_t} : C_{n_i} \in \mathcal{C}_n\}$ and construct the QPT M and N. The QPT M will access $U_{C_{n_1}\#\ldots\#C_{n_t}}$ one by one and concatenate the results to obtain $\mathcal{C}_n^t$. The QPT N will query the oracle of $\mathcal{C}_n^t$, and return the result according to the value of the control register to obtain $C_{n_1}\#\ldots\#C_{n_t}$. Since the quantum state in the control register is in the basic state, the measurement will not reveal any information on the input, so we can obtain $\mathcal{C}_n^t \ll \{C_{n_1}\#\ldots\#C_{n_t} : C_{n_i} \in \mathcal{C}_n\}$.

Under the condition of known $\mathcal{C}_n^t \ll \{C_{n_1}\#\ldots\#C_{n_t} : C_{n_i} \in \mathcal{C}_n\}$, $\mathcal{C}$ is obfuscatable, so $\{C_1\#\ldots\#C_t : C_i \in \mathcal{C}\}$ is obfuscatable according to the reduction for quantum obfuscation [22]. Similarly, since $\mathcal{C}^t$ is obfuscatable, the family of multi-valued quantum multi-point function $\mathcal{C}^*$ is obfuscatable in the multi-valued quantum random oracle model.

7.2.6.2 B. QFHE Scheme with Single Qubit

According to the definition of security in Definition 7.9, the QFHE scheme with single qubit is secure and can be proved as follows. $\varphi = \sum_{m=0}^{d-1} p_m |m\rangle\langle m|$ is the density matrix of all possible plaintexts of the quantum state. It is assumed that an attacker cannot know the probability distribution related to quantum data transmission via other channels in advance, so the plaintext of the quantum state in front of the attacker has the same probability $p_m = \frac{1}{d}, m \in \{0, \ldots, d-1\}$. $a, b \in \{0, \ldots, d-1\}$ is the key chosen by the encrypting party, which is only held by a user. When an attacker tries to intercept the information sent by the encrypting party, the output of the encryption algorithm according to Eq. (7.38) is in a fully mixed state $\frac{1}{d^2}\sum_{a,b\in\{0,\ldots,d-1\}} V_d^a W_d^b \varphi \cdot (V_d^a W_d^b)^\dagger$. Because the result that an attacker can intercept or detect is only a fully mixed quantum state, the attacker cannot obtain any valuable information on the plaintext of the encrypting party from it.

$$
\begin{aligned}
&\frac{1}{d^2}\sum_{a,b\in\{0,\ldots,d-1\}} V_d^a W_d^b \varphi \left(V_d^a W_d^b\right)^\dagger \\
&= \frac{1}{d^2}\sum_{a,b\in\{0,\ldots,d-1\}} V_d^a W_d^b \varphi \left(W_d^b\right)^\dagger \left(V_d^a\right)^\dagger \\
&= \frac{1}{d^2}\sum_{a,b\in\{0,\ldots,d-1\}} \left(\sum_{x=0}^{d-1} \omega^{x(a+bx)} |x\rangle\langle x| \right. \\
&\quad \left. \cdot \sum_{m=0}^{d-1} p_m |m\rangle\langle m| \sum_{x=0}^{d-1} \omega^{-x(a+bx)} |x\rangle\langle x| \right) \\
&= \frac{1}{d^2}\sum_{a,b\in\{0,\ldots,d-1\}} \left(\sum_{m=0}^{d-1} p_m \omega^{m(a+bm)} |m\rangle\langle m| \sum_{x=0}^{d-1} \omega^{-x(a+bx)} |x\rangle\langle x| \right) \\
&= \frac{1}{d^2}\sum_{a,b\in\{0,\ldots,d-1\}} \left(\sum_{m=0}^{d-1} p_m \omega^{m(a+bm)} \omega^{-m(a+bm)} |m\rangle\langle m| \right) \\
&= \frac{1}{d^2}\sum_{a,b\in\{0,\ldots,d-1\}} p_m I_d \\
&= \frac{1}{d} I_d
\end{aligned} \tag{7.40}
$$

According to Eq. (7.40), the output of the evaluation algorithm is also completely mixed in front of the attacker, as shown in Eq. (7.41):

$$
\begin{aligned}
&\frac{1}{d^2}\sum_{a,b,\alpha,\beta\in\{0,\ldots,d-1\}} V_d^\alpha W_d^\beta V_d^a W_d^b \varphi \left(V_d^a W_d^b\right)^\dagger \left(V_d^\alpha W_d^\beta\right)^\dagger \\
&= \frac{1}{d^2}\sum_{a,b,\alpha,\beta\in\{0,\ldots,d-1\}} p_m V_d^\alpha W_d^\beta I_d \left(V_d^\alpha W_d^\beta\right)^\dagger \\
&= \frac{1}{d} I_d
\end{aligned} \tag{7.41}
$$

From Eqs. (7.40) and (7.41), it can be seen that the outputs of the encryption algorithm and the evaluation algorithm of the QFHE scheme with single qubit are in completely mixed states, which means that an attacker cannot obtain any valuable information of the message sent by the encrypting party from the mixed state, so the scheme is information-theoretic security.

Theorem 7.9 *QFHE scheme with multi-valued quantum single-point obfuscation is IND-CPA(indistinguishability under chosen plaintext attack)-secure.*

Proof For the multi-valued quantum single-point obfuscator $O(U_{a,b})$, if $t = ploy(n)$, the combination of the obfuscation results of t different point functions is still a correct obfuscation. Then for any quantum polynomial-time algorithm D and a simulator S, Eq. (7.39) holds.

$$\begin{aligned}&|\Pr[D(A(O(U_{a_1,b_1}), O(U_{a_2,b_2}), \ldots, O(U_{a_t,b_t}))) = 1]\\&- \Pr[D(S^{U_{a_1,b_1}, U_{a_2,b_2}, \ldots, U_{a_t,b_t}}(0^n)) = 1]| \leq negl(n),\end{aligned} \tag{7.42}$$

where $k \leftarrow_{random} \{0, 1\}^n$, and $r_i \leftarrow_{random} \{0, 1\}^{poly(n)}$, $i = 1, \ldots, t$.

Assume that any adversary $A = (M, D)$ queries the encryption oracle for $t = poly(n)$ times. Then there are $r_1, \ldots, r_t$ (used by the encryption oracle) and r (used by the challenger) that maximize the difference

$$\begin{aligned}&|\Pr\{D^{Encrypt}[(Encrypt_\Delta \otimes I_E)\rho_{ME}] = 1\}\\&- \Pr\{D^{Encrypt}[(Encrypt_\Delta \otimes I_E)(|0\rangle\langle 0|_M \otimes \rho_E)] = 1\}|\end{aligned} \tag{7.43}$$

According to the adversary A, we construct another adversary A' attacking the obfuscator. Concretely, when A queries the encryption oracle for the ith times with ρ_i $(i = 1, \ldots, t)$, A' responds with $P_{r_i}\rho_i P_{r_i} \otimes O(U_{a_i,b_i})$. During the distinguishing challenge game, A' responds with either $(P_r \otimes I_E)\rho_{ME} \otimes O(U_{a,b})$ or $(P_r \otimes I_E)(|0\rangle\langle 0|_M \otimes \rho_E) \otimes O(U_{a,b})$ when queried with ρ_{ME}. So, when A' outputs the same as A,

$$\begin{aligned}&|\Pr\{D^{Encrypt}[(Encrypt_\Delta \otimes I_E)\rho_{ME}] = 1\}\\&- \Pr\{D^{Encrypt}[(Encrypt_\Delta \otimes I_E)(|0\rangle\langle 0|_M \otimes \rho_E)] = 1\}|\\&\leq |\Pr\{A'[O(U_{a_1,b_1}), \ldots, O(U_{a_t,b_t}); Encrypt_\Delta(\rho)] = 1\}\\&- \Pr\{A'[O(U_{a_1,b_1}), \ldots, O(U_{a_t,b_t}); Encrypt_\Delta(|0\rangle)] = 1\}|\\&\leq |\Pr\{S^{O(U_{a_1,b_1}),\ldots,O(U_{a_t,b_t})}[Encrypt_\Delta(\rho)] = 1\}\\&- \Pr\{S^{O(U_{a_1,b_1}),\ldots,O(U_{a_t,b_t})}[Encrypt_\Delta(|0\rangle)] = 1\}| + negl(n)\\&\leq negl(n)\end{aligned} \tag{7.44}$$

Therefore QFHE scheme with multi-valued quantum single-point obfuscation is IND-CPA-secure.

7.2.6.3 C. QFHE Scheme with Multiple Qubits

Similarly, according to Eq. (7.40), when there exists an attacker, the output state of the encryption algorithm of the QFHE scheme with multiple qubits is the tensor product of the cryptographic output, which is also completely mixed, as shown in Eq. (7.45):

$$\begin{aligned}
&\frac{1}{d^{2n}} \sum_{a_1,b_1\in\{0,\ldots,d-1\}} V_d^{a_1} W_d^{b_1} \varphi_1 \left(V_d^{a_1} W_d^{b_1}\right)^{\dagger} \otimes \ldots \\
&\otimes \sum_{a_n,b_n\in\{0,\ldots,d-1\}} V_d^{a_n} W_d^{b_n} \varphi_n \left(V_d^{a_n} W_d^{b_n}\right)^{\dagger} \\
&= \frac{1}{d^{2n}} \sum_{a_1,b_1\in\{0,\ldots,d-1\}} p_m I_d \otimes \ldots \otimes \sum_{a_n,b_n\in\{0,\ldots,d-1\}} p_m I_d \\
&= \frac{1}{d^n} I_{d^n}
\end{aligned} \tag{7.45}$$

In addition, according to Eqs. (7.41) and (7.45), the output of evaluation algorithm of the QFHE scheme with multiple qubits is also in a fully mixed state, as shown in Eq. (7.46):

$$\begin{aligned}
&\frac{1}{d^{2n}} \sum_{a_1,b_1,\alpha_1,\beta_1\in\{0,\ldots,d-1\}} V_d^{\alpha_1} W_d^{\beta_1} V_d^{a_1} W_d^{b_1} \varphi_1 \left(V_d^{a_1} W_d^{b_1}\right)^{\dagger} \left(V_d^{\alpha_1} W_d^{\beta_1}\right)^{\dagger} \otimes \ldots \\
&\otimes \sum_{a_n,b_n,\alpha_n,\beta_n\in\{0,\ldots,d-1\}} V_d^{\alpha_n} W_d^{\beta_n} V_d^{a_n} W_d^{b_n} \varphi_n \left(V_d^{a_n} W_d^{b_n}\right)^{\dagger} \left(V_d^{\alpha_n} W_d^{\beta_n}\right)^{\dagger} \\
&= \frac{1}{d^{2n}} \sum_{a_1,b_1\in\{0,\ldots,d-1\}} p_{m_1} I_d \otimes \ldots \otimes \sum_{a_n,b_n\in\{0,\ldots,d-1\}} p_{m_n} I_d \\
&= \frac{1}{d^n} I_{d^n}
\end{aligned} \tag{7.46}$$

So the QFHE scheme with multi-valued quantum multi-point obfuscation is also information-theoretic security. Similar to Theorem 7.7, it is IND-CPA-secure.

The above proof fully illustrates that the output quantum states of all possible information exposure points in the process of the QFHE scheme have the property of complete mixture state, which makes it impossible for an attacker to obtain any useful information on the plaintext through analysis, even if the encrypted message is intercepted or detected by the attacker during transmission. Therefore, the QFHE scheme with single qubit and the QFHE scheme with multiple qubits are both secure.

Table 7.2 Scheme comparison

Scheme	The evaluator knows the key	A regular interaction	Exponential price	Information-theoretic security
Our schemes	No	No	Yes	Yes
Liang's QHE [8]	No	No	No	Yes
Liang's QFHE [9]	No	Yes	Yes	Yes
Broadbent's QHE [12]	No	Yes	Yes	No
Sun's QHE [13]	Yes	No	No	No
Ouyang's QHE [11]	Yes	No	No	Yes

7.2.7 *Scheme Comparison*

We compare the QHE and QFHE schemes in term of four aspects such as whether the evaluator knows the decryption key, a regular interaction between evaluator and user, cost and security level.

It can be seen from Table 7.2 that our QFHE schemes are better. The evaluator does not know the decryption key and does not require a regular interaction with a user. The output state has the property of complete mixture. There is still an exponential price for obtaining perfect security, which should be paid more attention to for solution.

7.3 Quantum Homomorphic Encryption Based on Quantum Power Obfuscation

7.3.1 *Requirement of Quantum Nonlinear Obfuscation*

In terms of quantum nonlinear functions, quantum point obfuscation has yielded a number of positive results [22], but its application in cryptography is limited due to the singular function form. The significant applications of nonlinear functions in classical cryptography have prompted the construction of theoretical framework of quantum nonlinear functions. Under the assumption that the theory of quantum obfuscation began relatively late, the definition and obfuscation of quantum nonlinear functions need to be further studied. We will focus on the quantum obfuscation scheme based on the quantum nonlinear function and its cryptographic applications.

We address the issue on the reversibility of quantum linear function circuits and their applicability in constructing quantum one-way functions. To solve these problems, we introduce a novel approach that combines quantum nonlinear functions with quantum obfuscation theory [23]. We design a quantum nonlinear function obfuscator utilizing quantum teleportation. The objective is to obfuscate the parameter of nonlinear functions, thereby achieving obfuscation. The interpreter is based on the specific function of quantum nonlinear function, and the interpreter circuit operates on the input and the parameter. The construction of quantum obfuscator and quantum interpreter connects quantum teleportation with the theory of quantum obfuscation and strengthens the security of quantum communication by obfuscating circuits and functions.

7.3.2 Construction of Quantum Power Obfuscation

Quantum power function obfuscation focuses on the construction of quantum obfuscator and quantum interpreter. By selecting the parameters (such as the exponential quantum states of quantum power functions) and combining them with quantum teleportation, the quantum obfuscator employs different obfuscation circuits according to the number of qubits of the parameter to be obfuscated in order to obfuscate the parameter of quantum power functions. After the receiver measures the obfuscation result, the parameter is restored according to the obtained classical bits, and the restored parameter, along with the input, is put into the quantum interpreter and outputted the result after performing the quantum interpreter.

7.3.2.1 A. Quantum Obfuscator

We construct a quantum power function obfuscator based on quantum teleportation. To obfuscate a parameter in the form of a single qubit, for instance, $|y\rangle = |x\rangle^{|a\rangle}$, in addition to the input and output quantum states, $|a\rangle$ serves as the parameter that is put into the quantum power function obfuscator.

The recombination result is subjected to a joint quantum measurement, the classical result is transmitted to the receiver via a channel, and the parameter prior to obfuscation is restored by means of applying the unitary transformation to the corresponding quantum state of the collapsed states. The restored parameter and the input of the function are simultaneously transmitted into the quantum interpreter circuit to realize the quantum power function.

We obfuscate the quantum states and input them into the interpreter for quantum power functions with multi-parameter quantum states. For multi-qubit parameters, we extend the basic quantum teleportation circuit into a multi-qubit quantum teleportation circuit and obfuscate the parameter quantum states.

7.3.2.2 B. Quantum Interpreter

We design a circuit of quantum power function interpreter based on the functions and properties of quantum power functions. Firstly, the quantum interpreter performs quantum measurements on the obfuscated quantum states in order to obtain the classical two-bit measurements. On the basis of measurement results, the Pauli matrix is transformed to restore the quantum states of the obfuscated parameters. The quantum interpreter not only utilizes the functionality of a quantum power function but also encrypts the circuit of a quantum power function, thereby guaranteeing the security of the quantum communication system. Considering the quantum power function interpreter, we design the specific circuit of the equivalent functionality of a quantum power function in the quantum interpreter and obtain the output of the quantum power function.

According to the definition of the quantum power function, when the parameter $|a\rangle$ is $|0\rangle$, the output is $|1\rangle$ regardless of the input. When the parameter $|a\rangle$ is quantum state $|1\rangle$, the output is $|x\rangle$. Thus, we construct a quantum interpreter of the quantum power function based on its functionality. In order to reverse the quantum state $|a\rangle$, we firstly utilize the quantum state $|1\rangle$ to perform a quantum XOR operation with the parameter $|a\rangle$. Then, we perform a quantum XOR operation between $|\bar{a}\rangle$ and the input quantum state $|x\rangle$, which utilizes quantum XOR to realize the logical relationship between the base of the power function and the exponential operation. Quantum OR operation implementation is required to simultaneously output $|1\rangle \oplus |a\rangle$ and $|\bar{a}\rangle \oplus |x\rangle$. Since there is no quantum OR gate, we realize quantum OR gate through quantum NAND relationship, i.e., let the above two results be inverted with $|1\rangle$ respectively, and then add the two inverted results to generate the final output.

7.3.3 QHE Scheme Based on Quantum Power Obfuscation

We illustrate the cryptographic application of quantum nonlinear function obfuscation through the construction of a quantum homomorphic encryption scheme. This scheme contains key generation algorithm, encryption algorithm, evaluation algorithm and decryption algorithm. Furthermore, we give the security analysis of the entire scheme.

Assume that O is an obfuscator for a quantum nonlinear function, U_μ is a quantum nonlinear function, $\sigma = |m\rangle$ is a n-qubit quantum plaintext, and ρ is an encrypted quantum state. The quantum homomorphic encryption scheme based on quantum obfuscation Π consists of four QPT algorithms $\Pi =$ (KeyGen, Enc_{pk}, Dec_{sk}, Evaluate_Δ), which is shown in Fig. 7.5. Four algorithms are shown in Figs. 7.6, 7.7 and 7.8.

1. ***Key generation***: the algorithm generates the private key sk, the public key pk, and the publicly available computational key k_{eval} for the quantum asymmetric homomorphic encryption scheme. $\text{KeyGen}(1^n) = (sk, pk) \in K_n, sk = |k_1\rangle$, $pk = |k_2\rangle$, where $K_n = \{0, 1\}^n$ is uniformly distributed key space, and sk and pk are randomly selected by KeyGen from K_n. $k_{\text{eval}} = O(\text{Enc}_{pk} \circ U_\mu \circ \text{Dec}_{pk}) = X_\alpha Y_\beta Z_\gamma |k_1, k_2\rangle Z_\gamma^\dagger Y_\beta^\dagger X_\alpha^\dagger \otimes O(U_\mu)$, where O is a obfuscator for quantum nonlinear function and U_μ is a quantum nonlinear function.

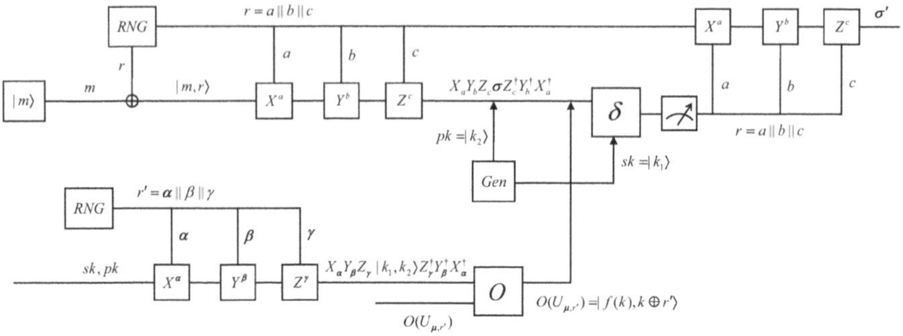

Fig. 7.5 QHE scheme based on quantum power obfuscation

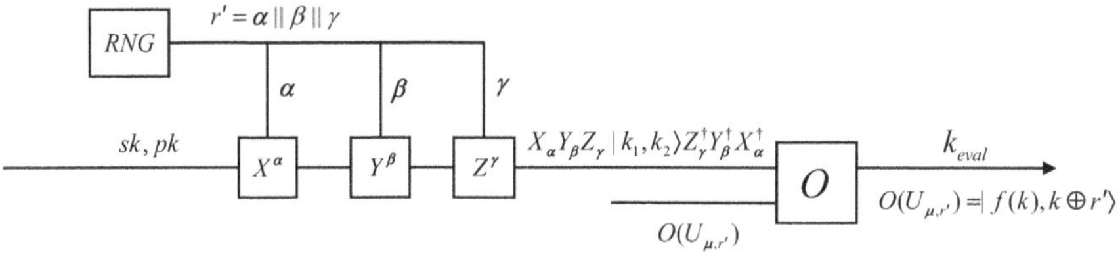

Fig. 7.6 Key generation

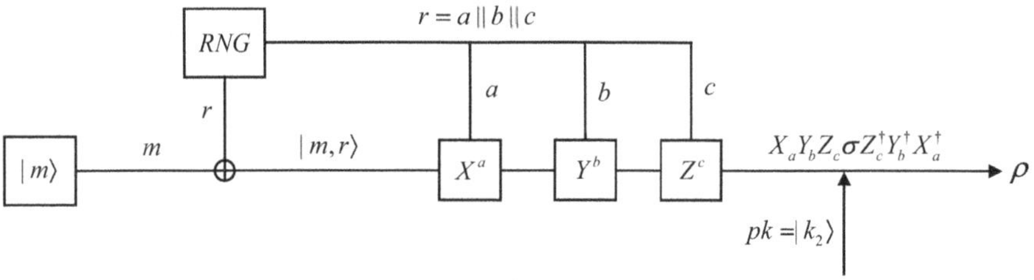

Fig. 7.7 Encryption

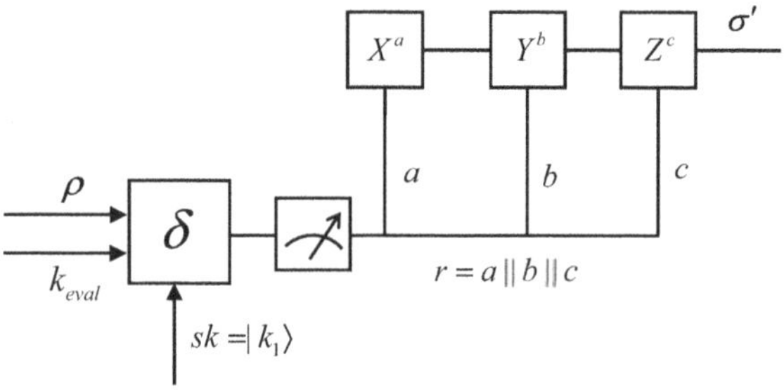

Fig. 7.8 Evaluation and decryption

2. ***Encryption***: the encrypting party uses the public key to execute an asymmetric encryption algorithm on the quantum plaintext message σ to obtain the ciphertext ρ. The encryption algorithm is denoted by $\mathrm{Enc}_{pk}(\sigma) = pk(|m, r\rangle) = [X_a Y_b Z_c(|r\rangle\langle r| \otimes |m\rangle) Z_c^\dagger Y_b^\dagger X_a^\dagger] \otimes |k_2\rangle$, and the ciphertext is ρ, where $r \in \{0, 1\}^{3n}$ is selected at radom and a, b, c represent the first, middle, and last n bites of r, respectively.
3. ***Evaluation***: the evaluator evaluates the quantum ciphertext ρ to obtain the evaluation result ρ' by utilizing the computational key k_{eval}. $\text{Evaluate}_\Delta = \delta(k_{eval} \otimes \rho \otimes |G\rangle\langle G|)$ is the evaluation algorithm, where $|G\rangle\langle G|$ represents the corresponding quantum gate. The evaluator transmits the evaluation result ρ' to the decryptor via the quantum channel for asymmetric decryption.
4. ***Decryption***: the decryptor receives the result ρ' calculated by the evaluator and employs the private key sk to perform the decryption algorithm on the evaluated result to obtain the plaintext denoted as $\sigma' = \mathrm{Dec}_{sk}(\rho') = \sigma \otimes |G\rangle\langle G| = X_a Y_b Z_c \sigma Z_c^\dagger Y_b^\dagger X_a^\dagger$.

Theorem 7.10 *After processing the quantum ciphertext ρ, the evaluator obtains the evaluation result ρ', which satisfies $\rho' = \text{Evaluate}_\Delta(\rho) = \mathrm{Enc}_{pk}(\sigma \otimes |G\rangle\langle G|)$.*

Proof When the corresponding unitary operation $X_a Y_b Z_c$ is performed on the quantum ciphertext ρ by the quantum homomorphic evaluation algorithm Evaluate_Δ, then

$$\begin{aligned}
&\rho' = \text{Evaluate}_\Delta(\rho) = \text{Evaluate}(\mathrm{Enc}_{pk}(\sigma)) = \delta(k_{eval} \otimes \rho \otimes |G\rangle\langle G|) \\
&= \delta\{[X_\alpha Y_\beta Z_\gamma |k_1, k_2\rangle Z_\gamma^\dagger Y_\beta^\dagger X_\alpha^\dagger \otimes O(U_\mu)] \otimes [X_a Y_b Z_c(|r\rangle\langle r| \otimes |m\rangle) Z_c^\dagger Y_b^\dagger X_a^\dagger] \otimes \\
&|k_2\rangle \otimes |G\rangle\langle G|\} \\
&= \delta\{[X_\alpha Y_\beta Z_\gamma |k_1, k_2\rangle Z_\gamma^\dagger Y_\beta^\dagger X_\alpha^\dagger] \otimes [X_a Y_b Z_c(|r\rangle\langle r| \otimes |m\rangle \otimes |G\rangle\langle G|) Z_c^\dagger Y_b^\dagger X_a^\dagger] \otimes \\
&|k_2\rangle \otimes O(U_\mu)\} \\
&= \delta\{[X_a Y_b Z_c(|r\rangle\langle r| \otimes |m\rangle \otimes [(X_\alpha Y_\beta Z_\gamma |k_1, k_2\rangle Z_\gamma^\dagger Y_\beta^\dagger X_\alpha^\dagger) \otimes |G\rangle\langle G|]) Z_c^\dagger Y_b^\dagger X_a^\dagger] \otimes \\
&|k_2\rangle \otimes O(U_\mu)\} \\
&= \delta\{[X_a Y_b Z_c(|r\rangle\langle r| \otimes |m\rangle \otimes [(X_\alpha Y_\beta Z_\gamma |k_1, k_2\rangle (X_\alpha Y_\beta Z_\gamma)^\dagger) \otimes |G\rangle\langle G|]) Z_c^\dagger Y_b^\dagger X_a^\dagger] \\
&\otimes |k_2\rangle \otimes O(U_\mu)\} \\
&= \delta\{[X_a Y_b Z_c(\sigma \otimes |G\rangle\langle G|) Z_c^\dagger Y_b^\dagger X_a^\dagger] \otimes |k_2\rangle \otimes O(U_\mu)\} \\
&= \mathrm{Enc}_{pk}(\sigma \otimes |G\rangle\langle G|).
\end{aligned} \tag{7.47}$$

The evaluator calculates the result of asymmetric encryption ρ to obtain ρ', and obtains σ' after asymmetric decryption. Equation (7.47) demonstrates that σ' is equivalent to the result when the evaluator directly calculates the quantum plaintext σ. Consequently, the correctness of quantum homomorphic encryption can be verified.

7.3.4 Security Analysis

Theorem 7.11 *If quantum virtual black-box obfuscation and secure quantum one-way functions exist, then there exist quantum asymmetric homomorphic encryption schemes that provide indistinguishable security against chosen-plaintext attacks.*

Proof A QPT interpreter δ with virtual black-box access to the quantum encryption algorithm Enc_{pk} can be used to simulate the access of any QPT adversary $A = (\Gamma, \Delta)$, where Γ is a quantum measurement and Δ is a quantum indistinguishable algorithm for quantum obfuscation.

Any QPT adversary $A = (\Gamma, \Delta)$ has arbitrary access to the inputs and outputs of the algorithm Δ . By the property of virtual black-box, there is

$$\begin{aligned}
&|\Pr[\Delta(A(O(U_\mu), |m\rangle)) = 1] - \Pr[\Delta(S^{U_\mu}(|m\rangle)) = 1]| \\
=&|\Pr[\Delta((\mathrm{Enc}_{pk} \otimes I)\rho_\Gamma) = 1] - \Pr[\Delta((\mathrm{Enc}_{pk} \otimes I)(|0\rangle\langle 0|_\Gamma \otimes \rho)) = 1]| \\
\leq& negl(n).
\end{aligned} \tag{7.48}$$

To prove the above equation, we introduce another QPT adversary A' to access the quantum obfuscator, input ρ to obtain $X_\alpha Y_\beta Z_\gamma \rho Z_\gamma^\dagger Y_\beta^\dagger X_\alpha^\dagger \otimes O(U_\mu)$. In this process, the outcomes of A' and A are identical.

$$\begin{aligned}
&|\Pr[\Delta((\mathrm{Enc}_{pk} \otimes I)\rho_\Gamma) = 1] - \Pr[\Delta((\mathrm{Enc}_{pk} \otimes I)(|0\rangle\langle 0|_\Gamma \otimes \rho)) = 1]| \\
\leq&|\Pr[A'(O(U_\mu, \mathrm{Enc}_{pk}(\rho))) = 1] - \Pr[A'(O(U_{m,r}, \mathrm{Enc}_{pk}(|0\rangle))) = 1]| \\
\leq&|\Pr[S^{U_\mu}(\mathrm{Enc}_{pk}(\rho)) = 1] - \Pr[S^{U_\mu}(\mathrm{Enc}_{pk}(|0\rangle)) = 1]| + negl(n) \\
\leq& negl(n).
\end{aligned} \tag{7.49}$$

Theorem 7.12 *The quantum states generated by the encryption algorithm and the quantum states generated by the evaluation algorithm of the quantum homomorphic encryption scheme based on quantum power obfuscation satisfy the fully mixed state.*

Proof For any quantum state of n qubits, its unitary operation is the orthonormal basis for the $2^n \times 2^n$ matrices, and there exists [24]

$$\frac{1}{2^{2n}} \sum_k U_k \rho U_k^\dagger = \frac{1}{2^n} I. \tag{7.50}$$

In the quantum homomorphic encryption scheme, a single qubit of quantum plaintext σ is encrypted by the public key pk. For any adversary, the output of the encryption algorithm $\mathrm{Enc}_{pk}(\sigma) = [X_a Y_b Z_c(|r\rangle\langle r| \otimes |m\rangle) Z_c^\dagger Y_b^\dagger X_a^\dagger] \otimes |k_2\rangle$, which can be denoted by $\frac{1}{2^2} \sum_{k_2} (XYZ)_{pk} \sigma (XYZ)_{pk}^\dagger$, i.e., $\frac{1}{2^2} \sum_{pk \in \{0,1\}} U_p k \sigma U_p k^\dagger$. In accordance with Eq. (7.50), the output of the encryption algorithm is completely mixed. Consequently, the output of the evaluation algorithm Evaluate$_\Delta$, $\frac{1}{2^2}\sum_{k_{eval}} U_G \rho U_G^\dagger = \frac{1}{2} I_2$ is completely mixed.

7.4 Non-interactive Quantum Homomorphic Encryption Based on Rotation Operator

7.4.1 Requirement of Non-interactive Homomorphic Encryption

Quantum homomorphic encryption scheme can be divided into interactive scheme and non-interactive scheme based on whether there is interaction between Client and Server in the evaluation algorithm. Interaction can reduce the difficulty of constructing QHE scheme for any quantum circuit. QHE for a T gate generates an undesired S gate. If interaction is allowed, an extra S gate can be used to eliminate the error. Childs [26] proposed a QHE scheme which performs a round of quantum information interaction for each quantum gate. Specifically, two rounds of interaction are required to complete the QHE for a T gate. Broadbent [27] proposed a QHE scheme that only requires M rounds of classical information interactions, where M is the number of T gates in the quantum circuit. Both quantum information interaction and classical information interaction between Client and Server can increase the communication overhead, inevitably reducing the efficiency of QHE scheme. Therefore, the research for non-interactive QHE scheme has become a focus.

Yu et al. [14] proved a no-go result: if no interaction is allowed, any QHE scheme with information-theoretic security must produce exponential storage overhead. Newman et al. [28] and Lai et al. [29] independently demonstrated an enhanced no-go result: it is impossible to construct a non-interactive quantum fully homomorphic encryption scheme with information-theoretic security. So any non-interactive QFHE scheme can only achieve computational security. Based on the classical FHE scheme, Broadbent et al. [12] constructed a non-interactive QFHE scheme with limited efficiency and security. Lai et al. [29] constructed a non-interactive QHE scheme with information-theoretic security and compactness. The scheme can only realize QHE for a specific class of quantum circuit.

Liang [30] proposed two teleportation-based QHE schemes with quasi-compactness and perfect security. These schemes use EPR entanglement pairs to achieve teleportation of S gate, and defer all quantum measurements until Server has finished all computation. Thus, the interaction can be avoided with the cost of alternating measurements and key updates in the decryption algorithm. The decryption complexity depends on the total number of non-Clifford gates in the evaluated circuit.

In order to reduce the decryption complexity of non-interactive QHE scheme, we achieve QHE for the $T/T^\dagger$ gate based on rotation operator, and constructs a non-interactive QHE scheme with information-theoretic security and $\mathcal{F}-$homomorphism [31]. The decryption complexity is $O(1)$, and the encryption complexity is $O(N)$, where N is the number of quantum gates in the quantum circuit.

7.4.2 Quantum One-Time Pad

Definition 7.10 A QHE scheme is compact, if for any quantum circuit C, the complexity of the decryption circuit after homomorphic evaluation of $Eval^{C_q}(\rho)$ is independent of the circuit C_q.

Definition 7.11 [24] Let σ be the density matrix of the plaintext quantum state $|\psi\rangle$ and $a, b \in \{0, 1\}^n$ be two classical keys. The quantum one-time pad (QOTP) encryption $QEnc_{a,b}$ and the QOTP decryption $QDec_{a,b}$ are defined as [24]

$$QEnc_{a,b} : \sigma \to X^a Z^b \sigma (X^a Z^b)^\dagger$$
$$QDec_{a,b} : X^a Z^b \sigma (X^a Z^b)^\dagger \to \sigma.$$

By specifying that the key (a, b) be chosen uniformly at random, the plaintext quantum state is encrypted to the completely mixed state, from which an adversary cannot acquire any information about $|\psi\rangle$ and (a, b), since for all σ:

$$\frac{1}{2^{2n}} \sum_{a,b\in\{0,1\}^n} X^a Z^b \sigma (X^a Z^b)^\dagger = \frac{I_{2^n}}{2^n}. \tag{7.51}$$

7.4.3 QHE Scheme for Clifford Circuit

The universal quantum gate set for quantum circuit includes Clifford gates $\{X, Z, H, S, CONT\}$ and T. The quantum circuit composed of the former is called the Clifford circuit. For any Clifford circuit C and Pauli gate Q, there is a Pauli gate Q' that satisfies $CQ = Q'C$ [32]. When $Q = X^a Z^b$, the key update functions [27, 33] are expressed in Eq. (7.52):

$$
\begin{aligned}
&X(X^a Z^b) = (X^a Z^b)X : f_X(a,b) = (a,b), \\
&Z(X^a Z^b) = (X^a Z^b)Z : f_Z(a,b) = (a,b), \\
&H(X^a Z^b) = (X^b Z^a)H : f_H(a,b) = (b,a), \\
&S(X^a Z^b) = (X^a Z^{a\oplus b})S : f_S(a,b) = (a, a\oplus b), \\
&CNOT(X^{a_1} Z^{b_1} \otimes X^{a_2} Z^{b_2}) \\
&= (X^{a_1} Z^{b_1\oplus b_2} \otimes X^{a_1\oplus a_2} Z^{b_2})CNOT \\
&: f_{CNOT}(a_1, b_1, a_2, b_2) = (a_1, b_1 \oplus b_2, a_1 \oplus a_2, b_2).
\end{aligned}
\tag{7.52}
$$

The QHE scheme for Clifford circuit performs $X^a Z^b$ to encrypt the plaintext quantum state $|\psi\rangle$. In the evaluation algorithm, the Clifford circuit C is applied to the ciphertext quantum state $X^a Z^b|\psi\rangle$, and the evaluation result is $CX^a Z^b|\psi\rangle = X^{a'} Z^{b'} C|\psi\rangle$. In the decryption algorithm, the key (a, b) is updated to (a', b') according to the key update function (7.52), and then $Z^{b'} X^{a'}$is used for QOTP decryption to obtain the correct output $C|\psi\rangle$.

7.4.4 Symmetric QHE Scheme Based on Rotation Operator

The rotation operator R_z and R_y are defined as follows:

$$
R_z(\theta) = e^{-i\theta Z/2} = \begin{bmatrix} e^{-i\theta/2} & 0 \\ 0 & e^{i\theta/2} \end{bmatrix},
$$

$$
R_y(\theta) = e^{-i\theta Y/2} = \begin{bmatrix} \cos\frac{\theta}{2} & -\sin\frac{\theta}{2} \\ \sin\frac{\theta}{2} & \cos\frac{\theta}{2} \end{bmatrix},
$$

and have

$$
R_z((-1)^a\theta)X^a Z^b = X^a Z^b R_z(\theta), \tag{7.53}
$$

$$
R_y((-1)^{a+b}\theta)X^a Z^b = X^a Z^b R_y(\theta). \tag{7.54}
$$

Any single qubit gate can be decomposed into the product of the rotation operator R_Z and R_y [34].

Theorem 7.13 *If U is an unitary operator that works on a single qubit, there exists real number α, β, γ and δ so that*

$$
U = e^{i\alpha} R_z(\beta) R_y(\gamma) R_z(\delta) \triangleq U(\alpha, \beta, \gamma, \delta).
$$

Proof According to Eqs. (7.53), and (7.54) and Theorem 7.13, we have

$$\begin{aligned}
&X^a Z^b U(\alpha, \beta, \gamma, \delta) \\
=&e^{i\alpha} X^a Z^b R_z(\beta) R_y(\gamma) R_z(\delta) \\
=&e^{i\alpha} R_z((-1)^a \beta) X^a Z^b R_y(\gamma) R_z(\delta) \\
=&e^{i\alpha} R_z((-1)^a \beta) R_y((-1)^{a+b}\gamma) X^a Z^b R_z(\delta) \\
=&e^{i\alpha} R_z((-1)^a \beta) R_y((-1)^{a+b}\gamma) R_z((-1)^a \delta) X^a Z^b \\
=&U\left(\alpha, (-1)^a \beta, (-1)^{a+b}\gamma, (-1)^a \delta\right) X^a Z^b.
\end{aligned} \tag{7.55}$$

Based on Eq. (7.55), Liang [8] proposed a symmetric QHE scheme for single qubit circuit. The scheme requires sharing the key (a, b) between Client and Server in advance. In the encryption algorithm, Client uses QOTP encryption to encrypt the single qubit and obtains the ciphertext quantum state $X^a Z^b|\psi\rangle$. In the evaluation algorithm, Sever replaces the single qubit gate $U(\alpha, \beta, \gamma, \delta)$ with $U(\alpha, (-1)^a\beta, (-1)^{a+b}\gamma, (-1)^a\delta)$. According to Eq. (7.55), the evaluation result is $X^a Z^b U(\alpha, \beta, \gamma, \delta)|\psi\rangle$. Thus the desired result can be obtained by means of acting $Z^b X^a$.

7.4.5 Non-interactive QHE Scheme Based on Rotation Operator

7.4.5.1 A. Quantum Gate Replacement

To extend Clifford circuits to universal quantum circuits, it is necessary to add a non-Clifford gate, such as T gate. If we apply T gate on the encrypted quantum state, the output cannot be corrected by means of applying Pauli corrections conditioned on key a, since

$$T X^a Z^b = X^a Z^{a \oplus b} S^a T. \tag{7.56}$$

Based on rotation operator, Liang [8] constructed a symmetric QHE scheme for any single-qubit gate, and the decryption complexity is independent of the evaluated circuit. Inspired by Ref. [8], we can achieve QHE for T gate based on rotation operator and transform the symmetric QHE scheme into a non-interactive QHE scheme: Client firstly replaces the T gate of the quantum circuit according to the replacement rule (7.55) in the encryption algorithm, and then Sever applies the replaced quantum circuit on the ciphertext quantum state in the evaluation algorithm. This can achieve QHE for any quantum circuit and avoid interaction between Client and Server. However, directly replacing the T gate will leak the key.

Lemma 7.3 *If the quantum circuit only contains Clifford gate and T gate, then replacing the T gate according to the key (a, b) and the replacement rule (7.55) will leak the key information a.*

Proof According to Theorem 7.13, the T-gate can be decomposed to $T = U(\pi/8, \beta, 0, \delta)$, where $\beta + \delta = \pi/4$. According to the key (a, b) and the replacement rule (7.55), the T gate is replaced with $T' = U(\pi/8, (-1)^a\beta, 0, (-1)^a\delta)$. Similarly, T' can be decomposed to $T' = U(\alpha', \beta', \gamma', \delta')$. Since only T gate is replaced in the quantum circuit, we can obtain that $\beta' + \delta' = (-1)^a\beta + (-1)^a\delta = (-1)^a(\beta + \delta) = (-1)^a\pi/4$. If $\beta' + \delta' = \pi/4$, then $a = 0$. If $\beta' + \delta' = -\pi/4$, then $a = 1$. Thus, Server can obtain the key a by comparing the quantum gates before and after replacement.

The reason why the key is leaked is that only T gate is replaced in the quantum circuit. So it is necessary to ensure that Server cannot distinguish what the the replaced gate is. Note that

$$T = \begin{bmatrix} 1 & 0 \\ 0 & e^{i\pi/4} \end{bmatrix} = e^{i\pi/8} \begin{bmatrix} e^{-i\pi/8} & 0 \\ 0 & e^{i\pi/8} \end{bmatrix} = e^{i\pi/8} R_z(\pi/4). \tag{7.57}$$

Since the global phase $e^{i\pi/8}$ is not measurable, it will not affect the measurement result that replacing the T gate with $R_z(\pi/4)$. Similarly, $R_z(-\pi/4)$ can be replaced by the $T^\dagger$ gate.

Suppose the quantum circuit consist of Clifford gate, T gate, and $T^\dagger$ gate. In the encryption algorithm, T gate and $T^\dagger$ gate are replaced by $R_Z(\pi/4)$ and $R_Z(-\pi/4)$ according to the replacement rule (7.58).

$$\begin{aligned} T &\rightarrow R_z((-1)^a\pi/4) \\ T^\dagger &\rightarrow R_z((-1)^a - \pi/4). \end{aligned} \tag{7.58}$$

Lemma 7.4 *If the quantum circuit consists of Clifford gate, T gate, and $T^\dagger$ gate, replacing the T gate and $T^\dagger$ gate according to the key (a, b) and the replacement rule (7.58) does not leak the key.*

Proof According to the replacement rule (7.58), the T gate and $T^\dagger$ gate are replaced with $R_z((-1)^a\pi/4)$ and $R_z((-1)^a - \pi/4)$, respectively. Because $a \in \{0, 1\}$, the replaced gate set is $S_{Gate} = \{R_z(\pi/4), R_z(-\pi/4)\}$. Since randomness of the key, Server cannot infer the original quantum gate from the replaced quantum gate. Thus the key a cannot be obtained by comparing the gates before and after the replacement.

7.4.5.2 B. Scheme

Here, we introduce a non-interactive QHE scheme based on rotation operator. In the encryption algorithm, Client firstly encrypts the plaintext quantum state by QOTP encryption and then updates the key (a_0, b_0) and replaces the $T/T^\dagger$ gate. In the evaluation algorithm, Server applies the replaced quantum circuit on the ciphertext quantum state. There is no interaction between Client and Server. In the decryption algorithm, Client performs QOTP decryption with the updated final key.

Assuming the quantum circuit C_q works on n qubit and consists of Clifford gates and M $T/T^\dagger$ gates, denoted as $g_1, g_2, \ldots, g_N$ in order from left to right. The key is $sk = (a_0, b_0), a_0, b_0 \in \{0, 1\}^n$, where the i-th plaintext qubit is encrypted with the key $(a_0(i), b_0(i))$. In the encryption algorithm, we can update the key according to the key update rule (7.52) and (7.53), use $(a_j, b_j)(1 \leq j \leq N)$ for the updated key after executing the j-th quantum gate, where the final key $(a_{final}, b_{final}) = (a_N, b_N)$ is used for decryption.

The QHE scheme is described as follows.

1. ***Key generation***: Randomly generate an encryption key $sk = (a_0, b_0), a_0, b_0 \in \{0, 1\}^n$.
2. ***Encryption***:
   a. Use QOTP encryption with the key $sk = (a_0, b_0)$, and encrypt the plaintext quantum state $|\psi\rangle$ to obtain the encryption result $X^{a_0} Z^{b_0} |\psi\rangle$.
   b. Perform $N - M$ key updates and M quantum gate replacements to obtain the final key (a_{final}, b_{final}) and the replaced quantum circuit C'_q.

   - For $g_j \notin \{T, T^\dagger\}$, update the key by Eq. (7.52):

   $$(a_j, b_j) = f_{g_j}(a_{j-1}, b_{j-1}).$$

   - For $g_j \in \{T, T^\dagger\}$, replace the quantum gate by Eq. (7.58):

   $$T \rightarrow R_z((-1)^{a_{j-1}} \pi/4)$$
   $$T^\dagger \rightarrow R_z((-1)^{a_{j-1}} - \pi/4).$$

   According to Eq. (7.53), the key remains unchanged:

   $$(a_j, b_j) = (a_{j-1}, b_{j-1}).$$

3. ***Evaluation***: Perform the quantum circuit C'_q on the encrypted quantum state $X^{a_0} Z^{b_0} |\psi\rangle$ and obtain the evaluation result $C'_q X^{a_0} Z^{b_0} |\psi\rangle$.
4. ***Decryption***: Use QOTP decryption with the key $Z^{b_{final}} X^{a_{final}}$, and decrypt the evaluation result to obtain the plaintext result $C_q |\psi\rangle$.

The process of the scheme can be shown in Fig. 7.9, where Client and Server are separated with dashed line. Before performing the homomorphic evaluation, Client transfers the ciphertext quantum state $X^{a_0} Z^{b_0} |\psi\rangle$ and the replaced quantum circuit C'_q to Server. After completing the homomorphic evaluation, Server transfers the evaluation result to Client. In the evaluation algorithm, there is no interaction between Client and Server.

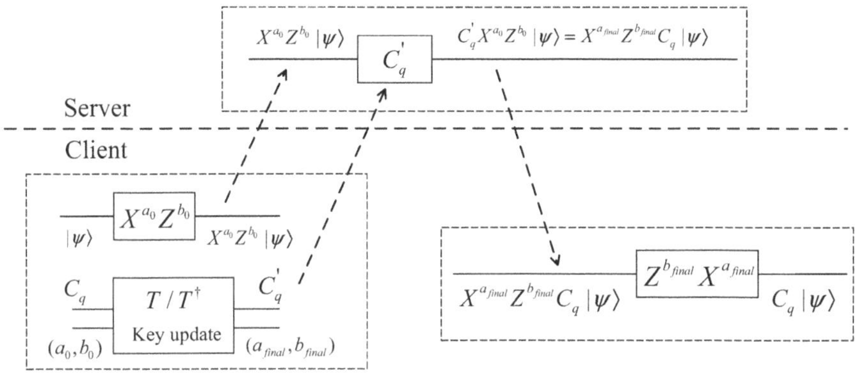

Fig. 7.9 QHE scheme based on rotation operator.

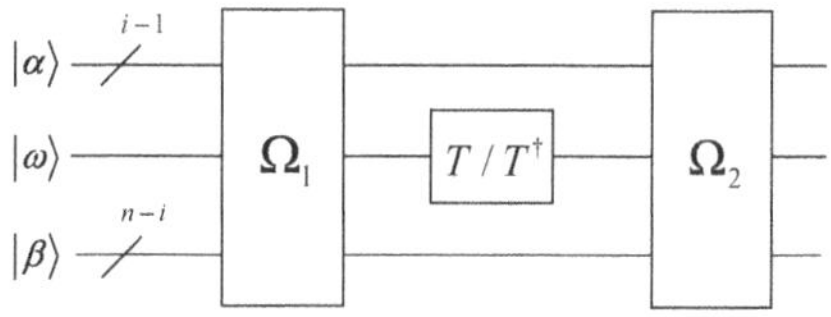

Fig. 7.10 Quantum circuit C_q containing at least one gate $T/T^\dagger$ gate

7.4.5.3 C. Correctness

We prove the correctness of the scheme and the detail is described in Theorem 7.14.

Theorem 7.14 *Let $\mathcal{F}$ be the class of all quantum circuits. The scheme is $\mathcal{F}$-homomorphic, i.e., homomorphic for any quantum circuit.*

Proof Any quantum circuit can be composed of Clifford gates, T gate, and $T^\dagger$ gate. Without losing generality, consider a quantum circuit C_q containing at least one $T/T^\dagger$gate, as shown in Fig. 7.10. Suppose the first non-Clifford gate is the j-th quantum gate, i.e., $g_j = T$, and works on the i-th qubit. Circuit Ω_1 only contains Clifford gates and Ω_2 consists of Clifford gates, T gate, and $T^\dagger$ gate.

We use QOTP encryption to encrypt the plaintext quantum state $|\psi\rangle = |\alpha\rangle \otimes |\omega\rangle \otimes |\beta\rangle$ and obtain the ciphertext quantum state $X^{a_0}Z^{b_0}|\psi\rangle$. After updating the Clifford circuit Ω_1, the key is (a_{j-1}, b_{j-1}). When updating the first T gate, first replace the T gate with $R_z((-1)^{a_{j-1}(i)}\pi/4)$ and then update the key $(a_j, b_j) = (a_{j-1}, b_{j-1})$. The replaced circuit C_q^{mid} is $\Omega_2(I_{i-1} \otimes R_z((-1)^{a_{j-1}(i)}\pi/4) \otimes I_{n-i})\Omega_1$. When applying C_q^{mid} on the ciphertext quantum state, we have

$$
\begin{aligned}
& C_q^{mid} X^{a_0} Z^{b_0} |\psi\rangle \\
=& \Omega_2 \left(I_{i-1} \otimes R_z((-1)^{a_{j-1}(i)}\pi/4) \otimes I_{n-i}\right) \Omega_1 \left(X^{\otimes_{k=1}^{i-1} a_0(k)} Z^{\otimes_{k=1}^{i-1} b_0(k)}\right. \\
& \left.\otimes X^{a_0(i)} Z^{b_0(i)} \otimes X^{\otimes_{k=i+1}^{n} a_0(k)} Z^{\otimes_{k=i+1}^{n} b_0(k)}\right) \left(|\alpha\rangle \otimes |\omega\rangle \otimes |\beta\rangle\right) \\
=& \Omega_2 \left(I_{i-1} \otimes R_z((-1)^{a_{j-1}(i)}\pi/4) \otimes I_{n-i}\right) \left(X^{\otimes_{k=1}^{i-1} a_{j-1}(k)} Z^{\otimes_{k=1}^{i-1} b_{j-1}(k)}\right. \\
& \left.\otimes X^{a_{j-1}(i)} Z^{b_{j-1}(i)} \otimes X^{\otimes_{k=i+1}^{n} a_{j-1}(k)} Z^{\otimes_{k=i+1}^{n} b_{j-1}(k)}\right) \Omega_1 \left(|\alpha\rangle \otimes |\omega\rangle \otimes |\beta\rangle\right) \\
=& \Omega_2 \left(X^{\otimes_{k=1}^{i-1} a_{j-1}(k)} Z^{\otimes_{k=1}^{i-1} b_{j-1}(k)} \otimes R_z((-1)^{a_{j-1}(i)}\pi/4) X^{a_{j-1}(i)} Z^{b_{j-1}(i)}\right. \\
& \left.\otimes X^{\otimes_{k=i+1}^{n} a_{j-1}(k)} Z^{\otimes_{k=i+1}^{n} b_{j-1}(k)}\right) \Omega_1 \left(|\alpha\rangle \otimes |\omega\rangle \otimes |\beta\rangle\right) \\
=& \Omega_2 \left(X^{\otimes_{k=1}^{i-1} a_{j-1}(k)} Z^{\otimes_{k=1}^{i-1} b_{j-1}(k)} \otimes X^{a_{j-1}(i)} Z^{b_{j-1}(i)} R_z(\pi/4)\right. \\
& \left.\otimes X^{\otimes_{k=i+1}^{n} a_{j-1}(k)} Z^{\otimes_{k=i+1}^{n} b_{j-1}(k)}\right) \Omega_1 \left(|\alpha\rangle \otimes |\omega\rangle \otimes |\beta\rangle\right) \\
=& \Omega_2 \left(X^{\otimes_{k=1}^{i-1} a_j(k)} Z^{\otimes_{k=1}^{i-1} b_j(k)} \otimes X^{a_j(i)} Z^{b_j(i)} \otimes X^{\otimes_{k=i+1}^{n} a_j(k)} Z^{\otimes_{k=i+1}^{n} b_j(k)}\right) \\
& \left(I_{i-1} \otimes R_z(\pi/4) \otimes I_{n-i}\right) \Omega_1 \left(|\alpha\rangle \otimes |\omega\rangle \otimes |\beta\rangle\right) \\
=& \Omega_2 X^{a_j} Z^{b_j} \left(I_{i-1} \otimes R_z(\pi/4) \otimes I_{n-i}\right) \Omega_1 \left(|\alpha\rangle \otimes |\omega\rangle \otimes |\beta\rangle\right).
\end{aligned}
\tag{7.59}
$$

Similarly, QHE for the quantum circuit Ω_2 can be completed. In the evaluation algorithm, the result after applying C_q' on the ciphertext quantum state $X^a Z^b |\psi\rangle$ is $C_q' X^a Z^b |\psi\rangle = X^{a_{final}} Z^{b_{final}} C_q |\psi\rangle$. Thus Client can obtain the desired plaintext result $C_q |\psi\rangle$ by means of applying $Z^{b_{final}} X^{a_{final}}$ in the decryption algorithm.

7.4.6 Security Analysis

We prove the security of the scheme and the detail is described in Theorem 7.15.

Theorem 7.15 *The QHE scheme is information-theoretically secure.*

Proof According to Eq. (7.51), the plaintext quantum state $|\psi\rangle$ is encrypted to the completely mixed state by QOTP. Therefore, Server cannot obtain any information about the input $|\psi\rangle$ and the key $sk = (a_0, b_0)$. According to Lemma 7.4, replacing the $T/T^\dagger$ gate does not leak the key. So Server cannot obtain the middle key (a_{j-1}, b_{j-1}), where $g_j \in \{T, T^\dagger\}$. Without the key (a_0, b_0) and (a_{j-1}, b_{j-1}), Server cannot calculate the final key (a_{final}, b_{final}) by the update function to correctly decrypt the evaluation result $X^{a_{final}} Z^{b_{final}} C_q |\psi\rangle$. QOTP depends on the unique physical mechanism rather than any computational assumptions of hard mathematical problems. Thus, the scheme is information-theoretically secure.

Since the $T/T^\dagger$ gate is replaced in the encryption algorithm, the evaluated circuit is C_q' rather than C_q. The compactness requires that the decryption circuit does not depend on the quantum circuit C_q which actually works on the plaintext quantum state$|\psi\rangle$. C_q' is obtained by C_q through the key update and quantum gate replacement,

Table 7.3 Comparison of non-interactive QHE schemes

QHE schemes	Information-theoretic security	$\mathcal{F}$-homomorphism	Compactness	Decryption complexity	Encryption complexity
Broadbent et al. [12]	No	Yes	Yes	$O(1)$	$O(1)$
Lai et al. [29]	Yes	No	Yes	$O(1)$	$O(1)$
Liang [30]	Yes	Yes	No	$O(M)$	$O(1)$
Our scheme	Yes	Yes	No	$O(1)$	$O(N)$

of which complexity is $O(N)$. Thus, the scheme is not compact, which is consistent with the no-go result [14, 28, 29]. The comparison with other non-interactive QHE schemes [12, 29, 30] is listed in Table 7.3.

7.5 Two-Round Quantum Homomorphic Encryption Based on Matrix Decomposition

7.5.1 Limitation of Decryption Efficiency

The homomorphism makes QHE have important theoretical value, which can be applied to quantum delegated computing [27], quantum multi-party computation [35, 36], quantum identity authentication [37] and quantum ciphertext retrieval [13, 38, 39]. Sun et al. [13] first proposed a symmetrically searchable encryption scheme based on QHE. Aiming at the disadvantage of low efficiency of linear search in this scheme, Zhou et al. [38] combined an interactive QHE scheme with Grover algorithm to propose a ciphertext retrieval scheme, in which the Grover algorithm [40] can greatly accelerate the speed of search. By introducing the non-interactive QHE scheme in Ref. [30] to avoid interaction, Gong *et al.* [39] improved the retrieval scheme and completed a two-qubit ciphertext retrieval experiment on IBM quantum simulator and real quantum computer, respectively. But the decryption efficiency of the improved scheme is still limited by the used QHE scheme.

In this section, we introduce a two-round QHE based on matrix decomposition [41]. By decomposing S gate into the linear combination of the unitary matrix I and Z, decryption matrix for any evaluated circuit can be obtained non-interactively. To achieve decryption, we use circuit synthesis to decompose the decryption matrix into a corresponding quantum circuit. Then, we construct a ciphertext retrieval scheme by combining the QHE scheme with the Grover algorithm.

7.5.2 Quantum Computation and Circuit Synthesis

Quantum operations include the Hadamard operation H, the phase shift operations $S, T = \sqrt{S}$ and $Z = S^2$, as well as the NOT operation X which flips the basis states $|0\rangle$ and $|1\rangle$. The corresponding unitary matrices are defined as

$$H = \frac{1}{\sqrt{2}}\begin{bmatrix}1 & 1\\ 1 & -1\end{bmatrix}, S = \begin{bmatrix}1 & 0\\ 0 & i\end{bmatrix}, T = \begin{bmatrix}1 & 0\\ 0 & e^{i\pi/4}\end{bmatrix}, Z = \begin{bmatrix}1 & 0\\ 0 & -1\end{bmatrix}, X = \begin{bmatrix}0 & 1\\ 1 & 0\end{bmatrix}$$

Besides these operations that work on a single target qubit, there are also controlled operations on multiple qubits. The state of the additional control qubits determines which operation is performed on the target qubit. An example is the CNOT operation on two qubits, which is defined by

$$CNOT = \begin{bmatrix}1 & 0 & 0 & 0\\ 0 & 1 & 0 & 0\\ 0 & 0 & 0 & 1\\ 0 & 0 & 1 & 0\end{bmatrix}$$

and it applies the NOT operation to the target if the control is in the $|1\rangle$ state.

A Clifford circuit is generated by Clifford gates $\{H, S, X, Z, CONT\}$. If a n-qubit Clifford operation is given in matrix form, an efficient procedure exists in order to produce a circuit that executes this Clifford [42]. The synthesis method in Ref. [42] includes three steps: Eliminating superposition, Diagonalization and Eliminating phase shifts. Firstly, superposition can be eliminated by using Hadamard gates for suitable pairs of rows (i.e., for 00 and 10 or 00 and 01) and only if the rows differ by no more than signs of the entries. Once superposition has been removed, each row or column of the matrix contains only one non-zero value as illustrated in Fig. 7.11b. Diagonalization is turning a matrix into a diagonal matrix as shown in Fig. 7.11c, which can be done by applying suitable X and $CNOT$ gates. Finally, possible phase shifts are eliminated, i.e., all diagonal entries of the matrix are equalized as shown in Fig. 7.11d, which is conducted by phase gates (performing shifts by $\pm i$) and controlled Z gates (performing partial shifts by -1).

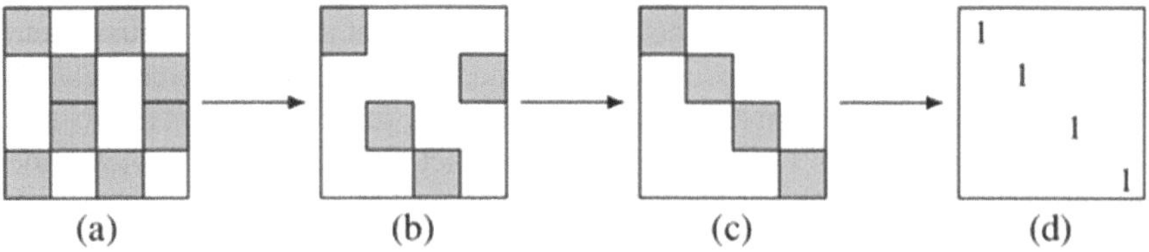

Fig. 7.11 Circuit synthesis procedure [42]

7.5.3 Key Update for T Gate Based on Matrix Decomposition

To extend Clifford circuits to universal quantum circuits, it is necessary to add a non-Clifford gate, such as T gate. If we apply T gate on the encrypted quantum state, the output cannot be corrected by means of applying Pauli corrections conditioned on key a, since

$$TX^aZ^b = X^aZ^{a\oplus b}S^aT. \tag{7.60}$$

Based on matrix decomposition, Broadbent et al. [33] proposed a new key update function to void this undesirable S-error. Note that S can be decomposed as a linear combination of the unitary matrix I and Z.

$$S = \left(\frac{1+i}{2}\right)I + \left(\frac{1-i}{2}\right)Z \tag{7.61}$$

Hence, Eq. (7.60) can be rewritten as

$$\begin{aligned} TX^aZ^b &= X^aZ^{a\oplus b}\left[\left(\frac{1+i}{2}\right)I + \left(\frac{1-i}{2}\right)Z\right]^a T \\ &= \left[\left(\frac{1+i}{2}\right)X^aZ^{a\oplus b} + \left(\frac{1-i}{2}\right)X^aZ^b\right]T \\ &= (\alpha_1 I + \alpha_2 X + \alpha_2 Z + \alpha_4 XZ)T, \end{aligned} \tag{7.62}$$

where $\alpha_j \in \left\{0, 1, \frac{1+i}{2}, \frac{1-i}{2}\right\}, j \in [4]$.

So the key update function for T gate based matrix decomposition can be defined as the mapping,

$$f_T : (a, b) \mapsto (\alpha_1, \alpha_2, \alpha_3, \alpha_4). \tag{7.63}$$

Note that for any n-qubit unitary operation U and n-qubit Pauli P, there exists a Clifford C such that $UP = CU$ [32]. It is also concluded in Ref. [33] that any n-qubit quantum circuit C_q with M T-gates satisfies

$$C_qX^aZ^b = \left(U_{F_{C_q}}\right)^\dagger C_q \tag{7.64}$$

where

$$U_{F_{C_q}} = \sum_{i=1}^{4^k} \beta_i X^{a_{i1}}Z^{b_{i1}} \otimes \cdots \otimes X^{a_{in}}Z^{b_{in}}, k = \min\{M, n\}.$$

So the update function for any n-qubit quantum circuit C_q can be defined as the mapping,

$$F_{C_q} : (a_1, b_1, \ldots a_n, b_n) \mapsto ((\beta_1, s_1), \ldots, (\beta_{4^k}, s_{4^k})) \tag{7.65}$$

where (a_j, b_j) is the key for the i-th qubit and $\beta_i \in \mathbb{C}$, $s_i = a_{i_1}b_{i_1}, \ldots a_{i_n}b_{i_n} \in \{0,1\}^{2n}$, $i \in [4^k]$.

7.5.4 QHE Scheme Based on Matrix Decomposition

In this section, we use matrix decomposition to obtain the key update function and achieve homomorphic evaluation for any quantum circuit with any number of T gates. Additionally, an extra round of QHE is used to perform the decryption circuit, which greatly reduces the decryption complexity.

7.5.4.1 A. Scheme

QOTP encryption is used as the encryption algorithm in the two rounds of QHE. In the first round of evaluation algorithm, Server applies the quantum circuit C_q on the ciphertext quantum state, and calculates the key update function F_{C_q} for C_q based on matrix decomposition. Then, Client computes the decryption matrix according to the key update function F_{C_q}, and uses the circuit synthesis method to construct the corresponding Clifford circuit. Instead of executing the decryption circuit by myself, Client uses the second round of QHE to complete the decryption and obtains eventually the desired plaintext result.

The QHE scheme for any quantum circuit C_q includes two rounds. Each round can be described as four algorithms: $Keygeneration$, $Encryption$, $Evaluation$, and $Decryption$. Note that the first round decryption is replaced by circuit synthesis and the second round can be seen as a part of the first round decryption. Thus the scheme conforms to the paradigm of QHE scheme though containing two rounds of the encryption, evaluation and decryption. The scheme is described as follows.

1. ***Key generation***: client randomly generates two $2n$-bit secret keys $ek_1 = (a_1, b_1)$ and $ek_2 = (a_2, b_2)$, $a_1, b_1, a_2, b_2 \in \{0,1\}^n$, where n is the qubit number of the plaintext quantum state $|\psi\rangle$.
2. ***First round encryption***: client uses QOTP encryption with the key $ek_1 = (a_1, b_1)$, and encrypts the plaintext quantum state $|\psi\rangle$ to obtain the encryption result $X^{a_1}Z^{b_1}|\psi\rangle$.
3. ***First round evaluation***: server performs the quantum circuit C_q on the encrypted quantum state, and calculates the corresponding key update function based on matrix decomposition.

$$F_{C_q} : (a_{11}, b_{11}, \ldots, a_{1n}, b_{1n}) \mapsto ((\beta_1, s_1), \ldots, (\beta_{4^k}, s_{4^k})).$$

4. ***Circuit synthesis***: according to the key update function F_{C_q} and the first encryption key ek_1, Client calculates the decryption key

$$dk_1 = F_{C_q}(a_{11}, b_{11}, \ldots, a_{1n}, b_{1n}) = ((\beta_1, s_1), \ldots, (\beta_{4^k}, s_{4^k})).$$

The decryption matrix is

$$U_{F_{C_q}} = \sum_{i=1}^{4^k} \beta_i X^{a_{i1}} Z^{b_{i1}} \otimes \cdots \otimes X^{a_{in}} Z^{b_{in}}.$$

Client computes a Clifford circuit C that applies $U_{F_{C_q}}$ by means of the circuit synthesis method [42].

5. ***Second round encryption***: client uses QOTP encryption with the key $ek_2 = (a_2, b_2)$, and encrypts the first round of evaluation result $C_q X^{a_1} Z^{b_1} |\psi\rangle$ to obtain the encryption result $X^{a_2} Z^{b_2} C_q X^{a_1} Z^{b_1} |\psi\rangle$.
6. ***Second round evaluation***: server performs the Clifford circuit C on the encrypted evaluation result, and calculate the corresponding key update function based on the update function for Clifford gates.

$$F_C : (a_2, b_2) \mapsto (a_{final}, b_{final}).$$

7. ***Decryption***: according to the key update function F_C and the second encryption key ek_2, Client calculates the decryption key $dk_2 = (a_{final}, b_{final})$. Then, Client performs QOTP decryption on the second round of evaluation result to obtain the desired plaintext result $C_q|\psi\rangle$.

The two-round QHE scheme is shown in Fig. 7.12, where Client and Server are divided by dashed line. Client performs two rounds of encryption and decryption (circuit synthesis), and Server performs two rounds of homomorphic evaluation. Obviously, there is no interaction between Client and Server during the two rounds of evaluation.

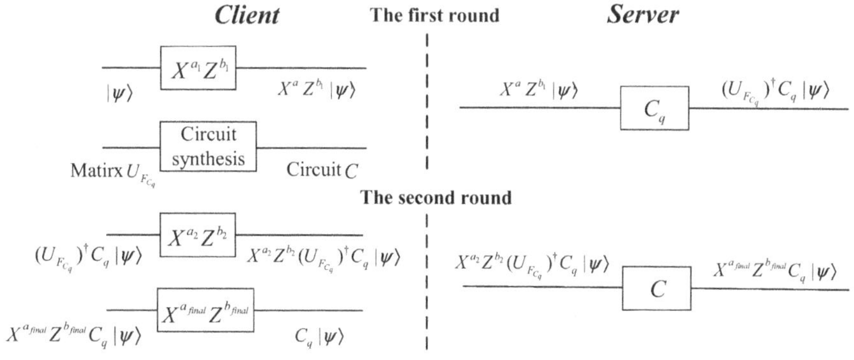

Fig. 7.12 Two-round QHE scheme

7.5.4.2 B. Correctness

Theorem 7.16 *Let $\mathcal{F}$ be the class of all quantum circuits. The QHE scheme is $\mathcal{F}$-homomorphic, i.e., homomorphic for any quantum circuit.*

Proof According to Eq. (7.52), the homomorphic evaluation result for Clifford circuit C has

$$CX^{a_2}Z^{b_2}C_qX^{a_1}Z^{b_1}|\psi\rangle = X^{a_{final}}Z^{b_{final}}CC_qX^{a_1}Z^{b_1}|\psi\rangle. \tag{7.66}$$

According to Eq. (7.64), the evaluation result for any n-qubit quantum circuit C_q has

$$C_qX^{a_1}Z^{b_1}|\psi\rangle = \left(U_{F_{C_q}}\right)^{\dagger} C_q|\psi\rangle. \tag{7.67}$$

Through the circuit synthesis method [33], Client can obtain the decryption circuit C that applies $U_{F_{C_q}}$. Hence,

$$\begin{aligned} &CX^{a_2}Z^{b_2}C_qX^{a_1}Z^{b_1}|\psi\rangle \\ &= X^{a_{final}}Z^{b_{final}}U_{F_{C_q}}\left(U_{F_{C_q}}\right)^{\dagger} C_q|\psi\rangle \\ &= X^{a_{final}}Z^{b_{final}}C_q|\psi\rangle. \end{aligned} \tag{7.68}$$

As long as the QOTP decryption is applied on the second round of evaluation result, Client can finally obtain the decryption result $C_q|\psi\rangle$, which is same as the result of directly applying the quantum circuit C_q on the plaintext quantum state $|\psi\rangle$.

7.5.4.3 C. Compactness

Theorem 7.17 *The QHE scheme is compact. That is, the decryption complexity of the scheme does not depend on the evaluated circuit.*

Proof It is sufficient to prove that the complexity of the circuit synthesis and the decryption in the scheme does not depend on the evaluated circuit.

In the first round of QHE, Client needs to use the circuit synthesis method to construct the decryption circuit. For any n-qubit quantum circuit C_q with M T gates, the decryption matrix is

$$U_{F_{C_q}} = \sum_{i=1}^{4^k} \beta_i X^{a_{i1}}Z^{b_{i1}} \otimes \cdots \otimes X^{a_{in}}Z^{b_{in}}.$$

Since $k = min(M, n) \leq n$, the complexity of the circuit synthesis does not depend on the evaluated circuit C_q.

In the second round of QHE, the evaluated circuit C is a Clifford circuit and the decryption circuit that applies $X^{a_{final}} Z^{b_{final}}$ is consist of $2n$ Pauli gates. Thus, the QOTP decryption also does not depend on the the evaluated circuit C.

7.5.5 Security Analysis

Theorem 7.18 *The QHE scheme is information-theoretically secure.*

Proof The security of the scheme is guaranteed by the security of QOTP. Specifically for the first round of QHE, the plaintext quantum state $|\psi\rangle$ is encrypted to the completely mixed state by QOTP. Therefore, Server cannot obtain any information on the input $|\psi\rangle$ and the first round encryption key $ek_1 = (a_1, b_1)$. Furthermore, Server cannot update to obtain the correct decryption key without the encryption key, therefore leading to incorrect decryption result. Similarly, the evaluation result $X^{a_{final}} Z^{b_{final}} C_q |\psi\rangle$ is protected by QOTP in the second round of QHE.

It is worth emphasizing that the encrypted quantum state $X^{a_1} Z^{b_1} |\psi\rangle$ is unknown to Server. According to the no-cloning theorem, Server cannot copy the exactly same ciphertext quantum state to obtain the same evaluation result $\left(U_{F_{C_q}}\right)^{\dagger} C_q |\psi\rangle$. Thus, even if the decryption circuit C is available in the second round of QHE, Server cannot complete the decryption to obtain the plaintext result $C_q |\psi\rangle$.

QOTP depends on the unique physical mechanism rather than any computational assumptions of hard mathematical problems. Thus, the scheme is information-theoretically secure.

7.5.6 Scheme Comparison

The scheme has the following properties: $\mathcal{F}$-homomorphism, information-theoretic security and compactness. The comparison with other non-interactive QHE schemes [12, 29, 30] is listed in Table 7.4. Note that the scheme has more rounds of QHE than others. Through the extra round of evaluation to make Server perform the decryption circuit C, the decryption overhead for Client is reduced. Compared to the other one-round QHE schemes, the scheme can achieve both decryption efficiency and security.

Table 7.4 Comparison of non-interactive QHE schemes

QHE scheme	$\mathcal{F}$-homomorphism	Information-theoretic security	Compactness	Number of rounds
Broadbent et al. [12]	Yes	No	Yes	1
Lai et al. [29]	No	Yes	Yes	1
Liang [30]	Yes	Yes	No	1
Our scheme	Yes	Yes	Yes	2

7.5.7 Application to Ciphertext Retrieval

In this section, we introduce a ciphertext retrieval scheme based on the two-round QHE scheme. In addition, we complete a three-qubit ciphertext retrieval experiment on IBM Qiskit simulator to verify the correctness of the QHE scheme.

7.5.7.1 A. Ciphertext Retrieval Scheme

Assume Alice delegates Bob to find the solution of a search problem and make sure that the specific solution is not accessible to Bob. Alice encrypts the plaintext superposition state and sends the ciphertext superposition state to Bob. Then, Bob applies the Grover search algorithm on the ciphertext superposition state and calculates the key update function. Next, Alice updates the encryption key according to the key update function, and uses the circuit synthesis method to construct the decryption circuit. Finally, Alice uses an extra round of QHE to complete the decryption and obtain the final retrieval result.

Based on the QHE scheme, the ciphertext retrieval scheme is described as follows. We assume that the retrieval space is $N = 2^n$. Thus, Alice only needs to prepare n qubits to store the data.

1. ***Plain superposition data***: Alice prepares a plain superposition state $|\psi\rangle = \frac{1}{\sqrt{N}} \sum_{j=0}^{N} |j\rangle$ by acting the Hadamard gate on the all-zero quantum state.
2. ***Key generation***: Alice randomly generates two $2n$-bit secret keys $ek_1 = (a_1, b_1)$ and $ek_2 = (a_2, b_2)$, $a_1, b_1, a_2, b_2 \in \{0, 1\}^n$.
3. ***Encryption***: Alice uses QOTP encryption with the key $ek_1 = (a_1, b_1)$, and encrypts the plaintext superposition state $|\psi\rangle$ to obtain the encryption result $X^{a_1} Z^{b_1} |\psi\rangle$.
4. ***Search***: Bob executes the Grover search algorithm on the ciphertext superposition state and calculates the corresponding key update function.
5. ***Circuit synthesis***: Alice updates the encryption key according to the key update function, and constructs the decryption circuit by means of the circuit synthesis method [42].

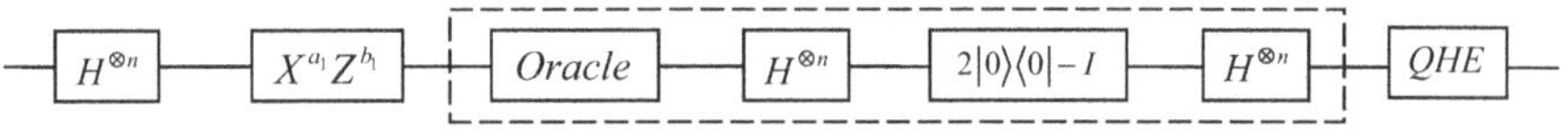

Fig. 7.13 Ciphertext retrieval procedure

Table 7.5 Comparison among ciphertext retrieval schemes

Scheme	$\mathcal{F}$-homomorphism	Search method	Decryption complexity	Interaction
Sun et al. [13]	No	Linear search	$O(1)$	No
Zhou et al. [38]	Yes	Grover search	$O(1)$	Yes
Gong et al. [39]	Yes	Grover search	$O(M)$	No
Our scheme	Yes	Grover search	$O(1)$	No

6. ***Decryption***: With the key $ek_2 = (a_2, b_2)$, Alice uses an extra round of QHE to complete the decryption and obtains the final retrieval result.

The ciphertext retrieval procedure is shown in Fig. 7.13. The first two steps generate the ciphertext superposition state. Then, Grover search algorithm surrounded by dotted box is iterated to expand the amplitude of the solution. Finally, Alice uses the second round of QHE to complete the decryption and obtains the final retrieval result.

7.5.7.2 B. Scheme Comparison

The ciphertext retrieval scheme is based on the two-round QHE scheme and the difference is that the universal quantum circuit C_q is replaced with the specific Grover circuit. Thus, the scheme also has the following properties: $\mathcal{F}$-homomorphism, information-theoretic security and compactness.

The comparison with other ciphertext retrieval schemes [13, 38, 39] is listed in Table 7.5. Combined with the Grover algorithm and non-interactive QHE, the retrieval speed is improved and the communication cost is reduced. Note that the scheme is more efficient than the scheme proposed in Ref. [39] when the evaluated circuit contains M non-Clifford gates.

7.5.7.3 C. Simulation Analysis

Based on the ciphertext retrieval scheme, we complete a three-qubit ciphertext retrieval experiment. All experiments are based on IBM Qiskit, which is an open source framework for quantum computation.

The plaintext retrieval quantum circuit for $|101\rangle$ and $|110\rangle$ from the superposition state $\frac{1}{\sqrt{8}}\sum_{j=0}^{8}|j\rangle$ is depicted in Fig. 7.14. We execute the circuit 1000 times and

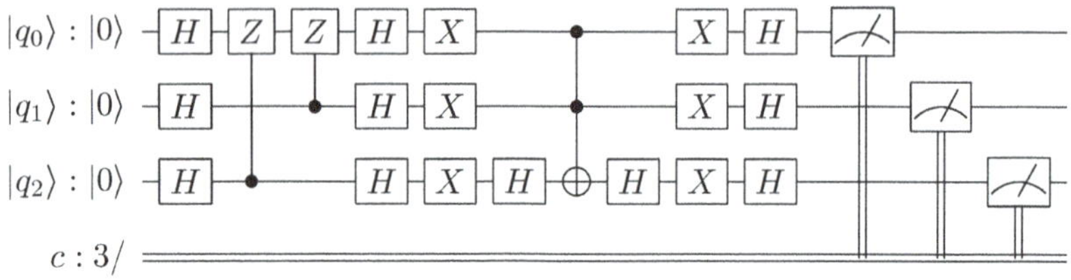

Fig. 7.14 Unencrypted search circuit for $|101\rangle$ and $|110\rangle$

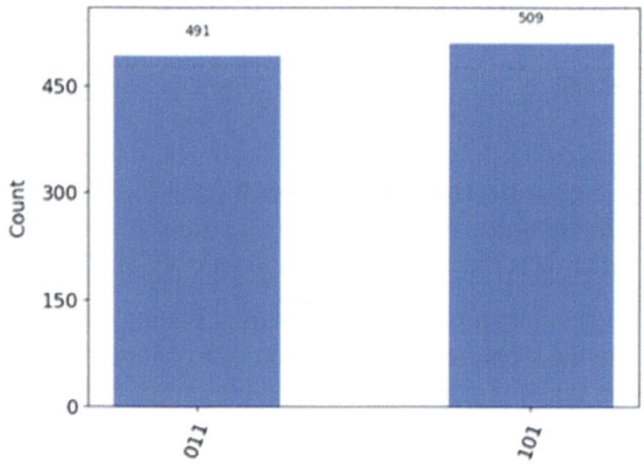

Fig. 7.15 Search result without encryption

the experimental result on Qiskit is shown in Fig. 7.15, where the horizontal axis represents the measurement result and the vertical axis represents the count. Since the rightmost qubit on IBM Qiskit represents the first qubit instead, the probability of measuring $|110\rangle$ and $|101\rangle$ is 50 percent, respectively.

We take the first round encryption key $ek_1 = (a_1, b_1) = ((1, 1), (1, 0), (1, 0))$. Then according to the proposed scheme, the decryption matrix U for the search circuit is calculated as follows.

$$U = \begin{bmatrix} 0 & \frac{-1}{2} & \frac{-1}{2} & 0 & \frac{-1}{2} & 0 & 0 & \frac{1}{2} \\ \frac{1}{2} & 0 & 0 & \frac{1}{2} & 0 & \frac{1}{2} & \frac{-1}{2} & 0 \\ \frac{1}{2} & 0 & 0 & \frac{1}{2} & 0 & \frac{-1}{2} & \frac{1}{2} & 0 \\ 0 & \frac{-1}{2} & \frac{-1}{2} & 0 & \frac{1}{2} & 0 & 0 & \frac{-1}{2} \\ \frac{1}{2} & 0 & 0 & \frac{-1}{2} & 0 & \frac{1}{2} & \frac{1}{2} & 0 \\ 0 & \frac{-1}{2} & \frac{1}{2} & 0 & \frac{-1}{2} & 0 & 0 & \frac{-1}{2} \\ 0 & \frac{1}{2} & \frac{-1}{2} & 0 & \frac{-1}{2} & 0 & 0 & \frac{-1}{2} \\ \frac{-1}{2} & 0 & 0 & \frac{1}{2} & 0 & \frac{1}{2} & \frac{1}{2} & 0 \end{bmatrix}. \tag{7.69}$$

Next, we need to construct a quantum circuit that applies the operation U. We write U_i for the transformation matrix that represents the uncontrolled operation of

$q_0q_1q_2$	000	001	010	011	100	101	110	111
000	0	0	$\frac{-1}{\sqrt{2}}$	0	$\frac{-1}{\sqrt{2}}$	0	0	0
001	0	0	0	$\frac{-1}{\sqrt{2}}$	0	$\frac{1}{\sqrt{2}}$	0	0
010	$\frac{1}{\sqrt{2}}$	0	0	0	0	0	$\frac{1}{\sqrt{2}}$	0
011	0	$\frac{-1}{\sqrt{2}}$	0	0	0	0	0	$\frac{-1}{\sqrt{2}}$
100	0	$\frac{-1}{\sqrt{2}}$	0	0	0	0	0	$\frac{1}{\sqrt{2}}$
101	$\frac{1}{\sqrt{2}}$	0	0	0	0	0	$\frac{-1}{\sqrt{2}}$	0
110	0	0	0	$\frac{1}{\sqrt{2}}$	0	$\frac{-1}{\sqrt{2}}$	0	0
111	0	0	$\frac{-1}{\sqrt{2}}$	0	$\frac{1}{\sqrt{2}}$	0	0	0

(a)

$q_0q_1q_2$	000	001	010	011	100	101	110	111
000	0	0	−1	0	0	0	0	0
001	0	0	0	1	0	0	0	0
010	0	−1	0	0	0	0	0	0
011	1	0	0	0	0	0	0	0
100	0	0	0	0	−1	0	0	0
101	0	0	0	0	0	1	0	0
110	0	0	0	0	0	0	0	−1
111	0	0	0	0	0	0	1	0

(b)

$q_0q_1q_2$	000	001	010	011	100	101	110	111
000	1	0	0	0	0	0	0	0
001	0	−1	0	0	0	0	0	0
010	0	0	−1	0	0	0	0	0
011	0	0	0	1	0	0	0	0
100	0	0	0	0	−1	0	0	0
101	0	0	0	0	0	1	0	0
110	0	0	0	0	0	0	1	0
111	0	0	0	0	0	0	0	−1

(c)

Fig. 7.16 Resulting matrices in the synthesis procedure

an U gate applied to a target qubit. Similarly, we use U_{ij} for a controlled U gate with control qubit i and target qubit j.

In order to eliminate superposition, we need to derive a pair of rows for which a Hadamard gate can be applied. We choose rows 001 and 111 and first use a $CNOT_{q_0q_1}$ gate to move row 111 to 101. Hence, applying a Hadamard gate on qubit q_0 reduces the superposition of the matrix and leads to a matrix as shown in Fig. 7.16(a). Then, it can be seen that row 001 matches pairwise to row 101. Hence, we sequentially use a $CNOT_{q_1q_2}$ gate and a $CNOT_{q_0q_1}$ gate to move row 111 to 101 and apply a Hadamard gate on qubit q_0. Finally, all superposition is eliminated and the resulting matrix is calculated in Fig. 7.16b.

In order to achieve a diagonal structure, we need to calculate linear functions f_{q_i} for each qubit q_i and determine which gates to apply so that $f_{q_i} = q_i$. These denote that for which inputs (columns) we obtain an output $|1\rangle$ on the respective qubit. From the current matrix in Fig. 7.16b, it can be seen that

$$
\begin{aligned}
f_{q_0} &= 100 \vee 101 \vee 110 \vee 111 &&= q_0 \\
f_{q_1} &= 000 \vee 001 \vee 110 \vee 111 &&= \overline{q_0 \oplus q_1} \\
f_{q_2} &= 000 \vee 011 \vee 101 \vee 110 &&= \overline{q_0 \oplus q_1 \oplus q_2}
\end{aligned}
$$

For q_1, we need to performs the XOR operation on q_0 by means of $CNOT_{q_0q_1}$ and then apply X_{q_1} to flip the state. For q_2, $f_{q_2} = q_2$ can similarly be accomplished by applying $CNOT_{q_0q_2}$, $CNOT_{q_1q_2}$ and X_{q_2}. The diagonal matrix is calculated in Fig. 7.16(c).

To remove the phase shift, three Z gates (Z_{q_0}, Z_{q_1}, Z_{q_2}) are applied, which leads to the identity matrix. Overall, performing the respective steps as described above eventually leads to the decryption circuit C illustrated in Fig. 7.17.

We take the second round encryption key $ek_2 = (a_2, b_2) = ((0, 1), (1, 0), (1, 1))$. According to the key update function in Eq. (7.52), the key update process for C is listed in Table 7.6. X gate and Z gate are omitted in the table because they do not affect

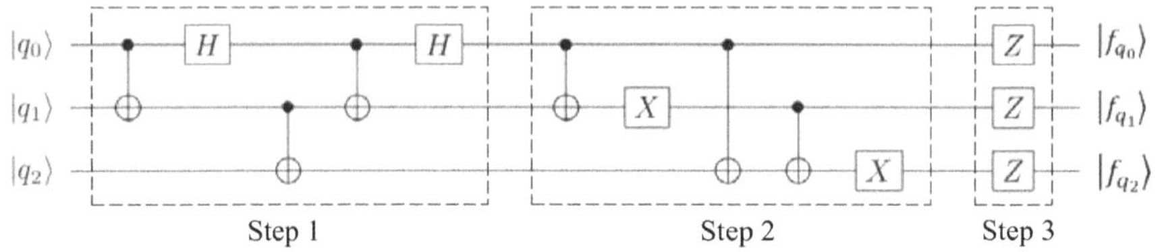

Fig. 7.17 Decryption circuit

Table 7.6 Key update process

	(a_2, b_2)	$CNOT_{q_0q_1}$	H_{q_0}	$CNOT_{q_1q_2}$	$CNOT_{q_0q_1}$	H_{q_0}	$CNOT_{q_0q_1}$	$CNOT_{q_0q_2}$	$CNOT_{q_1q_2}$
q_0	(0,1)	(0,1)	(1,0)	–	(1,1)	(1,1)	(1,0)	(1,1)	–
q_1	(1,0)	(1,0)	–	(1,1)	(0,1)	–	(1,1)	–	(1,0)
q_2	(1,1)	–	–	(0,1)	–	–	–	(1,1)	(0,1)

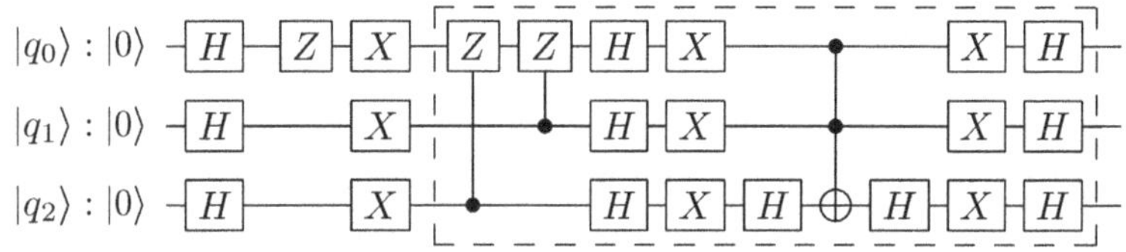

Fig. 7.18 Quantum circuit for the first round of QHE

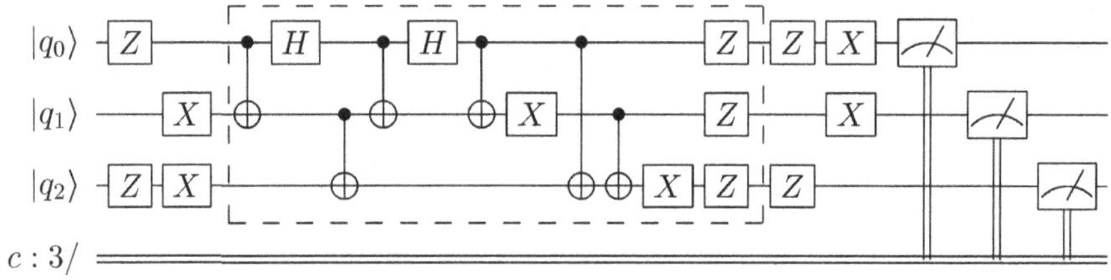

Fig. 7.19 Quantum circuit for the second round of QHE

the key update. Thus the decryption key is the final updated key $(a_{final}, b_{final}) = ((1, 1), (1, 0), (0, 1))$.

Hence, the ciphertext retrieval circuit for $|101\rangle$ and $|110\rangle$ are shown in Fig. 7.18 and Fig. 7.19. The first quantum circuit shown in Fig. 7.18 is the retrieval circuit, which achieves the Grover algorithm. The second quantum circuit shown in Fig. 7.19 is the decryption circuit, which is used to reduce the decryption overhead for Client. The Grover search circuit C_q and the decryption circuit C are emphasized by dotted boxes, respectively. We execute the circuit 1000 times on IBM Qiskit and the result is shown in Fig. 7.20. Obviously, the measurement result is same as the plaintext retrieval result, which verifies that the ciphertext retrieval scheme is correct.

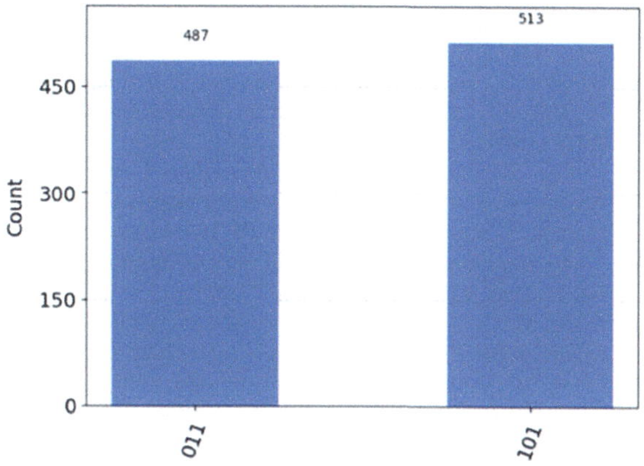

Fig. 7.20 Search result with encryption

7.6 Summary

Interactive quantum homomorphic encryption required classical or quantum information exchange between the user and the computing party during the execution of quantum circuits, increasing communication overhead and inevitably reducing the efficiency. In this chapter, we introduced several non-interactive quantum homomorphic encryption schemes. From the perspective of quantum obfuscation, we introduced a QHE scheme based on point obfuscation. From the perspective of quantum fully homomorphic encryption, we introduced two QFHE schemes based on multi-valued quantum point obfuscation, including single-qubit and multi-qubit QFHE schemes. Additionally, we introduced a QHE scheme based on quantum power obfuscation by combining quantum power functions and their obfuscation theory. Comprehensive information-theoretic security proofs were provided for all the schemes based on quantum obfuscation.

Also, we introduced a non-interactive QHE scheme based on the rotation operator R_z and R_y and a two-round QHE scheme with information-theoretic security and compactness. By decomposing S-error into the linear combination of the unitary matrix I and Z, the homomorphic evaluation for T gate could be completed non-interactively.

References

1. Liu, W.J., Gao, P.P., Liu, Z.H., et al.: A quantum-based database query scheme for privacy preservation in cloud environment. Secur. Commun. Netw., 4923590 (2019)
2. Gentry, C.: A Fully Homomorphic Encryption Scheme. Stanford University (2009)
3. Gentry, C.: Computing arbitrary functions of encrypted data. Commun. ACM **53**(3), 97–105 (2010)
4. Rivest, R.L., Dertouzos, M.L.: On data banks and privacy homomorphisms. Found. Secur. Comput. **4**(11), 169 (1978)

5. Rohde, P.P., Fitzsimons, J.F., Gilchrist, A.: Quantum walks with encrypted data. Phys. Rev. Lett. **109**(15), 150501 (2012)
6. Benaloh, J., Fischer, M.J.: A robust and verifiable cryptographically secure election scheme. In: The 26th Annual Symposium on Foundations of Computer Science (1985), pp. 372–382. IEEE (1985)
7. Paillier, P.: Public-key cryptosystems based on composite degree residuosity classes. In: Advances in Cryptology—International Conference on the Theory and Application of Cryptographic Techniques (EUROCRYPT 1999), vol. 1592, pp. 223–238 (1999)
8. Liang, M.: Symmetric quantum fully homomorphic encryption with perfect security. Quantum Inf. Process. **12**(12), 3675–3687 (2013)
9. Liang, M.: Quantum fully homomorphic encryption scheme based on universal quantum circuit. Quantum Inf. Process. **14**(8), 2749–2759 (2015)
10. Liang, M., Yang, L.: Quantum fully homomorphic encryption scheme based on quantum fault-tolerant construction (2015). arXiv:1503.04061
11. Ouyang, Y., Tan, S.H., Fitzsimons, J.: Quantum homomorphic encryption from quantum codes. Phys. Rev. A **98**, 042334 (2018)
12. Broadbent, A., Jeffery, S.: Quantum homomorphic encryption for circuits of low t-gate complexity. In: Advances in Cryptology—CRYPTO–35th Annual Cryptology Conference, Santa Barbara, CA, USA, , vol. 9216, pp. 609–629 (2015)
13. Sun, X., Wang, T., Sun, Z., et al.: An efficient quantum somewhat homomorphic symmetric searchable encryption. Int. J. Theor. Phys. **56**(4), 1335–1345 (2017)
14. Yu, L., Perez-Delgado, C.A., Fitzsimons, J.F.: Limitations on information-theoretically-secure quantum homomorphic encryption. Phys. Rev. A **90**(5), 050303 (2014)
15. Zhang, Y.J., Shang, T., Liu, J.W., et al.: Quantum homomorphic encryption based on quantum obfuscation. In: International Wireless Communications and Mobile Computing (IWCMC). IEEE (2020)
16. Tan, S.H., Kettlewell, J.A., Ouyang, Y.K., et al.: A quantum approach to fully homomorphic encryption. Sci. Rep. **6**, 33467 (2016)
17. Wang, Y., She, K., Luo, Q., et al.: Symmetric weak ternary quantum homomorphic encryption schemes. Mod. Phys. Lett. B **30**(7), 1650076 (2016)
18. Zhang, Y.J., Shang, T., Liu, J.W.: A multi-valued quantum fully homomorphic encryption scheme. Quantum Inf. Process. **20**(3), 101 (2021)
19. Boneh, D., Dagdelen, O., Fischlin, M., et al.: Random oracles in a quantum world. In: Advances in Cryptology-ASIACRYPT, pp. 41–69 (2011)
20. Shang, T., Lei, Q., Liu, J.W.: Quantum random oracle model for quantum digital signature. Phys. Rev. A **94**, 042314 (2016)
21. Shang, T., Chen, R.Y.L., Lei, Q.: Quantum random oracle model for quantum public-key encryption. IEEE Access **99**(7), 130024–130031 (2019)
22. Shang, T., Chen, R.Y.L., Liu, J.W.: On the obfuscatability of quantum point functions. Quantum Inf. Process. **18**(2), 55 (2019)
23. Pan, C.Y., Shang, T., Liu, J.W.: Quantum obfuscation based on quantum nonlinear function. J. Cryptologic Res. **10**(3), 506–516 (2023)
24. Boykin, P.O., Roychowdhury, V.: Optimal encryption of quantum bits. Phys. Rev. A **67**(4), 645–648 (2003)
25. Alagic, G., Fefferman B.: On quantum obfuscation (2016). arXiv:1602.01771
26. Childs, A.M.: Secure assisted quantum computation. Quantum Inf. Comput. **5**(6), 456–466 (2005)
27. Broadbent, A.: Delegating private quantum computations. Can. J. Phys. **93**(9), 941–946 (2015)
28. Newman, M., Shi, Y.: Limitations on transversal computation through quantum homomorphic encryption. Quantum Inf. Comput. **18**(11), 927–948 (2018)
29. Lai, C.Y., Chung, K.M.: On statistically-secure quantum homomorphic encryption. Quantum Inf. Comput. **18**(9), 785–794 (2018)
30. Liang, M.: Teleportation-based quantum homomorphic encryption scheme with quasi-compactness and perfect security. Quantum Inf. Process. **19**(1), 28 (2020)

31. Wang, S.L., Shang, T., Liu J.W.: Non-interactive quantum homomorphic encryption scheme based on the rotation operator. Sci. China-Phys. Mech. Astron. **53**(4), 240311 (2023)
32. Gottesman, D.: The Heisenberg representation of quantum computers. In: The XXII International Colloquium on Group Theoretical Methods in Physics, pp. 32–43 (1998)
33. Broadbent, A., Kazmi, R.A.: Constructions for quantum indistinguishability obfuscation. In: The 7th International Conference on Cryptology and Information Security in Latin America (LATINCRYPT), Bogotá, Colombia, pp. 24–43 (2021)
34. Nielsen, M.A., Chuang, I.: Quantum Computation and Quantum Information. Cambridge University Press (2001)
35. Wang, C., Zhou, R.G.: Secure multi-party convex hull protocol based on quantum homomorphic encryption. Quantum Inf. Process. **22**(1), 24–32 (2023)
36. Xu, G., Yun, F., Chen, X.B., et al.: Secure multi-party quantum summation based on quantum homomorphic encryption. Intell. Autom. Soft Comput. **34**(1), 531–541 (2022)
37. Chen, G., Wang, Y., Jian, L., et al.: Quantum identity authentication protocol based on flexible quantum homomorphic encryption with qubit rotation. J. Appl. Phys. **133**(6), 064402 (2023)
38. Zhou, Q., Lu, S.: Quantum search on encrypted data based on quantum homomorphic encryption. Sci. Rep. **10**(1), 5135 (2020)
39. Gong, C.Q., Du, J., Dong, Z.Y., et al.: Grover algorithm-based quantum homomorphic encryption ciphertext retrieval scheme in quantum cloud computing. Quantum Inf. Process. **19**(3), 105 (2020)
40. Grover, L.K.: A fast quantum mechanical algorithm for database search. In: The 28th Annual ACM Symposium on the Theory of Computing, pp. 212–219 (1996)
41. Shang, T., Wang, S.L., Jiang, Y.Z., et al.: A two-round quantum homomorphic encryption scheme based on matrix decomposition. Quantum Inf. Process. **22**(12), 422 (2023)
42. Niemann, P., Wille, R., Drechsler, R.: Efficient synthesis of quantum circuits implementing Clifford group operations. In: Asia and South Pacific Design Automation Conference (ASP-DAC), pp. 483–488 (2014)

Chapter 8
Quantum One-Way Function

One-way functions are fundamental tools for cryptography. Until now, quantum one-way functions have several input-output categories such as ‘classical-to-classical’, ‘classical-to-quantum’, ‘quantum-to-classical’ and ‘quantum-to-quantum’, which are used for post-quantum cryptography or quantum cryptography. The most significant functions are ‘classical-to-classical’ quantum one-way function and ‘quantum-to-quantum’ quantum one-way function. ‘Quantum-to-quantum’ quantum one-way function, also called full quantum one-way function, can deal with quantum state and be easily performed on the quantum computer. ‘Classical-to-classical’ quantum one-way function, which deals with classical information, can improve the security of current cryptographic systems to be secure even against quantum attacker. In this chapter, we introduce the full quantum one-way function to design quantum cryptographic schemes. By combining different functions, quantum obfuscation theory and quantum circuit mapping, several full quantum one-way functions are proposed. We prove its one-way property from ‘easy computation’ and ‘computationally difficult to invert’. Then we introduce a ‘classical-to-classical’ quantum hash function based on controlled alternate lively quantum walks and implement the progress from quantum one-way function to quantum hash function.

8.1 Full Quantum One-Way Function

8.1.1 Development of One-Way Function

Classical one-way functions (OWF) are easy to compute by classical polynomial-time algorithms but hard to invert by any classical polynomial-time adversary. Current candidates of one-way functions are based on mathematical hard problem hypothesis such as factoring and discrete logarithm. However, with the emergence of quantum technology, many candidates of one-way functions will be invertible under the attack

T. Shang, *Quantum Nonlinear Function Obfuscation Theory and Application*,
https://doi.org/10.1007/978-981-97-6722-9_8

of quantum computers. Thus classical cryptographic protocols based on one-way functions will be no longer secure.

In order to resist the threat of quantum adversaries, quantum one-way functions (QOWF) were proposed to design post-quantum or quantum cryptographic protocols. Quantum one-way functions can be computed in polynomial time but are hard to invert in polynomial time by any quantum adversary. According to different input and output forms, the quantum one-way functions can be classified into the following categories. The first kind of quantum one-way functions is the 'classical-classical' one-way function [1, 2]. These functions are based on the hypothesis secure against quantum algorithms, thus are hard to invert in the quantum environment. The second kind of quantum one-way functions is the 'classical-quantum' one-way function with classical bits as input and quantum states as output. One of the 'classical-quantum' one-way function is quantum fingerprinting based on binary error correction code [3]. Gottesman and Chuang [4] proposed the 'classical-quantum' one-way function for quantum digital signature. As the extension of the 'classical-quantum' one-way function, quantum hash function was extensively discussed in the references [5–8] based on quantum fingerprints and then used to design cryptographic protocols. The third kind of quantum one-way functions is the 'quantum-classical' one-way function proposed by Behera and Paul [9]. They extracted classical information from quantum states by means of quantum CNOT gate to mark quantum states. Such a function was used well in quantum money protocols. Moreover, Alagic et al. [10] proposed a problem about signing a quantum state, which reflects the demand of a one-way function with quantum states as input. It is feasible to conceive a one-way function of 'quantum-quantum' mode, or to say, a full quantum one-way function, under the assumption of general quantum computers. However, it is difficult to define a function which maps a quantum state to another quantum state and satisfies the definition of a one-way function. The main challenge is that any gate transformation of quantum states is linear and reversible, which means that it is probable to trace back to the original quantum state by the output quantum state [9]. Obviously, it is contrary to the property of the one-way function.

In cryptography, an important application of one-way functions is identity authentication. The identity authentication enables a prover to gain access to a verifier's resource by submitting credentials to the verifier. In 1995, Crépeau et al. [11] proposed the first quantum identify authentication scheme based on quantum oblivious transfer. Then Dušek *et al.* [12] proposed another quantum identify authentication scheme by utilizing quantum key distribution (QKD) to share the one-time secret key for a simple classical identification procedure. Subsequently, Ljunggren et al. [13] proposed several user authenticated QKD protocols, introducing an arbitrator to user authentication process. Shi et al. [14] also proposed authenticated QKD protocol based on entangled state and quantum memories, which does not need classical communication. Based on teleportation and entanglement swapping, Zhou et al. [15] proposed a cross-center quantum identification scheme, which involves over two participants. Based on ping-pong technique, a quantum identity authentication scheme without entanglements was designed and can additionally update the authentication key [16]. However, these quantum identify authentication schemes were proposed by means of referring to non-challenge-response mode, thus are insecure under possible verifier-impersonation attack. A challenge-response mode identity authentication can resist such active attack as it provides the situation where users share secret during the interaction phase but the adversary cannot learn about the secret [17].

In this section, we focus on the design of a full quantum one-way function which is 'quantum-to-quantum' and the application of the full quantum one-way function in quantum cryptography [18]. Inspired by Behera and Paul's approach in the reference [9], we distinguish the outputs of the function and the quantum circuit. Only partial data of the quantum circuit is declared as the output of the function. Consequently, it is difficult to trace back to the input of the quantum circuit by the partial information on the quantum circuit. By means of the one-wayness of the full quantum one-way function, we can construct a quantum identity authentication scheme, which is immune to active attacks because of the challenge-response technique.

8.1.2 Classical One-Way Function

As the basic theory in cryptography, one-way functions are widely used in public key cryptography. Goldreich [19] gave a widely accepted definition in the Foundations of Cryptography which is called 'strong one-way function'. The function is defined as follows.

Definition 8.1 (Strong one-way function) A function $f : \{0, 1\}^* \rightarrow \{0, 1\}^*$ is a one-way function, if f satisfies the following two conditions:

1. **Easy to compute**: There is a polynomial algorithm A that for the given input x, the algorithm $A(x)$ outputs $f(x)$, i.e., $A(x) = f(x)$.
2. **Hard to invert**: For every probabilistic polynomial-time algorithm A', every positive polynomial $p(\cdot)$, and all large sufficiently n, it satisfies

$$Pr[A'(f(x), 1^n) \in f^{-1}(f(x))] < \frac{1}{p(n)} \tag{8.1}$$

The two conditions of 'easy to compute' and 'hard to invert' illustrate the one-way property of the one-way function. Full quantum one-way function will be defined likewise.

8.1.3 Quantum One-Way Function

As introduced in Sect. 8.1.1, some attempts of constructing quantum one-way functions have been made to design a variety of quantum cryptographic protocols. Here we briefly discuss the construction and property of two quantum one-way functions, namely 'quantum-classical' one-way function and 'classical-quantum' one-way function. These two functions are not full quantum one-way functions, but can be used to construct the full quantum one-way function.

A. 'quantum-Classical' One-Way Function

The construction of a 'quantum-classical' one-way function was presented in the reference [9]. In this construction, a 'quantum-classical' one-way function F_{qc} maps from a n-qubit quantum GCH (GHZ-Computational-Hadamard basis) state to an n-bit classical string

$$F_{qc} : \{|\phi^{(n)}\rangle_{GCH}\} \mapsto \{0, 1\}^n \tag{8.2}$$

where the GCH state is a quantum state which can be denoted as a tensor product of either elements of Hadamard basis $(\{|+\rangle, |-\rangle\})$, computational basis $(\{|0\rangle, |1\rangle\})$ or GHZ states $(\{1/\sqrt{2}(|x_1, x_2, \ldots, x_n\rangle + |\bar{x_1}, \bar{x_2}, \ldots, \bar{x_n}\rangle), x_i \in \{0, 1\}\})$.

The one-wayness of the 'quantum-classical' one-way function was provided by the following lemmas [9]:

Lemma 8.1 *The 'quantum-classical' one-way function F_{qc} uses quantum gates with the number of $\mathcal{O}(n^3)$.*

Lemma 8.2 *For any quantum polynomial adversary A obtaining F_{qc}'s output c, the probability of A getting back the correct input $|\phi\rangle$ is*

$$\Pr[A(c) = |\phi\rangle] \leq \frac{1}{2^{\frac{n}{2}}} \tag{8.3}$$

B. 'classical-Quantum' One-Way Function

The 'classical-quantum' one-way function in the reference [20] utilizes the technique of single-bit rotation. In this construction, a 'classical-quantum' one-way function F_{cq} maps from an arbitrary n-bit string to 2-dimensional Hilbert space

$$F_{cq} : \{0, 1\}^n \mapsto \mathcal{H}^2 \tag{8.4}$$

Given the input string c, F_{cq} rotates $|0\rangle$ on Y axis with angle $\theta_c = \frac{c}{2^n} \cdot 2\pi$ on the Bloch sphere

$$\begin{aligned} F_{cq}(c) =& \hat{R}_Y(\theta_c)|0\rangle \\ =& \cos\left(\frac{\theta_c}{2}\right)|0\rangle + \sin\left(\frac{\theta_c}{2}\right)|1\rangle \end{aligned} \tag{8.5}$$

The 'hard-to-invert' property of the 'classical-quantum' one-way function is provided by the following lemma:

Lemma 8.3 *For any quantum polynomial adversary A obtaining F_{cq}'s output $F_{cq}(c)$, the probability of A getting back the correct input c is*

$$\Pr[A(F_{cq}(c)) = c] \leq \frac{1}{2^n} \tag{8.6}$$

The complexity of F_{cq} is determined by the single-bit rotation operator. According to the reference [21], $O(log^C(\frac{1}{\epsilon}))$ universal gates can approximate the single-bit quantum gate in precision ϵ, where C is a constant and close to 2.

8.1.4 Identity Authentication

Classical identity authentication, also known as the login protocol, is applicable where a **prover** wants to identify itself to a **verifier** for a later session or access to the verifier's resources. An identity authentication is defined in the reference [22].

Definition 8.2 An identity authentication scheme $\mathcal{I}$ is an interactive protocol consisting of three algorithms $\mathcal{I} = (G, P, V)$, where

1. G is the key generation algorithm $G() = (sk, vk)$. sk is the secret key and given to the prover, vk is the verification key and given to the verifier.
2. P is the prover algorithm, which takes as input a secret key sk and interacts with the verifier.
3. V is the verifier algorithm taking as input a verification key vk. After the interaction with the prover, V outputs 'accept' or 'reject'.

The correctness of the identity authentication scheme $\mathcal{I}$ requires that for all possible outputs (sk, vk) of $G()$, after interacting with $P(sk)$, $V(vk)$ outputs 'accept' with the probability 1.

In the cryptoanalysis of identity authentication, three attack models are suggested as follows, in the order of an adversary's capability.

1. **Direct attack**: the adversary with only public information tries to impersonate the prover to the verifier.
2. **Eavesdropping attack**: the adversary can eavesdrop successful identity authentication instances between the prover and the verifier. After eavesdropping, the adversary tries to impersonate the prover to the verifier.
3. **Verifier impersonation attack**: the adversary cannot only eavesdrop successful identity authentication instances, but also impersonate the verifier and interact with the prover. After eavesdropping and interaction, the adversary tries to impersonate the prover to the verifier.

Each attack model grants the adversary different capability, and corresponds to different security games. We will prove security against the strongest adversary, i.e., the one with active attacks. We will give the definition of the corresponding security game in a quantum circumstance and the proof of security.

8.1.5 Full Quantum One-Way Function

In this section, we give the construction of the full quantum one-way function and analyze the one-wayness.

The definition of the full quantum one-way function is based on the 'quantum-classical-quantum' idea, i.e., concatenation of 'quantum-to-classical' and 'classical-to-quantum'. The 'quantum-classical' one-way function is F_{qc} in the reference [9], while the 'classical-quantum' one-way function is F_{cq} in the reference [20]. The definition of full quantum one-way function is defined as follows:

Definition 8.3 The full quantum one-way function F maps a n-qubit GCH state to a 1-qubit superposition state, i.e.,

$$F : \{|\psi^{(n)}\rangle_{GCH}\} \mapsto \mathcal{H}^2 \tag{8.7}$$

For any input $|\psi\rangle$ of GCH state, the algorithm for a full quantum one-way function is described as follows:

Step 1: use F_{qc} to extract classical information from $|\psi\rangle$, i.e., $c = F_{qc}|\psi\rangle$, $c \in \{0, 1\}^n$.

Step 2: rotate the single qubit $|0\rangle$ with the angle θ_c according to the obtained classical information c, then calculate F_{cq} to obtain the quantum output $F|\psi\rangle$.

$$F|\psi\rangle = F_{cq}(c) = \cos\frac{\theta_c}{2}|0\rangle + \sin\frac{\theta_c}{2}|1\rangle, \tag{8.8}$$

where θ_c is $\theta_c = \frac{c}{2^n} \cdot 2\pi$.

8.1.6 One-Wayness

A. Easy to Compute

The 'easy to compute' property of the full quantum one-way function can be analyzed based on the time complexity of the execution of corresponding quantum circuit. As the execution time of single quantum gate is fixed, the total time complexity of quantum one-way function F can be measured by the number of quantum gates in the quantum circuit.

For Step 1, according to Lemma 8.1, the number of CNOT gates used by function F_{qc} is described as follow:

$$Y_{qc} \leq \frac{n^3 + n^2}{2} \tag{8.9}$$

From Sect. 8.1.3, the rotation used in Step 2 is a rotation operator on Y axis, and the operator is $R_j(\theta) = e^{i\theta_c Y/2}$. This operator is not a universal quantum gate. According to the reference [21], $O(log^C(\frac{1}{\epsilon}))$ universal quantum gates can approximate any single quantum gate in precision ϵ. So, for the full quantum one-way function F, the time complexity is

$$O(F)_{n,\epsilon} = O\left(n^3 + \log^C\left(\frac{1}{\epsilon}\right)\right) \tag{8.10}$$

It indicates that the function F can be computed in polynomial time. Thus the function F is easy to calculate.

B. Hard to Invert

Theorem 8.1 *Given an arbitrary output result $F|\psi\rangle$ of the full quantum one-way function F, for any quantum polynomial-time adversary A, the probability of A inverting F is negligible, i.e.,*

$$\Pr[A(F|\psi\rangle) = |\psi\rangle] \leq negl(n) \tag{8.11}$$

Proof Assume that a quantum algorithm A_F with polynomial time can invert the full quantum one-way function F with a non-negligible probability,

$$A_F(F|\psi\rangle) = |\psi\rangle \tag{8.12}$$

Let A_{qc} be an adversary against 'quantum-classical' one-way function F_{qc} and it tries to invert a classical string c. We denote the probability by $\Pr[A_{qc}(c) = |\psi'\rangle]$. Since F_{cq} is public, the adversary A_{qc} can use c to calculate $F_{cq}(c)$ and get $F|\psi'\rangle = F_{cq}(c)$. Through the adversary A_F of the full quantum one-way function F, the adversary A_{qc} can obtain input $|\psi'\rangle$ in Step 1 by means of algorithm A_F to invert the final result $F|\psi'\rangle$. Then

$$\begin{aligned} \Pr[A_{qc}(c) = |\psi'\rangle] &= \Pr[A_{qc}(c, F_{cq}) = |\psi'\rangle] \\ &= \Pr[A_{qc}(F|\psi'\rangle) = |\psi'\rangle] \\ &= \Pr[A(F|\psi'\rangle) = |\psi'\rangle] \end{aligned} \tag{8.13}$$

It shows that the inversion of function F_{qc} can be achieved, which contrasts the one-wayness of the one-way function F_{qc}. Thus the assumption above is not true. No polynomial-time quantum algorithm A_F can invert the full quantum one-way function F with a non-negligible probability. The full quantum one-way function F is hard to invert.

8.1.7 Application to Quantum Identity Authentication

In this section, we construct a quantum identity authentication scheme, in which any information, such as the secret key, the verification key and the interacting message between two parties, is a quantum state. Firstly, we give the construction of the

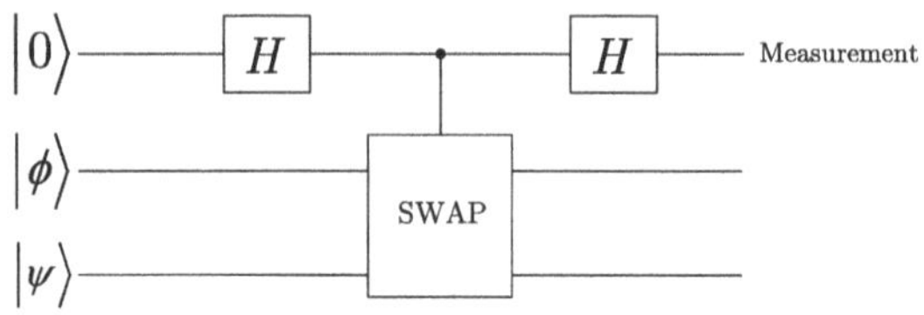

Fig. 8.1 Circuit of SWAP-test

identity authentication scheme based on the full quantum one-way function defined in Sect. 8.1.5. Then we set up the attack game for the scheme and analyze its security.

A. Scheme

In this full quantum identity authentication scheme, a prover chooses a private key as $|sk\rangle$. For the message $|m\rangle$ sent by a verifier, the prover performs a rotation operation on it and then sends it to the verifier to do the verification work.

The quantum identity authentication scheme is described as follows:

Step 1: the prover chooses a GCH state as its private key $|sk\rangle$. It takes $|sk\rangle$ as the input of the full quantum one-way function F and then creates a set of verification key $|vk\rangle = F|sk\rangle$. The prover places the verification key on a trusted platform.

Step 2: the verifier has a message $|m\rangle = \cos\frac{\theta_m}{2}|0\rangle + \sin\frac{\theta_m}{2}|1\rangle$, where $m \in \{0, 1\}^n$ and $\theta_m = \frac{m}{2^n} \cdot 2\pi$. The verifier sends $|m\rangle$ to the prover.

Step 3: the prover uses the private key $|sk\rangle$ to calculate F_{cq} to obtain c. Then it performs a rotation operation on the received message $|m\rangle$ as follows $\hat{R}_Y(\theta_c)|m\rangle$, where $\theta_c = \frac{c}{2^n} \cdot 2\pi$.
The result of the rotation is $\hat{R}_Y(\theta_c|m\rangle) = \cos\frac{\theta_c+\theta_m}{2}|0\rangle + \sin\frac{\theta_c+\theta_m}{2}|1\rangle$. The result is recorded as $|P\rangle$. Then the prover sends $|P\rangle$ to the verifier.

Step 4: the verifier receives $|P\rangle$. It applies a $-\theta_m$ rotation and denotes the result as $|P_s\rangle$. The verifier uses the SWAP-test to compare $|P_s\rangle$ with the prover's verification key $|vk\rangle$. If $|P_s\rangle = |vk\rangle$, it completes the verification of the prover.

The circuit of SWAP-test used in Step 4 is shown in Fig. 8.1. Before the final measurement, the state is $\frac{1}{2}|0\rangle(|\psi\rangle|\psi\rangle + |\psi\rangle|\psi\rangle) + \frac{1}{2}|1\rangle(|\phi\rangle|\psi\rangle \quad |\psi\rangle|\phi\rangle)$ When two quantum states $|\phi\rangle$ and $|\psi\rangle$ are the same, the measurement result of the first qubit in SWAP-test is always $|0\rangle$. However, if the two quantum states $|\phi\rangle$ and $|\psi\rangle$ have inner product $\delta = |\langle\psi|\phi\rangle| < 1$, the measurement result is probabilistic. Thus SWAP-test determines whether the two quantum states are equal with one-sided error $(1 + \delta^2)/2$.

Obviously, in the quantum identity authentication scheme, the prover can generate $|P\rangle = \cos\frac{\theta_c+\theta_m}{2}|0\rangle + \sin\frac{\theta_c+\theta_m}{2}|1\rangle$, and the verifier generates $|P_s\rangle = \cos\frac{\theta_c}{2}|0\rangle + \sin\frac{\theta_c}{2}|1\rangle$. The prover thus passes SWAP-test with the probability 1. The correctness of the quantum identity authentication scheme holds.

B. Security Analysis

Now we set up the attack game for the quantum identity authentication scheme under active attacks.

Definition 8.4 (Attack game) For the given quantum identity authentication scheme and a quantum adversary A, the attack game allowing active attacks runs as follows:

1. **Key generation**: the challenger runs G to generate secret key $|sk\rangle$ and verification key $|vk\rangle = F|sk\rangle$, where F is the full quantum one-way function defined in Sect. 8.1.5. The challenger sends sufficient copies of $|vk\rangle$ to the adversary A.
2. **Verifier impersonation**: A in this phase impersonates the verifier to interact with the challenger. A queries the challenger with single qubit $|a_i\rangle$, and obtains responses $\hat{R}_Y(\frac{c}{2^n} \cdot 2\pi)|a_i\rangle$, where $c = F_{qc}|sk\rangle$.
3. **Prover impersonation**: the challenger in this phase randomly chooses $|m\rangle = \hat{R}_Y(\theta_m)|0\rangle = \hat{R}_Y(\frac{m}{2^n} \cdot 2\pi)|0\rangle$ and sends it to A. With A's response $|P_m\rangle$, the challenger runs $\hat{R}_Y(-\theta_m)|P_m\rangle$ and compares the result and $|vk\rangle$ by means of SWAP-test. The challenger repeats this phase p times and outputs 'accept' only if all SWAP-test results are $|0\rangle$.

The adversary's advantage over the scheme is defined as

$$\text{Adv}(A, \mathcal{I}) = \Pr[\textit{the challenger outputs 'accept'}]$$

Before the security proof of the scheme, we introduce the following lemma.

Lemma 8.4 *For any quantum adversary A obtaining quantum states* $\hat{R}_Y(\theta_m)|0\rangle = \hat{R}_Y(\frac{m}{2^n} \cdot 2\pi)|0\rangle$ *and* $\hat{R}_Y(\theta_c)|0\rangle = \hat{R}_Y(\frac{c}{2^n} \cdot 2\pi)|0\rangle$, $m, c \in \{0, 1\}^n$, *the probability of A generating* $\hat{R}_Y(\theta_m + \theta_c)|0\rangle$

$$\Pr[A(\hat{R}_Y(\theta_m)|0\rangle, \hat{R}_Y(\theta_c)|0\rangle) = \hat{R}_Y(\theta_m + \theta_c)|0\rangle] \leq \frac{1}{2} \tag{8.14}$$

Proof With $\hat{R}_Y(\theta_m)|0\rangle$, according to *Lemma* 8.3, the adversary A cannot compute m with a non-negligible probability. So A cannot generate $\hat{R}_Y(\theta_m + \theta_c)|0\rangle$ with knowledge of m or c.

Assume A uses $poly(n)$ auxiliary qubits $|0\rangle$, a unitary operator U, and measurement $\mathbf{M} = \{M_i, i \in [1, m]\}$ that one or more $M_i \in \mathbf{M}$ satisfies

$$\begin{aligned} &M_i U(|0\rangle^{poly(n)} \otimes \hat{R}_Y(\theta_m)|0\rangle \otimes \hat{R}_Y(\theta_c)|0\rangle) \\ &= M_i|\phi\rangle \\ &= \hat{R}_Y(\theta_m + \theta_c)|0\rangle \otimes \cdots \end{aligned} \tag{8.15}$$

where $|0\rangle^{poly(n)} \otimes \hat{R}_Y(\theta_m)|0\rangle \otimes \hat{R}_Y(\theta_c)|0\rangle$. In this way, A can obtain $\hat{R}_Y(\theta_m + \theta_c)|0\rangle$ with probability

$$\Pr[A\ obtains\ \hat{R}_Y(\theta_m+\theta_c)|0\rangle] = \sum_i ||M_i|\phi\rangle||_2 \tag{8.16}$$

According to the Reference [21], the measurement $\mathbf{M}$ can be implemented by another $\log_2(m)$ auxiliary qubits, some unitary operator V and projective measurement $\mathbf{P} = \{P_i, i \in [1, m]\}$, $P_i = |i\rangle\langle i|$. We denote $U' = V(U \otimes I_{\log_2(m)})$ and $P_i' = I_{2+ploy(n)} \otimes |i\rangle\langle i|$, then

$$P_i'U'(\hat{R}_Y(\theta_m)|0\rangle \otimes \hat{R}_Y(\theta_c)|0\rangle \otimes |0\rangle^{poly(n)}) \tag{8.17}$$

computes the same result as

$$M_iU(\hat{R}_Y(\theta_m)|0\rangle \otimes \hat{R}_Y(\theta_c)|0\rangle \otimes |0\rangle^{poly(n)+\log_2(m)}) \tag{8.18}$$

By denoting $|input\rangle = |0\rangle^{poly(n)+\log_2(m)} \otimes \hat{R}_Y(\theta_m)|0\rangle \otimes \hat{R}_Y(\theta_c)|0\rangle$, and $n' = 2 + poly(n) + \log_2(m)$, it is clear that $|input\rangle$ satisfies Equation (8.19).

$$\begin{aligned}|input\rangle = [&\cos(\theta_m/2)\cos(\theta_c/2), \cos(\theta_m/2)\sin(\theta_c/2), \sin(\theta_m/2)\cos(\theta_c/2),\\ &\sin(\theta_m/2)\sin(\theta_c/2), \underbrace{0, \ldots, 0}_{2^{n'}-4}]^{\mathrm{T}}\end{aligned} \tag{8.19}$$

Then

$$\begin{aligned}\Pr[A\ obtains\ \hat{R}_Y(\theta_m+\theta_c)|0\rangle] &= \sum_i ||M_i|\phi\rangle||_2\\ &= \sum_i ||P_i'U'|input\rangle||_2\end{aligned} \tag{8.20}$$

Suppose $U' = \{u'_{i,j}\}, i, j \in [1, 2^{n'}]$, then we apply it in $|input\rangle$, the result is described in Equation (8.21).

$$\begin{aligned}U'|input\rangle = [&u'_{1,1}\cos(\theta_c/2)\cos(\theta_m/2) + u'_{1,2}\cos(\theta_c/2)\sin(\theta_m/2)\\ &+ u'_{1,3}\sin(\theta_c/2)\cos(\theta_m/2) + u'_{1,4}\sin(\theta_c/2)\sin(\theta_m/2), \ldots,\\ &u'_{2^{n'},1}\cos(\theta_c/2)\cos(\theta_m/2) + u'_{2^{n'},2}\cos(\theta_c/2)\sin(\theta_m/2)\\ &+ u'_{2^{n'},3}\sin(\theta_c/2)\cos(\theta_m/2) + u'_{2^{n'},4}\sin(\theta_c/2)\sin(\theta_m/2)]^{\mathrm{T}}\end{aligned} \tag{8.21}$$

$P_i' = I_{2+ploy(n)} \otimes |i\rangle\langle i|$ corresponds to certain rows in vector presentation of $U'|input\rangle$. Recall that P_i helps A generate $\hat{R}_Y(\theta_m+\theta_c)|0\rangle$, for some $i \in [1, m]$. Let G be the indexes to which all P_i correspond, then

$$
\begin{aligned}
&\Pr[A\ obtains\ \hat{R}_Y(\theta_m+\theta_c)|0\rangle] \\
&= \sum_i ||P_i'U'|input\rangle||_2 \\
&= \sum_{j\in G} |u_{j,1}' \cos(\theta_c/2)\cos(\theta_m/2) + u_{j,2}' \cos(\theta_c/2)\sin(\theta_m/2) \\
&+ u_{j,3}' \sin(\theta_c/2)\cos(\theta_m/2) + u_{j,4}' \sin(\theta_c/2)\sin(\theta_m/2)|^2
\end{aligned} \tag{8.22}
$$

Now we look into restrictions on $u_{j,k}', j \in G, k = 1, 2, 3, 4$. Note that the first qubit of $P_i'U'|input\rangle$ is

$$
\begin{aligned}
&\hat{R}_Y(\theta_m+\theta_c)|0\rangle \\
&= \cos((\theta_m+\theta_c)/2)|0\rangle + \sin((\theta_m+\theta_c)/2)|1\rangle \\
&= (\cos(\theta_m/2)\cos(\theta_c/2) - \sin(\theta_m/2)\sin(\theta_c/2))|0\rangle \\
&+ (\sin(\theta_m/2)\cos(\theta_c/2) + \cos(\theta_m/2)\sin(\theta_c/2))|1\rangle
\end{aligned} \tag{8.23}
$$

Equation (8.23) indicates that for all $j \in G,\ j \le 2^{n'-1}$, $u_{j,k}'$ satisfies Equation (8.24) for arbitrary θ_m, θ_c.

$$
\begin{aligned}
&[u_{j,1}' \cos(\theta_c/2)\cos(\theta_m/2) + u_{j,2}' \cos(\theta_c/2)\sin(\theta_m/2) \\
&+ u_{j,3}' \sin(\theta_c/2)\cos(\theta_m/2) + u_{j,4}' \sin(\theta_c/2)\sin(\theta_m/2)] \\
&\div [u_{j+2^{n'-1},1}' \cos(\theta_c/2)\cos(\theta_m/2) + u_{j+2^{n'-1},2}' \cos(\theta_c/2)\sin(\theta_m/2) \\
&+ u_{j+2^{n'-1},3}' \sin(\theta_c/2)\cos(\theta_m/2) + u_{j+2^{n'-1},4}' \sin(\theta_c/2)\sin(\theta_m/2)] \\
&= \frac{\cos(\theta_m/2)\cos(\theta_c/2) - \sin(\theta_m/2)\sin(\theta_c/2)}{\sin(\theta_m/2)\cos(\theta_c/2) + \cos(\theta_m/2)\sin(\theta_c/2)}
\end{aligned} \tag{8.24}
$$

This condition holds only when

$$
\begin{cases}
u_{j,1}' = -u_{j,4}', u_{j,2}' = u_{j,3}' = 0 & x \in [1, 2^{n'-1}] \\
u_{j,1}' = u_{j,4}' = 0, u_{j,2}' = u_{j,3}' & x \in [2^{n'-1}+1, 2^{n'}] \\
u_{j,1}' = u_{j+2^{n'-1},2}' & x \in [1, 2^{n'-1}]
\end{cases} \tag{8.25}
$$

Then

$$
\begin{aligned}
&\Pr[A\ obtains\ \hat{R}_Y(\theta_m+\theta_c)|0\rangle] \\
&= \sum_{j\in G} |u_{j,1}' \cos(\theta_c/2)\cos(\theta_m/2) + u_{j,2}' \cos(\theta_c/2)\sin(\theta_m/2) \\
&+ u_{j,3}' \sin(\theta_c/2)\cos(\theta_m/2) + u_{j,4}' \sin(\theta_c/2)\sin(\theta_m/2)|^2 \\
&= \sum_{j\in G} |u_{j,1}'|^2
\end{aligned} \tag{8.26}
$$

Since U' is unitary, the inner product of the $1st$ and the $4th$ column of U' equals to 0, i.e.,

$$\begin{aligned}
&\sum_{j\in[1,2^{n'}]} u'^{*}_{j,1}u'_{j,4} = 0 \\
&= \sum_{j\in G} u'^{*}_{j,1}u'_{j,4} + \sum_{j\notin G} u'^{*}_{j,1}u'_{j,4} \\
&= \sum_{j\in G} -u'^{*}_{j,1}u'_{j,1} + \sum_{j\notin G} u'^{*}_{j,1}u'_{j,4} \\
&\Rightarrow \sum_{j\in G} u'^{*}_{j,1}u'_{j,1} = \sum_{j\notin G} u'^{*}_{j,1}u'_{j,4} \\
&\Rightarrow \sum_{j\in G} |u'^{*}_{j,1}|^2 = \sum_{j\notin G} u'^{*}_{j,1}u'_{j,4}
\end{aligned} \tag{8.27}$$

Assume that $\Pr[A\ obtains\ \hat{R}_Y(\theta_m+\theta_c)|0\rangle] = \sum_{j\in G}|u'_{j,1}|^2 > 1/2$, then $\sum_{j\notin G} u'^{*}_{j,1}u'_{j,4} > 1/2$. According to Cauchy-Buniakowsky-Schwarz inequality, we have

$$\sum_{j\notin G}|u'_{j,1}|^2\sum_{j\notin G}|u'_{j,4}|^2 \geq |\sum_{j\notin G}u'^{*}_{j,1}u'_{j,4}|^2 > \frac{1}{4} \tag{8.28}$$

This indicates either $\sum_{j\notin G}|u'_{j,1}|^2 > 1/2$ or $\sum_{j\notin G}|u'_{j,4}|^2 > 1/2$. If $\sum_{j\notin G}|u'_{j,1}|^2 > 1/2$, consider the norm of $1st$ column of U', we have

$$\sum_{j\in[1,2^{n'}]}|u'_{j,1}|^2 = \sum_{j\in G}|u_{j,1}|^2 + \sum_{j\notin G}|u_{j,1}|^2 > \frac{1}{2}+\frac{1}{2} = 1 \tag{8.29}$$

which contradicts the unitary of U'. If $\sum_{j\notin G}|u'_{j,4}|^2 > 1/2$, consider the $4th$ column of U' we have the similar contradiction. Thus the assumption that that $\Pr[A\ obtains\ \hat{R}_Y(\theta_m+\theta_c)|0\rangle] = \sum_{j\in G}|u'_{j,1}|^2 > 1/2$ fails.

So the probability of A obtaining $\hat{R}_Y(\theta_m+\theta_c)|0\rangle$ with $\hat{R}_Y(\theta_m)|0\rangle$ and $\hat{R}_Y(\theta_c)|0\rangle$ satisfies

$$\Pr[A(\hat{R}_Y(\theta_m)|0\rangle, \hat{R}_Y(\theta_c)|0\rangle) = \hat{R}_Y(\theta_m+\theta_c)|0\rangle] \leq \frac{1}{2} \tag{8.30}$$

Theorem 8.2 *The adversary's advantage over the full quantum identity authentication scheme $\mathcal{I}$ is equal to or less than $\frac{1}{2^p}$, i.e.,*

$$Adv(A,\mathcal{I}) = \Pr[the\ challenger\ outputs\ `accept'] \leq \frac{1}{2^p} \tag{8.31}$$

Proof With the attack game in Definition 8.4, the adversary A wins the game when challenger outputs 'accept'. The adversary A obtains $\hat{R}_Y(\theta_c)|0\rangle$ in the verifier impersonation attack phase and $\hat{R}_Y(\theta_m)|0\rangle$ in the prover impersonation phase. The adversary may not necessarily follow the prover algorithm but it needs to generate

$\hat{R}_Y(\theta_m + \theta_c)|0\rangle$ to pass challenger's verification. From Lemma 8.4, at each 'prover impersonation' phase, the probability for adversary A to obtain $\hat{R}_Y(\theta_m + \theta_c)|0\rangle$ is equal to or less than $\frac{1}{2}$. When repeating the 'prover impersonation' phase p times, the success probability of adversary is reduced to $\frac{1}{2^p}$, i.e., the probability for challenger outputting 'accept' is equal to or less than $\frac{1}{2^p}$.

Thus adversary's advantage over the full quantum identity authentication scheme $\mathcal{I}$ is

$$Adv(A, \mathcal{I}) = \Pr[\textit{the challenger outputs `accept'}] \leq \frac{1}{2^p} \tag{8.32}$$

According to Theorem 8.2, when p is large sufficiently, the advantage of adversary A is a negligible probability. Thus the full quantum identity authentication scheme is secure against active attacks.

C. Effect of Noisy Channels

In practice, there are some noises in the quantum channels, which always leads to the error of transmitted qubits. For the full quantum identity authentication scheme in the challenge-response mode, the error of transmitted qubits will affect each verification phase under the challenge-response mode.

With the noise in a quantum channel, the challenger in the attack game of the above security analysis will not output the 'accept' even if only one transmission error between prover and verifier. It is difficult for attacker, prover and verifier, to obtain the success of authentication. The original challenge-response mode of the proposed full quantum identity authentication scheme is not secure in noisy channels. Through improvement, the full quantum identity authentication scheme is still secure in noisy channels.

The first method is quantum error correction code. Since the quantum error correction code avoids the errors between transmission, the above scheme and security analysis are valid in noisy channels. The second method is to change the challenge-response mode in the security analysis. Firstly, we suppose the error rate of transmitted qubits is α. For the p-time verifications in the 'prover impersonation' phase in Sect. 8.1.7, the number of failure verification is αp. Secondly, we set error threshold T_0 and error counter T. Here $T_0 = \alpha p$ and the initial value of T is 0. Each time the challenger verifies unsuccessfully, the error counter is incremented by one. Thirdly, we change the condition for the challenger to output 'accept' in Sect. 8.1.7. The challenger outputs 'accept' only if $T \leq T_0$. With such modifications, the legal participants can pass authentication, but it is hard for attackers. Because Lemma 8.4 and error rate α mean the attacker may obtain the higher value of error counter than legal participants, attackers more probably fail in authentication than legal participants. Thus, the full quantum identity authentication scheme and security analysis are valid in noisy channels.

8.2 Full Quantum One-Way Function Based on Quantum Point Obfuscation

8.2.1 Requirement of Universal Construction

Shang et al. [18] proposed a full quantum one-way function, which means quantum state can be used to authenticate quantum states. Shang's full QOWF is defined by concatenating a 'quantum-classical' QOWF [20] and a 'classical-quantum' QOWF [9]. So there is still classical information during the execution. In addition, the 'quantum-classical-quantum' mode limits the application of Shang's full QOWF only to quantum identity authentication scheme. Better model of full QOWF can be paid attention to, so that full QOWF will be applied to not only quantum identity authentication scheme but also other quantum cryptographic protocols, such as quantum digital signature, quantum message authentication, and so on. In order to realize more applications of full QOWF, we further consider how to define a more universal full QOWF. One feasible work is to find a purely full QOWF which does not transform information between classical strings and quantum states during the execution.

The quantum obfuscation, including an *obfuscator* and *interpreter*, transforms a quantum circuit into a functionally equivalent quantum state. Then this quantum state depends on *interpreter* to implement the functionality of the quantum circuit. In 2014, with topological quantum computation, the algorithm of quantum circuit obfuscation [23] was proposed. In 2016, Alagic et al. [24] formally defined quantum obfuscation. There are three features of quantum obfuscation: functionality, polynomial slowdown and virtual black-box property. Notably, Alagic et al. pointed out that the existence of the quantum obfuscation algorithm means the existence of the quantum-secure one-way function. Moreover, the black-box property of quantum obfuscation implies that it is difficult to figure out the input of the obfuscator with a given output. Obviously, it is similar to the property of OWF. So it is feasible to consider the application of the quantum obfuscation in constructing a full QOWF.

Our goal is to use quantum obfuscation to construct a full QOWF. In this section, we start with the definition of a pure QOWF. We utilize quantum obfuscation to construct a new full QOWF and give its detailed quantum circuit for implementation [25]. After analyzing the properties of the full QOWF, we use quantum point obfuscation in the specific full QOWF and explore its implementation on the Quantum Experience platform. Finally, we apply the full QOWF to quantum message authentication to show its application in cryptography.

8.2.2 Challenges in Quantum One-Way Function

Definition 8.5 (Quantum one-way function) A function $f : x \rightarrow y, x, y \in \{0, 1\}^* or \{|\phi\rangle\}^*$ is a quantum one-way function, if f satisfies the following two conditions:

1. **Easy to compute**: There exists a quantum polynomial-time algorithm A which outputs $f(x)$ for the input x, i.e., $A(x) = f(x)$.
2. **Hard to invert**: For every probabilistic quantum polynomial-time algorithm A', every positive polynomial $p(\cdot)$, and all sufficiently large n,

$$\Pr[A'(f(x), |0\rangle) \in f^{-1}(f(x))] < \frac{1}{p(n)} \tag{8.33}$$

The main challenges in the construction of QOWF contain two aspects:

1. How to measure whether a function is "easy to compute" or not?
   It is usual to compute time complexity. The OWF can reflect the concept of computational complexity [19]. For QOWF, the time complexity can be measured by the number of quantum gates in the corresponding quantum circuit [9].
2. How to ensure the property of "hard to invert"?
   For classical OWF, it is based on the mathematical problems, such as prime factorization and discrete logarithms, so as to obtain the property of "hard to invert". But, Shor's polynomial-time algorithm [26] indicates the problem of factorization and discrete logarithms can be solved on quantum computer.
   For QOWF, the property and operations of quantum system are utilized to ensure the property of "hard to invert", such as principles of quantum mechanics [4], quantum measurement [9], and so on. The main challenge is mentioned in the reference [18], such as linearity and reversibility of quantum transformation gates.
   Behera et al. [9] pointed out that the linearity and reversibility of quantum transformation gate might be broken through by revealing partial output information of quantum gates. Shang's full QOWF is constructed by means of concatenating two QOWFs to ensure the property of "hard to invert" [18]. Moreover, when discussing the quantum obfuscation for quantum circuit, Alagic et al. [24] indicated the black-box property of quantum obfuscation can be used to prove the property of "hard to invert" of a QOWF.

We focus on the construction of a purely full QOWF without generating any classical information. There is no transformation between quantum information and classical information. Meanwhile, this full QOWF is not universal for quantum cryptographic protocols. We try to construct a full QOWF with basic quantum gates to make it universal.

8.2.3 Quantum Black-Box Obfuscation

Alagic and Fefferman [24] have formally given the definition of quantum obfuscation. The quantum algorithm $\mathcal{O}$ and interpreter $\circ$ compose the quantum obfuscation scheme. The input of $\mathcal{O}$ is a quantum circuit $\mathcal{C}$, and the interpreter δ is a quantum polynomial-time algorithm.

Definition 8.6 (Quantum black-box obfuscator [24]**)** A quantum black-box obfuscator is a quantum algorithm $\mathcal{O}$ and a quantum polynomial-time algorithm δ satisfying:

1. **Polynomial expansion**: $m = poly(n)$.
2. **Functional equivalence**: For the quantum circuit $\mathcal{C}$ with $n - qubit$ as input, the output quantum state $\mathcal{O}(\mathcal{C})$ of the quantum algorithm $\mathcal{O}$ satisfies

$$\|\delta(\mathcal{O}(\mathcal{C}) \otimes \rho) - U_{\mathcal{C}} \rho U_{\mathcal{C}}^{\dagger}\|_{\mathrm{tr}} \leq negl(n) \tag{8.34}$$

3. **Virtual black-box**: For every quantum polynomial-time algorithm A, there exists a quantum polynomial-time algorithm S^{U_C} satisfies

$$|\Pr[A(\mathcal{O}(\mathcal{C})) = 1] - \Pr[S^{U_C}(|0^n\rangle) = 1]| \leq negl(n) \tag{8.35}$$

The existence of a black-box quantum obfuscator algorithm implies the existence of quantum-secure OWF. Quantum obfuscation can protect the functionality of quantum circuits and support black-box access to quantum circuits. It provides the possibility to break through the reversibility of quantum logic gates.

8.2.4 Quantum Point Obfuscation

The obfuscation of quantum point function is considered by Shang et al. [27], including the definition of quantum point obfuscation and the quantum circuit of an interpreter $\circ$. The interpreter $\circ$ is independent from quantum obfuscator.

Definition 8.7 (Quantum point obfuscation) The quantum point obfuscation is composed of quantum obfuscator $\mathcal{O}$ and interpreter $\circ$. $\mathcal{C}_\alpha$ is the quantum circuit of the quantum point function, its result of obfuscation is $\mathcal{O}(\mathcal{C}_\alpha)$, $\mathcal{O}(\mathcal{C}_\alpha) = |R(\alpha), \alpha \oplus \beta\rangle$. $\mathcal{C}_n = \{\mathcal{C}_\alpha : \alpha, \beta \in \{0, 1\}^n\}$ is the set of quantum circuits of quantum point function. $|R(\alpha)\rangle$ is the query result of the quantum random oracle $R_q : |x, y\rangle \to |x, y \oplus R(x)\rangle$, where $R(x)$ is a classical random permutation.

The quantum circuit for the interpreter $\circ$ contains three parts, namely Bit-Wise XOR, Reverse and ANDs. These circuits are shown in Figs. 8.2, 8.3, 8.4 and 8.5.

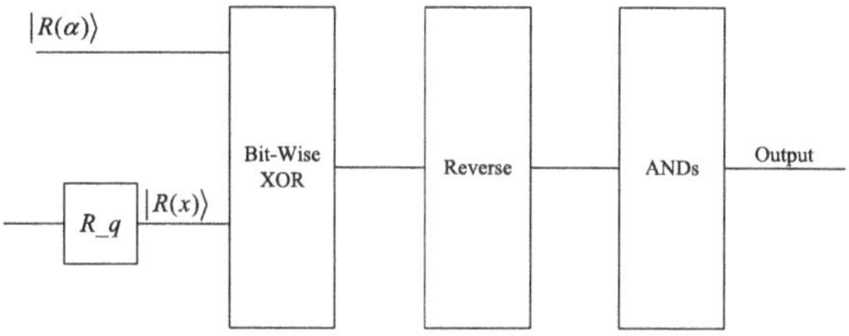

Fig. 8.2 Circuit of interpreter δ

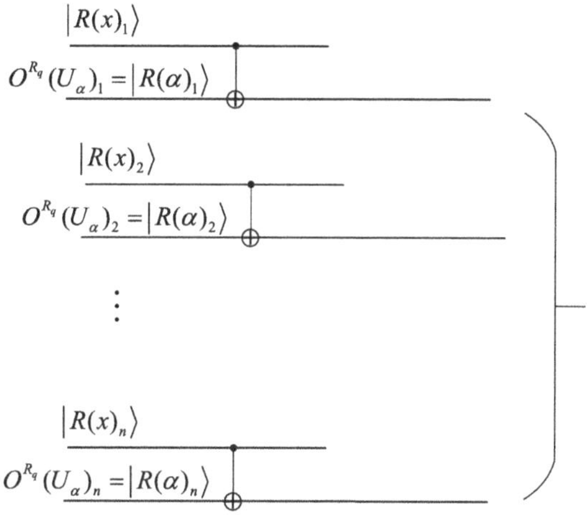

Fig. 8.3 Circuit of bit-wise XOR

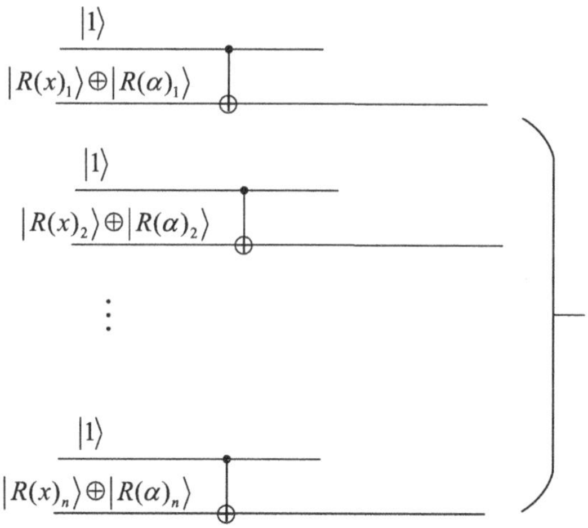

Fig. 8.4 Circuit of reverse

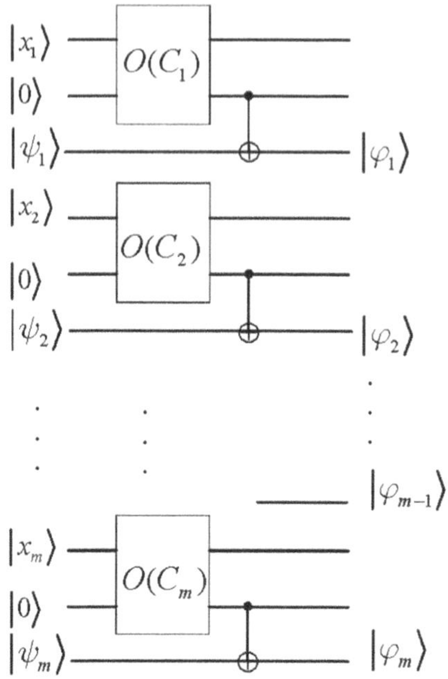

Fig. 8.5 Circuit of ANDs

8.2.5 Obfuscation-Based Full Quantum One-Way Function

We introduce a full QOWF by means of quantum obfuscation and revealing partial information of a quantum circuit, which was inspired by the References [9, 24, 27].

A. Notation and Definition

Let W denote a quantum state, named **input-cell**, which is regarded as a triple $W = |x\rangle|0\rangle|\psi\rangle$.$|x\rangle$ is $n - qubit$, $|0\rangle$ and $|\psi\rangle$ are both single-qubit.

Let $\mathcal{O}$ denote the quantum obfuscator of the quantum circuit C which is with $(n + 1)$ qubits as input and output. $\circ$ is the interpreter of $\mathcal{O}$.

Let p denote the last qubit of the quantum result which the interpreter $\circ$ has gotten after using $\mathcal{O}(C)$ to implement C in a quantum state.

The definition of a full QOWF is formally introduced as follows.

Definition 8.8 (Full quantum one-way function) A quantum function $f : |\psi\rangle \rightarrow |\varphi\rangle$ is a full quantum one-way function (full QOWF) if the function f satisfies the following two properties:

1. **Easy to compute**: For the input $|\psi\rangle$, there is a quantum polynomial-time algorithm A which outputs $f(|\psi\rangle)$, i.e., $A(|\psi\rangle) = f(|\psi\rangle)$.
2. **Hard to invert**: Given the output $|\varphi\rangle$ of the function, for each quantum polynomial-time algorithm A', each polynomial $p(\bullet)$, and all sufficiently large n, function f satisfies

$$\Pr[A'(f(|\varphi\rangle), |0\rangle) \in f^{-1}(f(|\varphi\rangle))] < \frac{1}{p(n)} \tag{8.36}$$

Now we will define a new full QOWF based on quantum obfuscation.

Definition 8.9 (Obfuscation-based full quantum one-way function) The obfuscation-based full quantum one-way function F is a function that directly maps quantum states to quantum states. F takes m input-cells W as the input quantum state and $m - qubit$ quantum state as output, i.e.,

$$F : \overbrace{W_1 \otimes \cdots \otimes W_m}^{m} \to |\varphi^{(m)}\rangle \tag{8.37}$$

To distinguish the obfuscation-based full QOWF from the full QOWF of the Reference [18], we introduce the concept of a pure quantum one-way function.

Definition 8.10 (Pure quantum one-way function) A full quantum one-way function $f : |\psi\rangle^{(a)} \to |\varphi\rangle^{(b)}$, which takes an a-qubit quantum state as input and a b-qubit quantum state as output, is called **pure quantum one-way function** if there is no classical string output or mapping relations between classical strings and quantum states in the processing.

According to Definition 8.10, the QOWF of the Reference [18] is not a pure quantum one-way function. Note that the expectation for the obfuscation-based full QOWF is to be a pure quantum one-way function. The quantum circuits and algorithm of obfuscation-based full QOWF are described as follows.

B. Algorithm

In this algorithm, we perform the quantum gates, like CNOT and controlled-swap gate. The input of the obfuscation-based full QOWF F is composed of m input-cells, i.e., $W_1 \otimes \cdots \otimes W_m$. The input quantum state can respectively be denoted as

$$|x_1\rangle|0\rangle|\psi_1\rangle, |x_2\rangle|0\rangle|\psi_2\rangle, \ldots, |x_m\rangle|0\rangle|\psi_m\rangle. \tag{8.38}$$

We put the input qubits into two quantum registers, input register R_I and result register R_D. The first two tuples of input-cell W_i are stored in R_I as control qubits. The remaining tuple of W_i is stored in R_D as the target qubit. The overall circuit C_F of the obfuscation-based QOWF is shown in Fig. 8.6. For the quantum state $W_1 \otimes \cdots \otimes W_m$, the algorithm is described as follows:

- **Step 1 (Obfuscate)**: Select m quantum circuits $C_i(i = 1, 2, \ldots, m)$ which are from the same function family $U_g : |x, y\rangle \to |x, y \oplus g(x)\rangle$, $g : \{0, 1\}^n \to \{0, 1\}^n$. The input quantum state of quantum circuit $C_i(i = 1, 2, \ldots, m)$ is $(n + 1)$-qubit. Then, use quantum obfuscator O to obfuscate C_i and obtain the result $\mathcal{O}(C_i)$. Next, for the first two tuples $|x_i, 0\rangle$ of each input-cell W_i in the input register R_I, the

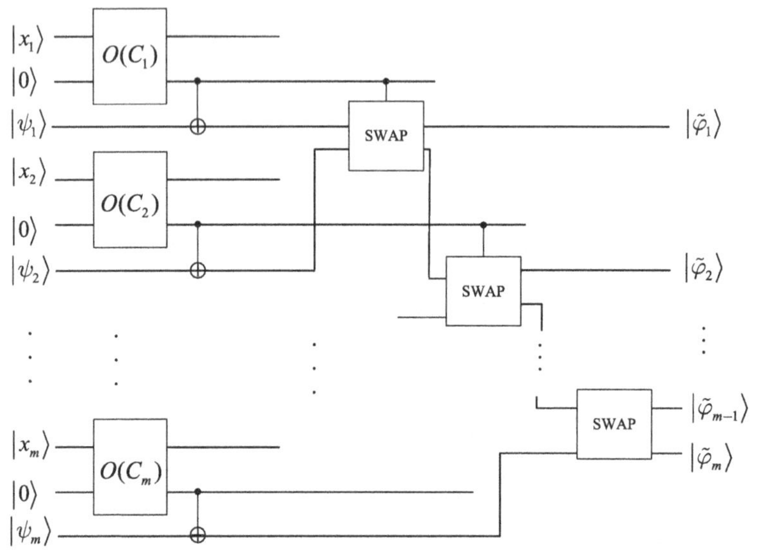

Fig. 8.6 Overall circuit C_F of obfuscation-based QOWF

interpreter $\circ$ utilizes $\mathcal{O}(\mathcal{C}_i)$ to implement the quantum circuit $\mathcal{C}_i$. The final output of the quantum circuit $\mathcal{C}_i$ is denoted as $|x_i, p_i\rangle$.

- **Step 2 (Reverse)**: For each input-cell, take the last qubit of the result $|x_i, p_i\rangle$ as the control qubit, which is calculated from **Step 1**. Take the last tuple $|\psi_i\rangle$ of W_i as the target qubit, which is in the result register R_D. Then, apply the CNOT operation to reverse some qubits. The result is denoted as $W_i^{'} = |x_i, p_i, \psi_i \oplus p_i\rangle$.
- **Step 3 (Swap)**: Take the second tuple p_i of $W_i^{'}$ as the control qubit, and the third tuple in W_i and W_{i+1} as the qubits to be exchanged. Apply the controlled swap gate. The final result is denoted as $W_i^{''}$.
- **Step 4 (Output)**: Take the quantum state $|\tilde{\varphi}_1, \tilde{\varphi}_2, \ldots, \tilde{\varphi}_m\rangle$ of the result register R_D, the third tuple of $W_i^{''}$, as the output of the obfuscation-based QOWF F, i.e.,

$$F : \overbrace{W_1 \otimes \cdots \otimes W_m}^{m} \rightarrow |\tilde{\varphi}_1, \tilde{\varphi}_2, \ldots, \tilde{\varphi}_m\rangle \tag{8.39}$$

C. Property

Property 8.1 *The time complexity of the obfuscation-based full QOWF F is* $O(m + m \times poly(\cdot))$.

Proof We assume that the execution time of the quantum gate and quantum obfuscation operation is fixed. The algorithm for the obfuscation-based full QOWF F depends on the specific quantum circuit C_F. The time complexity of the quantum circuit can be measured by the number of quantum gates in Fig. 8.6.

Let $poly(\cdot)$ denote the number of total quantum gates used in **Step 1** for the interpreter $\circ$, as the interpreter $\circ$ is a quantum polynomial-time algorithm [27].

Corresponding to the quantum circuit in Fig. 8.6, m obfuscation results is used in **Step 1 Obfuscate**. Then m interpreters are used. So the total number of quantum gates in **Step 1** is $m \times poly(\cdot)$, denoted as Y_1.

In **Step 2 Reverse**, the CNOT gates are applied to each input-cell W_i. The number of CNOT gates is m, denoted as Y_2.

In **Step 3 Swap**, the corresponding operation in Fig. 8.6 takes place between the input-cell W_i and $W_{i+1} (i = 1, 2, \cdots, m-1)$. It uses $m-1$ controlled swap gates, denoted as Y_3.

Then the total number of quantum gates in the quantum circuit is

$$Y = Y_1 + Y_2 + Y_3 = 2m + m \times poly(\cdot) - 1 \tag{8.40}$$

So, for the obfuscation-based full QOWF F, the time complexity is

$$O(F)_{m,poly(\cdot)} = O(m + m \times poly(\cdot)) \tag{8.41}$$

Lemma 8.5 *For the obfuscation-based full QOWF*

$$F : \overbrace{W_1 \otimes \cdots \otimes W_m}^{m} \rightarrow |\varphi^{(m)}\rangle \tag{8.42}$$

there exists a quantum polynomial-time algorithm A outputting $F(|\psi\rangle)$ for the input $|\psi\rangle$, i.e., $A(|\psi\rangle) = F(|\psi\rangle)$.

Proof According to **Property** 8.1, the corresponding quantum circuit C_F of the obfuscation-based full QOWF F can be performed in quantum polynomial-time. Thus the quantum algorithm described in Sect. 8.2.5 is a quantum polynomial-time algorithm.

Property 8.2 *For the same input $W_1 \otimes \cdots \otimes W_m$, the output quantum state of the obfuscation-based full QOWF F remains consistent, when C_F is executed multiple times.*

Proof According to the property of ***virtual black-box*** described in Sect. 8.2.3, for any quantum polynomial-time algorithm A, there is a quantum polynomial-time algorithm S^{U_C}

$$\Pr[A(\mathcal{O}(C)) = 1] - \Pr[S^{U_C}(|0^n\rangle) = 1]| \leq negl(n) \tag{8.43}$$

For the input $W_1 \otimes \cdots \otimes W_m$, the quantum states are unknown after the **Obfuscate** operation. Because the input circuit of quantum obfuscation is not revealed in detail. When the circuit C_F of the obfuscation-based full QOWF is performed multiple times, it is difficult to judge whether the obfuscation result $\mathcal{O}(C_i)$ is the same or not. As $\mathcal{O}(C_i)$ is the quantum state, it is difficult to compare the quantum state without destroying it.

According to the property of ***functional equivalence*** described in Sect. 8.2.3, the output quantum state $\mathcal{O}(\mathcal{C})$ of the quantum obfuscator $\mathcal{O}$ satisfies, $\|\delta(\mathcal{O}(\mathcal{C}) \otimes \rho) - U_{\mathcal{C}} \rho U_{\mathcal{C}}^{\dagger}\|_{\text{tr}} \leq negl(n)$.

The functionality of the result $\mathcal{O}(\mathcal{C}_i)$ of quantum obfuscation and the original circuit is the same. Thus, with the interpreter $\circ$, the output quantum state after the **Obfuscate** operation remains consistent. For the same input $W_1 \otimes \cdots \otimes W_m$, the output of the obfuscation-based full QOWF F is identical for multiple executions.

According to **Property** 8.2, a full QOWF F is proved to be well defined. This property reflects the correctness of the full QOWF F that there is a mapping relationship formed between input $W_1 \otimes \cdots \otimes W_m$ and output $|\varphi^{(m)}\rangle$. In other words, the output is definite and unique for each input $W_1 \otimes \cdots \otimes W_m$.

Property 8.3 *If any adversary A can obtain all the output qubits ρ of the quantum circuit C_F, the probability that adversary A successfully performs the inverse operation on the quantum circuit C_F and obtains the input $W_1 \otimes \cdots \otimes W_m$ is negligible.*

Proof Because the quantum CNOT gate and quantum controlled swap gate in Fig. 8.6 are unitary and capable to be inverted, the key for the adversary A to invert the quantum circuit C_F is to invert the quantum obfuscation, i.e., to obtain the circuit $\mathcal{C}_i$.

Suppose there is a polynomial-time algorithm S^{U_i}. Adversary A obtains the circuit $\mathcal{C}_i$ by black-box accessing. Due to the property of ***virtual black-box*** described in Sect. 8.2.3, the probability $\Pr[A(\mathcal{O}(\mathcal{C}_i)) = 1]$ that adversary A obtains the input $\mathcal{C}_i$ correctly satisfies

$$\Pr[A(\mathcal{O}(\mathcal{C}_i)) = 1] \leq \Pr[S^{U_i}(|0^n\rangle) = 1] + negl(n) \tag{8.44}$$

$$\leq \tfrac{1}{2} + negl(n) \tag{8.45}$$

There are m quantum obfuscation results $\mathcal{O}(\mathcal{C}_i)$ in the quantum circuit C_F. The probability $\Pr[A(\mathcal{O}(\mathcal{C}_1)) = 1, A(\mathcal{O}(\mathcal{C}_2)) = 1, \ldots, A(\mathcal{O}(\mathcal{C}_m)) = 1]$ that adversary A successfully guesses obfuscation results satisfies

$$\Pr[A(\mathcal{O}(\mathcal{C}_1)) = 1, A(\mathcal{O}(\mathcal{C}_2)) = 1, \ldots, A(\mathcal{O}(\mathcal{C}_m)) = 1] \tag{8.46}$$

$$\leq \left(\frac{1}{2} + negl(n)\right)^m \tag{8.47}$$

When m is large enough, $\Pr[A(\mathcal{O}(\mathcal{C}_1)) = 1, A(\mathcal{O}(\mathcal{C}_2)) = 1, \ldots, A(\mathcal{O}(\mathcal{C}_m)) = 1]$ is negligible. The probability that adversary A correctly guesses the m obfuscation results $\mathcal{O}(\mathcal{C}_i)$ is negligible. Then the probability that adversary A successfully implements the inverse operation on the quantum circuit C_F is negligible.

Lemma 8.6 *If any adversary A can obtain the output $|\varphi^{(m)}\rangle$ of the obfuscation-based full QOWF F, the probability that adversary A successfully inverts the function F and obtains the input $W_1 \otimes \cdots \otimes W_m$ is negligible.*

Proof The inverse operation that adversary A performs for the obfuscation-based full QOWF F consists of two parts. The first part is to supplement the other half output $|\Phi\rangle$ of the quantum circuit C_F, which is not revealed in ***Step 4 Output*** in Sect. 8.2.5. The second part is to invert the corresponding quantum circuit C_F.

If the adversary A can obtain the right $|\Phi\rangle$ corresponding to $|\varphi^{(m)}\rangle$, the inversion of the obfuscation-based full QOWF F is transformed into the inversion of the quantum circuit C_F. Let the complete output of C_F be denoted as ρ. ρ consists of $|\Phi\rangle$ and $|\varphi^{(m)}\rangle$. According to **Property** 8.3, the probability that adversary A successfully inverts the quantum circuit C_F is negligible. Thus the probability that adversary A successfully inverts the function F and obtains the input $W_1 \otimes \cdots \otimes W_m$ is negligible.

If the adversary A does not know the right $|\Phi\rangle$ corresponding to $|\varphi^{(m)}\rangle$, it is necessary for adversary A to supplement the output quantum state of quantum circuit C_F. Then adversary A intends to invert the quantum circuit C_F. According to **Property** 8.3, the probability that Adversary A successfully inverts the quantum circuit C_F is negligible. The process of supplementing the output of the quantum circuit C_F reduces the probability that adversary A successfully inverts obfuscation-based full QOWF F. Thus the probability that adversary A successfully inverts the function F and obtains the input $W_1 \otimes \cdots \otimes W_m$ is negligible.

Property 8.4 *(One-wayness) The obfuscation-based full quantum one-way function*

$F : \overbrace{W_1 \otimes \cdots \otimes W_m}^{m} \rightarrow |\varphi^{(m)}\rangle$ *is 'easy to compute', but 'hard to invert'.*

Proof **Lemma** 8.5 is the same as 'easy to compute' described in Sect. 8.2.5. So the obfuscation-based full quantum function F is 'easy to compute'. According to **Lemma** 8.6, the obfuscation-based full quantum function F can be inverted with negligible probability. So the obfuscation-based full quantum function F is 'hard to invert'.

8.2.6 Application to Quantum Message Authentication

We utilize quantum point obfuscation (defined in Sect. 8.2.4) in the universal QOWF, then apply this specific QOWF to a quantum message authentication scheme. The circuit of quantum point function is represented as $\mathcal{C}_{\alpha_i}$ and the corresponding quantum obfuscation result is represented as $\mathcal{O}(\mathcal{C}_{\alpha_i})$.

A. Quantum Message Authentication Scheme

The quantum message authentication scheme involves two parties: Alice (sender) and Bob (receiver). There are three phases in the scheme: initialization, authentication tag generation and verification. The scheme is described as follows:

1. ***Initialization*** Alice and Bob agree on the sequence of quantum point obfuscation result $\mathcal{O}(\mathcal{C}_{\alpha_i})$ used in the quantum circuit C_F, the corresponding interpreter δ, and m-bit classical string K.

2. ***Authentication tag generation***

- **Step 1**: To send m-qubit message $|m\rangle$, Alice prepares three messages $|m\rangle$ and two $m(n+1)$-qubit auxiliary qubits $|\alpha\rangle$. Alice utilizes a copy of auxiliary qubits $|\alpha\rangle$ and a copy of message $|m\rangle$ to construct the input-cell $W_i(i = 1, \ldots, m)$. Then Alice computes $F_q : W_1 \otimes \cdots \otimes W_m \to |\varphi^{(m)}\rangle$. Alice generates the authentication tag $|\varphi^{(m)}\rangle$.
- **Step 2**: Alice does quantum symmetric encryption by means of K. The remaining two messages $|m\rangle$ and a copy of auxiliary qubits $|\alpha\rangle$ are encrypted as $E_K(|m\rangle, |m\rangle, |\alpha\rangle)$. Alice sends the ciphertext $E_K(|m\rangle, |m\rangle, |\alpha\rangle)$ and the message authentication tag $|\varphi^{(m)}\rangle$ to Bob.

3. ***Verification***

- **Step 1**: After receiving the ciphertext $E_K(|m\rangle, |m\rangle, |\alpha\rangle)$ and the message authentication tag $|\varphi^{(m)}\rangle$, Bob firstly uses K to decrypt the ciphertext $E_K(|m\rangle, |m\rangle, |\alpha\rangle)$ and obtains $|m_0\rangle, |m_1\rangle, |\alpha'\rangle$.
- **Step 2**: Bob uses the SWAP-test [3] to test whether $|m_1\rangle$ and $|m_0\rangle$ are equal or not. If unequal, the authentication fails, otherwise, continue the next step.
- **Step 3**: When the test in Step 2 is successfully passed, Bob constructs the input-cell $W_1 \otimes \cdots \otimes W_m$ using $|m_z\rangle, z = 0, 1$ and the auxiliary qubits $|\alpha'\rangle$. Then Bob computes

$$F_q : \overbrace{W_1 \otimes \cdots \otimes W_m}^{m} \to |\varphi^{'(m)}\rangle$$

Compare the message authentication tag $|\varphi^{(m)}\rangle$ with $|\varphi^{'(m)}\rangle$, by means of SWAP-test. If the measurement result of SWAP-test is $|0\rangle$, the authentication is successful, otherwise the authentication fails.

B. Security Analysis

No-cloning theorem means that it is impossible to fully copy an unknown quantum state. For this quantum message authentication scheme, no-cloning theorem indicates that an adversary cannot eavesdrop quantum information in quantum channel. Furthermore, the adversary cannot perform the eavesdropping attack. In this section, we analyze the performance of the quantum message authentication scheme against forgery attack. We suppose that adversary A has the ability to decrypt.

The first challenge for adversary A performing forgery attack is the detail of quantum circuit in the quantum message authentication scheme. As the sequence of quantum point obfuscation result $\mathcal{O}(\mathcal{C}_{\alpha_i})$ used in the scheme is secretly shared by Alice and Bob, adversary A has no idea of $\mathcal{O}(\mathcal{C}_{\alpha_i})$. The only way adversary A can do is to randomly guess $\mathcal{O}(\mathcal{C}_{\alpha_i})$ or guess the input circuit $\mathcal{C}_{\alpha_i}$ of quantum point obfuscation. If there are l elements in the input set of $\mathcal{O}$. For $\mathcal{O}$, there are l possibilities of the input quantum circuit $\mathcal{C}_{\alpha_i}$. In other words, in the sequence of $\mathcal{O}(\mathcal{C}_{\alpha_i})$, there are l possibilities at one position. For a m-qubit message, Alice and Bob secretly share m quantum point obfuscators. So there are l^m possible permutations of the obfuscator sequence. The probability $P_{\mathcal{O}(\mathcal{C}_{\oslash})}$ that adversary A gets the right permutation is $\frac{1}{l^m}$. $P_{\mathcal{O}(\mathcal{C}_{\oslash})}$ is negligible when l^m is large enough.

The second challenge for successful forgery attack is forging new message segment $(|m\rangle, |m\rangle, |\alpha\rangle)$. We show that the property of obfuscation-based full QOWF reduces the probability that adversary A successfully forges a message.

Theorem 8.3 *The probability P_{mod} that adversary A successfully forges the message $|m\rangle$ and deceives Bob is negligible.*

Proof If adversary A tries to tamper with the message $(|m\rangle, |m\rangle, |\alpha\rangle)$ that Alice sends to Bob, adversary A intercepts the message and modifies it. Since the unknown quantum state cannot be copied. To pass the authentication by Bob successfully, adversary A should recover $|m\rangle$ and auxiliary qubits $|\alpha\rangle$ from the message authentication tag $|\varphi^{(m)}\rangle$ and then modify all the data $|m\rangle$. At this moment, adversary A is in the phase of ***Authentication tag generation*** and adversary A can regenerate a new message authentication tag and send it to Bob to pass authentication. The key for adversary A successfully obtaining $|m\rangle$ and $|\alpha\rangle$ is to invert the obfuscation-based QOWF F_q. According to Lemma 8.6, the probability for adversary A to invert F_q is negligible. Thus the probability P_{mod} that adversary A successfully forges message is negligible.

8.3 Dynamic Full Quantum One-Way Function Based on Quantum Circuit Mapping

8.3.1 Requirement of Dynamic Mapping

Shang et al. [18] pioneered the full quantum one-way function, of which the information transformation follows the pattern 'quantum→classical→quantum'. The input quantum state will be destroyed and firstly transformed into a classical string during the execution of this function. However, the full quantum one-way function, in the literal sense, directly maps between pure quantum information without an intermediate process of classical information. Thus this full quantum one-way function does not perfectly match the words 'full quantum'. Besides, it is difficult to construct a full quantum trapdoor one-way function. It is worth thinking about how to eliminate the concatenation step and construct a purely full quantum one-way function. The expected 'purely full quantum one-way function' will directly map between quantum states and can be used to construct a full quantum trapdoor one-way function.

In quantum computation, the function can be regarded as a quantum algorithm which is usually described by quantum circuit. Quantum circuit consists of a series of quantum gates that directly interact with quantum states without destroying them. In the noisy intermediate-scale quantum (NISQ) era [29], there is a gap between physical devices and logical quantum circuits [30]. Because the coupling relationship between logical qubits might not exist in physical qubits, several gates of quantum circuits cannot be directly performed on real quantum systems. Quantum circuits need to be optimized to make the remapped quantum circuit meet the constraints of physical devices. This task focuses on the qubit mapping problem, whose exact solution is exponential in the worst case [31]. Recently, quantum circuit optimization employs the heuristic search algorithm to implement quantum circuit mapping. The heuristic search algorithms insert Bridge gate [31] or SWAP gate [30, 32] into the original quantum circuit. These heuristic search algorithms can accelerate the execution of some quantum circuit tasks on IBM's physical quantum platform. Quantum circuit optimization maps a logical quantum circuit to another different quantum circuit which satisfies the coupling relationship between physical qubits. Without the coupling relationship between physical qubits or the mapping relationship between logical qubits and physical qubits, it is difficult to discover the mapping relationship between a physical quantum circuit and a logical quantum circuit. Thus, we use quantum circuit optimization to construct a quantum one-way function in which the average-case complexity of the inverting task is out of polynomial time [33].

In this section, we utilize a quantum circuit optimization algorithm to construct a dynamic full quantum one-way function, which can dynamically generate a quantum circuit [34]. The dynamic circuit generation contributes to one-wayness of a new full quantum one-way function and is treated as the trapdoor to construct a full quantum trapdoor one-way function.

8.3.2 Quantum One-Way Function

Quantum one-way function has a similar definition to classical one-way function, defined as follows.

Definition 8.11 (Weak quantum one-way function [1]) A one-to-one function $f : \{0, 1\}^* \to \{0, 1\}^*$ is a weak quantum one-way function, if f satisfies

1. **Easy to compute**: f can be computed by a polynomial-time classical circuit.
2. **Hard to invert**: For probabilistic polynomial-time algorithm I, every polynomial $p(\cdot)$, and all sufficiently large $n \in N$,

$$\frac{1}{2^n} \sum_{x \in \{0,1\}^n} \Pr[I(f(x)) \in f^{-1}(f(x))] \leq 1 - \frac{1}{p(n)} \tag{8.48}$$

The definition of ***weak quantum one-way function*** was proposed for a 'classical-classical' quantum one-way function. Ablayev et al. [5] gave a definition that is suitable for all types of quantum one-way functions.

Definition 8.12 (Quantum one-way function [5])
f is a quantum one-way function , if it is

1. **Easy to compute**: For an input w, there is a quantum polynomial-time algorithm that outputs $|f(w)\rangle$.
2. **Hard to invert**: One cannot obtain w from $|f(w)\rangle$ based on quantum information theory.

According to the definition of ***Strong one-way function*** and ***Quantum one-way function***, the definition of full quantum one-way function is further summarized as follows.

Definition 8.13 (Full quantum one-way function) A quantum function $f : |\varphi\rangle \rightarrow |\psi\rangle$ is a full quantum one-way function (full QOWF) if the function f satisfies

1. **Easy to compute**: For an input $|\varphi\rangle$, there is a quantum polynomial-time algorithm A that outputs $|\psi\rangle$.
2. **Hard to invert**: For every quantum polynomial-time algorithm A', every polynomial $p(\bullet)$, and all sufficiently large n, the function f satisfies

$$\Pr[A' \text{ obtains } |\varphi\rangle \text{ from } |\psi\rangle] < \frac{1}{p(n)} \tag{8.49}$$

8.3.3 *Quantum Circuit Optimization*

Quantum circuit optimization aims to solve the difficult task named 'quantum circuit mapping'.

Definition 8.14 (Quantum circuit mapping [35]) To make quantum operations of a given quantum circuit obey the constraints of physical qubits, it maps the qubits in the given quantum circuit to the actual qubits in physical quantum devices.

On the NISQ computer, there is a coupling relationship between physical qubits which limits the execution of quantum gates on physical devices. So the quantum algorithm, described by quantum circuit, cannot be directly performed between actual qubits. By optimizing the quantum circuit, the quantum algorithm is modified to perfectly fit the physical quantum devices. The prevalent method for quantum circuit optimization is employing a heuristic algorithm to insert extra quantum gates (such as Bridge gate [31], CNOT gate [35] and SWAP gate [30]) into the original quantum circuit. Li et al. [30] proposed a quantum circuit optimization algorithm named SWAP-based BidiREctional heuristic search algorithm (SABRE). They introduced the reverse traversal technique and a *decay* effect into this algorithm to balance the cost between depth and capacity of quantum circuits. The overview of SABRE algorithm is described as follows.

Algorithm 1 (SABRE) *It includes two steps: preprocessing and SWAP-based heuristic search.*

1. **Preprocessing**: *Given the quantum circuit and coupling relationship between physical qubits, obtain the distance matrix D, the dependency graph DAG of quantum gates in the quantum circuit, the front layer Fr of DAG, and the initial mapping.*
2. **SWAP-based heuristic search**: *Traverse the entire DAG from the front layer Fr and insert SWAP gates to the quantum circuit until Fr is empty. The traversal iterates from the forward and backward of a quantum circuit. The decay effect is used to design the heuristic cost function H.*

$$
\begin{aligned}
H &= max(decay(SWAP.q_1), decay(SWAP.q_2)) \\
&* \left\{ \frac{1}{|Fr|} \sum_{gate \in Fr} D[\pi(gate.q_1)][\pi(gate.q_2)] \right. \\
&\left. + W * \frac{1}{|E|} \sum_{gate \in E} D[\pi(gate.q_1)][\pi(gate.q_2)] \right\}
\end{aligned} \tag{8.50}
$$

π is a quantum circuit mapping. $gate.q_i$ is the qubit i where the quantum gate is performed on. E is an Extension Set which contains closet successors of the gates in Fr.

The SABRE algorithm can calculate a solution which satisfies the coupling relationship between physical qubits but may not be unique and globally optimal. With different coupling relationships between physical qubits, the quantum circuit optimization algorithm generates different remapped quantum circuits for the same original circuit. We use quantum circuit mapping to define a hard task for constructing the new full quantum one-way function. In the hard task, the corresponding remapped circuit is difficult to be exactly calculated when an original quantum circuit is given without giving the coupling relationship.

8.3.4 Quantum Money

Based on conjugate coding, quantum money was first proposed by Wiesner [36]. It is not only the origin of quantum money but also quantum cryptography. Subsequently, more quantum money schemes were proposed, such as public-key quantum money [37] and quantum bitcoin [38]. For a quantum money scheme with quantum mechanics, Lutomirski et al. [39] pointed out three requirements that quantum money should satisfy: (1) the mint can print it with an efficient algorithm, (2) anyone can verify it with minimal damage, (3) no one can copy it except the mint.

Based on the quantum one-way function, Behera et al. [9] came up with a quantum money scheme named quantum currency notes. In Behera's scheme, the currency notes can be verified multiple times. This scheme includes a minting algorithm and verification algorithm. The overview of these algorithms is described as follows:

1. ***Minting Algorithm*** The bank prints a quantum currency note $\$ = (|\psi\rangle, \mathcal{M}, L, F, \sigma)$, where $L = F|\psi\rangle$. F is the chosen quantum one-way function. σ is the signature that is calculated from the classical string $(\mathcal{M}||L||F)$. $(\mathcal{M}||L||F)$ is signed by the private key K_{priv} from the key pair (K_{priv}, K_{pub}).
2. ***Verification Algorithm*** The user checks whether the format of the quantum currency note is $(|\psi\rangle, \mathcal{M}, L, F, \sigma)$ or not. With the classical string $(\mathcal{M}||L||F)$ and public key K_{pub}, the user verifies whether the signature σ is valid or not. Besides, the user checks whether L, F, $|\psi\rangle$ matches or not. Note that the quantum state $|\psi\rangle$ can be recovered with *OWF Verification Algorithm* [9] of quantum one-way function F.

8.3.5 Dynamic Full Quantum One-Way Function

We introduce a new full quantum one-way function $F : |\phi\rangle \rightarrow |\psi\rangle$. The process of circuit mapping in quantum circuit optimization is used to construct the one-wayness of the new full quantum one-way function. During the execution of this function, the final quantum circuit is dynamically generated based on an input quantum state $|\phi\rangle$. Since this new QOWF features the dynamic nature, we call it to be 'dynamic full quantum one-way function', named DF-QOWF.

Quantum circuit optimization algorithms indicate the qubit mapping problem which is hard to be solved exactly via a polynomial-time algorithm. Based on the list of allowed quantum transformations and the cost of implementing a transformation, qubit mapping problem is modified to the solvable version [31] in quantum circuit optimization algorithms. In quantum cryptography, quantum one-way function is 'easy to compute' but 'hard to invert' in quantum polynomial time. We apply the quantum circuit optimization algorithm *SABRE algorithm* to construct a hard task that is impossible to be solved in quantum polynomial time. The hard task contributes to defining the dynamic full quantum one-way function.

Definition 8.15 (Dynamic full quantum one-way function) F is a dynamic full quantum one-way function (DF-QOWF) that maps n-qubit quantum state $|\phi\rangle$ to another n-qubit quantum state $|\psi\rangle$ based on the dynamic quantum circuit. $|\phi\rangle$ is n-qubit, where $n = 3k, k = 1, 2, \ldots$.

$$F : |\phi\rangle \rightarrow |\psi\rangle \tag{8.51}$$

Before introducing the algorithm of the dynamic full quantum one-way function, we provide its auxiliary algorithm which generates a coupling graph from a quantum state. In this auxiliary algorithm, the quantum point function is employed to establish a relationship between specific input quantum state and generated coupling graph. The generated coupling graph is fundamental for applying SABRE algorithm to the full quantum one-way function. It delineates a qubit permutation. If there is an edge between a pair of qubits, the two-qubit quantum gate can be performed in this position. The auxiliary algorithm is defined as follows.

Algorithm 2 (Coupling generation algorithm) *The input of this algorithm is n separate copies of n − qubit quantum state* $|\phi\rangle$. *Quantum measurement will consume these input states. For* $|\phi\rangle$, *the algorithm generates a coupling graph represented by an* $n \times n$ *matrix* $G_{n\times n}$. *The element in* $G_{n\times n}$ *is 0 or 1. The detailed steps are described below:*

Step 1*:* *Choose n quantum point functions* $U_{f_i} : |x, y\rangle \rightarrow |x, y \oplus f_i(x)\rangle$, *where* $y = 0$ *and* $f_i(x)$ *is a classical quantum point*

$$f_i(x) = P_{\alpha_i} = \begin{cases} 1 & if \quad x = \alpha_i \\ 0 & otherwise \end{cases} \tag{8.52}$$

$\alpha_i \in \{0, 1\}^n$, $i = 1, \ldots, n$.

Step 2*:* *Perform the function* U_{f_k} *on each qubit* q_i *of quantum state* $|\phi\rangle$ *to obtain the result* $|q_i, y \oplus f_k(q_i)\rangle$, $k = 1$. *Then, measure the second qubit of* $|q_i, y \oplus f_k(q_i)\rangle$ *to obtain a classical string* $d_k = d_1 = (g_{11}, \ldots, g_{n1})^T$. d_1 *is stored in the first column of matrix* $G_{n\times n}$.

Step 3*:* *For the remaining copies of* $|\phi\rangle$, *repeat* Step 2 *with k increasing from 2 to n. Store the classical string* d_k *in the* k^{th} *column of matrix* $G_{n\times n}$.

Step 4*:* *Check matric* $G_{n\times n}$. *If the element* $g_{i,i}$ *is not 1 in matrix* $G_{n\times n}$, *change* $g_{i,i}$ *to be 1. Depth-first search (DFS) algorithm is used to check whether there is a path through all qubits or not. If not, add edges to produce the default path. In the default path, each* Q_i *has an edge to* Q_1, *i.e.,* $G[i][1] = 1$, $i = 2, \ldots, n$.

Coupling generation algorithm *generates a virtual qubit permutation that quantum circuits should follow for execution.* $G[i][k] = 1$ *means two-qubit quantum gates can be performed between qubit* Q_k *and* Q_i. *If* $G[k][i] = 1$ *or* $G[i][k] = 1$, *quantum gates can be performed normally.*

Based on Li's quantum circuit optimization algorithm [30], detailed algorithm of the new full quantum one-way function is described as follows.

Algorithm 3 (DF-QOWF algorithm) *The algorithm of dynamic full quantum one-way function includes six steps which are divided into three phases. Except for the input state* $|\phi\rangle$, *other n separate copies of* $|\phi\rangle$ *are needed as auxiliary quantum states.*

1. ***Preparation phase***

Step 1*:* *Prepare an n-qubit input state* $|\phi\rangle$ *and n separate copies of* $|\phi\rangle$. *These copies of* $|\phi\rangle$ *will be consumed to generate a coupling graph in the next phase. Prepare an original quantum circuit* C_{orig} *(shown in Fig. 8.7) which is in public. According to the execution order,* C_{orig} *is divided into three sub-circuits. For n-qubit input state* $|\phi\rangle$, C_{orig} *is combined by three tuples of*

CNOT gates, denoted by $C_{orig} = C_1\#C_2\#C_3$. '#' is the connector denoting the operation of combining quantum circuits [27]. In each tuple of C_{orig}, the CNOT gates can be executed simultaneously. C_1, C_2 and C_3 are described as follows.

$$\begin{aligned} C_1 &= \{c_{1_k} | c_{1_k} = CNOT(q_{3k-2}, q_{3k-1})\} \\ C_2 &= \{c_{2_k} | c_{2_k} = CNOT(q_{3k-1}, q_{3k})\} \\ C_3 &= \{c_{3_k} | c_{3_k} = CNOT(q_{3k}, q_{3k+1})\} \end{aligned} \tag{8.53}$$

$k = 1, 2, 3, \ldots$ *and* $3k + 1 \leq n$.

Step 2: *Generate the dependency graph DAG and front layer F_{ront} of quantum circuit C_{orig}. The logical circuit $LC = (M, C_{orig})$ is the profile of original circuit C_{orig}. M is the set of qubit $q_1, \ldots, q_n$. $q_1, \ldots, q_n$, called mapping-input qubits. The detail of DAG and F_{ront} are described as follows.*

(a) *DAG: It is a matrix that stores the execution path of quantum gates in C_{orig}. Quantum gates in the same layer are performed simultaneously.*

(b) *front layer F_{ront}: It is a set of quantum gates in dependency graph DAG which has no previous quantum gate to be performed. In other words, it is a set of all quantum gates in the first layer of dependency graph DAG.*

2. ***Generation phase***

Step 3: *Calculate the coupling graph $G[V, E]$ by performing* ***Coupling generation algorithm*** *on n copies of $|\phi\rangle$. $G[V, E]$ is stored in matrix $G_{n\times n}$. V is the set of qubits $Q_1, \ldots, Q_n$ which the input qubits $q_1, \ldots, q_n$ are actually mapped to be. $Q_1, \ldots, Q_n$ are called mapping-result qubits. E indicates the two-position Q_i, Q_k where the quantum gates can be performed.*

Step 4: *Perform Floyd-Warshall algorithm [40] and generate distance matrix D based on the coupling graph $G[V, E]$ and dependency graph DAG. The element of metric D is the shortest path to move qubit from the position q_i to Q_i. Initially, the mapping-input qubits q_i and mapping-result qubits Q_i are in the same line, as shown in Fig. 8.7.*

3. ***Execution phase***

Step 5: *Perform SABRE algorithm (described in Sect. 8.3.3) to add SWAP gates into C_{orig}. Finally, the logical circuit $LC = (M, C_{orig})$ is mapped to a practical circuit $PC = (V, C_p)$ with the execution circuit C_p.*

Step 6: *Perform the execution circuit PC for input quantum state $|\phi\rangle$, and output quantum state $|\psi\rangle$ as the result of the dynamic full quantum one-way function F.*

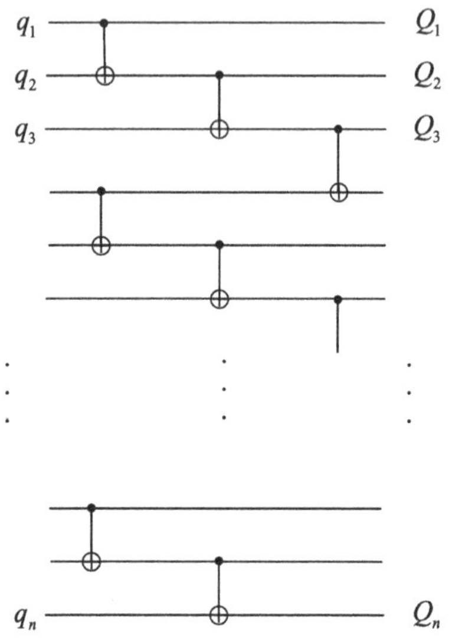

Fig. 8.7 Original quantum circuit C_{orig}

For the input quantum state $|\phi\rangle$, the DF-QOWF algorithm dynamically generates a quantum circuit C_p. C_p is finally performed on $|\phi\rangle$ to obtain the output of the dynamic full quantum one-way function.

Besides, an image verification algorithm is defined to verify the image $|\psi\rangle$ of the dynamic full quantum one-way function. It can repeatedly verify whether $F|\phi\rangle = |\psi\rangle$ or not.

Algorithm 4 (Image verification algorithm) *Given an input quantum state $|\phi\rangle$ and an image $|\psi\rangle$ (the output quantum state) of the dynamic full quantum one-way function F, the verification of the image $|\psi\rangle$ includes three steps with auxiliary information $G_{n\times n}$ and LC.*

Step 1: *With $G_{n\times n}$ and LC, perform the execution phase of* ***DF-QOWF algorithm*** *to obtain PC and $|\psi'\rangle$.*

Step 2: *Perform SWAP-test on $|\psi\rangle$ and $|\psi'\rangle$ to check whether they are equal or not. If $|\psi\rangle = |\psi'\rangle$, the measurement result of SWAP-test is '0'. If the measurement result is '0', mark $|\psi'\rangle$ 'pass' in this step.*

Step 3: *If $|\psi'\rangle$ passes* ***Step 2****, treat $|\psi\rangle = |\psi'\rangle$ and accept $|\psi\rangle$ as the image of F when given $|\phi\rangle$. Then, execute circuit PC reversely on $|\psi'\rangle$ to obtain a quantum state $|\phi'\rangle$.*

When given an input $|0\rangle|\psi\rangle|\psi'\rangle$ in SWAP-test, the final state before measurement is

$$\frac{1}{2}|0\rangle(|\psi\rangle|\psi'\rangle + |\psi'\rangle|\psi\rangle) + \frac{1}{2}|1\rangle(|\psi\rangle|\psi'\rangle - |\psi'\rangle|\psi\rangle) \tag{8.54}$$

The outcome '0' of SWAP-test is held with an error probability P_e [41], where

$$P_e = \frac{1+\varepsilon^2}{2}, \varepsilon = |\langle\psi|\psi'\rangle|, 0 \le \varepsilon < 1 \tag{8.55}$$

In **Image verification algorithm**, $|\psi\rangle$ and $|\psi'\rangle$ are n-qubit. If $|\psi\rangle = |\psi'\rangle$, the measurement result of SWAP-test is '0' with probability 1. $|\psi'\rangle$ is marked with 'pass' in Step 2. As a result, $|\psi\rangle$ is accepted as the image of F for the input $|\phi\rangle$. The final state after SWAP-test is $|0\rangle|\psi\rangle|\psi\rangle$. There is no entanglement after SWAP-test [42], so that the corresponding input state $|\phi\rangle$ can be recovered from $|\psi'\rangle$ in Step 3, i.e., $|\phi'\rangle = |\phi\rangle$. Consequently, **Image verification algorithm** can be repeated between $|\psi\rangle$ and $|\phi\rangle$.

If $|\psi\rangle$ and $|\psi'\rangle$ are different, **Image verification algorithm** inherits the error probability P_e from SWAP-test and $0 \le |\langle\psi|\psi'\rangle| < 1$. The measurement of SWAP-test outputs '0' with probability $\frac{1+|\langle\psi|\psi'\rangle|^2}{2}$. If the result of measurement is '0', $|\psi'\rangle$ will be misjudged and marked with 'pass'. In other words, $|\psi\rangle$ is mistakenly accepted as the image of F for the input $|\phi\rangle$. The misjudged image $|\psi\rangle$ leads to the failure of **Image verification algorithm**. The failure probability of **Image verification algorithm** is denoted by P_f.

Theorem 8.4 *For any input pair* $(|\phi\rangle, |\psi\rangle)$ *of* **Image verification algorithm**, l *rounds execution of* **Image verification algorithm** *reduces the failure probability* P_f *to be*

$$P_f = \left(\frac{1+\varepsilon^2}{2}\right)^l, \varepsilon = |\langle\psi|\psi'\rangle| < 1 \tag{8.56}$$

$|\psi'\rangle$ is calculated with $|\phi\rangle$ in Step 1 of **Image verification algorithm**. $|\phi'\rangle$ is calculated with $|\psi'\rangle$ in Step 3 of **Image verification algorithm**.

Proof Because the failure of **Image verification algorithm** is caused by the erroneous judgment of SWAP-test when $|\psi\rangle \ne |\psi'\rangle$, P_f is equal to the error probability P_e. Meanwhile, the erroneous judgment reduces the probability of $|\phi'\rangle = |\phi\rangle$ in Step 3 of **Image verification algorithm**. If $|\psi\rangle \ne |\psi'\rangle$, the final state after SWAP-test is an entangled state $|0\rangle\frac{|\psi\rangle|\psi'\rangle+|\psi'\rangle|\psi\rangle}{\sqrt{2}}$ when the measurement result of SWAP-test is '0' [42]. $|\psi'\rangle$ is inseparable in the entangled state $|0\rangle\frac{|\psi\rangle|\psi'\rangle+|\psi'\rangle|\psi\rangle}{\sqrt{2}}$. In Step 3 of **Image verification algorithm**, performing PC reversely is impossible to recover the input state $|\phi\rangle$ precisely. The obtained state $|\phi'\rangle$ is not equal to $|\phi\rangle$. The input state $|\phi\rangle$ can be recovered if and only if $|\psi\rangle$ is the right image of $|\phi\rangle$, i.e., $|\psi\rangle = |\psi'\rangle$. Although the error probability P_e influences the accuracy of **Image verification algorithm**, the failure probability P_f can be reduced by l rounds execution of this verification algorithm. l copies of $|\psi\rangle$ and $|\phi\rangle$ should be provided as the input for reducing the failure probability. If and only if all the measurement results of SWAP-test are '0', $|\psi\rangle$ is accepted as the image of F and the input state $|\phi\rangle$ can be recovered. The failure probability P_f of l rounds **Image verification algorithm** is

$$P_f = (P_e)^l = \left(\frac{1+\varepsilon^2}{2}\right)^l, \varepsilon = |\langle\psi|\psi'\rangle| < 1 \tag{8.57}$$

The proof indicates that the failure probability P_f declines exponentially based on the repetition of **Image verification algorithm**. The negligibility of P_f is determined by the round of repetitions. In order to avoid the requirement of enormous rounds, state overlap is employed to improve **Image verification algorithm**. The detail of the improved algorithm is described as follows:

Algorithm 5 (Image-overlap verification algorithm) *Given an input quantum state* $|\phi\rangle$ *and an image* $|\psi\rangle$ *(the output quantum state) of the dynamic full quantum one-way function* F*, the verification of the image* $|\psi\rangle$ *is carried out with auxiliary information* $G_{n\times n}$ *and* LC*.*

Step 1: *With* $G_{n\times n}$ *and* LC*, perform the execution phase of* ***DF-QOWF algorithm*** *to obtain* PC *and* $|\psi'\rangle$*.*

Step 2: *Calculate the (squared) overlap* $|\langle\psi|\psi'\rangle|^2$ *between* $|\psi\rangle$ *and* $|\psi'\rangle$*. If* $|\langle\psi|\psi'\rangle|^2 = 1$*, accept* $|\psi\rangle$ *as the image of* F *when given* $|\phi\rangle$*.*

For the pure state $|\psi\rangle$ and $|\psi'\rangle$, the overlap reflects the similarity between the two states. $|\langle\psi|\psi'\rangle|^2 = 1$ indicates that $|\psi\rangle$ is equal to $|\psi'\rangle$. The standard algorithm for computing overlap is SWAP-test [3]. Besides, there are more precise estimation algorithms of the overlap based on the collective measurement [43], quantum mean estimation [44] or machine learning [45].

8.3.6 Scheme Analysis

We introduce the correctness and one-wayness of the full quantum one-way function F based on quantum circuit optimization.

A. Correctness

The full quantum one-way function F is well defined. As the coupling graph G is fixed, QC is unique in **Execution phase** of **Algorithm** 3. For an input state $|\phi\rangle$, the output state $|\psi\rangle$ is unique after performing C_p.

To prove the correctness of F, we prove the consistency of the input quantum state $|\phi\rangle$ and the output quantum state $|\psi\rangle$. The consistency ensures that there is a one-to-one correspondence between the input quantum state $|\phi\rangle$ and the image $|\psi\rangle$. **Algorithms** 4 and 5 well verifies the consistency which indicates $F|\phi\rangle = |\psi\rangle$. Its failure probability will be reduced after repeated executions on the input quantum state $|\phi\rangle$ and the image $|\psi\rangle$.

B. One-Wayness

One-wayness is the fundamental property of quantum one-way functions. It can be interpreted as 'easy to compute but hard to invert' [19].

Property 8.5 *Given the initial circuit* LC *of the dynamic full quantum one-way function* F*, the probability* $\Pr(\mathrm{PC} \leftarrow \mathrm{LC})$ *that an adversary* A *successfully guesses* PC *is negligible.*

Proof Suppose there is an adversary A with strong computing power, who tries to access the dynamic full quantum one-way function F. According to **Algorithm** 3, the unique corresponding relationship (LC, QC) is ensured by SABRE algorithm and the coupling graph $G_{n\times n}$. The mapping relationship $LC \stackrel{G_{n\times n}}{\longrightarrow} QC$ contains partial information on the input quantum state $|\phi\rangle$ of F. The partial information is obtained by quantum measurement in Generation phase of **Algorithm** 3. Thus the three-tuple $(LC, QC, G_{n\times n})$ is unique. When adversary A accesses F, it is impossible to obtain the very PC simply with LC. Nevertheless, we still consider adversary A successfully obtain the unique pair (LC, QC). Adversary A tries two methods to obtain (LC, QC): (1) construct a coupling graph $G_{n\times n}$ to execute the heuristic search algorithm SABRE; (2) randomly guess.

1. Construct a coupling graph $G_{n\times n}$ to execute the heuristic search algorithm **SABRE**.
   In this case, adversary A needs to choose a quantum state to generate matrix $G_{n\times n}$. It is as difficult as directly constructing matrix $G_{n\times n}$, because knowing the chosen quantum point functions U_{f_i} is not helpful to generate $G_{n\times n}$ when the input quantum state $|\phi\rangle$ is unknown. There are totally n^2 elements in $G_{n\times n}$, which means 2^{n^2} possibilities of $G_{n\times n}$. So the probability that adversary A successfully obtains (LC, QC) by constructing a coupling graph $G_{n\times n}$ and executing SABRE algorithm satisfies
   $$\mathrm{Pr(PC \leftarrow LC)} \leq \frac{1}{2^{\mathrm{n}^2}} \tag{8.58}$$
   When n is a sufficiently large number, Pr(PC $\leftarrow$ LC) is negligible.
2. Randomly guess.
   In this case, adversary A tries to simulate the process that **Algorithm** 3 performs to insert SWAP gates into LC to obtain QC without $G_{n\times n}$. There are $n-1$ CNOT gates in original quantum circuit C_{orig}. All these CNOT gates are performed between different qubit pairs. Thus, a SWAP gate can be inserted into any position of $n-1$ CNOT gates in C_{orig}. In C_{orig}, at most $n-2$ SWAP gates can be performed for any qubit-pairs. When randomly guessing PC, adversary A should insert SWAP gates in the correct qubit pairs. The probability Pr(PC $\leftarrow$ LC) for adversary A obtaining the right PC satisfies
   $$\mathrm{Pr(PC \leftarrow LC)} \leq \frac{1}{2^{(\mathrm{n}-2)*(\mathrm{n}-1)}} \tag{8.59}$$
   When n is a sufficiently large number, Pr(PC $\leftarrow$ LC) is negligible.

Property 8.6 *The new full quantum one-way function F satisfies one-wayness. It is 'easy to compute but hard to invert' in quantum polynomial time.*

Proof During the execution of F, the number of quantum gates in original circuit C_{orig} and execution circuit PC is polynomial. The time complexity of F mainly depends on the heuristic search algorithm SABRE and the calculation of coupling graph matrix $G_{n\times n}$ and distance matrix D. The time complexity of SABRE algorithm is $O(n^2)$. The time complexity of coupling graph matrix $G_{n\times n}$ depends on the number of quantum point functions U_{f_i} which are used in **Algorithm** 3. It is $O(n^2)$. Distance matrix D is calculated by the Floyd-Warshall algorithm. Its time complexity is $O(n^3)$ [40]. According to the time complexity of $G_{n\times n}$, D and SABRE algorithm, F is computable in quantum polynomial time. Thus F is 'easy to compute'.

In **Algorithm** 3, only the profile of original circuit $LC = (M, C_{orig})$ is revealed. The final execution circuit $PC = (V, C_p)$ and coupling graph $G_{n\times n}$ are not revealed. A pair of LC and QC is maintained by $G_{n\times n}$, which ensures the consistency of their functionality. **Property** 8.5 points out that the probability of successfully constructing the one-to-one correspondence PC and QC in (LC, G, QC) is negligible. It is difficult to construct PC and obtain the input quantum state $|\phi\rangle$ even given the output quantum state $|\psi\rangle$ and original circuit $LC = (M, C_{orig})$. It indicates F is 'hard to invert' in quantum polynomial time.

Thus the new full quantum one-way function F satisfies one-wayness.

C. Comparison Among Full Quantum One-Way Functions

There are few full quantum one-way functions which can deal well with quantum states, but ones in the references [9, 18, 25]. Some comparisons are made between the full quantum one-way function F and these typical full quantum one-way functions (listed in Table 8.1). Firstly, the time complexity of QOWF in the Reference [18] is $O(n^3 + log^C(\frac{1}{\epsilon}))$. According to **Property** 8.6, the time complexity of DF-QOWF can be $O(n^3)$, same as the function in the Reference [9]. Although the time complexity of QOWF in the reference [25] is $O(n + n \times poly(\cdot))$ and seems to be the smallest, it highly depends on the time complexity of interpreter algorithm. Secondly, there are limitations of input for QOWF in the references [9, 18, 25]. The input of QOWF in the References [9, 18] is n-qubit GHZ state. The input of QOWF in the Reference [25] is a series of self-defined tuples W_i. However, there is no restriction in DF-QOWF for an input. DF-QOWF does not require the input to be from specific state families. Furthermore, the method for providing one-wayness in QOWF has influenced the output and input. DF-QOWF is a full quantum one-way function that outputs a n-qubit quantum state. As the final operation on the input state is a remapped quantum circuit, the DF-QOWF does not destroy the input state. Meanwhile, the quantum circuit mapping method provides one-wayness to the function. function in the Reference [9] utilizes OWF unitary operation, which is composed of CNOT gates and measurement. Its input state can be restored so the input is also not destroyed. But its output is $l - bit$ classical strings. Although QOWF in the Reference [18] is also a full quantum one-way function, the process of this function will destroy the input. The concatenation method restricts the output of function to be 1-qubit.

Table 8.1 Comparison of full quantum one-way functions

	Our function	[9]	[18]	[25]
Time complexity	$O(n^3)$	$O(n^3)$	$O(n^3 + log^C(\frac{1}{\epsilon}))$	$O(n + n \times poly(\cdot))$
Method for one-wayness	Quantum circuit mapping	OWF unitary operation	Concatenation	Quantum obfuscation
Requirements for input	No	GHZ state	GHZ state	n input-cell W_i
Output	n-qubit	l-bit, $l <= n$	1-qubit	n-qubit
Destroying the input	No	No	Yes	NA

8.3.7 Full Quantum Trapdoor One-Way Function

In this section, we discuss the construction of a full quantum trapdoor one-way function based on the full quantum one-way function F.

A. Definition

Quantum trapdoor one-way function, widely applied to quantum cryptographic schemes, is an important extension of quantum one-way function. It is 'easy to compute and invert' with a trapdoor but 'hard to invert' without a trapdoor. **Property** 8.5 indicates that there is a possibility to invert DF-QOWF to obtain the input $|\phi\rangle$ from the output $|\psi\rangle$, if the coupling graph $G_{n\times n}$ is given. Except for the input $|\phi\rangle$, the coupling graph $G_{n\times n}$ is related to the quantum point function U_f in **Algorithm** 2. We consider (U_f, G) to be the trapdoor for the new full quantum trapdoor one-way function based on DF-QOWF.

According to **Algorithm** 3 of the full quantum one-way function and **Algorithm** 4 of verification for an image, a full quantum trapdoor one-way function is defined as follows, named Trapdoor DF-QOWF.

Definition 8.16 (Trapdoor DF-QOWF) A full quantum trapdoor one-way function, denoted $F_{U_f,G}$, is extended from the dynamic full quantum one-way function F. It maps n-qubit quantum state $|\phi\rangle$ to n-qubit quantum state $|\psi\rangle$:

$$F_{U_f,G} : |\phi\rangle \rightarrow |\psi\rangle \tag{8.60}$$

G is a coupling graph generated by **Algorithm** 2 for a quantum state $|\phi\rangle$. The quantum point functions used in **Algorithm** 2 are represented as U_f. The algorithm of $F_{U_f,G}$ is the same as **Algorithm** 3, which requires n separate copies of $|\phi\rangle$ as auxiliary quantum states.

The inverse algorithm $F^{-1}_{U_f,G}$ is defined as follows.

Algorithm 6 (Inverse algorithm) *Given the output quantum state $|\psi\rangle$ of $F_{U_f,G}$ and the trapdoor G, there are four steps to calculate the input quantum state $|\phi\rangle$.*

Step 1: *With the public original quantum circuit C_{orig}, perform* **Step 2** *of* **Algorithm** *3 to obtain dependency graph DAG and front layer F_{ront}.*

Step 2: *With G and DAG, perform* **Step 4** *of* **Algorithm** *3 to calculate distance matrix D.*

Step 3: *With D, F_{ront}, DAG and G, perform* **Step 5** *of* **Algorithm** *3 to dynamically generate a execution circuit $PC = \{V, C_p\}$.*

Step 4: *Invert PC. It mainly inverts the quantum circuit C_p and obtains its inverse quantum circuit C_{iv}.*

Step 5: *Perform C_{iv} on $|\psi$ to obtain $|\psi\rangle$.*

B. Property

According to **Property** 8.6, the probability of obtaining *PC* from *LC* is negligible when the trapdoor (U_f, G) is not revealed. Given the output quantum state $|\psi\rangle$, the probability that obtaining the input quantum state $|\phi\rangle$ by successfully inverting execution circuit *PC* is negligible.

Property 8.7 *Given trapdoor (U_f, G) and output quantum state $|\psi\rangle$, $F_{U_f,G}$ is 'easy to compute and invert' with a trapdoor (U_f, G).*

Proof According to **Property** 8.6, the key for successfully inverting $F_{U_f,G}$ is to construct *PC*. **Property** 8.5 shows that *PC* is difficult to be calculated only given U_f. However, given the trapdoor (U_f, G), *PC* can be calculated through **Step 4** in **Algorithm** 6. The inverse of *PC* is denoted by PC^{-1}. The input quantum state $|\phi\rangle$ of $F_{U_f,G}$ can be calculated by performing PC^{-1} on $|\psi\rangle$. Since *PC* describes a quantum circuit, PC^{-1} can be constructed by the inverse gates corresponding to *PC*. As the time complexity of PC^{-1} is measured by the number of quantum gates, PC^{-1} is performed in quantum polynomial time as well as *PC*. Thus $F_{U_f,G}$ is 'easy to compute and invert' with a trapdoor (U_f, G).

8.3.8 Simulation Anlysis

The quantum computation programming tool Qiskit [46] and *quantum-qubit-mapping* are used for the implementation of a dynamic full quantum one-way function, in which the original quantum circuit is 6-qubit.

A. Preparation Phase

In this phase, **Steps 1 and 2** of **Algorithm** 3 is performed to preparation. The input quantum state $|\phi\rangle = \frac{1}{\sqrt{2}}(|0\rangle + |1\rangle) \otimes |00011\rangle$ and an original quantum circuit C'_{orig} are prepared. The original quantum circuit C'_{orig} is shown in Fig. 8.8. The CNOT gates are marked as $g_1, \ldots, g_5$. $LC = (M, C'_{orig})$, where $M = \{q_1, \ldots, q_6\}$.

The dependency graph *DAG* is generated from Fig. 8.8, shown in Fig. 8.9. According to *DAG*, the front layer F_{ront} is obtained that $F_{ront} = \{g_1, g_2\}$.

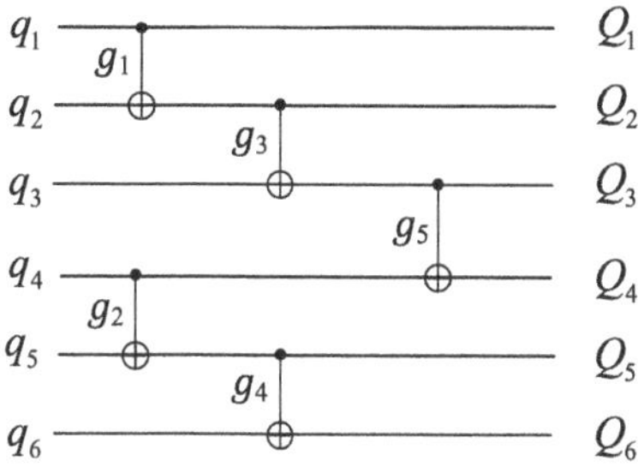

Fig. 8.8 Original quantum circuit C'_{orig}

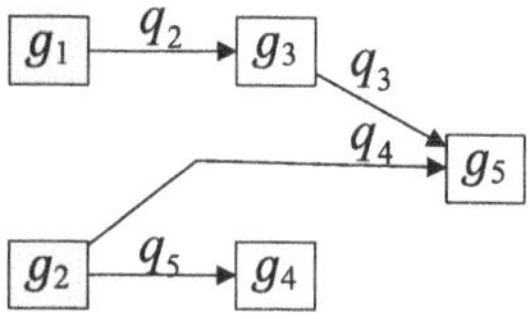

Fig. 8.9 *DAG*

B. Generation Phase

As *quantum-qubit-mapping* calculates the distance matrix D when executing the SABRE algorithm, there is no need to generate D. **Step 3** of **Algorithm** 3 is performed to generate a coupling graph G.

For the input quantum state $|\phi\rangle = \frac{1}{\sqrt{2}}(|0\rangle + |1\rangle) \otimes |00011\rangle$, we perform **Coupling generation algorithm**. The chosen quantum point functions are represented as $U_{f_1}, U_{f_2}, \ldots, U_{f_6}$. Only two quantum point functions U_{P_1} and U_{P_2} are chosen. $U_{f_1}, \ldots, U_{f_6}$ is simply set to U_{P_1} or U_{P_2}. $U_{f_1} = U_{f_3} = U_{f_5} = U_{P_1} : |x, 0\rangle \rightarrow |x, P_1(x)\rangle$, where

$$P_1(x) = \begin{cases} 1 & if \quad x = 1 \\ 0 & otherwise \end{cases} \tag{8.61}$$

$U_{f_2} = U_{f_4} = U_{f_6} = U_{P_1} : |x, 0\rangle \rightarrow |x, P_2(x)\rangle$, where

$$P_2(x) = \begin{cases} 1 & if \quad x = 0 \\ 0 & otherwise \end{cases} \tag{8.62}$$

U_{P_1} and U_{P_2} are implemented by two quantum circuits (shown in Fig. 8.10a and b).

$U_{P_1}|0\rangle = |0, 0\rangle$ and the measurement result for the second qubit of $|0, 0\rangle$ is always 0. $U_{P_1}|1\rangle = |1, 1\rangle$ and the measurement result for the second qubit of $|1, 1\rangle$ is always 1. Similarly, we can obtain the measurement result of $U_{P_2}|0\rangle$ and $U_{P_2}|1\rangle$, namely 1 and 0. For the first qubit $\frac{1}{\sqrt{2}}(|0\rangle + |1\rangle)$ in $|\phi\rangle$, the probability of measurement results '0' and '1' are both 0.5 in U_{P_1} and U_{P_2}.

When performing **Step 3** in **Algorithm** 3, Qikist is employed to simulate the two quantum circuits shown in Fig. 8.10a and b. Due to the probabilistic of quantum measurement in a superposition state, a generated coupling graph G will change

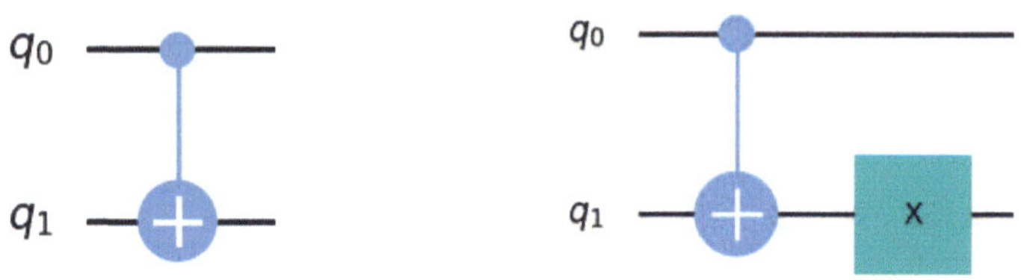

Fig. 8.10 Quantum circuits for quantum point functions P_1 and P_2

when repeatedly performing **Algorithm** 2 for $|\phi\rangle$. The API *result().get_counts(). most_frequent()* in Qiskit is used to obtain the measurement result. **Algorithm** 2 is only performed once to obtain the coupling graph $G_{6\times6}$. The initial coupling graph G_{ini} before performing Step 4 of **Algorithm** 2 is

$$G_{ini} = \begin{pmatrix} 1&1&0&0&1&0\\ 0&1&0&1&0&1\\ 0&1&0&1&0&1\\ 0&1&0&1&0&1\\ 1&0&1&0&1&0\\ 1&0&1&0&1&0 \end{pmatrix} \tag{8.63}$$

We perform Step 4 of **Algorithm** 2 and check G_{in}. The diagonal elements in G_{ini} are modified to be 1. Then we add the default path (mentioned in **Algorithm** 2) in G_{ini}. The coupling graph $G_{6\times6}$ is obtained.

$$G_{6\times6} = \begin{pmatrix} 1&1&0&0&1&0\\ 1&1&0&1&0&1\\ 1&1&1&1&0&1\\ 1&1&0&1&0&1\\ 1&0&1&0&1&0\\ 1&0&1&0&1&1 \end{pmatrix} \tag{8.64}$$

C. Execution Phase

There is already a quantum mapping package *quantum-qubit-mapping* in Python, which implements the SABRE algorithm based on the quantum programming tool PyQuil. The initial mapping is set as $\{q_1 \to Q_1, q_2 \to Q_2, \ldots, q_6 \to Q_6\}$. Then the algorithm of SABRE in *quantum-qubit-mapping* is performed with the coupling graph $G_{6\times6}$ and original circuit C'_{orig}. Distance matrix D is calculated during the execution. The obtained execution circuit $PC = (V, C_p)$ will finally be performed with the 32-qubit '*ibmq_qasm_simulator*' for 1024 shots. C_p is shown in Fig. 8.11.

In **Step 6**, we run C_p and obtain the output as the output $|\psi\rangle$ of this dynamic full quantum one-way function. For the input quantum state $|\phi\rangle = \frac{1}{\sqrt{2}}(|0\rangle + |1\rangle) \otimes |00011\rangle$, the output $|\psi\rangle$ is described by measuring each qubit and obtaining possible states after measurement. The result of the possible state is shown in Fig. 8.12 and Table 8.2.

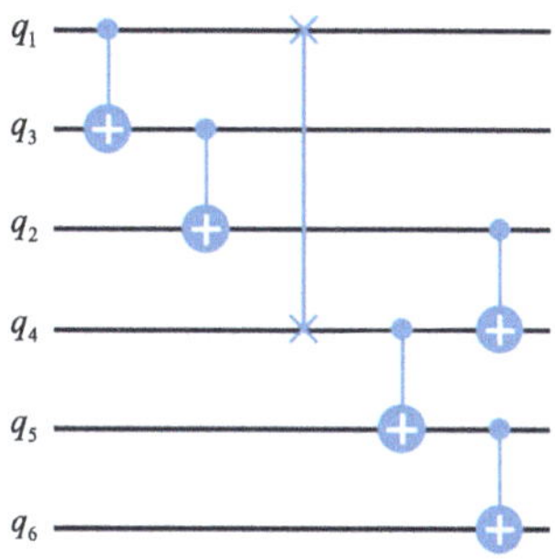

Fig. 8.11 Execution circuit *CP*

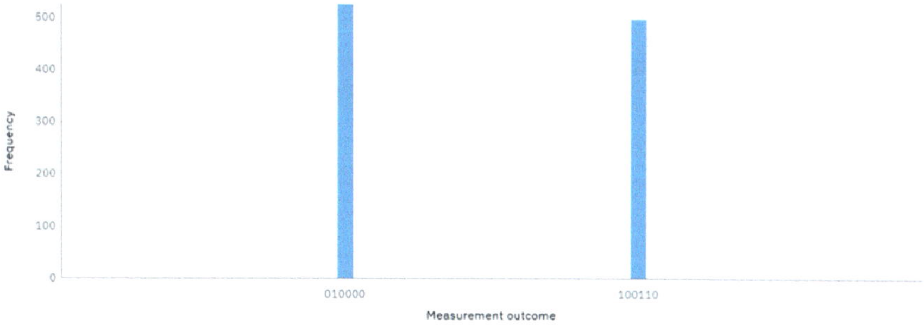

Fig. 8.12 Possible state after measurement

Table 8.2 Measurement outcome vs frequency in simulator

Outcome	Frequency
010000	526
100110	498

In future work, the optimization of the DF-QOWF will be studied to deal with noise and decoherence needs. Quantum error-correcting codes [47] can be an effective method to reduce bit-flip errors.

The influence of initial mapping to the **SABRE** algorithm is not the problem for the **DF-QOWF algorithm**. No reverse operation is required to reduce the influence of initial mapping. The initial mapping can be set as any mapping relationship at the start. In this implementation, the initial mapping is set as $\{q_1 \rightarrow Q_1, q_2 \rightarrow Q_2, \ldots, q_6 \rightarrow Q_6\}$. The coupling graph can be generated not only by **Algorithm** 2 but also by the coupling graph of qubits from a real quantum device. At this moment, the generated execution circuit C_p will run directly on the device without a transpiler circuit which is generated by the quantum optimization algorithm of the quantum service.

8.3.9 Application to Quantum Currency Notes

Quantum cryptography originates from the proposal of 'quantum money'. In this section, the full quantum one-way function is applied to quantum currency notes. This scheme includes two algorithms: (1) Minting algorithm and (2) Verification algorithm. Minting algorithm is used by central institutions (the bank) to generate an effective quantum currency note. Verification algorithm is used for the verification of a quantum currency note.

This quantum money scheme combines **Algorithm** 4 Image verification algorithm to achieve multiple verifications which do not destroy the quantum state of a quantum currency note. We suppose that there is a secure quantum public-key encryption scheme. The specific algorithm of quantum currency notes is described as follows.

Algorithm 7 (Minting algorithm) *Suppose the information of a quantum currency note is stored as a bit string M. The Minting algorithm includes following steps:*

Step 1: *The bank encodes M to a quantum state $|\phi\rangle$. The bank produces a key pair (p_{sk}, p_{pk}) based on the key generation algorithm of the quantum public-key encryption scheme. p_{pk} is public to the user.*
Step 2: *The bank runs the* ***DF-QOWF algorithm*** *to obtain the output quantum state $|\psi\rangle$, original circuit LC and coupling graph $G_{n\times n}$. The bank encrypts $G_{n\times n}$ to obtain a quantum state σ with p_{sk}. Let $I = (LC, \sigma)$.*
Step 3: *The bank sends a triple $(|\phi\rangle, |\psi\rangle, I)$ to the user. $(|\phi\rangle, |\psi\rangle, I)$ is a quantum currency note.*

Algorithm 8 (Verification algorithm) *Suppose the user receives $(|\phi\rangle, |\psi\rangle, I)$ from a bank, it includes following steps:*

Step 1: *The user decrypts $G_{n\times n}$ from σ with p_{pk}.*
Step 2: *The user verifies whether $|\psi\rangle$ and $|\phi\rangle$ are consistent or not, utilizing* ***Image verification algorithm****. The user runs* ***Image verification algorithm*** *l times. Only if the results of the l times are consistent, i.e., the results are always '$|\psi\rangle$ is the image of F when given $|\phi\rangle$', the user accepts $(|\phi\rangle, |\psi\rangle, I)$ as a legal quantum currency note, otherwise the user declares $(|\phi\rangle, |\psi\rangle, I)$ is invalid.*

As mentioned in **Algorithm** 4, if $|\psi\rangle$ is the image of F for the input $|\phi\rangle$, there is no entanglement after SWAP-test. **Algorithm** 4 can be executed repeatedly. Even if k times execution of **Image verification algorithm** in the scheme, the user will not destroy the legal quantum currency note when verifying a quantum currency note. The user consumes a legal quantum currency note but does not know its detail. Only the bank knows how to decode the information on a quantum currency note from a quantum state.

According to the no-cloning theorem, an adversary cannot accurately copy the unknown quantum state in $(|\phi\rangle, |\psi\rangle, I)$. It indicates the security of this quantum currency note scheme.

The probability that an adversary successfully utilizes $(|\phi\rangle, |\psi\rangle, LC)$ to forge a legal $(|\psi\rangle, PC)$ is negligible, according to **Property** 8.5 **and Property** 8.6. Because $G_{n\times n}$ is unknown for an adversary, the probability for an adversary successfully obtaining $(LC, G_{n\times n}, C_p)$ is negligible. It is impossible for an adversary to execute the right circuit PC for $|\phi\rangle$. Thus an adversary is impossible to forge a message to cheat the bank and the user. This quantum money scheme is secure against forgery attack. It implies that it is difficult to counterfeit the quantum currency note.

8.4 Full Quantum One-Way Function Based on Quantum Hypergraph State

8.4.1 Advantage of Multipartite Entanglement

Full quantum one-way function (F-QOWF) has an advantage in dealing with quantum messages, which can map a quantum state to another quantum state but hold one-wayness based on quantum operations. In the Reference [25], Tang et al. further presented a universal construction of F-QOWF. Based on the instantiation of quantum obfuscation, abundant F-QOWF can be implemented from the universal construction. However, the entanglement in the input quantum state is not discussed. The quantum cryptographic application of this universal construction scheme is limited to quantum message authentication.

Entangled states are critical in quantum information processing. The graph states can be used to represent a larger family of entangled states, including cluster states, *GHZ* states and stabilizer states [48]. Quantum hypergraph states were proposed to generalize the graph states [49]. Quantum hypergraph states are the set of highly entangled states, constructed from mathematical hypergraph [50]. According to the advantage of multipartite entanglement, quantum hypergraph states were applied to quantum blockchain to replace classical one-way functions and connect the block [50, 51]. Besides, quantum hypergraph states are prepared by a series of controlled-Z gates in the quantum circuits. Considering the construction and quantum cryptographic application of quantum hypergraph states, it is clear that we can generalize the universal construction of F-QOWF by means of quantum hypergraph states for entangled input states.

Digital signature is used to provide non-repudiation in cryptography. Shor's algorithm [26] indicates classical digital signature schemes face a huge threat from quantum adversaries. Therefore, quantum digital signature schemes are proposed, which are unconditionally secure in the quantum channel. The first quantum digital signature, based on the quantum one-way function, can be traced back to Gottesman's work [4]. There is little research on quantum aggregate signature, which can compress multiple signatures to one signature and reduce the cost of communication [52]. You et al. first implemented a quantum aggregate signature scheme using a four-qubit cluster state [53]. Considering the advantage of F-QOWF in handling quantum states and the advantage of quantum hypergraph states in multiparty computation, the new model of quantum aggregate signature naturally comes into focus.

In this section, we focus on the construction of F-QOWF of quantum hypergraph states [54]. The universal construction of F-QOWF [25] is generalized for entangled states. We utilize the new full quantum one-way function to design a quantum aggregate signature scheme, which is a multi-party quantum cryptographic scheme.

8.4.2 Quantum Hypergraph States

Quantum hypergraph states are associated with the corresponding mathematical hypergraph [49]. Given a hypergraph $G = [V, E]$, a quantum hypergraph state can be obtained with controlled-Z gates and initial states $|+\rangle^{\otimes n}$. V is a set of vertexes in the mathematical hypergraph G. E is a set of hyperedges of order k. In a mathematical hypergraph, a hyperedge connects more than two vertexes (six-vertex hypergraph shown in Fig. 8.13). Each vertex i_k is assigned to a qubit with the state $|+\rangle$. Given a hyperedge e_k which connects the qubits $i_1, \ldots, i_k$, the quantum gates $C^k Z_{i_1,\ldots,i_k}$ is performed. Hence, a quantum state $|g\rangle$ is obtained from $G = [V, E]$ (the related quantum circuit is shown in Fig. 8.14),

$$|g\rangle = \prod_{k=1}^{m} \prod_{\{i_1,i_2,\ldots,i_k\}\in E} C^k Z_{i_1,i_2,\ldots,i_k} |+\rangle \tag{8.65}$$

Qu et al. [48] proved that there is equivalence between the real equally weighted (REW) states and the hypergraph states [48]. Then the weighted hypergraph state was introduced and applied to quantum blockchain [50, 51]. When each hyperedge carries weight in a hypergraph, the state obtained from the hypergraph is called

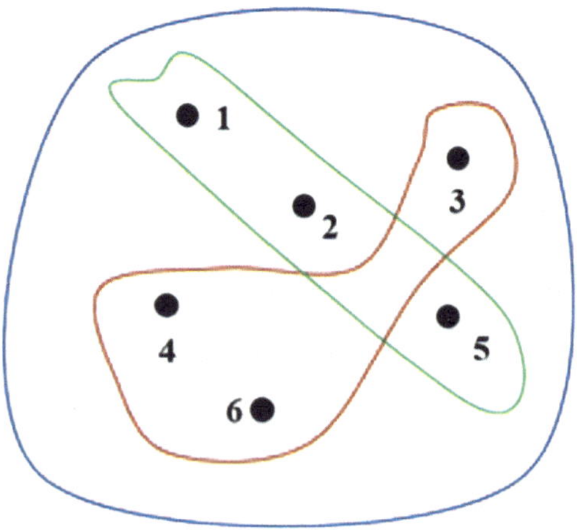

Fig. 8.13 Six-vertex classical hypergraph

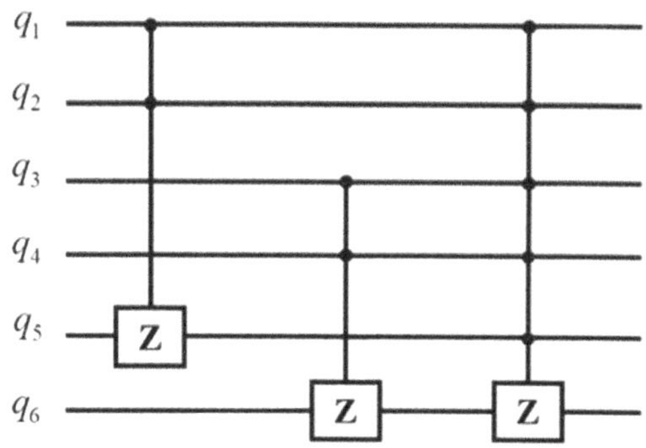

Fig. 8.14 Corresponding six-vertex quantum hypergraph state

'weighted hypergraph state'. For an N-vertex weighted hypergraph, the weighted hypergraph state is defined as

$$|\phi\rangle = \frac{1}{\sqrt{2^N}} \sum_{j\in\{0,1\}^N} e^{i\pi f(j)}|j\rangle \tag{8.66}$$

$f(j)$ is a Boolean function that is $f(j) : \{0, 1\}^n \mapsto \{0, 1\}$. $|j\rangle$ is the computation basis. In the references [50, 51], $\pi f(j)$ is replaced by a rotation operation $R(\theta)$, which introduces a phase to the initial state. The rotation gates are added before performing the controlled-Z gates and the initial state is changed to

$$|\Phi\rangle = R(\theta)|+\rangle = \begin{bmatrix} 1 & 0 \\ 0 & e^{i\theta} \end{bmatrix} \frac{|0\rangle + |1\rangle}{\sqrt{2}} = \frac{|0\rangle + e^{i\theta}|1\rangle}{\sqrt{2}} \tag{8.67}$$

8.4.3 *Full Quantum One-Way Function*

In order to reduce the classical string used in F-QOWF, a universal construction of full quantum one-way function was proposed based on quantum obfuscation [25]. The most important property of full quantum one-way function is one-wayness, which is described as "easy to compute" and "hard to invert".

The obfuscation-based full quantum one-way function F is a function that directly maps quantum states to quantum states, defined as follows.

Definition 8.17 (Obfuscation-based full quantum one-way function [25]**)** F takes m input-cells W as the input quantum state and m-qubit quantum state as output, i.e.,

$$F : \overbrace{W_1 \otimes \cdots \otimes W_m}^{m} \rightarrow |\varphi^{(m)}\rangle \tag{8.68}$$

where W_i is an input-cell with three tuples $W_i = |x\rangle|0\rangle|\psi\rangle$. $|x\rangle$ is n-qubit. $|0\rangle$ and $|\psi\rangle$ are single-qubit.

Obfuscation-based full quantum one-way function can be implemented in a quantum computing platform. $O(C_i)$ is a series of quantum obfuscation states which are implemented with the interpreter δ. $SWAP$ is the step of controlled-SWAP gates to exchange the qubit in $|\tilde{\varphi}_i\rangle$, $|\tilde{\varphi}_j\rangle$.

8.4.4 Aggregate Signature

The aggregate signature scheme can compress multiple signatures, generated by different users for different messages, into a single aggregate signature. Sato and Shikata [52] summarize the scheme of classical aggregate signature.

Definition 8.18 (Classical aggregate signature) A aggregate signature $ASIG$ scheme includes five polynomial-time algorithms $(KGen, Sign, Vrfy, Agg, Avrfy)$: For a security parameter λ, message space M and signature space S.

1. $(pk, sk) \leftarrow KGen(1^\lambda)$: The randomized algorithm $KGen$ takes 1^λ as the input and outputs a public key pk and a private key sk.
2. $\sigma \leftarrow Sign(sk, m)$: The algorithm $Sign$ inputs the private key sk and the message m and outputs a signature $\sigma \in S$.
3. $1/0 \leftarrow Vrfy(pk, m, \sigma)$: The algorithm $Vrfy$ inputs the public key pk, message $m \in M$ and signature $\sigma \in S$, and outputs '1' (accept) or '0' (reject).
4. $\hat{\sigma} \leftarrow Agg((pk_1, m_1, e_1), \ldots, (pk_l, m_l, e_l))$: The algorithm Agg inputs the tuples $(pk_1, m_1, e_1), \ldots, (pk_l, m_l, e_l)$ and outputs an aggregate signature $\hat{\sigma} \in S$.
5. $1/0 \leftarrow AVrfy((pk_1, m_1), \ldots, (pk_l, m_l), \hat{\sigma})$: The algorithm $Avrfy$ inputs the tuples $(pk_1, m_1), \ldots, (pk_l, m_l)$ and the aggregate signature $\hat{\sigma}$, and outputs '1' (accept) or '0' (reject).

8.4.5 Hypergraph-Based Full Quantum One-Way Function

Although there is an input format in the universal construction of F-QOWF, the entanglement among the tuples of input-cells is not discussed. In this work, we apply quantum hypergraph states to the universal construction scheme of F-QOWF, which is based on quantum obfuscation [25]. Quantum hypergraph states are highly entangled quantum states which play an important role in quantum key distribution and quantum computation. Moreover, they can be applied to quantum blockchain schemes to replace classical hash functions [50]. In the new F-QOWF based on quantum hypergraph states, the entanglement in input-cells is considered.

A. Definition

According to Sect. 8.4.3, the definition of full quantum one-way function based on quantum hypergraph states is provided.

Definition 8.19 (F-QOWF based on quantum hypergraph states) The full quantum one-way function F_h takes m input-cells W_i as the input quantum state. F_h maps the input quantum state $\overbrace{W_1 \otimes \cdots \otimes W_m}^{m}$ to an $m - qubit$ quantum state, i.e.,

$$F_h : \overbrace{W_1 \otimes \cdots \otimes W_m}^{m} \rightarrow |\varphi^{(m)}\rangle \tag{8.69}$$

The input $W_1 \otimes \cdots \otimes W_m$ of F_h is composed of m input-cells W_i. W_i is a triple $W_i = |x\rangle|0\rangle|\psi_i\rangle$ (or $W_i = |x, 0, \psi_i\rangle$), $i = 1, 2, \ldots, m$. $|x\rangle$ is n-qubit. $|0\rangle$ is single-qubit. $|\psi_i\rangle$ is a single qubit from a quantum hypergraph state $|\psi\rangle$.

$$|\psi\rangle = \frac{1}{\sqrt{2^m}} \sum_{j \in (0,1)^m} e^{i\pi f(j)}|j\rangle, f(j) : \{0, 1\}^m \rightarrow \{0, 1\} \tag{8.70}$$

$|\psi\rangle$ is employed to construct an input-cell $W_i = |x_i, 0, \psi_i\rangle$ where each qubit is in the third tuple ψ_i.

Quantum hypergraph states contribute to the simplification and the quantum computing resources conservation of this universal construction. The full quantum one-way function based on quantum hypergraph states is more conducive to the design of multi-participant quantum cryptographic schemes. It can easily be adapted to other quantum entangled states.

B. Algorithm

The algorithm of the F-QOWF F_h, which is based on quantum hypergraph states, is named as *hypergraph-FQOWF*. Besides, we demonstrate the *hypergraph-FQOWF* algorithm with a quantum circuit (shown in Fig. 8.15). The detail of *hypergraph-FQOWF* algorithm is described as follows.

Algorithm 9 (Hypergraph-FQOWF) *Given m n-qubit copies of quantum state $|x_i\rangle$ and m copies of single-qubit quantum state $|0\rangle$, there are four steps of F-QOWF F_h, including preparation, obfuscation, reverse and output.*

- *Step 1:* ***Preparation***. *Prepare a classical hypergraph $G = [V, E]$, which includes m vertexes. According to $G = [V, E]$, generate an m-qubit quantum hypergraph state $|\psi\rangle$. Following the format $|x_i\rangle|0\rangle|\psi\rangle$, a tensor of $|x_i\rangle$, $|0\rangle$ and one qubit of $|\psi\rangle$ is obtained, which is an input-cell W_i. Then the input $W_1 \otimes \cdots \otimes W_m$ of F-QOWF F_h is obtained. The generation from $G = [V, E]$ to a quantum hypergraph state $|\psi\rangle$ is described as follows.*

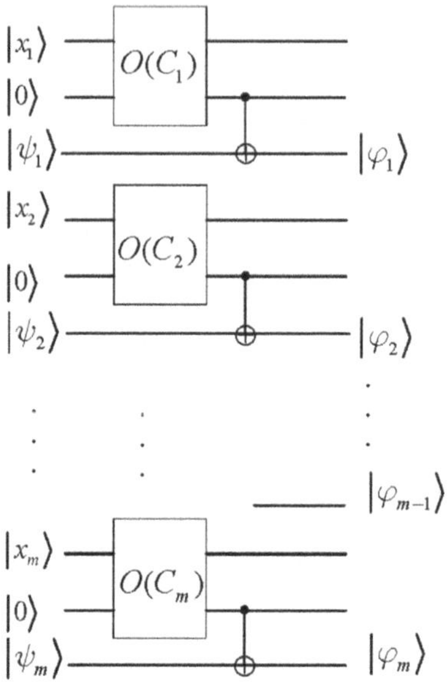

Fig. 8.15 Quantum circuit of hypergraph-FQOWF

- *i. Prepare an m-qubit initial quantum state* $|q\rangle$ *and initialize each qubit in* $|+\rangle = \frac{|0\rangle+|1\rangle}{\sqrt{2}}$.
- *ii. Assign a qubit* $|q_i\rangle$ *of* $|q\rangle$ *to each vertex i in* $G = [V, E]$. *For each edge* e_k *in* $G = [V, E]$, *perform the controlled-Z gate* $C^k Z_{i_1,i_2,\ldots,i_k}$ *in the qubits which are connected by the edge* e_k. *Then, obtain an quantum hypergraph state* $|\psi\rangle = \prod_{k=1}^{m} \prod_{\{i_1,i_2,\ldots,i_k\}\in E} C^k Z_{i_1,i_2,\ldots,i_k}|+\rangle$.

- *Step 2:* ***Obfuscation***. *Choose m quantum circuits* C_i, *the functionality of* C_i *is* $U_g : |a, b\rangle \to |a, b \oplus g(a)\rangle$, $g : \{0, 1\}^n \to \{0, 1\}^n$. *Obfuscate* C_i *with the obfuscator O of quantum function* U_g *and obtain the obfuscation state* $O(C_i)$. *Based on the interpreter* δ, *implement* $O(C_i)$ *on the first two tuples* $|x_i, 0\rangle$ *of the input-cell* W_i *to perform the functionality of* C_i *on* $|x_i, 0\rangle$. *The output is denoted by* $|x_i, p_i\rangle$. *Then* $W_i = |x_i, p_i, \psi_i\rangle$.
- *Step 3:* ***Reverse***. *For the last two tuples* $|p_i, \psi_i\rangle$ *of each input-cell* W_i, *take the first tuple* $|p_i\rangle$ *as the control qubit. Take the last tuple* $|\psi_i\rangle$ *as the target qubit. Then, perform CNOT gates. The input-cells* W_i *are changed to* $W_i = |x_i, p_i, \varphi_i\rangle$, $\varphi_i = \psi_i \oplus p_i$.
- *Step 4:* ***Output***. *Output the qubit* φ_i *of each input-cell* W_i *and obtain* $|\varphi_1, \ldots, \varphi_m\rangle$. $|\varphi_1, \ldots, \varphi_m\rangle$ *is the output of hypergraph-FQOWF* F_h.

Different from the algorithm of obfuscation-based F-QOWF [25], *hypergraph-FQOWF* algorithm includes a preparation process of $W_1 \otimes \cdots \otimes W_m$ to generate m input-cells W_i. Compared to the quantum circuit in Fig. 8.6, the SWAP operation is reduced in the quantum circuit of hypergraph-FQOWF. The controlled-SWAP gate in Fig. 8.6 is deleted in Fig. 8.15. Because the quantum hypergraph state $|\psi\rangle = \frac{1}{\sqrt{2^m}} \sum_{j\in\{0,1\}^m} e^{i\pi f(j)}|j\rangle$ is highly entangled, there is no need to implement the SWAP operation to entangle each qubit in $|\psi\rangle$.

8.4.6 One-Wayness

One-wayness, described as 'easy to compute' and 'hard to invert', is the key property of F-QOWF. In this section, we prove that hypergraph-FQOWF is one-way in quantum polynomial time.

Theorem 8.5 *The quantum gates used in hypergraph-FQOWF F_h is $\mathcal{O}(k + m \times poly(\cdot))$.*

Proof Let Y be the total number of quantum gates used in hypergraph-FQOWF F_h. Y consists of the quantum rotation gates, controlled-Z gates, CNOT gates and the quantum gates in obfuscation of Algorithm 9.

In Step 1, a controlled-Z gate is performed based on one hyperedge. For k hyperedge in the hypergraph $G = [V, E]$, k controlled-Z gates are needed. The number of quantum gates used in Step 1 is denoted by Y_1.

$$Y_1 = k. \tag{8.71}$$

In Step 2, the number of quantum gates is denoted by Y_2. Since the algorithm of interpreter δ is polynomial-time [55], the quantum gates used in an interpreter δ can be denoted by $poly(\cdot)$. There are m interpreters used according to Fig. 8.15,

$$Y_2 = m \times poly(\cdot). \tag{8.72}$$

In Step 3, there are m CNOT gates used, the number of quantum gates is denoted by Y_3

$$Y_3 = m. \tag{8.73}$$

The total number of quantum gates used in hypergraph-FQOWF F_h is described as

$$Y = Y_1 + Y_2 + Y_3 \tag{8.74}$$

$$= m + k + m \times poly(\cdot) \tag{8.75}$$

Hence, $Y \in \mathcal{O}(k + m \times poly(\cdot))$.

Lemma 8.7 *The hypergraph-FQOWF F_h is easily computed in quantum polynomial time.*

Proof The time complexity of F_h can be determined by the number of quantum gates used in the quantum circuit of F_h. The execution time of a quantum gate is constant. According to Theorem 8.5, the time complexity of F_h is

$$\mathcal{O}(F_h) = \mathcal{O}(k + m \times poly(\cdot)) \tag{8.76}$$

Thus, the hypergraph-FQOWF F_h can be computed in quantum polynomial time.

Theorem 8.6 *Given the output $|\varphi\rangle$, it is difficult for an adversary A to obtain the right input $W_1 \otimes \cdots \otimes W_m$ by implementing the inverse of the hypergraph-FQOWF F_h in quantum polynomial time.*

Proof The hypergraph-FQOWF F_h was constructed by the obfuscation-based full quantum one-way function [25]. The key step for protecting the hypergraph-FQOWF F_h from being inverted is Step 2 obfuscation, similar to the obfuscation-based full quantum one-way function. Given the output $|\varphi\rangle$, adversary A can obtain $W_1 \otimes \cdots \otimes W_m$ by reversely performing the quantum circuit of F_h (Fig. 8.15). Because the quantum circuit of F_h is in public except the obfuscation state $O(C)$. The only thing can adversary A do for reversely performing the quantum circuit of F_h is to obtain the input quantum C_i for the obfuscation state $O(C)$. According to the *virtual black-box* property of quantum obfuscation [55], the probability of adversary A correctly obtains C_i satisfies

$$|\Pr[A(O(C_i)) = 1] - \Pr[S^{U_i}(|0^n\rangle) = 1]| \leq negl(n) \tag{8.77}$$

Besides, the Reference [25] proved that an adversary A successfully implements the inverse operation on the quantum circuit of F_h and obtains the input $W_1 \otimes \cdots \otimes W_m$ is negligible.

Thus it is difficult for an adversary A to obtain the right input $W_1 \otimes \cdots \otimes W_m$ by implementing the inverse of the hypergraph-FQOWF F_h in quantum polynomial time.

8.4.7 Application to Quantum Aggregate Signature

A. Scheme

Sato et al. [52] summarized the components of classical aggregation signature schemes, while You et al. [53] paid attention to quantum aggregation signature schemes. According to Sato's and You's work, we summarize the definition of quantum aggregation signature which is similar to Definition 1 in Sect. 8.4.4.

Definition 8.20 (Quantum aggregate signature) A quantum aggregate signature scheme $QASIG$ composes of six quantum polynomial-time algorithms $(KGen, Sign, Enc, Vrfy, Agg, Avrfy)$. M is message space. S is signature space. E is ciphertext space.

1. $(pk, sk) \leftarrow KGen(|0\rangle^{\otimes n})$: The algorithm $KGen$ takes $|0\rangle^{\otimes n}$ as input and generates a public key pk and a private key sk. sk and pk can be either classical string or quantum state.
2. $\sigma \leftarrow Sign(sk, m)$: The algorithm $Sign$ takes the private key sk and the message m as input and outputs a signature $\sigma \in S$.
3. $\hat{\sigma} \leftarrow Agg((pk_1, m_1, \sigma_1), \ldots, (pk_l, m_l, \sigma_l))$: The algorithm Agg takes the tuple $(pk_1, m_1, \sigma_1), \ldots, (pk_l, m_l, \sigma_l)$ as input and outputs an aggregate signature $\hat{\sigma} \in S$.
4. $e \leftarrow Enc(pk, \hat{\sigma})$: The quantum polynomial-time algorithm Enc encrypts the signature $\hat{\sigma}$ with public key pk and outputs the ciphertext $e \in E$.
5. $1/0 \leftarrow Vrfy(pk, m, \sigma)$: The algorithm $Vrfy$ takes the public key pk, message $m \in M$ and signature $\sigma \in S$ as input and outputs '1' (accept) or '0' (reject).
6. $1/0 \leftarrow AVrfy((pk_1, m_1), \ldots, (pk_l, m_l), \hat{\sigma})$: The algorithm $Avrfy$ takes the tuple $(pk_1, m_1), \ldots, (pk_l, m_l)$ and the aggregate signature $\hat{\sigma}$ as input and outputs '1' (accept) or '0' (reject).

Definition 8.20 shows that quantum aggregation signature is similar to the classical aggregation signature, except the encryption of signatures. According to the reference [56], any authentication scheme for quantum messages must also encrypt them. The process of encryption is an indispensable part of the quantum aggregate signature for quantum security. Hence, in the quantum aggregation signature scheme, six algorithms ($KGen$, $Sign$, Enc, $Vrfy$, Agg, $Avrfy$) can be adapted and reduced, but include an encryption algorithm at least.

We introduce a quantum aggregate signature scheme with quantum symmetric encryption, adapting from Definition 8.20. The new quantum aggregate signature scheme includes four types of participants: the owner of message *Alice*, aggregator *David*, signer U_i and verifier *Bob*. The new quantum aggregate signature scheme is described as follows.

Scheme 1 (Quantum aggregate signature scheme): For the message m_i, there are four phases in the quantum aggregate signature scheme.

1. Initialization phase. The purpose of this phase is to implement key sharing and quantum message generation, including the following steps.

   (a) *Alice*, *David*, U_i and *Bob* share a secret key K_{U_i}. *David* and *Bob* share a secret key K_{BD}.
   (b) *David* prepares two copies of auxiliary quantum state $|x_i\rangle$ $(i = 1, 2, \ldots, n)$ and $|0\rangle$.
   (c) Each signer U_i prepares an initial quantum state $|+\rangle$, which is 1-qubit.
   (d) The signers U_i negotiate a classical hypergraph G with each other. According to G, the controlled-Z gate is performed on the initial quantum state $|+\rangle$ which is owned by signers U_i. Then a quantum hypergraph state $|\psi\rangle$ is obtained.
   (e) *Alice* encodes message m_i to a quantum hypergraph state $|m\rangle$. For message m_i, *Alice* regards it as a phase and introduces m_i to $|\psi\rangle$ to obtain the weighted

hypergraph states $|m\rangle$ (such as (8.67) in Sect. 8.4.4). Another copy of $|m\rangle$ is prepared following the same steps (c-e).

2. Aggregation phase. *David* receives $|m\rangle$ and constructs n input-cells $W_i = |x_i\rangle|0\rangle|m_i\rangle$ with the auxiliary quantum state $|x_i\rangle$ and $|0\rangle$. Then, *David* takes $W_1 \otimes \cdots \otimes W_n$ as input and performs the hypergraph-FQOWF F_h to generate the aggregate signature $|\sigma^{\otimes n}\rangle$.
3. Encryption phase. U_i encrypts $|m_i\rangle$ with secret key K_{U_i} and obtains the cipertext $|e\rangle = |e_1, e_2, \ldots, e_n\rangle$.
4. Verification phase. Bob verifies the aggregate signature of Step (3) by double verification.

   (a) *David* records the unrevealed output ρ of the executing quantum circuit of the hypergraph-FQOWF F_h. Then *David* encrypts ρ, $|\sigma^{\otimes n}\rangle$, $|x_1, \ldots, x_n\rangle$, $|0\rangle$ with K_{BD}. $Enc_{K_{BD}}(\rho, |\sigma^{\otimes n}\rangle, |x_1, \ldots, x_n\rangle, |0\rangle)$ is sent to *Bob*.
   (b) U_i sends the cipertext $|e_i\rangle$ to *Bob*.
   (c) *Bob* decrypts $Enc_{K_{BD}}(\rho, |\sigma^{\otimes n}\rangle, |x_1, \ldots, x_n\rangle, |0\rangle)$ with K_{BD}. *Bob* decrypts $|e_i\rangle$ and obtains $|m_i\rangle$ with K_{U_i}.
   (d) *Bob* uses $(|m_i\rangle, |x_i\rangle, |0\rangle)$ to constrcut the input-cells $W_1' \otimes \cdots \otimes W_n'$. Then, perform F_h to obtain the signature $|\hat{\sigma}^{\otimes n}\rangle$. If $|\hat{\sigma}^{\otimes n}\rangle \neq |\sigma^{\otimes n}\rangle$, *Bob* outputs '0' to reject $|\sigma^{\otimes n}\rangle$. Otherwise, continue to the next step.
   (e) *Bob* takes ρ and $|\sigma^{\otimes n}\rangle$ as inputs and reversely performs the quantum circuit of hypergraph-FQOWF F_h. The outputs is denoted by $\hat{W}_1 \otimes \cdots \otimes \hat{W}_n$.
   (f) *Bob* measures the seccond tuple of $\hat{W}_i$. If all measurement results of $\hat{W}_i$ are 0, *Bob* accepts $|\sigma^{\otimes n}\rangle$ as a valid signature and outputs '1'. Otherwise, *Bob* outputs '0' to reject the signature $|\sigma^{\otimes n}\rangle$.

B. Security Analysis

Obviously, the quantum aggregate signature scheme can resist the eavesdropping attack because of quantum non-cloning theorem and Heisenberg's uncertainty principle [21]. Besides, the entanglement of $|m\rangle$ and one-wayness of the F-QOWF F_h guarantee that the quantum aggregate signature scheme is secure against the forgery attack. When an adversary A captures $|e_i\rangle$ that U_i sends to *David*, assuming A has the ability to decrypt $|e\rangle$ and encrypt $|m\rangle$, A can tamper the message by replacing some qubits in $|m\rangle$ with its own qubits or forging a totally new message $|m'\rangle$. In the former case, the replacement operation destroys the correlation and entanglement between the qubit $|m_i\rangle$. As a result, the tampered message is easy to be rejected at the first verification of *Bob* in Scheme 1. In the latter case, A should forge $|m'\rangle$ to match the unrevealed output ρ. Theorem 8.6 means that it is almost impossible for the adversary A to obtain a rigth input $|m\rangle$ when given the output $|\sigma^{\otimes n}\rangle$, so that it is difficult for A to forge $|m'\rangle$ which matches the unrevealed ρ. Meanwhile, *Bob*'s double verification further reduces the probability of mistakenly verifying an invalid signature as valid.

8.5 Quantum Hash Function Based on Quantum Walks

8.5.1 From One-Way Function to Hash Function

Hash function plays an important role in modern cryptography, which is considered a key component of almost all encryption schemes and many security applications, such as message authentication code, data integrity, data storage, and random number generation. In the classical context, hash function can map a message of arbitrary length to a fixed-size output. Generally, there are two types of hash functions in terms of security attributes. One is the collision-resistant hash function that has provable security reductions and the other is based on an iterated construction of compression functions. The former satisfies computational security but is too inefficient to be used in practice. Some provably secure examples can reduce to hard problems, such as *integer factorization problem* [57], *very smooth number nontrivial modular square root problem* (VSSR) [58], and *Knapsack problem* [59]. The latter is easily designed and more efficient because the design of hash functions can be transformed into that of compression functions [60]. Meanwhile, cryptanalysis attacks also have gradually emerged in recent years, which poses a huge challenge to the security of such hash functions [61].

With the development of quantum computation, more and more researchers have shown increasing interests in using quantum mechanisms to develop cryptographic algorithms with high security, especially quantum hash function, which is one of the most important in cryptographic discussions [7, 66, 67, 69, 76–78]. There are two approaches of research on quantum hash functions. One is based on quantum one-way functions (QOWF) [5–7, 62, 63, 65], while the other one is based on quantum simulation, including discrete-time quantum walk (DQW) [67, 69, 71, 75, 77, 78], continuous-time quantum walk (CQW) [76] and grouped coarse-grained boson sampling (GCGBS) [66]. The former has attempted to formally define the one-way and collision resistance property of quantum hash functions, which have been conclusively proved with a rigorous mathematical form. The latter constructs quantum hash functions by virtue of quantum mechanics, specifically, the chaotic characteristic of quantum walk or the irreversibility of GCGBS without formal security proof. Alternatively, one can evaluate such types of schemes through statistical analysis which can provide quantitative evidence. Moreover, QOWF-based quantum hash functions map a classical bit string to a quantum state whose lengths are positively related to the length of an input message. By contrast, DQW-based, CQW-based and GCGBS-based quantum hash functions generate a fixed-length classical hash value from a classical bit input. Of particular concern is QOWF-based schemes are only guaranteed to correctly distinguish the quantum hash states of two different input messages with a high probability by means of SWAP-test, which means such schemes are non-deterministic with a one-side error. In addition, GCGBS-based quantum hash function could only be efficiently calculated through a linear optical network, but is awkward to perform on a classical computer due to high time complexity. In accordance with the above, the practical value of DQW-based and CQW-based quantum hash functions are higher compared to those based on QOWF and GCGBS, because the former has deterministic outputs for fixed inputs and can be simulated classically before the advent of commercial quantum computers.

As we know, the construction of quantum walks based quantum hash function relies on different quantum walks procedures with various unitary evolution operators which can be generally decomposed into coin and shift operators. Such schemes begin with an initial quantum state, then the evolution of the system proceeds by repeatedly using different unitary operators controlled by the input bit string, it will then obtain a classical hash value by post-processing algorithm, i.e., modular and truncation arithmetic. Li et al. [77] explored, for the first time, a brand-new perspective on the design of a dedicated hash function based on quantum walks. They presented a quantum hash function whose underlying model is one-dimensional two-particle controlled interacting quantum walks (CIQW), and discussed the security and feasibility of the scheme. Over the past decade, more information has become available on the quantum hash functions based on quantum walks, particularly for the quantum hash functions based on controlled alternate quantum walks (CAQW) [67, 69, 73, 78], which are the improvement and extension of CIQW-based quantum hash functions [75, 77]. Until now, almost all such schemes control the evolution of quantum walks by alternate coin operators, little attention has been paid to the role of shift or other operators besides coin operator. Recently, an extra operator called the direction-determine transform has been introduced in the work of Zhou et al. [69], which can also be considered for a CAQW-based quantum hash function. In order to explore whether more operators are valid for designing a CAQW-based quantum hash function, we introduce lively quantum walks with variable liveliness parameters to construct a CAQW-based quantum hash function [78].

8.5.2 Cryptographic Hash Function

A cryptographic hash function must satisfy three criteria: preimage resistance, second-preimage resistance and collision resistance.

1. Preimage resistance
   A hash function is a one-way function. For any valid output, it is computationally infeasible to find the corresponding input. In particular, a function mapping $f : \{0,1\}^* \to \{0,1\}^*$ is a strong one-way function if it satisfies all of the following conditions:

   (a) **Easy to compute**: f can be computed in polynomial time.
   (b) **Hard to invert**: A polynomial $p(\cdot)$ exists such that for any polynomial time adversary's algorithm A, in the case of sufficiently large number $n \in N$, has

$$Prob[A(f(x), 1^n) \in f^{-1}(f(x))] < \frac{1}{p(n)}. \tag{8.78}$$

Given a message digest y, it is difficult to find its preimage x such that $H(x) = y$, instead, its inverse process is computable.

2. Second-preimage resistance
   Finding any two inputs that have the same output is computationally infeasible, i.e., given an input x, find its second preimage x' such that $H(x) = H(x')$.
3. Collision resistance
   Finding two different inputs x and x' such that their hash values are the same is computationally infeasible, i.e., $H(x) = H(x')$. In fact, collision resistance implies second-preimage resistance but does not guarantee preimage resistance.

8.5.3 Lively Quantum Walk on an N-Length Cycle

Standard discrete-time quantum walk (DQW) is a quantum analogue of classical random walk, taking place in the product space $\mathcal{H}_p \bigotimes \mathcal{H}_c$ in which a particle (walker) is placed at a vertex in a cycle and allowed to jump along the edges to adjacent vertexes. Here a particle starts from its initial state $|x\rangle \otimes |c\rangle$, where the spatial degree of freedom $\{|x\rangle, x \in Z_N\}$ spans the position space $\mathcal{H}_p$, and the two-dimensional coin state $\{|c\rangle, c \in \{0, 1\}\}$ spans the coin space $\mathcal{H}_c$. In DQW on an N-length cycle, each evolution of a system proceeds by a unitary operator, which is defined as $U = S(I_N \otimes C)$, where S is the shift operator updating the position chirality states of the particle, C is the coin operator on the coin space $\mathcal{H}_c$ determining the direction at each walking step, and I_N is the N order identity matrix of $\mathcal{H}_p$ space. The shift operator is defined as follows:

$$S = \sum_{x \in Z_N} |x + 1(\mathrm{mod}\, N)\rangle \langle x| \otimes |0\rangle \langle 0| + |x - 1(\mathrm{mod}\, N)\rangle \langle x| \otimes |1\rangle \langle 1|, \quad (8.79)$$

then the evolution process of quantum walk can be defined in the situation by shift operator

$$S(|x\rangle \otimes |0\rangle) = |x + 1(\mathrm{mod}\, N)\rangle \otimes |0\rangle, S(|x\rangle \otimes |1\rangle) = |x - 1(\mathrm{mod}\, N)\rangle \otimes |0\rangle. \quad (8.80)$$

Such operator implies that the particle moves from one vertex to the left or right corresponding to the coin quantum state $|0\rangle$ or $|1\rangle$, respectively.

One-dimensional three-state quantum walks(or lazy quantum walks), the generalized Hadamard walks(DQW) with three inner coin states, were first proposed by Konno et al. [79]. In recent years, Sadows et al. [80] introduced a new family of quantum walks on cycles parametrized by their liveliness (named lively quantum walks). The introduced family contains lazy quantum walks, which can be considered as lively quantum walks with liveliness equal to zero.

Consistent with DQW, the process of a lively quantum walk on an N-length cycle occurs in Hilbert space $\mathcal{H}_p \otimes \mathcal{H}_c$, where $\mathcal{H}_p$ represents the position space, whose orthogonal basis is given by the label of each vertex on the N-length cycle, and defined as $\mathcal{H}_p = Span\,|x\rangle$, $x \in Z_n$. $\mathcal{H}_c$ represents the three-dimensional coin space, which is defined as $\mathcal{H}_c = Span\,|c\rangle\,, c \in \{|0\rangle\,, |1\rangle\,, |2\rangle\}$. Then a formulation for the lively quantum walk can be defined.

The shift operator S of the lively quantum walk acting on each vertex x is given by

$$\begin{aligned} S = \sum_{x \in Z_n} & |x + 1(\text{mod } N)\rangle \langle x| \otimes |0\rangle \langle 0| \\ & + |x - 1(\text{mod } N)\rangle \langle x| \otimes |1\rangle \langle 1| \\ & + |x + \tau(\text{mod } N)\rangle \langle x| \otimes |2\rangle \langle 2|, \end{aligned} \tag{8.81}$$

with a liveliness parameter $\tau \leq \left\lceil \frac{N}{2} \right\rceil$ ($\lceil\cdot\rceil$ represents a ceiling function), which controls the particle to make an additional choice of hop. Thus the entire evolution of the quantum system at each time step can be described by $U = S\,(I_N \otimes C) \in \mathcal{H}_p \bigotimes \mathcal{H}_c$, with a usually used coin operator called Grover operator G. $G = 2\,|s_v\rangle\,\langle s_v| - I$, where $|s_v\rangle = \frac{1}{\sqrt{3}}(|0\rangle + |1\rangle + |2\rangle)$, and we can obtain $G = \begin{bmatrix} -\frac{1}{3} & \frac{2}{3} & \frac{2}{3} \\ \frac{2}{3} & -\frac{1}{3} & \frac{2}{3} \\ \frac{2}{3} & \frac{2}{3} & -\frac{1}{3} \end{bmatrix}$.

8.5.4 *Periodic Quantum Walk on a Cycle*

Under certain conditions, some coin operators may give rise to periodic quantum walks. Here, some necessary conditions for specific quantum walks with periodicity [81–85] have been discussed. In particular, for the lazy quantum walk, Konno and Kajiwara [84] studied the necessary condition that the coin operator to have a finite period. For a more general case, the periodicity phenomenon for lively quantum walks on cycles, generated by the combination of variable parameters of liveliness and generalized Grover coins, has been thoroughly studied. Sarkar and Mandal [85] regarded the coin operator as a linear combination of orthogonal permutation matrices, extending the study of periodic lively quantum walk. Permutation matrices of this type are called Grover-type matrices. According to the Reference [82], the periodic quantum walk on a cycle can be defined as follows:

Definition 8.21 (Periodic quantum walk on a cycle) Define a set as $\mathcal{N} = \{n \geq 1 \in N : U^n = I\}$, where N is the set of nature numbers, U is the evolution operator corresponding to the quantum walk on a cycle, and I is an identity matrix. If $\mathcal{N} \neq \emptyset$, the period T of the quantum walk on a cycle is written as $min\mathcal{N}$. Otherwise, for the case of $\mathcal{N} = \emptyset$, the quantum walk on a cycle has a period defined as ∞ and is called an aperiodic quantum walk. In particular, the periodicity for quantum walk on a cycle means that the particle returns precisely to its quantum initial state after a finite number of steps.

The set of Grover-type matrices [85] can be represented as $M_{Grov} = \{\frac{2}{3}J - P; P \in \mathcal{P}\}$ where J is a matrix whose elements are all one, $\mathcal{P} = \{P_1 = I, P_2 = (123), P_3 = (132), P_4 = (23), P_5 = (12), P_6 = (13)\}$ is the symmetric group S_3 corresponding permutation matrices. Therefore, all parametric orthogonal matrices can be regarded as linear combinations of permutation matrices. The single-parameter orthogonal matrix group is described as follows:

$$\mathcal{X}_\theta = \begin{bmatrix} \frac{2cos\theta+1}{3} & \frac{(1-cos\theta)}{3} + \frac{1}{\sqrt{3}}sin\theta & \frac{(1-cos\theta)}{3} - \frac{1}{\sqrt{3}}sin\theta \\ \frac{(1-cos\theta)}{3} - \frac{1}{\sqrt{3}}sin\theta & \frac{2cos\theta+1}{3} & \frac{(1-cos\theta)}{3} + \frac{1}{\sqrt{3}}sin\theta \\ \frac{(1-cos\theta)}{3} + \frac{1}{\sqrt{3}}sin\theta & \frac{(1-cos\theta)}{3} - \frac{1}{\sqrt{3}}sin\theta & \frac{2cos\theta+1}{3} \end{bmatrix}, \quad (8.82)$$
$$0 < \theta < 2\pi$$

then we have

1. $\mathcal{X}_\theta \cup \mathcal{Y}_\theta$, where

$$\mathcal{Y}_\theta = \begin{bmatrix} \frac{2cos\theta-1}{3} & -\frac{(1+cos\theta)}{3} + \frac{1}{\sqrt{3}}sin\theta & -\frac{(1+cos\theta)}{3} - \frac{1}{\sqrt{3}}sin\theta \\ -\frac{(1+cos\theta)}{3} - \frac{1}{\sqrt{3}}sin\theta & \frac{2cos\theta-1}{3} & -\frac{(1+cos\theta)}{3} + \frac{1}{\sqrt{3}}sin\theta \\ -\frac{(1+cos\theta)}{3} + \frac{1}{\sqrt{3}}sin\theta & -\frac{(1+cos\theta)}{3} - \frac{1}{\sqrt{3}}sin\theta & \frac{2cos\theta-1}{3} \end{bmatrix}.$$
$$0 < \theta < 2\pi \quad (8.83)$$

2. $\mathcal{X}_\theta \cup \mathcal{Z}_\theta$, where

$$\mathcal{Z}_\theta = \begin{bmatrix} \frac{2cos\theta+1}{3} & \frac{(1-cos\theta)}{3} + \frac{1}{\sqrt{3}}sin\theta & \frac{(1-cos\theta)}{3} - \frac{1}{\sqrt{3}}sin\theta \\ \frac{(1-cos\theta)}{3} + \frac{1}{\sqrt{3}}sin\theta & \frac{(1-cos\theta)}{3} - \frac{1}{\sqrt{3}}sin\theta & \frac{2cos\theta+1}{3} \\ \frac{(1-cos\theta)}{3} - \frac{1}{\sqrt{3}}sin\theta & \frac{2cos\theta+1}{3} & \frac{(1-cos\theta)}{3} + \frac{1}{\sqrt{3}}sin\theta \end{bmatrix}. \quad (8.84)$$
$$0 < \theta < 2\pi$$

3. $\mathcal{X}_\theta \cup \mathcal{W}_\theta$,where

$$\mathcal{W}_\theta = \begin{bmatrix} \frac{2cos\theta-1}{3} & -\frac{(1+cos\theta)}{3} + \frac{1}{\sqrt{3}}sin\theta & -\frac{(1+cos\theta)}{3} - \frac{1}{\sqrt{3}}sin\theta \\ -\frac{(1+cos\theta)}{3} + \frac{1}{\sqrt{3}}sin\theta & -\frac{(1+cos\theta)}{3} - \frac{1}{\sqrt{3}}sin\theta & \frac{2cos\theta-1}{3} \\ -\frac{(1+cos\theta)}{3} - \frac{1}{\sqrt{3}}sin\theta & \frac{2cos\theta-1}{3} & -\frac{(1+cos\theta)}{3} + \frac{1}{\sqrt{3}}sin\theta \end{bmatrix}.$$
$$0 < \theta < 2\pi \quad (8.85)$$

4. $\mathcal{PO}_\theta = \mathcal{X}_\theta \cup \mathcal{Y}_\theta \cup \mathcal{Z}_\theta \cup \mathcal{W}_\theta$

Without loss of generality, the necessary condition for the coin operators that satisfy the periodic lively quantum walks when $C \in \mathcal{X}_\theta$ is given by

$$\begin{cases} lcm\{c_l p_l : 0 < l \le N-1\},\ \frac{2l}{n} = \frac{m_l}{p_l},\ gcd(m_l, p_l) = 1, \\ c_l = 1,\ if\ m_l\ is\ even\ and\ c_l = 2,\ if\ m_l\ is\ odd,\ if\ C = I \\ 3,\ if\ C \in \{P_2, P_3\} \\ lcm\{3, q\},\ if\ N = 3\ and\ \theta = \frac{2m\pi}{q},\ \frac{m}{q} \in Q,\ gcd(2m, q) = 1,\ C \notin \{I, P_2, P_3\} \\ lcm\{3, 2q\},\ if\ N = 3\ and\ \theta = \frac{(2m+1)\pi}{q},\ \frac{(2m+1)}{q} \in Q,\ gcd(2m+1, q) = 1,\ C \notin \{I, P_2, P_3\} \\ \infty,\ otherwise \end{cases} \tag{8.86}$$

Where $lcm\{\cdot, \cdot\}$ represents the least common multiple, and $gcd(\cdot, \cdot)$ represents the greatest common divisor. For example, we can consider two special coin operators in $\mathcal{X}_\theta$ with parameters $\theta = \frac{\pi}{2}$ and $\theta = \frac{3\pi}{2}$, whose corresponding coin operators are described as follows: $\begin{bmatrix} \frac{1}{3} & \frac{1+\sqrt{3}}{3} & \frac{1-\sqrt{3}}{3} \\ \frac{1-\sqrt{3}}{3} & \frac{1}{3} & \frac{1+\sqrt{3}}{3} \\ \frac{1+\sqrt{3}}{3} & \frac{1-\sqrt{3}}{3} & \frac{1}{3} \end{bmatrix}$, and $\begin{bmatrix} \frac{1}{3} & \frac{1-\sqrt{3}}{3} & \frac{1+\sqrt{3}}{3} \\ \frac{1+\sqrt{3}}{3} & \frac{1}{3} & \frac{1-\sqrt{3}}{3} \\ \frac{1-\sqrt{3}}{3} & \frac{1+\sqrt{3}}{3} & \frac{1}{3} \end{bmatrix}$. Their corresponding periods are given by $\begin{cases} 12,\ N = 3 \\ \infty,\ N \neq 3 \end{cases}$.

8.5.5 *Quantum Hash Function Based on Controlled Alternate Lively Quantum Walks*

In this section, we introduce the controlled alternate lively quantum walks with variable liveliness on a cycle, then give the specific scheme for the quantum hash function based on it, named QHFL.

A. Controlled Alternate Lively Quantum Walk on an N-length cycle

The controlled alternate lively quantum walk can be constructed by cleverly modifying lively quantum walk on an N-length cycle. Assume that the particle performs the lively quantum walk on an N-length cycle with liveliness parameter τ. At the t-th time step, the quantum state amplitude of a particle at the position x is given by $\left|\psi_{x,t}\right\rangle = \left[a^1_{x,t}\ a^2_{x,t}\ a^3_{x,t}\right]^\dagger = \sum_c a^c_{x,t} \left|c\right\rangle \in \mathcal{H}_c$, where $a^c_{x,t}$ represents the quantum state amplitude of the particle in the coin register, so the state of the whole system can be defined as

$$|\Psi(t)\rangle = \sum_{x \in z_n} |x\rangle \otimes \left|\psi_{x,t}\right\rangle. \tag{8.87}$$

For the initial state $|\Psi(t=0)\rangle$ with a unitary operator U to update the quantum state at each step, the time evolution of the quantum state is defined as $|\Psi(t)\rangle = U^t\,|\Psi(t=0)\rangle$. Thus the transformation of amplitude for the particle at the position x can be obtained as follows

$$\left|\psi_{x,t+1}\right\rangle = C_1\left|\psi_{x+1,t}\right\rangle + C_2\left|\psi_{x-1,t}\right\rangle + C_3\left|\psi_{x+\tau,t}\right\rangle, \tag{8.88}$$

where $C_i = \sum_{k=1}^{3} \tilde{C}_{i,k} |i\rangle \langle k|, i \in \{1, 2, 3\}$, $\tilde{C}_{i,k}$ is the element in the i-th row and k-th column of matrix C. Now we can introduce the controlled alternate lively quantum walk with liveliness on a cycle.

Specifically, given an input message msg, each bit $\{m_1, m_2, \cdots m_t\} \in \{0, 1\}^t$ of the message is a string of binary numbers, so the quantum walk evolution operator controlled by t bits message is $U_{msg} = U_{m_1} U_{m_2} U_{m_3} \cdots U_{m_t}$, where $U_{m_j} (1 \leq j \leq t)$ denotes the evolution operator of j-th step which can be designed with variable liveliness parameters given by Eq. 8.81. Accordingly, the final quantum state can be expressed as $|\Psi\rangle_{final} = U_{msg} |\Psi (t = 0)\rangle$. Then, after t steps, the probability of finding the particle being in the position x is given by

$$p_x = \langle \psi_{x,t} | \psi_{x,t} \rangle = \sum_{c=1}^{3} \left| a_{x,t}^c \right|^2, \tag{8.89}$$

satisfying the condition $\sum_{c=1}^{3} \sum_{x \in z_n} \left| a_{x,t}^c \right|^2 = 1$, where $a_{x,t}^c$ can be obtained by means of measuring the basis state $|x, c\rangle$, as shown in equation (8.90)

$$\left| \langle x, c \left| (U^t) \right| \Psi (t = 0) \rangle \right|^2. \tag{8.90}$$

B. Quantum Hash Function

For an initial state $|\Psi (t = 0)\rangle = |x\rangle \otimes |c\rangle$, where $|c\rangle = a_1 |0\rangle + a_2 |1\rangle + a_3 |2\rangle$, taking message msg as an input, the specific steps of QHFL can be described as follows:

- *Step 1*: Select a set of initial parameters $(N, l, s, C, a_1, a_2, a_3)$, where N is an integer, representing the number of vertexes in a cycle, l represents the amplification factor of the probability with the constraint $10^l \gg 2^s$, C is a coin operator selected from a set that meets the security requirement, a_1, a_2, a_3 are the amplitudes of the three-state coin registers in the initial state, which satisfy $|a_1|^2 + |a_2|^2 + |a_3|^2 = 1$.
- *Step 2*: Apply U_{msg} to the initial state $|\Psi (t = 0)\rangle$ and generate the final probability distribution for each position, denoted by $P = (p_0, p_1, p_2, \cdots p_{n-1})$, where p_x $(x \in z_n)$ is the probability of the particle in its final state finding at each vertex of the cycle given by Eqs. 8.89 and 8.90.
- *Step 3*: Perform the post-processing algorithm on the obtained probability distribution to generate $N \times s$ hash values. In particular, perform $\lfloor p_x \cdot 10^l \rfloor \bmod 2^s$ on p_x. Then, concatenate these s-bit h_x $(x \in z_n)$ together to form the final hash value $h = h_0 \| h_1 \| h_2 \| \cdots \| h_{n-1}$.

8.5.6 Security Analysis

In this section, we will discuss the security of the scheme against the preimage attack, the force search attack and the forgery attack.

A. Preimage Attack Resistance

Hash functions should have one-wayness, which guarantees the security of plaintext information from malicious adversaries, i.e., the adversary cannot guess the original message through the hash value with a non-negligible probability. We define a message space M, quantum state space Q and hash space H. Function mapping $f : M \to Q \to H$ firstly maps the message $msg \in \{0, 1\}^L$ to the quantum state of a quantum system, denoted by $|\Psi\rangle_{final}$, then to the hash space $h \in \{0, 1\}^m$, $m < L$, which is a classical-classical mapping. Moreover, the inversion of this mapping is tough to accomplish due to two shields. The first shield is using the post-processing algorithms to obtain the hash value by truncation arithmetic and modular arithmetic on the probability of vertexes, which obviously is a many-to-one mapping. The second shield is based on the irreversibility of quantum measurement on the final state, which breaks the linear relationship between the final state and the initial state, even if the adversary takes the hash value in hand and has a priori knowledge of initial state. For example, assume that the message length L is disclosed to the adversary, there is no efficient polynomial-time algorithm $A(f(x))$ to try all of 2^L guesses, which satisfies Eq. 8.78. Therefore, when the message space is sufficiently large, the adversary cannot backtrack the original message by hash value with a non-negligible probability.

B. Force Search Attack Resistance

Cryptographic hash functions are designed to keep their output as short as possible, but it is still difficult to find collisions. There is a powerful attack for hash functions acting on hash value, *birthday attack* [86]. The birthday attack can find the collision of the target hash h with a 50% probability of only $O(\sqrt{sN})$ expected times. For classical computers, the general hash length of $\frac{sN}{2} \geq 128$ can satisfy the condition of cryptographic security. Because of the extensibility of the hash length in the scheme, we can easily construct hash functions that satisfy the security conditions.

C. Forgery Attack Resistance

Here forgery attack means that a valid message-hash pair can be obtained from other message-hash pairs that are of equal or variant lengths. The forgery attack is closely related to the second-preimage resistance of the hash function. To demonstrate such attack on the original scheme, the following procedure is introduced.

Periodic quantum walk on a cycle is defined in Definition **Periodic quantum walk on a cycle**. If there is more than one quantum walk with a finite period, it will be easy to generate collisions in all DQW-based hash functions. Specifically, assume a quantum walk algorithm with a chosen evolution operator U_1 (executed when the message bit is 1) has a finite period T. In that case, ${U_1}^T \, |\Psi\,(t=0)\rangle = I\,|\Psi\,(t=0)\rangle \; = |\Psi\,(t=0)\rangle$, so for a message $msg = 10\cdots 10$, any $nT, n \in \{1, 2, 3\ldots\}$ message bits can be inserted into the message string, then a collision can be formed as

$$U_{Msg} = U_1 U_0 \cdots U_1 U_0 = U_1 U_0 \cdots \underbrace{U_1 \cdots U_1}_{I} \cdots U_1 U_0. \tag{8.91}$$

Anyone can easily construct a collision at this point, making such algorithms no longer satisfy the collision resistance property. Therefore, when designing a hash function based on quantum walks, proper parameters should be selected to avoid this situation. The coin operator of controlled alternate lively quantum walk on a cycle is selected from Grover type of matrix set, which will provide strict security and collision resistance. Consequently, collisions may only be affected by computational precision or by truncation and modular operations.

8.5.7 Performance Analysis

It is difficult to evaluate the security of the scheme by rigorous mathematical proof. So widely accepted statistical tests can be used to evaluate the performance and feasibility of the scheme. We take the same public arxiv Dataset as the Reference [69] used and randomly select from about 2 million records as the input string. Note that since DQW-based hash functions are classical input and classical output, the hash value of a message in classical computation is usually generated and stored in ASCII format.

In Sect. 8.5.6, the security lower bound for the birthday attack of the hash function is given. To ensure the security of the scheme, we generate $Len = sN > 256$-bit hash values, i.e., $Len \in \{296, 264\}$. As with other existing DQW-based hash functions, two instances of QHFL share the same l value, and the remaining parameters are $C = Grov$, $\alpha_1 = \alpha_2 = \alpha_3 = \frac{1}{\sqrt{3}}$. The statistical performance analyses include: collision resistance, sensitivity, diffusion and confusion property, uniform distribution. The test results will be compared mainly with the typical scheme QHFM [69].

A. Collision Resistance

Collision resistance is an important property of cryptographic hash functions. Such property of hash functions can be quantified by collision test. In general, collision resistance is assessed by two types of tests, namely T_1 and T_2. In the test T_1, a random input message is selected and computed to obtain an ASCII hash value h_1. In the test T_2, a random bit reversal is performed on the message in the test T_1, and the corresponding hash value h_2 is also generated and stored in ASCII format by $h_1 = \{b_1, b_1 \ldots, b_s\}$ and $h_2 = \{b'_1, b'_1 \ldots, b'_s\}$, respectively, where b_i and b'_i are the i-th ASCII characters, and $s = \frac{Len}{8}$ represents the size of the hash value in ASCII format.

Moreover, we compare the number of characters of h_1 and h_2 with the same value at the same location, i.e., the number of hits, and calculate as follows:

$$\omega = \sum_i^N \delta(T(b_i), T(b'_i)), \tag{8.92}$$

where $\delta(x, y) = \begin{cases} 1, & x = y \\ 0, & x \neq y \end{cases}$ indicates that b_i and b'_i are converted to the corresponding decimal values with $T(b_i), T(b'_i) \in \{0, 1, 2, \ldots 255\}$.

Through $J = 10000$ times independent experiments of drawing records from the arxiv dataset and assuming that the hash value distribution is uniform and random, the theoretical number of tests can be given by the binomial distribution formula:

$$W_t(\omega) = J \times Prob^t\{\omega\} = J \frac{s!}{\omega!\,(s-\omega)!} \left(\frac{1}{2^8}\right)^{\omega} (1 - \frac{1}{2^8})^{s-\omega}, \tag{8.93}$$

where $\omega = 0, 1, \ldots, s$, $Prob^t\{\omega\}$ is the probability distribution of the theoretical number of hits (the probability distribution of the experimental number of hits is denoted by $Prob^e\{\omega\}$), and the distance with the theoretical value can be measured by means of *Kullback-Leibler* relative entropy (KL divergence) [87]

$$D(Prob^t\{\omega\} \| Prob^e\{\omega\}) = \sum_{\omega=0}^{s} \frac{W_t(\omega)}{J} \log_2 \left(\frac{W_e(\omega)}{J \times Prob^t\{\omega\}}\right). \tag{8.94}$$

The smaller $D(Prob^t\{\omega\} \| Prob^e\{\omega\})$ is, the closer $W_t(\omega)$ and $W_e(\omega)$ are, which means that the hash function has the exceptional collision resistance property.

The collision resistance property can also be quantified by the absolute difference between two hash values (i.e., the distance between two hash values):

$$d = \sum_{i}^{s} |T(b_i) - T(b'_i)|. \tag{8.95}$$

The experimental mean difference per byte of two hash values can be calculated by d, then obtain the absolute difference between it and its theoretical value is denoted by $\Delta\bar{d} = |\bar{d}^t - \bar{d}^e|$. Since the spatial distribution of ASCII characters is independent and uniform, and $\bar{d}^t$ can be calculated by the following equation [88]:

$$\bar{d}^t = E\left(T(b_i) - T(b'_i)\right) = \frac{1}{3} \times Lev \approx 85.3, \tag{8.96}$$

where $Lev = 256$ is the number of levels. As the number of experiments increases, $\bar{d}^e$ will converge to $\bar{d}^t$, which means better property of collision resistance. As we can see from Table 8.3, two instances of the scheme have a smaller $D(Prob^t\{\omega\}||Prob^e\{\omega\})$ and $\Delta\bar{d}$ compared with those in QHFM, which implies that the scheme has better performance in the collision test.

So far this section has focused on collision test to assess the collision resistance. The main criterion for collision resistance of a hash function is that the hash value has less number of hits when a random bit reversal is performed on the input message. When the discrete-time quantum walks perform on an even-length cycle starting in the position $|0\rangle$ after odd steps, then the probability at the even vertexes is zero, while

Table 8.3 Collision resistance test results

Instance		Numbers of hits ω					$D(Prob^t\{\omega\}\|Prob^e\{\omega\})$	$\Delta\bar{d}$
		0	1	2	3	4		
QHFL-296	$W_e(\omega)$	8637	1278	81	4	0	0.00009977	0.15
	$W_t(\omega)$	8652	1255	89	4	0		
QHFM-296 [69]	$W_e(\omega)$	8662	1250	85	2	1	0.00001848	0.13
	$W_t(\omega)$	8652	1255	89	4	0		
QHFL-264	$W_e(\omega)$	8784	1133	82	1	0	0.00024273	0.02
	$W_t(\omega)$	8788	1137	71	3	0		
QHFM-264 [69]	$W_e(\omega)$	8853	1074	73	0	0	0.00072578	0.11
	$W_t(\omega)$	8788	1137	71	3	0		

the odd vertex is not zero. This periodic behavior is similar to lively quantum walk with an odd lively parameter on an even-length cycle τ. The issue that emerges from these patterns is that the collision test can not pass. However, the lively quantum walks with even lively parameters τ do not show such a periodic pattern for both even-length cycles and odd-length cycles. It can thus be suggested that the quantum hash function can satisfy multi-level security, i.e., it can output variable-length hash values. By contrast, most quantum hash functions based on discrete-time quantum walks cannot satisfy this property. For example, they cannot output a 256-bit hash value [68, 69, 73].

B. Sensitivity

An effective hash function needs to be extremely sensitive to the initial input, which means that any slight change in the input message will produce a hash value completely unrelated to the result of the original message. To verify the sensitivity of the scheme, four experiments were designed and calculated with the following input information:

$M1$: Randomly draw a record from the dataset

$M2$: Randomly flip the bits of message $M1$ at a location

$M3$: Randomly insert a random bit at a location in message $M1$

$M4$: Delete a bit at a random location in message $M1$

The hash values corresponding to the above four input messages are $H_{Mj}, j = 1, 2, 3, 4$. Taking the instance that the output hash value length is $L = 296$-bit, the hexadecimal format of the four hash values is described as follows:

H_{M1}:D8CCADC2F92994BCBA291E6E790B848ED2ECF9A4D406D00DB40 084B7129C9CADB8BE6A504D

H_{M2}:AD8E79F3A902AC2AA9C16FD35389ECA58C5ACAE9243EC67CB5F 1FF68576C5C2A5252F54B47

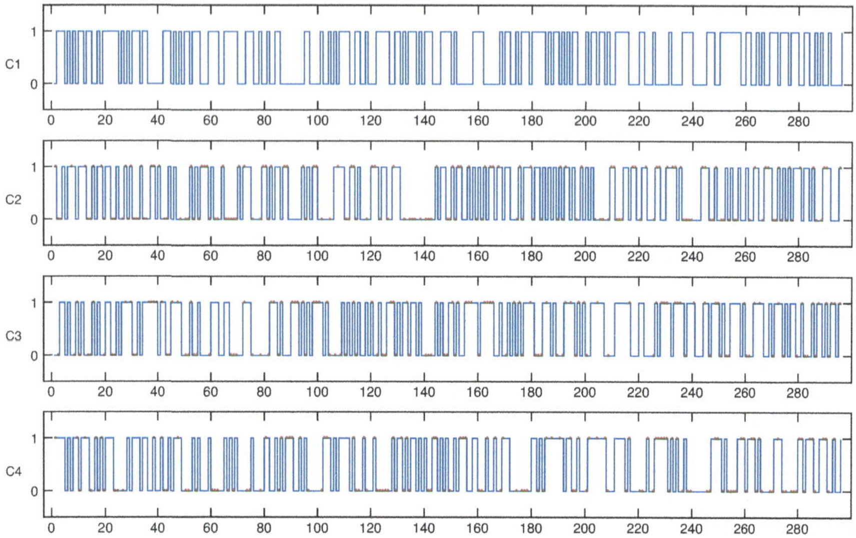

Fig. 8.16 Hash values in the binary format generated by QHFL-296. The symbol * represents a different bit between H_{M2} and $H_{M2} - H_{M4}$

H_{M3}:712DBD57C4300F84478C36FF9FAC6CF46DC2463EEA006FEA237 F1679FC93E019AA42FC017D

H_{M4}:C8555E380EA9854F3F913CA2D30F86F1AA386748E0345E6F223 9FC84D1C986511F00F23AB0

The binary format of the hash values corresponding to the input messages $M1 - M4$ is shown in Fig. 8.16, which demonstrates that even a slight change of the input message can also cause the new hash value to have a large deviation from the original hash value. This result further demonstrates that QHFL can satisfy the one-wayness well.

Since the hash value of the scheme is calculated by the probability distribution of each vertex in the final state on the cycle, the distance between the discrete probability distribution corresponding to the modified message and the original message, respectively, can also be used as an indicator to measure the sensitivity of DQW-based hash functions.

For two discrete probability distributions $P = (p_1, p_2, \ldots p_N)$ and $Q = (q_1, q_2, \ldots q_N)$ on a finite alphabet of size N, the distance between them can be measured by *Jensen–Shannon divergence* (JSD) [89], which is denoted by JSD in the sensitivity test. Different from KL divergence, it is a symmetric function, defined everywhere, with values between 0 and 1. The larger JSD value indicates the farther distance between the two probability distributions. KL divergence can be modified slightly to obtain the JSD formula

$$JSD(Prob^{M1} \parallel Prob^{Mk}) = \frac{1}{2}D(Prob^{M1} \parallel Prob^{Mk}) + \frac{1}{2}D(Prob^{Mk} \parallel Prob^{M1}), \tag{8.97}$$

Table 8.4 JSD-sensitivity test results

Instance	$M2$	$M3$	$M4$
QHFL-296	0.0810050584976550	0.136948519786094	0.137304527477550
QHFM-296	0.0433801323884277	0.0578510007648174	0.0574491187555278

where Mk denotes a modified message with a range of $k \in \{2, 3, 4\}$, and $D(\cdot \parallel \cdot)$ denotes the KL divergence in Eq. 8.94. After repeating 2048 independent sensitivity test experiments, as listed in Table 8.4, the QHFL scheme is more sensitive to messages in comparison with the QHFM scheme.

C. Diffusion and Confusion Property

Diffusion and confusion methods, first introduced by Shannon [90], can effectively impede the statistical analysis of encryption algorithms. In the context of a hash function, diffusion (often referred to as the avalanche effect) allows any slight impact on the original message and is propagated throughout the whole output, which means that the output hash is highly correlated with the input text. For the binary format of the input and output hash values, any change in the original message bit leads to a change in each bit of the hash value with a 50% probability. Confusion attempts to hide the input message and the relation between the key and the output hash value, which means that it is difficult for an adversary to break the security of the hash function by means of statistical analysis.

To evaluate the diffusion and confusion performance of QHFL, we independently repeat the following experiments $J = 10000$ times. In the i-th experiment, the original message $M1$ generates its corresponding hash value h, and then randomly selects and flips a bit in $M1$ to obtain a new hash value h'. The new L-bit hash value is then compared with the original message, and followed by calculating their Hamming distance $B_i = \sum_{k=1}^{|h|} h(k) \bigoplus h'(k)$ between the two hash values per experiment. Four statistical indicators can be further calculated to evaluate the diffusion and confusion property of the hash function:

1. Mean number of bits changed $\bar{B} = \frac{\sum_{i=1}^{J} B_i}{J}$ bit
2. Mean probability of change per bit $P = \frac{\bar{B}}{|h|} \times 100\%$
3. Standard deviation of the changed bit number $\Delta B = \sqrt{\frac{1}{J-1} \sum_{i=1}^{J} (B_i - B)^2}$ bit
4. Standard deviation of the mean change per bit probability $\Delta P = \sqrt{\frac{1}{J-1} \sum_{i=1}^{J} (P_i - P)^2} \times 100\%$

The ideal values of $\bar{B}$ and $P(\%)$ are $\frac{L}{2}$ and 50%, respectively. Meanwhile, a smaller standard deviation of ΔB and $\Delta P(\%)$ can also explain the stability of the diffusion and confusion effects. Comparison between QHFL and QHFM is listed in Table 8.5. It can be concluded from the results that the ΔB and $\Delta P(\%)$ of QHFL are slightly less than or approximately equal to QHFM. In addition, it is obvious that $\bar{B}$ and $P(\%)$ of QHFL are approximate to the ideal values, which are on the same level as

Table 8.5 Results of diffusion and confusion tests

Instance	$\bar{B}$	$P(\%)$	ΔB	$\Delta P(\%)$
QHFL-296	148.19	50.06	8.55	2.89
QHFM-296	147.91	49.97	8.81	2.98
QHFL-264	132.03	50.01	8.11	3.07
QHFM-264	131.96	49.98	8.16	3.09

QHFL. Differential analysis is based on the analysis of the correlation between some input differences and output differences, exploiting the weaknesses in the diffusion and confusion property. These differential attacks can pose a serious threat to the security of hash functions as well. If there is a strong correlation between different inputs and outputs, one can easily detect message collisions. Therefore diffusion and confusion are strong indicators for assessing the resistance of hash functions against the differential analysis attacks. Excellent diffusion and confusion property evaluated from tests indicate that the scheme has robust resistance and reliability to differential analysis attack.

D. Uniform Distribution

In general, the uniform distribution of output hash values over the compression range is one of the most critical security features. When the output space of a hash function is uniformly distributed, the input message will hide the statistics of the original message after diffusion and confusion. As shown in Fig. 8.17, we count the number of tests to flip a hash bit at each location, and the result is visually described in the form of a histogram, which proves that the QHFL scheme is able to resist statistical analysis attacks.

8.5.8 *Computing Complexity*

For the case where QHFL with L-bit input and $O(N)$-bit output, it is easy to perform both in the quantum and classical computer, specifically, only up to $O(LN)$ time complexity is required in the classical case, and at most, $O\left(\lceil \log_2 N \rceil\right)$-sized elementary gates along with memory are necessary for the quantum case. In the classical context, it is trivial to obtain the time and space complexity of these schemes by analyzing the number of arithmetic operations performed during the entire hash process [69]. Such schemes can also be efficiently implemented under quantum computing models by performing controlled alternate lively quantum walks, such that we can give the design of quantum circuit for QHFL by some trivial alterations on the quantum circuit of DQW.

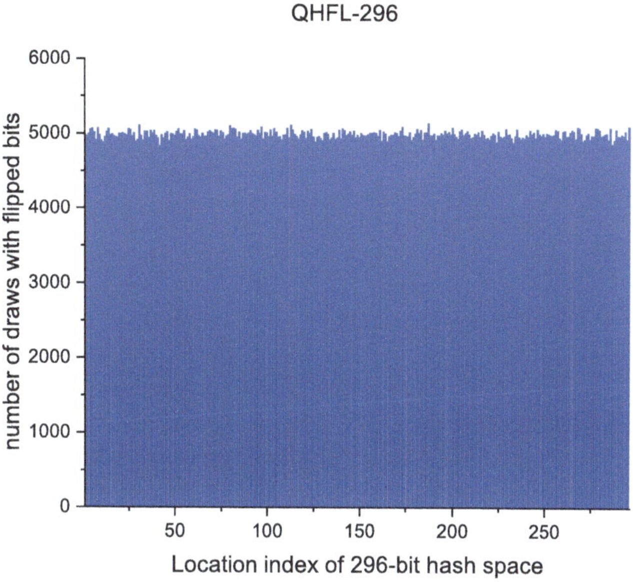

Fig. 8.17 Histogram of the 296-bit hash space

A. Classical Time and Space Complexity

The quantum evolution at each step of controlled alternate lively quantum walk on an N-length cycle is simulated by matrix multiplication. The quantum state at the t-th step can be denoted by $|\Psi(t)\rangle = \sum_{x \in z_n} a^c_{x,t} |x, c\rangle$ or in Eq. 8.87. Each step performs a quantum evolution via a unitary operator $U_1 = S_1 (I_N \otimes C)$ or $U_0 = S_0 (I_N \otimes C)$ controlled by message bits, where S_1 and S_0 represent the shift operators of different τ, C is the coin operator, denoted by $\begin{bmatrix} C_1 \\ C_2 \\ C_3 \end{bmatrix}$, where $C_i = \sum_{k=1}^{3} C_{i,k} |i\rangle \langle k|, i \in \{1, 2, 3\}$, $C_{i,k}$ are the elements in the i th row and k th column of the matrix C. After combining Eqs. 8.87 and 8.88, the transformation of coin operator acting on $|\psi_{x,t}\rangle$ can be formulated as

$$
\begin{aligned}
|\Psi(t+1)\rangle = &\sum_{x \in z_n} C_1 \begin{bmatrix} \left(a^1_{x+1,t}\right)^\dagger \\ \left(a^2_{x+1,t}\right)^\dagger \\ \left(a^3_{x+1,t}\right)^\dagger \end{bmatrix} |x+1, 0\rangle + \sum_{x \in z_n} C_2 \begin{bmatrix} \left(a^1_{x-1,t}\right)^\dagger \\ \left(a^2_{x-1,t}\right)^\dagger \\ \left(a^3_{x-1,t}\right)^\dagger \end{bmatrix} |x-1, 1\rangle \\
&+ \sum_{x \in z_n} C_3 \begin{bmatrix} \left(a^1_{x+a,t}\right)^\dagger \\ \left(a^2_{x+a,t}\right)^\dagger \\ \left(a^3_{x+a,t}\right)^\dagger \end{bmatrix} |x+\tau, 2\rangle ,
\end{aligned}
\quad (8.98)
$$

where $x+1, x-1$, and $x+\tau$ are all calculated by modular arithmetic under modulus N. According to Eq. 8.98, the amplitude of the quantum state $|\Psi(t)\rangle$ is given by

$$\begin{aligned}
\left[a^1_{x+1,t}\ a^2_{x+1,t}\ a^3_{x+1,t}\right]^\dagger &= \left[a^1_{x+1,t}\ a^2_{x+1,t}\ a^3_{x+1,t}\right]^\dagger \\
&\quad + \left[a^1_{x,t-1}\ a^2_{x,t-1}\ a^3_{x,t-1}\right]^\dagger C_1 \\
\left[a^1_{x-1,t}\ a^2_{x-1,t}\ a^3_{x-1,t}\right]^\dagger &= \left[a^1_{x-1,t}\ a^2_{x-1,t}\ a^3_{x-1,t}\right]^\dagger \\
&\quad + \left[a^1_{x,t-1}\ a^2_{x,t-1}\ a^3_{x,t-1}\right]^\dagger C_2 \\
\left[a^1_{x+\tau,t}\ a^2_{x+\tau,t}\ a^3_{x+\tau,t}\right]^\dagger &= \left[a^1_{x+\tau,t}\ a^2_{x+\tau,t}\ a^3_{x+\tau,t}\right]^\dagger \\
&\quad + \left[a^1_{x,t-1}\ a^2_{x,t-1}\ a^3_{x,t-1}\right]^\dagger C_2.
\end{aligned} \tag{8.99}$$

The calculation process of the QHFL scheme consists of two parts of arithmetic operations. The first part is to update the quantum state amplitudes, and the second is to use multiplication and modular arithmetic to obtain the final hash value. Since the liveliness parameter τ is controlled by each message bit, a QHFL with L steps has the same complexity as the controlled alternate lively quantum walk on an N-length cycle with message length L. Given the quantum state amplitude at the $t-1$-th step and the position x, the new quantum state amplitude at the t-th step can be updated by only 9 multiplications and 9 additions. For a cycle with N vertexes, each step will take $O(N)$ basic arithmetic operations. Obviously, for an input message of L bits, the basic operations required for obtaining the value of amplitude only increase by $O(LN)$. In addition, such computation needs $3N$ registers to store the amplitude values, so the space complexity is $O(N)$. The time and space complexity of other existing schemes can be analyzed by using similar processes related to the length of the output hash value. As a result, QHFL has the same classical time and space complexity as its peers [67–73, 75, 77] except Cao-195 [74].

B. Quantum Circuit and Resource Consumption

For the reason of exponential speedups, quantum implementation of the proposed scheme must scale logarithmically with graph scale on which it performs. As a structure with a high degree of symmetry, a small number of parameters can characterize the cycle [91, 92]. QHFL, whose underlying model is controlled alternate lively quantum walk on the N-length cycle, can be regarded as the DQW proceeding around a slightly modified N-length cycle with additional connections for each transition, such that each vertex on the cycle has three adjacent edges. Then we give an efficient quantum circuit to implement QHFL by referring to the Reference [91].

There are three associated spaces: the vertex space, in which x lies, the coin space, in which c lies, the message space, in which msg lies. We firstly assign each vertex x a bit string in lexicographic order to encode the vertex space, then use $\lceil \log_2 3 \rceil$ (rounded up to a nearest integer) additional qubits to encode the coin space, where the first three bit strings represent the three edges of each vertex. In the end, one

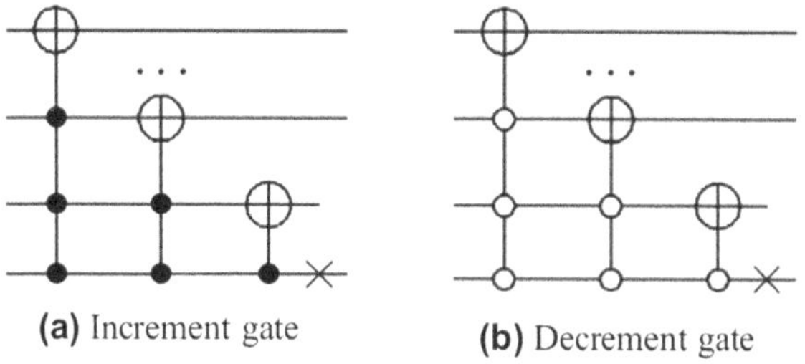

Fig. 8.18 Increment and decrement gates on n qubits

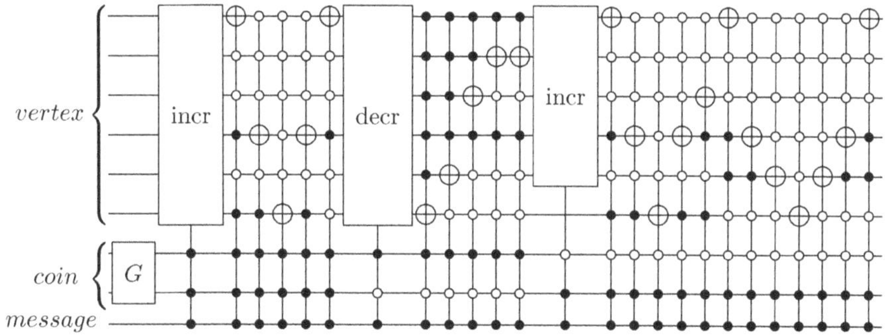

Fig. 8.19 Quantum circuit implementing QHFL with the liveliness parameter of $\tau = 2$ alone a 37-length cycle controlled by message bit 1

qubit is required to encode the message space, with each computational basis $|0\rangle$ and $|1\rangle$ representing the input message bits 0 and 1, respectively. The shift operator can be implemented by a cyclic permutation gate, which increases or decreases a vertex bit string value into its adjacent vertexes in Fig. 8.18, and the coin operator is the Grover operator defined on $\lceil \log_2 3 \rceil$ dimensions. Such quantum circuit is made up of generalized CNOT gates, which $O\left(\lceil \log_2 N \rceil\right)$ additional ancillary qubits and $O\left(\lceil \log_2 N \rceil\right)$ elementary gates are also required. An example of the quantum circuit for the implementation of QHFL at per step controlled by per message bit is shown in Figs. 8.19 and 8.20.

8.5.9 Advantage

Through the above analysis, QHFL performs better in tests of statistical performance than other QW-based quantum hash functions. Furthermore, QHFL has more advantages than other CAQW-based quantum hash functions and benefits from the structure of controlled alternate lively quantum walks on cycles.

Applying the controlled alternate lively quantum walk as an underlying algorithm for quantum hash functions presents several useful attributes. Firstly, sim-

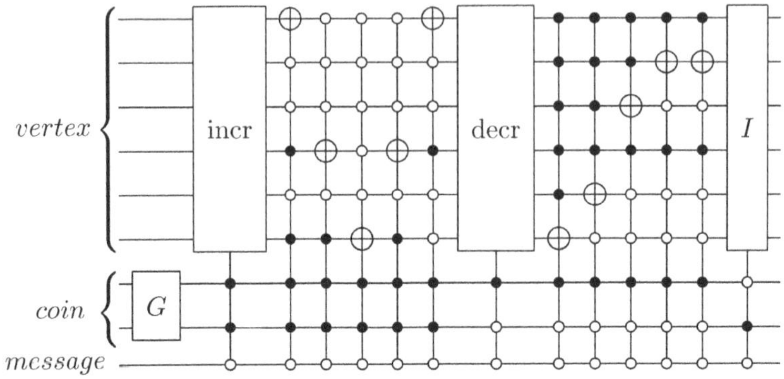

Fig. 8.20 Quantum circuit implementing QHFL with the liveliness parameter $\tau = 0$ alone a 37-length cycle controlled by message bit 0 per step

ply changing the liveliness parameters, not just the coin operators of the controlled alternate lively quantum walk employed results in a totally different hash output. Without introducing an additional direction-determine operator as in QHFM, QHFL can implement different quantum hash functions for different purposes by setting unique liveliness parameters, for each purpose. Secondly, the structure of controlled alternate lively quantum walks can be modified, allowing for a longer hash output, simply by changing the cycles on which controlled alternate lively quantum walks perform. As described on the collision resistance in previous section, QHFL performed on an even-sized cycle will not result in regular hash values. Consequently, differently from some CAQW-based quantum hash functions [68–74], it can generate hash values with arbitrary length under suitable conditions.

We addressed to designing a new quantum hash function QHFL with variable output length, which is based on the controlled alternate lively quantum walks with variable parameters of liveliness. Its performance and security property are evaluated and compared with the existed state-of-art scheme. The selection criteria of coin operators were also discussed to guarantee the security conditions of QHFL, mainly to avoid collisions. The nature of DQW-based quantum hash functions is that different input messages correspond to completely divergent probability distributions of final quantum state. Thus we adopted an additional indicator JSD to evaluate the sensitivity of the probability distribution to a message. The analyses show that QHFL is with the near-ideal properties of collision resistance, sensitivity, diffusion-confusion property, and hash value uniform distribution property. Moreover, QHFL is a compatible hash function that can perform efficiently on both a quantum and a classical computer. We also designed an efficient quantum circuit implementation of QHFL, which only requires ancillary qubits and elementary quantum gates in logarithmic complexity scaling with cycle size. Remarkably, the scheme has better flexibility than the scheme based on the controlled alternate quantum walks with memory, because it is easy to replace the underlying lively quantum walks by changing the liveliness parameters. Thus, such research can facilitate the construction of novel CAQW-base hash functions without restricting the use of controlled coins. Furthermore, QHFL is suited for various security levels required among different applications. Research on QW-based quantum hash functions is still in progress. Despite some positive results in the design of quantum hash functions, questions remain. Firstly, all the processes on a classical computer of QHFL are realized by multiplication and addition/subtraction operations, there is abundant room for further progress in efficiency. Secondly, the collision resistance and differential analysis attack resistance of the quantum hash function is analyzed only by some statistical tests. In future work, more efficient constructions of combining other different quantum walks and using a parallel realization are therefore required to explore. And to develop a full analysis of QW-based quantum hash function, additional studies will be needed to perform a rigorous mathematical proof for the scheme.

8.6 Summary

In this chapter, quantum one-way function was designed based on the theory of quantum computation and quantum mechanics, including full quantum one-way function and 'classical-to classical' quantum one-way function. Following the 'quantum-classical-quantum' idea, the first full quantum one-way function was introduced and proven to be 'easy to compute and hard to invert'. To define a purely full QOWF, we introduced quantum obfuscation into QOWF. The property of the full QOWF was rigorously proved by means of the property of quantum obfuscation. Of course, quantum obfuscation is still a challenge in implementing the full QOWF in practice. The more effective implementation for the full QOWF should be discussed in further work. Meanwhile, we introduced a full quantum one-way function called DF-QOWF, which exploits quantum circuit mapping to ensure its one-wayness and generate a dynamic quantum circuit. This function facilitates the construction of a full quantum trapdoor one-way function. It is also easy to be implemented in the quantum platform through programming. The function can bind the coupling graph and input quantum state to dynamically generate an execution quantum circuit. Besides, quantum hypergraph state was introduced for the preparation of the input quantum state in the algorithm of F-QOWF. The multiparty entanglement property of quantum hypergraph state empowers F-QOWF an application scenario in quantum multiparty cryptographic protocols. In order to design a new quantum one-way function with variable output length and collision resistance, we adopted the controlled alternate lively quantum walks with variable parameters of liveliness. In future work, we may consider more multi-party scenarios such as quantum blockchain and quantum voting protocols.

References

1. Kashefi, E., Kerenidis, I.: Statistical zero knowledge and quantum one-way functions. Theor. Comput. Sci. **378**(1), 101–116 (2005)
2. Hosoyamada, A., Yasuda, K.: Building quantum-one-way functions from block ciphers: Davies-Meyer and Merkle-Damgård constructions. In: Advances in Cryptology—ASIACRYPT 2018 (2018)
3. Buhrman, H., Cleve, R., Watrous, J., Wolf, R.D.: Quantum fingerprinting. Phys. Rev. Lett. **87**(16), 167902 (2001)
4. Gottesman, D., Chuang, I.: Quantum digital signatures (2002). arXiv preprint arXiv: quant-ph/0105032
5. Ablayev, F.M., Vasiliev, A.V.: Cryptographic quantum hashing. Laser Phys. Lett. **11**(2), 025202 (2014)
6. Ablayev, F., Ablayev, M.: On the concept of cryptographic quantum hashing. Laser Phys. Lett. **12**(12), 125204 (2015)
7. Ablayev, F., Ablayev, M., Vasiliev, A., Ziatdinov, M.: Quantum fingerprinting and quantum hashing, computational and cryptographical aspects. Modern Comput. **4**(4), 860–875 (2016)
8. Ablayev, F., Ablayev, M., Vasiliev, A.: On the balanced quantum hashing. J. Phys. Conf. Ser. 012019 (2016)
9. Behera, A., Paul, G.: Quantum to classical one-way function and its applications in quantum money authentication. Quant. Inform. Process. **17**(8), 200 (2018)
10. Alagic, G., Gagliardoni, T., Majenz, C.: Can you sign a quantum state? (2018) arXiv preprint arXiv: quant-ph/1811.11858
11. Crépeau, C., Salvail, L.: Quantum oblivious mutual identification. In: Advances in Cryptology—EUROCRYPT'95, pp. 133–146 (1995)
12. Dusek, M., Haderka, Hendrych, O.M., Myska, R.: Quantum identification system. Phys. Rev. A **60**(1), 149–156 (1999)
13. Ljunggren, D., Bourennane, M., Karlsson, A.: Authority-based user authentication in quantum key distribution. Phys. Rev. A **62**(2), 22305 (2000)
14. Shi, B.S., Li, J., Liu, J.M., et al.: Quantum key distribution and quantum authentication based on entangled state. Phys. Lett. A **281**(281), 83–87 (2001)
15. Zhou, N., Zeng, G., Zeng, W., Zhu, F.: Cross-center quantum identification scheme based on teleportation and entanglement swapping. Opt. Commun. **254**(4), 380–388 (2005)
16. Yuan, H., Liu, Y.M., Pan, G.Z., et al.: Quantum identity authentication based on ping-pong technique without entanglements. Quant. Inform. Process. **13**(11), 2535–2549 (2014)
17. Hopper, N.J., Blum, M.: Secure human identification protocols. In: Advances in Cryptology—ASIACRYPT 2001, pp. 52–66 (2001)
18. Shang, T., Tang, Y., Chen, R.Y.L., Liu, J.W.: Full quantum one-way function for quantum cryptography. Quant. Eng. **2**, e32 (2020)
19. Goldreich, O.: Foundations of Cryptography, vol. 2 (2004)
20. Nikolopoulos, G.M.: Applications of single-qubit rotations in quantum public-key cryptography. Phys. Rev. A **77**(78), 156–156 (2008)
21. Nielsen, M., Chuang, I.: Quantum Computing and Quantum Information. Cambridge Press, New York (2000)
22. Bohen, D., Shoup, V.: A Graduate Course in Applied Cryptography (2019). Online draft, http://toc.cryptobook.us/
23. Alagic, G., Jeffery, S., Jordan, S.: Circuit obfuscation using braids. In: 9th Conference on the Theory of Quantum Computation, Communication and Cryptography (TQC 2014), pp. 141–160 (2014)
24. Alagic, G., Fefferman B.: On Quantum Obfuscation (2016). arXiv preprint arXiv:1602.01771
25. Tang, Y., Shang, T., Liu, J.W.: Universal construction of a full quantum one-way function. Quant. Inform. Process. **21**, 258 (2022)
26. Shor, P.W.: Polynomial-Time algorithms for prime factorization and discrete logarithms on a quantum computer. SIAM Rev. **41**, 303–332 (1999)

27. Shang, T., Chen, R.Y.L., Liu, J.W.: On the obfuscatability of quantum point functions. Quant. Inform. Process. **18**, 55 (2019)
28. Smolin, J., DiVincenzo, D.: Five two-bit quantum gates are sufficient to implement the quantum Fredkin gate. Phys. Rev. A **53**(4), 2855–2856 (1996)
29. Preskill, J.: Quantum computing in the NISQ era and beyond. Quantum **2**, 79 (2018)
30. Li, G., Ding, Y., Xie, Y.: Tackling the qubit mapping problem for NISQ-era quantum devices. In: The 24th International Conference on Architectural Support for Programming Languages and Operating Systems (ASPLOS '19), pp. 1001–1014 (2019)
31. Siraichi, M., Santos, V., Collange, C., Pereira, F.: Qubit allocation. In: The International Symposium on Code Generation and Optimization (CGO 2018), pp. 113–125 (2018)
32. Zulehner, A., Paler, A., Wille, R.: An efficient methodology for mapping quantum circuits to the IBM QX architectures. IEEE Trans. Comput.-Aided Des. Integrated Circ. Syst. **38**, 1226–1236 (2019)
33. Akavia, A., Goldreich, O., Goldwasser, S., Moshkovitz, D.: On basing one-way functions on NP-hardness. In: The 38th Annual ACM Symposium on Theory of Computing (STOC '06), pp. 701–710 (2006)
34. Tang, Y., Shang, T., Liu, J.W.: Dynamic full quantum one-way function based on quantum circuit mapping. Quant. Inform. Process. **22**, 324 (2023)
35. Itoko, T., Raymond, R., Imamichi, T., Matsuo, A.: Optimization of quantum circuit mapping using gate transformation and commutation. Integration **70**, 43–50 (2020)
36. Wiesner, S.: Conjugate coding. SIGACT News **15**(1), 78–88 (1983)
37. Aaronson, S., Farhi, E., Gosset, D., et al.: Quantum money. Commun. ACM **55**(8), 84–92 (2012)
38. Jogenfors, J.: Quantum bitcoin: an anonymous, distributed, and secure currency secured by the no-cloning theorem of quantum mechanics. In: IEEE International Conference on Blockchain and Cryptocurrency (ICBC), pp. 245–252 (2019)
39. Lutomirski, A., Aaronson, S., Farhi, E., et al.: Breaking and making quantum money: toward a new quantum cryptographic protocol. Innov. Comput. Sci. (ICS), 20–31 (2010)
40. Floyd, R.: Algorithms 97: shortest path. Commun. ACM **5**, 345 (1962)
41. Zeng, G.H.: Reply to "Comment on 'Arbitrated quantum-signature scheme"'. Physi. Rev. A **8**, 016301 (2008)
42. García-Escartín, J., Chamorro-Posada, P.: Swap test and Hong-Ou-Mandel effect are equivalent. Phys. Rev. A **87**, 052330 (2013)
43. Fanizza, M., Rosati, M., Skotiniotis, M., et al.: Beyond the swap test: optimal estimation of quantum state overla. Phys. Rev. A **124**, 060503 (2020)
44. Liu, W., Yin, H.: A quantum scheme of state overlap based on quantum mean estimation and support vector machine. Physica A: Stat. Mech. Appl. **606**, 128117 (2022)
45. Cincio, L., Subaşl, Y., Sornborger, A.T., et al.: Learning the quantum algorithm for state overlap. New J. Phys. **20**, 113022 (2018)
46. Treinish, M., Gambetta, J., Nationand, P., et al.: Qiskit/qiskit: Qiskit 0.34.0 (0.34.0). Zenodo (2021)
47. Bergou, J. A., Hillery, M., Saffman, M.: Decoherence and quantum error correction. In: Introduction to the Theory of Quantum Information Processing, Graduate Texts in Physics, pp. 133–148. Springer (2021)
48. Qu, R., Wang, J., Li, Z., Bao, Y.: Encoding hypergraphs into quantum states. Phys. Rev. A **87**, 039905 (2013)
49. Rossi, M., Huber, M., Bruß, D., Macchiavello, C.: Quantum hypergraph states. New J. Phys. **15**, 113022 (2013)
50. Li, Q., Wu, J., Quan, J., et al.: Efficient quantum blockchain with a consensus mechanism QDPoS. IEEE Trans. Inform. Forensics Secur. **17**, 3264–3276 (2022)
51. Banerjee, S., Mukherjee, A., Panigrahi, P.K.: Quantum blockchain using weighted hypergraph states. Phys. Rev. Res. **2**(1), 013322 (2020)
52. Sato, S., Shikata, J.: Quantum-secure aggregate one-time signatures with detecting functionality. Advanced Information Networking and Applications (AINA 2022), vol. 450 (2022)

53. You, M., Lu, D., Fan, T., Qian, S.: A quantum aggregate signature scheme based on quantum teleportation using four-qubit cluster state. Int. J. Theor. Phys. **61**, 155 (2022)
54. Shang T., Tang, Y., Liu, J.W.: Full quantum one-way function based on quantum hypergraph state. In: International Conference on Wireless Communications and Signal Processing (WCSP). IEEE (2023)
55. Shang, T., Chen, R.Y.L., Liu, J.W.: On the obfuscatability of quantum point functions. Quant. Inform. Process. **18**, 55 (2019)
56. Barnum, H., Crepeau, C., Gottesman, D., et al.: Authentication of quantum messages. In: The 43rd Annual IEEE Symposium on Foundations of Computer Science, pp. 449–458 (2002)
57. Pointcheval, D.: The composite discrete logarithm and secure authentication. In: International Workshop on Public Key Cryptography, pp. 113–128. Springer (2000)
58. Contini, S., Lenstra, A.K., Steinfeld, R.: Vsh, an efficient and provable collision-resistant hash function. In: Annual International Conference on the Theory and Applications of Cryptographic Techniques, pp. 165–182 (2006)
59. Damgård, I.B.: A design principle for hash functions. In: Conference on the Theory and Application of Cryptology, pp. 416–427 (1989)
60. Sobti, R., Geetha, G.: Cryptographic hash functions: a review. Int. J. Comput. Sci. **9**, 461 (2012)
61. Bao, Z., Wang, L., Guo, J. and Gu, D.: Functional graph revisited: updates on (second) preimage attacks on hash combiners. In: Annual International Cryptology Conference, pp. 404–427 (2017)
62. Vasiliev, A.: Quantum hashing for finite abelian groups. Lobachevskii J. Math. **37**, 753–757 (2016)
63. Ziatdinov, M.: From graphs to keyed quantum hash functions. Lobachevskii J. Math. **37**, 705–712 (2016)
64. Ablayev, F., Vasiliev, A.: Cryptographic quantum hashing. Laser Phys. Lett. **11**, 025202 (2013)
65. Ablayev, F.M., Ziatdinov, M.: Universal Hash Functions from Quantum Procedures. Kazan University, Physics and Mathematics Series/Uchenye Zapiski Kazanskogo Universiteta (2020)
66. Shi, J.J., Lu, Y.H., Feng, Y.Y., et al.: A quantum hash function with grouped coarse-grained boson sampling. Quant. Inform. Process. **21**, 1–17 (2022)
67. Li, D., Ding, P., Zhou, Y., Yang, Y.: Controlled alternate quantum walk based block hash function. Quant. Inform. Process. **22**(10), 363 (2023)
68. Yang, Y. G., Dong, J. R., Yang, Y. L., et al.: Usefulness of decoherence in quantum-walk-based hash function. Int. J. Theor. Phys. 1–13 (2021)
69. Zhou, Q., Lu, S.: Hash function based on controlled alternate quantum walks with memory. Quant. Eng. **3**, 1–10 (2021)
70. Yang, Y.G., Bi, J.L., Li, D., et al.: Hash function based on quantum walks. Int. J. Theor. Phys. **58**, 1861–1873 (2019)
71. Yang, Y.G., Bi, J.L., Chen, X.B., et al.: Simple hash function using discrete-time quantum walks. Quant. Inform. Process. **17**, 1–19 (2018)
72. Yang, Y., Zhang, Y.C., Xu, G., et al.: Improving the efficiency of quantum hash function by dense coding of coin operators in discrete-time quantum walk. Sci. China-Phys. Mech. Astron. **61**, 1–8 (2018)
73. Li, D., Yang, Y.G., Bi, J.L., et al.: Controlled alternate quantum walks based quantum hash function. Sci. Rep. **8**, 1–7 (2018)
74. Cao, W.F., Zhang, Y.C., Yang, Y.G., et al.: Constructing quantum hash functions based on quantum walks on Johnson graphs. Quant. Inform. Process. **17**, 1–11 (2018)
75. Yang, Y.G., Xu, P., Yang, R., et al.: Quantum hash function and its application to privacy amplification in quantum key distribution, pseudo-random number generation and image encryption. Sci. Rep. **6**, 1–14 (2016)
76. Shi, W.M., Wang, S., Pan, T., et al.: Continuous-time quantum hash function based on one-dimensional cycle lattice. Modern Phys. Lett. B **36**, 2150241 (2022)
77. Li, D., Zhang, J., Guo, F.Z., et al.: Discrete-time interacting quantum walks and quantum hash schemes. Quant. Inform. Process. **12**, 1501–1513 (2013)

78. Hou, P.L., Shang, T., Zhang, Y.J., et al.: Quantum hash function based on controlled alternate lively quantum walks. Sci. Rep. **13**(1), 5887 (2023)
79. Inui, N., Konno, N., Segawa, E.: One-dimensional three-state quantum walk. Phys. Rev. E **72**, 056112 (2005)
80. Sadowski, P., Miszczak, J.A., Ostaszewski, M.: Lively quantum walks on cycles. J. Phys. A-Math. Theor. **49**, 375302 (2016)
81. Tregenna, B., Flanagan, W., Maile, R., Kendon, V.: Controlling discrete quantum walks: coins and initial states. New J. Phys. **5**, 83 (2003)
82. Konno, N., Shimizu, Y., Takei, M.: Periodicity for the Hadamard walk on cycles. Interdiscip. Sci. Rev. **23**, 1–8 (2017)
83. Dukes, P.R.: Quantum state revivals in quantum walks on cycles. Results Phys. **4**, 189–197 (2014)
84. Kajiwara, T., Konno, N., Koyama, S., Saito, K.: Periodicity for the 3-state quantum walk on cycles (2019). arXiv preprint arXiv:1907.01725
85. Sarkar, R.S., Mandal, A., Adhikari, B.: Periodicity of lively quantum walks on cycles with generalized Grover coin. Linear Algebra Appl. **604**, 399–424 (2020)
86. Girault, M., Cohen, R., Campana, M.: A generalized birthday attack. In: Workshop on the Theory and Application of of Cryptographic Techniques, vol. 129–156 (1988)
87. Van Erven, T., Harremos, P.: Rényi divergence and Kullback-Leibler divergence. IEEE Trans. Inform. Theory **60**, 3797–3820 (2014)
88. Preneel, B.: Analysis and design of cryptographic hash functions. Ph.D. Thesis, Katholieke Universiteit te Leuven (1993)
89. Fuglede, B., Topsoe, F.: Jensen-Shannon divergence and Hilbert space embedding. In: International Symposium on Information Theory (ISIT 2004), vol. 31 (2004)
90. Shannon, C.E.: Communication theory of secrecy systems. Bell Syst. Tech. J. **28**, 656–715 (1949)
91. Douglas, B., Wang, J.: Efficient quantum circuit implementation of quantum walks. Phys. Rev. A **79**, 052335 (2009)
92. Douglas, B., Wang, J.: Complexity analysis of quantum walk based search algorithms. J. Comput. Theor. Nanosci. **10**, 1601–1605 (2013)

Chapter 9
Quantum Access Control

Access control specifies whether resources are accessible based on permissions and enables resource management, is a fundamental requirement for information system security. In this chapter, we define the quantum access control problem using quantum point function and an abstract model of the graph-based access control problem. By defining the auxiliary problem of the quantum access control problem, the exponential scale problem of valid inputs encountered during the process of proving the obfuscatability of the quantum access control problem is resolved, and the obfuscatability of the quantum access control problem is demonstrated.

9.1 Access Control Problem

Quantum access control solves corresponding problems in quantum computers. At present, quantum key distribution and quantum secure direct communication solve the secure issues in quantum communication, while quantum access control restricts user access to qubits or quantum circuits based on user identities or user groups, enabling resource management for quantum computer systems. With the rapid development of quantum information, research on quantum computers has yielded some results [1]. Progressive implementation of quantum access control can be employed on quantum computer and quantum network in order to facilitate effective resource management. The findings will serve as a significant theoretical foundation for the advancement of quantum cryptography.

In order to illuminate the quantum access control problem utilizing quantum point functions, we need to investigate the positive results of classical obfuscation and quantum obfuscation, design the obfuscation scheme of quantum point functions. By defining the auxiliary problem of quantum access control problem, we solve the

T. Shang, *Quantum Nonlinear Function Obfuscation Theory and Application*,
https://doi.org/10.1007/978-981-97-6722-9_9

exponential scale problem of valid inputs during the process of proving the obfuscatability of quantum access control problem and prove the obfuscatability of quantum access control problem [2].

9.2 Quantum Obfuscation

Alagic et al. [3] were the first to clarify the definition of quantum obfuscation and prove some basic work. In the theory of quantum obfuscation, a quantum obfuscator was defined to satisfy the following properties:

Definition 9.1 A repeatable quantum circuit obfuscator is a quantum algorithm O and a QPT δ satisfying the following properties:

1. (Functional equivalence) Given an input quantum circuit C of n qubits, the output is a quantum state $O(C)$ of m qubits that satisfies

$$\|\delta(O(C) \otimes \rho) - U_C \rho U_C^{\dagger}\|_{tr} \leq negl(n). \tag{9.1}$$

   for all $\rho \in D(\mathcal{H}_n)$, $D(\mathcal{H}_n)$ denotes the space of density operators in Hilbert space $\mathcal{H}_n$.
2. (Polynomial expansion)

$$m = poly(n).$$

3. (Virtual black-box) For any QPT A, there exists a QPT S^{U_C} satisfying

$$|\Pr[A(O(C)) = 1] - \Pr[S^{U_C}(|0^n\rangle) = 1]| \leq negl(n)$$

   for all circuits C.
4. (Repeatable) The functionality remains after utilizing δ.

As demonstrated by the inequality (9.1), the major difference between quantum obfuscation and classical obfuscation is that the output of a quantum obfuscator is no longer a description of a quantum circuit, but rather a quantum state, which enables users to perform specific functionality. The interpreter δ is required because the output of the obfuscator is a quantum state. It is noteworthy that while the interpreter algorithm δ is required to operate in polynomial time, the obfuscation algorithm O does not necessarily need to operate in polynomial time. The implementation of the obfuscator requires achieving polynomial time complexity. However, the non-polynomial time obfuscation yields a more robust result in theory. The interpreter, as defined in the inequality (9.1), can be expressed in various ways. For instance, a common quantum interpreter can be set for a quantum circuit family. Alternatively, the obfuscation algorithm consists of a quantum state and a quantum circuit so that the end user can perform the quantum circuit and provide the required input.

It is straightforward to demonstrate that the definitions of these two interpreters are equivalent, showing that if one quantum obfuscator exists, the other exists as well.

We follow the definition of quantum obfuscation as represented in Definition 9.1. An intuitive explanation can be given: the obfuscation algorithm O computes the potential output value of the circuit C under all possible inputs and stores results in $O(C)$. The interpreter δ only serves as a selector, selecting the output corresponding to the input of the obfuscated circuit. Although the obfuscation algorithm O may not have a polynomial time complexity, it is still necessary for the interpreter δ to operate in polynomial time. We emphasize that the interpreter is a natural and necessary addition to the extension of classical obfuscator to quantum obfuscator. There must exist an efficient algorithm to compute the function of U_C utilizing $O(C)$ for the definition to be valid. We define this efficient algorithm as an interpreter, which is denoted by δ.

Repeatability is a new property of quantum obfuscation compared to classical obfuscation. Clearly, repeatable quantum obfuscators are superior to non-repeatable quantum obfuscators, as repeatability enables quantum adversaries to mount a more formidable attack [3]. All discussions in this book will be based on quantum obfuscators that can be repeated.

9.3 Access Control Based on Graphs

In the graph-based access control problem [4, 5], the system graph determines the security policy, and the security policy framework generates the system graph. The security policy framework is represented by the quaternion SP = (TG, RS, Pos, Neg). Among them, TG is a type graph, RS is a rule set, Pos and Neg are positive and negative constraints, respectively. All system graphs are transformed from type graphs based on the set of rules, and must contain graphs with positive constraints as subgraphs, but not graphs with negative constraints.

A typical access control system graph is shown in Fig. 9.1 where U denotes a user, R denotes a role, T denotes a task, and t denotes a behaviour. The edge between the user and the role represents the affiliation relationship between them. The edge between roles represents the affiliation relationship between them. The edge between the role and the task represents the assignment relationship between them. The edge between the user and the behaviour represents the execution relationship between them. The system graph is used to determine user permissions. When a user submits a behaviour application to the system, the system determines the user's role and determines if there is a distribution relationship between the applied task and the user's role. In the process of execution, the specific user executes the corresponding behaviour of the task.

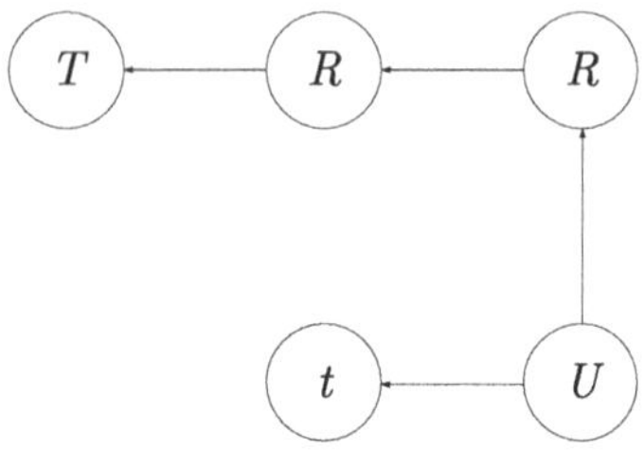

Fig. 9.1 Typical system graph

9.4 Definition of Quantum Access Control Problem

As described previously, a graph-based access control system executes multiple operations based on the system graph. The information contained in the system graph can be extracted again. The nodes in the graph can be user, role, task, and behaviour, referred to as the secrets of nodes. The edges in the graph can be the affiliation relationship between user and role, the hierarchical relationship between roles, the assignment relationship between role and task, and the execution relationship between user and behaviour, referred to as the passwords of edges. Secrets of nodes and passwords of edges are stored in quantum states. During the execution, the user submits an action request, which is reflected in the graph as a movement from the present node to the target node: the system approves the application and returns the target node's secret if and only if the user can provide the password of adjacent edge between two nodes.

Quantum access control problems include graph topology, passwords of edges, and secrets of nodes. Secure obfuscation of quantum access control problems necessitates concealing all relevant information, including graph topology, all edge passwords, and node secrets. We define the access control problem in a formal manner.

Definition 9.2 A graph-based quantum access control problem X_G is defined as follows:

1. Consider a directed graph with k nodes, denoted by G. Each node $u \in [k]$ has a maximum of d adjacent ordered edges denoted by $\mu_u^{(1)}, \ldots, \mu_u^{(d)}$(note that multiple adjacent edges may point to the same node), and define $E = \{(u, v, i) : v = u_u^{(i)}\}$ as the set of all adjacent edges, where $u_u^{(i)}$ denotes the ith adjacent node of u.
2. Each adjacent edge has a password, and the password set is denoted by $\{|\pi_e\rangle | e \in E\}$.
3. Each node has a secret, and the set of secrets is denoted by $\{|\sigma_v\rangle | v \in k\}$.
4. For the input $|i_1, x_1\rangle \cdots |i_n, x_n\rangle |y_1, y_2\rangle$, examine whether there are $v_0,\ldots,v_n \in [k]$ and $e_0, \ldots, e_{n-1} \in E$, so that $v_0 = 1$, $e_j = (v_j, v_{j+1}, i_j)$, and $x_j = \pi_{e_j}$ are satisfied.

   Therefore, we define the quantum access control problem,

$$X_G : |i_1, x_1\rangle \cdots |i_n, x_n\rangle |y_1, y_2\rangle \mapsto$$

$$\begin{cases} |i_1, x_1\rangle \cdots |i_n, x_n\rangle |y_1 \oplus v_n, y_2 \oplus \sigma_{v_n}\rangle, \text{if } v_0 = 1, e_j = (v_j, v_{j+1}, i_j), x_j = \pi_{e_j} \\ |i_1, x_1\rangle \cdots |i_n, x_n\rangle |y_1, y_2\rangle \quad , \text{otherwise} \end{cases}$$

Define $\mathscr{X} = \bigcup_G X_G$.

Note that the form of the quantum access problem is similar to the classical point function, we are inspired to study the obfuscability of the quantum access problem starting from the obfuscability of the point function.

9.5 Obfuscability of Quantum Point Function and Quantum Multi-qubit Point Function

Definition 9.3 A quantum point function is defined by

$$U_{\alpha,\beta} : |x, y\rangle \mapsto \begin{cases} |x, y \oplus \beta\rangle \ , \text{if } x = \alpha \\ |x, y\rangle \quad , \text{otherwise} \end{cases},$$

where $\alpha, \beta \in \{0, 1\}^n$.

Assume the function $U_{\alpha,\beta}$ is implemented by a particular circuit denoted as $C_{\alpha,\beta}$. Define $\mathscr{C}_n = \{C_{\alpha,\beta} : \alpha, \beta \in \{0, 1\}^n\}$ and $\mathscr{C} = \bigcup_n \mathscr{C}_n$.

The quantum point function is obfuscatable under quantum-accessible random oracle model. By using the quantum-accessible random oracle model $R_q : |x, y\rangle \mapsto |x, y \oplus R(x)\rangle$ defined in Ref. [6] where $R : \{0, 1\}^{2n} \mapsto \{0, 1\}^{2n}$, we construct an obfuscation $O^R(U_{\alpha,\beta})$ for the point function $U_{\alpha,\beta}$ as follows. Select $r \in \{0, 1\}^n$ at random, and use $|r, \alpha\rangle|0^n, \beta\rangle$ to access the random oracle R_q and obtain the result $|r, \alpha\rangle|0^n \oplus R_1(r, \alpha), \beta \oplus R_2(r, \alpha)\rangle$, where R_1, R_2 are the first n and the last n bits, i.e., $|R(\cdot)\rangle = |R_1(\cdot), R_2(\cdot)\rangle$. Subsequently, discard the register $|\alpha\rangle$ and store $tr_\alpha(|r, \alpha, 0^n \oplus R_1(\alpha), \beta \oplus R_2(\alpha)\rangle) = |r, R_1(\alpha), \beta \oplus R_2(\alpha)\rangle$. Then, for the input $|x, y\rangle$, $O^R(U_{\alpha,\beta})$ queries the random oracle R_q with $|r, x\rangle|0^{2n}\rangle$ and obtains the result $|r, x\rangle|R(r, x)\rangle = |r, x\rangle|R_1(r, x), R_2(r, x)\rangle$ and stores it. Finally, $O^R(U_{\alpha,\beta})$ compares whether $R_1(r, x) = R_1(r, \alpha)$, if so, output $|x, y \oplus (\beta \oplus R_2(r, \alpha)) \oplus R_2(r, x)\rangle$, otherwise it outputs $|x, y\rangle$.

Definition 9.4 The quantum multi-qubit point function with a general output is defined by

$$U_{(\alpha_1,\beta_1),\ldots,(\alpha_t,\beta_t)} : |x, y\rangle \mapsto \begin{cases} |x, y \oplus \beta_i\rangle \ , \text{if } x = \alpha_i \\ |x, y\rangle \quad , \text{otherwise} \end{cases},$$

where $\alpha_i, \beta_i \in \{0, 1\}^n$.

Assume the function $U_{(\alpha_1,\beta_1),\ldots,(\alpha_t,\beta_t)}$ is implemented by a particular circuit denoted by $C_{(\alpha_1,\beta_1),\ldots,(\alpha_t,\beta_t)}$. Define $\mathscr{C}_n^t = \{C_{(\alpha_1,\beta_1),\ldots,(\alpha_t,\beta_t)} : \alpha_i, \beta_i \in \{0, 1\}^n\}$, and $\mathscr{C}^t = \bigcup_n \mathscr{C}_n^t$. Define $\mathscr{C}^* = \bigcup_{poly\ t} \mathscr{C}^t$.

The obfuscability of $\mathscr{C}^*$ can be proved by treating each element in $\mathscr{C}^*$ as a combination of elements in $\mathscr{C}$. Then we prove $\mathscr{C}^*$ is obfuscatable.

Lemma 9.1 *A quantum circuit family $\mathscr{C}^*$ is obfuscatable.*

Proof Considering the combination circuit $\{C_1\#\cdots\#C_t : C_i \in \mathscr{C}\}$, the circuit has two input registers: a log_2^k-bit control register and a n-bit input register. The second register is applied to the corresponding quantum circuit under the control of the first register, i.e.,

$$C_1\#C_2\#\cdots\#C_t(|i, x\rangle) = C_i(|x\rangle).$$

Since C_i is obfuscatable, there exist $O(C_1), O(C_2), \ldots, O(C_t)$. The probability that any two obfuscators in the circuit $O(C_1)\#O(C_2)\#\cdots\#O(C_t)$ employ the same r is negligible because t is a polynomial level of n. Since the obfuscator is a random algorithm, a simulator with oracle access to $C_1\#C_2\#\cdots\#C_t$ can simulate an arbitrary adversary who can arbitrarily obtain $O(C_1)\#O(C_2)\#\cdots\ \#O(C_t)$. Hence, $O(C_1)\#O(C_2)\#\cdots\#O(C_t)$ is an effective obfuscation for $C_1\#C_2\#\cdots\#C_t$.

Given that the circuit $M^{C_1\#C_2\#\cdots\#C_t}$ that has oracle access to $C_1\#C_2\#\cdots\# C_t$. M works as follows: For any input ρ, M inputs $|\rho, 0\rangle$ into C_1 to obtain $|\rho, C_1(\rho)\rangle$, and then obtain $|\rho, C_2(\rho)\rangle$,...,$|\rho, C_t(\rho)\rangle$ in turn, and finally return $|\bigoplus_{i=1,\ldots,t} C_i(\rho)\rangle$. It is obvious that $M = C_{(\alpha_1,\beta_1),\ldots,(\alpha_t,\beta_t)}$. Then we replace $C_1\#C_2\#\cdots\#C_t$ with its obfuscation $O(C_1)\#O(C_2)\#\cdots\#O(C_t)$ and place inside M. The obtained $M'_{O(C_1)\#O(C_2)\#\cdots\#O(C_t)}$ is also an effective obfuscation of $C_{(\alpha_1,\beta_1),\ldots,(\alpha_t,\beta_t)}$, i.e., $\mathscr{C}^* = \bigcup_{poly\ t} \mathscr{C}^t$ is obfuscatable.

9.6 Obfuscability of Auxiliary Problem for Quantum Access Control Problem

By the construction of circuit family $\mathscr{C}^*$ and Lemma 9.1, we can demonstrate that the quantum access control problem is obfuscatable. However, the following issues exist: there are k nodes in the directed graph, so $n \leq k$. In the worst case, the problem X_G may have d^k valid inputs (where the output is not 0), but $\mathscr{C}^*$ requires t that satisfies $t = poly(k)$. Thus, it cannot be explicitly proven that the problem can be obfuscated.

In order to solve the exponential scale problem of valid inputs, we introduce an auxiliary problem of the access control problem.

Definition 9.5 We randomly allocate a key $\kappa_u \in \{0, 1\}^l$ to each node $1 < u \leq k$. Define $\kappa_1 = |0\rangle^{\otimes l}$. The input key of edge (u, v, i) is denoted by z. We define the auxiliary problem as

$$W_G^{\overline{\kappa}} : |u, z, i, x\rangle|y_1, y_2, y_3\rangle$$
$$\mapsto \begin{cases} |u, z, i, x\rangle|y_1 \oplus v, y_2 \oplus \kappa_v, y_3 \oplus \sigma_v\rangle & \text{, if } z = \kappa_u,\ \pi_{u,v,i} = x \\ |u, z, i, x\rangle|y_1, y_2, y_3\rangle & \text{, otherwise} \end{cases}.$$

An access control problem satisfying this definition has at most kd valid inputs (inputs whose output is not 0). We define the problem $W_G(u, z, i, x)$. We randomly select $\kappa_u \leftarrow \{0, 1\}^k$ for $v \in [k]$ and return $W_G^{\overline{\kappa}}(u, z, i, x)$ for input (u, z, i, x). Define $\mathscr{W} = \bigcup_G W_G$.

According to Lemma 9.1, the auxiliary problem $\mathscr{W}$ can be obfuscated. Obviously, the security of this obfuscator will not be compromised by the insertion of the key κ, as the adversary will not obtain any information about κ_v unless it has previously experienced the node v. The only requirement for experiencing the node v is that the password π_e on the adjacent edge is simple to obtain.

9.7 Obfuscability of Quantum Access Control Problem

Now we prove the obfuscability of quantum access control problem by proving the obfuscability of auxiliary problem for quantum access control problem.

Theorem 9.1 *Quantum circuit $\mathscr{X}$ is obfuscatable.*

Proof Firstly, we prove the relationship between the quantum access control problem and its auxiliary problem. Consider any $X_G \in \mathscr{X}$, $W_G \in \mathscr{W}$, there exists a circuit M such that $\|\delta(M^{W_G}(|0\rangle^{\otimes|W_G|}) \otimes \rho) - U_{X_G}\rho U_{X_G}^{\dagger}\|_{tr} \leq negl$, and there also exists a circuit N such that $\|\delta(N^{X_G}(|0\rangle^{\otimes|X_G|}) \otimes \rho) - U_{W_G}\rho U_{W_G}^{\dagger}\|_{tr} \leq negl$. M works as follows: for input $|i_1, x_1\rangle \cdots |i_n, x_n\rangle$, M access W_G with $|1, 0^k, i_1, x_1\rangle$. If W_G returns $|v_2, \kappa_{v_2}, \sigma_{v_2}\rangle$, then M access W_G with $|v_2, \kappa_{v_2}, i_2, x_2\rangle$, and so on, until $\perp$ is returned or all inputs are processed to obtain $|v_n, \kappa_{v_n}, \sigma_{v_n}\rangle$. In all instances, the output will consist of the returned result. N works as follows. Internally, N maintains two tables: one for storing the key κ_i, and the other for storing experienced adjacent edges and the relationship of adjacent edges. Set $\kappa_1 = |1^k\rangle$ during initialization, and set all other keys to $\perp$. For input $|u, z, i, x\rangle$, N verifies whether $z = \kappa_u \neq \perp$ exists. If so, N has recorded the route from node 1 to node u and sends it to X_G. If X_G returns v, σ_v, N examines whether κ_v has been assigned, otherwise it assigns a random key to node v. Note that for N to simulate W_G successfully, N must have visited edge e of node u with valid password $|\pi_e\rangle$ and key $|\kappa_u\rangle$. The probability of this event is negligible, so $\|\delta(N^{X_G}(|0\rangle^{\otimes|X_G|}) \otimes \rho) - U_{W_G}\rho U_{W_G}^{\dagger}\|_{tr} \leq negl(n)$.

Additionally, we make use of M and N to construct the obfuscation of $X_G \in \mathscr{X}$. Since $\mathscr{W}$ is obfuscatable, we assume $O(W_G)$ is one of the obfuscations of $W \in \mathscr{W}$. We construct circuit $M'_{O(W_G)}(|0\rangle^{\otimes|W_G|})$, M' operates as follows: firstly, it passes $|0\rangle^{\otimes|W_G|}$ to M. Then, whenever M requires ρ oracular access to W_G, M' calculates $\delta(O(W_G) \otimes \rho)$ and returns to M, and finally M' outputs the output value of M.

$M'_{O(W_G)}(|0\rangle^{\otimes|W_G|})$ obviously satisfies polynomial slowdown and function equivalence, so we demonstrate that it also satisfies the property of virtual black-box. Considering the adversary $A(M'_{O(W_G)})$, we firstly construct $A'(O(W_G))$. A' operates as follows: A' can obtain $M'_{O(W_G)}$ from $O(W_G)$, then pass it to A, and ultimately emit the output. Consequently, there exists

$$\Pr[A'(O(W_G)) = 1] = \Pr[A(M'_{O(W_G)}) = 1]. \tag{9.2}$$

And the obfuscation $O(W_G)$ satisfies the property of the virtual black-box:

$$|\Pr[A'(O(W_G)) = 1] - \Pr[S'^{U_{W_G}}(|0\rangle^{\otimes|W_G|}) = 1]| \leq negl(n). \tag{9.3}$$

Next, we construct $S^{U_{X_G}}$ by $S'^{U_{W_G}}$. $S^{U_{X_G}}$ operates as follows: $S^{U_{X_G}}$ passes $|0\rangle^{\otimes|W_G|}$ to $S'^{U_{W_G}}$ after receiving the input $|0\rangle^{\otimes|X_G|}$. Whenever $S'^{U_{W_G}}$ requires oracular access to U_{W_G} with ρ, $S^{U_{X_G}}$ performs the calculation $\delta(N^{X_G}(|0\rangle^{\otimes|X_G|}) \otimes \rho)$ and then returns to $S'^{U_{W_G}}$, then outputs the output value of $S'^{U_{W_G}}$. Thus,

$$\Pr[S^{U_{X_G}}(|0\rangle^{\otimes|X_G|}) = 1] = \Pr[S'^{U_{W_G}}(|0\rangle^{\otimes|W_G|}) = 1]. \tag{9.4}$$

By combining (9.2),(9.3) and (9.4), we can obtain

$$|\Pr[A(M'_{O(W_G)}) = 1] - \Pr[S^{U_{X_G}}(|0\rangle^{\otimes|X_G|}) = 1]| \leq negl(n).$$

The formula demonstrates that $M'_{O(W_G)}$ is a secure obfuscation of X_G. Hence, we can conclude that the quantum access control problem X_G is obfuscatable.

9.8 Future Direction

There are very few studies on quantum obfuscation theory for quantum access control at present. The primary research strategy is to follow the research path of classical obfuscation theory and apply the results of classical obfuscation theory to the quantum scenario. The research directions for the future of quantum obfuscation are described as follows:

1. Quantum mechanics implementation of an information-theory secure quantum black-box obfuscator and the utilization of polynomial degrees of obfuscated quantum states. Such a quantum obfuscator will be extremely effective, and it will also be a compelling demonstration that quantum mechanics can play a more significant part in cryptography.
2. Quantum obfuscation of classical circuits. Since the output of the classical circuit is a classical string, the quantum state can be used to execute classical calculations. After retaining the classical output, the original obfuscation result can be restored by reversing each unitary gate, allowing the result to be used multiple times.

3. Non-reusable quantum obfuscation. In practice, it is frequently necessary that the obfuscator's output cannot be replicated. Broadbent et al. [7] have discussed quantum one-time programs, which will play an important role in cryptography.
4. Removal of the quantum-accessible random oracle model. The quantum-accessible random oracle modele has made numerous modifications to superposition queries compared to the classical random oracle. Additionally, the quantum state generated by quantum obfuscation may also be a superposition state. How to use the quantum obfuscation mechanism to remove the quantum-accessible random oracle model will become a research hotspot in the field of provably secure quantum cryptography.

9.9 Summary

In this chapter, we defined the quantum access control problem and proved the obfuscability of quantum access control problem by the auxiliary problem. In comparison to other areas of cryptography, the uniqueness and significance of obfuscation theory are self-evident. In the future, the quantum access control problem can combine the valuable research directions of quantum obfuscation theory, including quantum black box obfuscator's realization, quantum obfuscation for classical circuits, non-reusable quantum obfuscation, and removing quantum random oracles.

References

1. Ghosh, D., Agarwal, P., Pandey, P., et al.: Automated error correction in IBM quantum computer and explicit generalization. Quantum Inf. Process. **17**(6), 153 (2018)
2. Chen, R.Y.L., Shang, T., Liu, J.W.: Obfuscatability of quantum access control problem. J. Cryptologic Res. **6**(3), 362–369 (2019). (in Chinese)
3. Alagic, G., Fefferman, B.: On quantum obfuscation (2016). arXiv:1602.01771
4. Koch, M., Mancini, L.V., Parisi-Presicce, F.: A graph-based formalism for RBAC. ACM Trans. Inf. Syst. Secur. **5**(3), 332–365 (2002)
5. Koch, M., Mancini, L.V., Parisi-Presicce, F.: Graph transformations for the specification of access control policies. Electron. Notes Theor. Comput. Sci. **51**, 222–232 (2002)
6. Dan, B., Özgur, D., Fischlin, M., et al.: Random oracles in a quantum world. Comput. Sci. **7073**(1), 41–69 (2011)
7. Broadbent, A., Gutoski, G., Stebila D.: Quantum one-time programs. In: Advances in Cryptology—CRYPTO 2013 : 33rd Annual Cryptology Conference, Santa Barbara, CA, USA, pp. 344–360 (2013)

Chapter 10
Quantum Zero-Knowledge Proof

Zero-knowledge (ZK) proof provides an elegant way of formally secure identification. In quantum zero-knowledge (QZK) proof, the prover and the verifier are allowed to use only unitary operations and the zero-knowledge property is defined in a seemingly weaker way than in the classical case. Many interesting results has developed for this complexity class such as complete problems, closure properties. The first question is whether it is possible to use it in realistic zero-knowledge protocols. In this chapter, we revisit the definition of quantum point functions and analyze the quantum zero-knowledge protocols. Furthermore, we discuss the application of quantum obfuscation in quantum zero knowledge. As a start of study on quantum zero-knowledge proof based on quantum obfuscation, this work will be very useful in the future development of quantum cryptography.

10.1 Zero-Knowledge Proof

Zero-knowledge proof is a fundamental concept in classical cryptography, which can be used to construct many useful cryptographic protocols, such as identity authentication schemes. In these interactive protocols, a prover P knows a secret s and he wants to convince a verifier V that he knows s without revealing any information about s. Zero knowledge has been extensively studied and applied in theoretical computer science and cryptography. So it is meaningful to extend zero-knowledge proof to quantum circumstance and consider quantum zero-knowledge proof.

An interactive proof has a zero-knowledge property if a malicious verifier cannot learn anything from the interaction with the prover except for the public input which belongs to the given language. In other words, anything that can be effectively calculated from the interaction can also be calculated from the public input.

We introduce the notions of various quantum zero-knowledge proof by following a manner in Ref. [1].

T. Shang, *Quantum Nonlinear Function Obfuscation Theory and Application*,
https://doi.org/10.1007/978-981-97-6722-9_10

Let V be an arbitrary quantum verifier. The space of density operators in Hilbert space $\mathcal{H}$ is denoted by $D(\mathcal{H})$ and the space of transformations from $\mathcal{H}_1$ to $\mathcal{H}_2$ is denoted by $T(\mathcal{H}_1, \mathcal{H}_2)$. We suppose that V possesses some auxiliary quantum states in $D(\mathcal{A})$ at the beginning for some Hilbert space $\mathcal{A}$, and possesses some quantum states in $D(\mathcal{Z})$ after the protocol for some Hilbert space $\mathcal{Z}$. For such V, any quantum prover P and every $x \in \{0, 1\}^*$, let $\langle V, P\rangle(x)$ denote the admissible transformation in $T(\mathcal{A}, \mathcal{Z})$ induced by the interaction between V and P on input x. We call this $\langle V, P\rangle(x)$ the induced admissible transformation (completely-positive trace-preserving mappings) from V, P, and x.

Zero-knowledge is really a family of complexity classes. We define the classes QPZK(m, c, s), QSZK(m, c, s), and QZK(m, c, s) of problems having m-message quantum perfect, statistical, and computational zero-knowledge proof systems, respectively, with completeness accepting probability at least c and soundness accepting probability at most s, as follows.

Definition(QPZK) 10.1 Given a polynomially bounded function $m : Z^+ \to N$ and functions $c, s : Z^+ \to [0, 1]$, a problem $A = \{A_{yes}, A_{no}\}$ is in $QPZK(m, c, s)$ if there exists an m-message quantum verifier V and an m-message honest quantum prover P such that

1. (**Completeness and Soundness**) (V, P) forms an m-message quantum interactive proof system with completeness accepting probability at least c and soundness accepting probability at most s.
2. (**Perfect Zero-Knowledge**) for any m-message quantum verifier V', there exists a polynomial-time uniformly generated family $\{Q_x\}$ of quantum circuits, where each Q_x exactly implements an admissible transformation $S_{V'(x)}$, such that $S_{V'(x)} = \langle V', P\rangle(x)$ for every $x \in A_{yes}$, where $\langle V', P\rangle(x)$ is the induced admissible transformation from V', P, and x.

Definition(QSZK) 10.2 Given a polynomially bounded function $m : Z^+ \to N$ and functions $c, s : Z^+ \to [0, 1]$, a problem $A = \{A_{yes}, A_{no}\}$ is in $QSZK(m, c, s)$ if there exists an m-message quantum verifier V and an m-message honest quantum prover P such that

1. (**Completeness and Soundness**) (V, P) forms an m-message quantum interactive proof system with completeness accepting probability at least c and soundness accepting probability at most s.
2. (**Statistical Zero-Knowledge**) for any m-message quantum verifier V', there exists a polynomial-time uniformly generated family $\{Q_x\}$ of quantum circuits, where each Q_x exactly implements an admissible transformation $S_{V'(x)}$, such that $\left\| S_{V'(x)} - \langle V', P\rangle(x) \right\|_{\diamond}$ is negligible with respect to $|x|$ for all but finitely many $x \in A_{yes}$, where $\langle V', P\rangle(x)$ is the induced admissible transformation from V', P, and x.

Definition(QZK) 10.3 Given a polynomially bounded function $m : Z^+ \to N$ and functions $c, s : Z^+ \to [0, 1]$, a problem $A = \{A_{yes}, A_{no}\}$ is in $QZK(m, c, s)$ if there exists an m-message quantum verifier V and an m-message honest quantum prover P such that

1. (**Completeness and Soundness**) (V, P) forms an m-message quantum interactive proof system with completeness accepting probability at least c and soundness accepting probability at most s.
2. (**Computational Zero-Knowledge**) for any m-message quantum verifier V', there exists a polynomial-time uniformly generated family $\{Q_x\}$ of quantum circuits, where each Q_x exactly implements an admissible transformation $S_{V'(x)}$, such that the ensembles $\{S_{V'(x)} : x \in A_{yes}\}$ and $\{\langle V', P\rangle(x) : x \in A_{yes}\}$ are polynomially quantum indistinguishable, where $\langle V', P\rangle(x)$ is the induced admissible transformation from V', P, and x.

If the verifier is honest, we can obtain the definitions of the corresponding honest-verifier quantum zero-knowledge proof HVQPZK(m, c, s), HVQSZK(m, c, s), and HVQZK(m, c, s).

Many researchers have studied the relationship between the classes of problems having a quantum perfect/statistical/computational zero-knowledge proof system and an honest-verifier quantum perfect/statistical/computational zero-knowledge proof system. Watrous [2] proved that honest verifier equals cheating verifier, i.e., HVQSZK = QSZK. Kobayashi [3] showed that HVQPZK = QPZK and HVQZK = QZK. So from the perspective of computational complexity, restricting the honest verifier does not change the problem set of quantum zero-knowledge proof.

Since ZK was introduced, questions regarding the round complexity of ZK protocols were studied extensively. In light of the difficulties in achieving 3-round ZK, it is natural to examine relaxations of ZK that might enable the construction of such protocols. Witness Hiding (WH) [4] is one of the previously studied relaxations. Roughly speaking, a protocol is WH if no verifier can extract a witness from its interaction with the honest prover. By directly providing the verification circuit to the verifier, Bitansky and Paneth [5] constructed a 3-round interactive protocol for NP language through delegation computation, and combined the indistinguishability of point obfuscation to satisfy the property requirements of WH. Shang et al. [6] extended the protocol of Nir and Omer to the quantum case and designed a 3-round quantum zero-knowledge proof protocol based on quantum delegation computation and quantum point obfuscation.

10.2 Quantum Cryptographic Protocols Based on Zero-Knowledge Proof

In this section, we will introduce some quantum cryptographic protocols based on zero-knowledge proof. The logic of classical zero-knowledge proof due to Schnorr is applied in quantum circuits and algorithms [7]. This is achieved by moving away from the hardness of the Discrete Logarithm Problem towards the hardness of estimating quantum states.

10.2.1 Zero-Knowledge Proof Protocol Based on Quantum Teleportation

In 2018, Chen et al. [8] proposed a zero-knowledge proof protocol based on quantum teleportation. The protocol operates on a scenario which can be described as follows. Alice expects to prove to Bob that she legitimately holds a certain file. The content of the file can be considered as a secret number S and S can not be disclosed. It is expected that Bob will learn nothing about the file from Alice's proof if he does not have the identical file.

The initialization phase of the protocol consists of three steps to ensure the quantum communication between both parties.

1. ***Quantum channel preparation***. The prover Alice prepares N' EPR entangled pairs and send one particle in each EPR pair to Bob.
2. ***Quantum channel security detection***. Alice selects $N' - N$ particles from her own particle sequence and measures them using basis states B_Z and B_X randomly. After Bob is informed of Alice's basis states and results, he measures his own particles and compares with Alice's results openly. If the results appear to be the same, the channel can be considered secure and the rest N EPR pairs will be used in the quantum zero-knowledge proof protocol.
3. ***Quantum key distribution***. Quantum keys can be distributed through any tested quantum key distribution protocol, such as BB84 or BBM92.

In Alice's phase of proof, she uses $S = S_1 S_2 ... S_N$ to prepare qubit sequence M. If $S_i = 0, i = 1, 2, ..., N$, add $|0\rangle$ to M. Otherwise, add $|+\rangle$ to M. Alice measures M and her own particle sequence using Bell basis, the results can be represented by 00, 01, 10 and 11. The classical bits are then encrypted and sent to Bob.

In Bob's phase of verification, he operates quantum gates on his particle sequence according to the classical information decrypted from the message. If he has the identical secret number S, he can measure his particles based on the same rules as Alice has followed. The results should be either $|0\rangle$ or $|+\rangle$. Bob refuses Alice's proof if he obtains any other result.

The aforementioned protocol is proved to be zero-knowledge. The message sent from Alice only contains non-orthogonal information. If Bob has no secret number S, it is impossible for him to choose the correct measurement basis. Alice's proof message is independent of the secret number S, which ensures that Bob obtains no information related to S from the proof.

10.2.2 Non-interactive Zero-Knowledge Proof Protocol on Quantum State

In 2021, Colisson et al. [9] proposed the first non-interactive zero-knowledge (NIZK) proof on quantum state (NIZKoQS) and provided a protocol to prove some advanced properties on a received quantum state non-destructively and non-interactively. Due to the quantum no-cloning principle, it is nearly impossible for the receiver to efficiently check non-trivial properties on a quantum state without destroying it when receiving it. A sender is allowed to send maliciously crafted states without being detected. The goal of NIZKoQS protocol is for the receiver to obtain a quantum state and verify it without destroying it non-interactively.

The formal definition of NIZKoOS is provided. A protocol between an honest prover and an honest verifier is said to be a zero-knowledge proof on quantum state (ZKoOS) if the properties including completeness, soundness and quantum zero knowlegde are satisfied. If in a ZKoOS protocol, only one single message is sent from the prover to the verifier, it is said to be an NIZKoOS protocol.

In the NIZKoOS protocol, a method to classically prepare large states on n qubits using a single superposition is provided and lifted to a multiparty setting in which each sender can control one part of the hidden GHZ state. The protocol operates between one server and n applicants. At the end of the protocol, the applicants end-up sharing a GHZ state in such a way that, if the server is honest, only the applicants knowing a classical secret such as password, secret key or signature can be part of the GHZ state. These applicants are said to be supported, while the other applicants will not be entangled in any way with the supported applicants, and therefore cannot disturb a potential future protocol.

The protocol has two crucial properties. Firstly, it is blind, which means that no adversary can learn whether the honest applicants are supported or not. Secondly, it is impossible for any malicious or noisy applicant to significantly change the GHZ state obtained by supported applicants. It is proved that the protocol exhibits NIZKoQS.

10.2.3 Quantum Oblivious Transfer Protocol

In 2023, Colisson et al. [10] proposed a generic construction to turn any classical zero-knowledge (ZK) protocol into a quantum oblivious transfer (OT) protocol, which is also zero knowledge and used to prove properties on a received quantum state without revealing additional information on it. The functionality of OT can be described as follows: a sender Bob owns two bits m_0 and m_1, and Alice wants to learn m_b where the bit b is provided as an input. A malicious Bob should be unable to learn the value b, and a malicious Alice should be unable to obtain information on both m_0 and m_1.

We can notice that if we are given a state in the computational basis $|l\rangle$ for some bit l, rotating it by applying a Z^m gate for some bit m will leave the state unchanged. On the other hand, if we are given a state in the Hadamard basis $H|r\rangle$ for some bit r, applying a Z^m gate will flip the encoded bit if $m = 1$. Therefore, there is a naive protocol for OT without ZK on quantum state. Alice could prepare two states $|\psi^{(b)}\rangle := H|r^{(b)}\rangle$ and $|\psi^{(1-b)}\rangle := |l\rangle$ for some random bits $r^{(b)}$ and l, send $|\psi^{(0)}\rangle$ and $|\psi^{(1)}\rangle$ to Bob, Bob could rotate the i-th qubit according to Z^{m_i}, and measure them in the Hadamard basis, obtaining outcomes $z^{(i)}$ that will be sent back to

Alice. Unfortunately, this protocol is not secure, because Alice can cheat by sending two $|+\rangle$ states to learn m_0 and m_1.

To avoid this trivial cheating strategy, the quantum OT protocol uses a quantum equivalent of ZK to prove to Bob that at least one of the received states is in the computational basis. It changes a bit the procedure to send bigger, more structured states encoding the original qubit instead of $|\psi^{(0)}\rangle$ and $|\psi^{(1)}\rangle$. Bob would conduct some non-destructive tests on this large state before collapsing it to a 2-qubit system to check that the encoding is valid, and that at least one state is not in superposition. In the protocol, the encoded state is defined as a superposition of pre-images of multiple images of a given hash function h.

This protocol can easily be generalized to string OT or k-out-of-n OT by sending one "hashed qubit" per bit to transmit, and proving via ZK the wanted properties on the number and position of the dummy hashes.

10.3 Quantum Point Obfuscation

According to quantum computation theory, any classical function f can be implemented by a quantum circuit. To implement such a function, a quantum circuit maps input register x and target register b, namely $|x \circ b\rangle$ to $|x \circ b \oplus f(x)\rangle$, where $\circ$ denotes concatenation. For convenience, the target register b can be set to zero. On this premise, we can define a quantum point function as follows:

Definition 10.4 A quantum point function U_α is defined as

$$U_\alpha : |x, 0\rangle \mapsto |x, P_\alpha(x)\rangle$$

where $\alpha \in \{0, 1\}^n$, and P_α is a classical point function.

Obviously, with an input in superposition $\sum_x a_x |x \circ 0\rangle$, the point function will also return a result of superposition $\sum_x a_x |x \circ P_\alpha(x)\rangle$, where a_x is a complex coefficient. After defining $\mathcal{U}_n = \{U_\alpha : \alpha \in \{0, 1\}^n\}$ and $\mathcal{U} = \bigcup_n \mathcal{U}_n$, we can construct the obfuscation of $\mathcal{U}$ and prove the following lemma.

Lemma 10.1 *A quantum point function family $\mathcal{U}$ is obfuscatable, under the quantum-accessible random oracle model.*

Note that the quantum-accessible random oracle R_q is interpreted as a length-preserving permutation oracle, $R_q : |x, y\rangle \mapsto |x, y \oplus R(x)\rangle$, where $R : \{0, 1\}^n \mapsto \{0, 1\}^n$ and $x, y \in \{0, 1\}^n$. The obfuscator for the quantum point function U_α works as follows: $O^R(U_\alpha)$ firstly makes query to oracle R_q with a classical bit string α to obtain $R(\alpha)$, then removes any information about α except $R(\alpha)$. When it receives an input $|x, 0\rangle$, $O^R(U_\alpha)$ accesses to quantum-accessible random oracle R_q with $|x, 0^n\rangle$ to obtain $|x, R(x)\rangle$. Finally, $O^R(U_\alpha)$ implements the checking function

$$Ch(x) = \begin{cases} 1 \ if \ x = R(\alpha) \\ 0 \ otherwise \end{cases}$$

by quantum gate $Ch_q : |x, y\rangle \mapsto |x, y \oplus Ch(x)\rangle$ and uses it on both the second register of return result of the oracle and the target register of input of the quantum circuit.

We can prove the functional equivalence property of U_α. Since quantum random query is made once for any input, polynomial slowdown condition holds. Now we prove the black-box property. For any adversary A, a simulator S^{U_α} can be constructed, and thus the black-box condition holds.

In the context of multi-qubit output, $|0^n\rangle$ becomes a possibly valid output. In classical case, the invalid output $\perp$ is introduced and a point function with multi-bit output is defined by

$$P_{\alpha,\beta}(x) = \begin{cases} \beta \ if \ x = \alpha \\ \perp \ otherwise \end{cases}.$$

where $\alpha, \beta \in \{0, 1\}^n$. As the quantum circuits are required to be invertible and unitary, concession must be made to keep consistence with well-formed QPT. Concretely, to avoid the use of $\perp$, we manually set $|0^n\rangle$ to generate an invalid input, therefore β is restricted in any bit-string in $\{0, 1\}^n$ except 0^n. In this sense, $P_{\alpha,\beta}$ will be modified as $P'_{\alpha,\beta}$ to output 0^n when $x \neq \alpha$.

Definition 10.5 A quantum point function with general output is defined as follows.

$$U_{\alpha,\beta} : |x, 0^n\rangle \mapsto |x, P'_{\alpha,\beta}(x)\rangle$$

where $\alpha \in \{0, 1\}^n$, $\beta \in \{0, 1\}^n \backslash 0^n$, and $P'_{\alpha,\beta}$ is the modified multi-bit point function.

Let $C_{\alpha,\beta}$ be a quantum circuit which implements $U_{\alpha,\beta}$. We define $C_n = \{C_{\alpha,\beta} : \alpha, \beta \in \{0, 1\}^n\}$.

Lemma 10.2 *A quantum point function family $\mathcal{C}$ with multi-qubit output is obfuscatable, under the quantum-accessible random oracle model.*

It is obvious that this obfuscation is valid, with the method similar to the proof of Lemma 10.1. We can see that $\mathcal{C}$ can be simply obfuscated. Note that we have only polynomial-many obfuscations, the probability that two of them happen to pick up a same result is negligible. Under this condition, the simulator will be able to simulate any adversary.

Definition 10.6 A quantum multi-point function with multi-qubit output is defined as

$$U_{(\alpha_1,\beta_1),\ldots,(\alpha_t,\beta_t)} : |x, y\rangle \mapsto |x, y \oplus P_{(\alpha_1,\beta_1),\ldots,(\alpha_t,\beta_t)}\rangle,$$

where $\alpha_i \in \{0, 1\}^n$, $\beta_i \in \{0, 1\}^n \backslash 0^n$ and $P_{(\alpha_1,\beta_1),\ldots,(\alpha_t,\beta_t)}$ is a classical function that maps $\{0, 1\}^n$ to $\{0, 1\}^{tn}$:

$$P_{(\alpha_1,\beta_1),\ldots,(\alpha_t,\beta_t)}(x)|_i = \begin{cases} \beta_i & if\ x = \alpha_i \\ 0^n & otherwise \end{cases}$$

and $P_{(\alpha_1,\beta_1),\ldots,(\alpha_t,\beta_t)}(x) = P_{(\alpha_1,\beta_1),\ldots,(\alpha_t,\beta_t)}(x)|_1 \circ \cdots \circ P_{(\alpha_1,\beta_1),\ldots,(\alpha_t,\beta_t)}(x)|_t$.

Let $C_{(\alpha_1,\beta_1),\ldots,(\alpha_t,\beta_t)}$ be a quantum circuit which implements $U_{(\alpha_1,\beta_1),\ldots,(\alpha_t,\beta_t)}$. Define $\mathcal{C}_n^t = \{C_{(\alpha_1,\beta_1),\ldots,(\alpha_t,\beta_t)} : \alpha_i, \beta_i \in \{0,1\}^n\}$. We define $\mathcal{C}^* = \bigcup_{poly\ t} \mathcal{C}_n^t$.

Lemma 10.3 *A quantum circuit family $\mathcal{C}^*$ is obfuscatable.*

To construct a QPT M that $M^{U_{\mathcal{C}_n^1\#\ldots\#\mathcal{C}_n^t}}$ computes $\mathcal{C}_n^t$, M has access to each oracle successively and simply concatenate all return values. To construct a QPT N that $N^{U_{\mathcal{C}_n^t}}$ computes $\mathcal{C}_n^1\#\ldots\#\mathcal{C}_n^t$, N query the oracle of $\mathcal{C}_n^t$ with the input register once and discard the unwanted part of output according to the control register. Since the control register is fixed to be basic state, measurement will not cause any information loss of the input register.

10.4 Quantum Zero-Knowledge Proof Based on Quantum Point Obfuscation

Quantum obfuscation allows users to run quantum circuits functionally as an unpenetrable black-box. In a quantum zero-knowledge circumstance, a protocol allows a verifier to accept a statement without leaking extra information. Moreover, the definition of both quantum obfuscation and QZK are simulation-based paradigm. All these similarities inspire us to study on applications of quantum obfuscation in QZK. In this section, we will introduce a QZK scheme based on quantum obfuscation.

The classical idea of constructing zero knowledge by obfuscation was initiated in the beginning of researches on obfuscation [11], but was realized relatively recently in the work of Bitansky [5]. Bitansky constructed a zero-knowledge scheme for languages in NP, based on obfuscation of point functions and 2-message delegation. Extending Bitansky's idea to quantum circumstance includes transferring the primitives such as NP, zero knowledge, delegation and obfuscation, into their quantum version.

1. Quantum version of NP: quantum Merlin-Arthur (QMA) [12]. QMA is defined analogously to NP, except that the witness is presented as a quantum state. For a language L in QMA, any statement $x \in L$ has (at least) a witness ρ helping x pass the family of verifier circuits $\{Ver_L(x, \rho)\}$, while any statement $x \notin L$ has no witness helping x pass the verifier.
2. Quantum version of zero knowledge: quantum zero knowledge (QZK). Transferring prover and verifier into quantum computer extends ZK to QZK. Here one interesting thing is that in quantum circumstances we do not limit a verifier to be honest because honest-verifier quantum zero knowledge equals general quantum zero knowledge [13].

3. Quantum version of delegation: secure multiparty quantum computation (SMQC). We roughly explain what we need from SMQC: essentially a 2-party quantum computation task. Consider Alice (holding secret state ρ_A) and Bob (holding a secret circuit $f = f(x)$). After particular operations, Bob obtains the result $f(\rho_A)$ while Alice obtains nothing about f. This task can be specialized from Liang's universal SMQC structure [14]. Since Liang's scheme is valid based on quantum oblivious transfer [15], the expectation for SMQC is feasible.
4. Obfuscation: quantum obfuscation. We define quantum obfuscation in Definition 10.4, and quantum point function with general outputs in Definition 10.5. According to Lemma 10.2, the quantum obfuscation for quantum point functions is valid.

In order to construct a QZK scheme, we start with the following awkward strategy: verifier V selects a verifier circuit $Ver_L(x, \rho)$, prover P sends $Ver_L(x, \rho)$ to V directly. It is unsound since P can always send 'yes'. To fulfill the requirement of soundness, we introduce SMQC strategy mentioned above. That is, P holds a secret ρ, V randomly generates a secret $|y\rangle$ and offers circuit working as

$$f_{|y\rangle}(\rho) = \begin{cases} |y\rangle & if\ Ver_L(x,\rho)\ says\ 'yes' \\ |0\rangle^{|y|} & otherwise \end{cases}$$

After calculation, P obtains the output of f and sends it to V, and V compares the result and its secret $|y\rangle$. Since SMQC leaks no information on $|y\rangle$, malicious P can not cheat V.

However, the scheme is now non-ZK: a cheating V may send any circuit of ρ (like trivial circuit $f(\rho) = \rho$) to learn about ρ. Here the key is to make sure that V compares the output of P without 'knowing' it. An intuitive way of doing so is obfuscation. Concretely, after calculation, P obtains the output of $f_{|y\rangle}(\rho)$, and sends a quantum obfuscation of quantum point function $O(U_{f_{|y\rangle}(\rho)})$ instead of $f_{|y\rangle}(\rho)$ itself. Now the whole scheme works as Table 10.1.

At last, we point out two notable details. One is that the scheme is somewhat similar to the quantum version of witness hiding scheme rather than zero-knowledge scheme in Bitansky's work [5], but satisfies QZK property. This is because that Bitansky's

Table 10.1 QZK scheme

Step 1	public input: x, P holds witness ρ, V holds verifier $Ver_L(x, \rho)$
Step 2	V randomly generates $|y\rangle$ and sends $f_{|y\rangle}(\rho)$ to P
Step 3	P receives function f', computes $f'(\rho)$ and sends a quantum obfuscation quantum point function $O(U_{f'(\rho)})$ to V
Step 4	V receives O' and accepts if $\delta_{O'}$ is identical to $U_{|y\rangle}$

attack on ZK requires repeated comparison of the obfuscation's output, which is ruled out by quantum no-cloning theory. The other is that Bitansky's structure is insecure in post-quantum cryptographic. The reason is that the 2-message delegation on which the scheme based is proved insecure against quantum adversaries [16].

10.5 Summary

In this chapter, we investigated the relationship between quantum-computable problems and those with zero-knowledge proof. We gave the construction of some quantum cryptographic protocols based on zero-knowledge proof. From the perspective of quantum obfuscation, we discussed an obfuscation-based QZK scheme and demonstrated the usability of a quantum point obfuscator in a quantum cryptographic protocol. This work can be applied to the quantum-resistance of cryptography, where algorithms occasionally rely on non-interactive zero-knowledge proof protocols. With the anticipated advent of a 'quantum Internet', such protocols and ideas may soon have utility and execution in the real world, and show some additional benefits over purely classical approaches, despite its classical origins.

References

1. Watrous, J.: Limits on the power of quantum statistical zero-knowledge. In: IEEE Symposium on Foundations of Computer Science (FOCS), pp. 459–468 (2002)
2. Watrous, J.: Zero-knowledge against quantum attacks. IAM J. Comput. **39**(1), 25–58 (2005)
3. Kobayashi, H.: General properties of quantum zero-knowledge proofs. In: Conference on Theory of Cryptography. Springer, Berlin, Heidelberg (2008)
4. Feige, U., Shamir, A.: Witness indistinguishable and witness hiding protocols. In: ACM Symposium on Theory of Computing (STOC), pp. 416–426 (1990)
5. Bitansky, N., Paneth, O.: Point obfuscation and 3-round zero-knowledge. In: Conference on Theory of Cryptography, pp. 190–208 (2012)
6. Shang, T., Chen, R.Y.L., Liu, J.W.: On the obfuscatability of quantum point functions. Quantum Inf. Process. **18**(2), 55 (2019)
7. Schnorr, C.P.: Efficient identification and signatures for smart cards. In: Advances in Cryptology-CRYPTO-9th Annual International Cryptology Conference, Santa Barbara, California, USA, August 20–24, pp. 239–252 (1989)
8. Chen, Y., Fan, X., Wen, X.: A zero-knowledge proof protocol based on quantum teleportation. Chin. J. Quantum Electron. **35**(2), 173–178 (2018)
9. Colisson, L., Grosshans, F., Kashefi, E.: Non-destructive zero-knowledge proofs on quantum states, and multi-party generation of authorized hidden GHZ states (2021). arXiv:2104.04742
10. Colisson, L., Muguruza, G., Speelman, F.: Oblivious transfer from zero-knowledge proofs, or how to achieve round-optimal quantum oblivious transfer and zero-knowledge proofs on quantum states. In: IACR Cryptology ePrint Archive (2023)
11. Hada, S.: Zero-knowledge and code obfuscation. In: International Conference on the Theory and Application of Cryptology and Information Security (ASIACRYPT 2000), vol. 1976, pp. 443–457 (2000)
12. Bookatz, A.D.: QMA-complete problems. Quantum Inf. Comput. **14**, 361–383 (2012)

13. Kobayashi, H.: General properties of quantum zero-knowledge proofs. In: Conference on Theory of Cryptography, pp. 107–124 (2008)
14. Liang, M.: Secure multiparty quantum computation based on bit commitment (2013). arXiv:1306.0447
15. Liang, M.: Symmetric quantum fully homomorphic encryption with perfect security. Quantum Inf. Process. **12**, 3675–3687 (2013)
16. Lo, H.K.: Insecurity of quantum secure computations. Phys. Rev. A **52**, 1154–1162 (1996)

Index

A

Access control, 2, 7, 40, 235–238, 240–243
Adjoint, 15
Adversary-challenger game, 37, 38, 46, 47, 114, 115
Aggregate signature, 201, 202, 204, 208–210
AND operation, 45, 55, 79
Attack game, 166, 167, 170, 171
Authenticated encryption, 70
Authentication tag generation, 181–183
Auxiliary problem, 235, 240, 241, 243
Auxiliary qubit, 45, 62, 65, 66, 80, 167, 168, 182, 183

B

BB84, 6, 248
Bell measurement, 55
Bell states, 25, 52, 54, 56, 64
Best-possible obfuscation, 2
Binary converter, 36, 37, 114
Bit error rate, 97, 98
Black-box quantum obfuscator, 21, 22, 174
Bloch sphere, 47, 57–59, 88, 91, 162
Braid group, 7

C

Challenge-response mode, 161, 171
Classical obfuscation, 1, 8, 12, 15, 21, 29, 41, 66, 235–237, 242
Classical one-way function, 159, 161, 184, 201
Clifford circuit, 136–138, 141, 144–149
Closure properties, 245
Cloud-based quantum computation, 101
CNOT, 18, 45, 52, 54, 62, 64, 79, 136, 144, 153, 160, 164, 177–180, 185, 189, 193, 194, 196, 206, 207, 227
Code obfuscation, 2
Coherent state, 67
Collision-free quantum one-way function, 20
Collision-free quantum states, 21
Collision-type error, 42
Collision resistance, 42, 211–213, 219–221, 228, 229
Combined point function, 2
Combined quantum circuits, 3, 8, 10, 11
Completely mixed state, 104, 124, 127, 136, 142, 149
Complete problems, 245
Complex coefficient, 32, 250
Composite function, 51, 68
Computational basis, 57, 64, 113, 162, 226, 227, 249, 250
Computing complexity, 224
Continuous-time Quantum Walk (CQW), 211
Controlled Alternate Lively Quantum Walks (CAQW), 159, 212, 216, 217, 219, 224–229
Controlled Interacting Quantum Walks (CIQW), 212
Controlled-Z gates, 201–203, 206, 207, 209

T. Shang, *Quantum Nonlinear Function Obfuscation Theory and Application*,
https://doi.org/10.1007/978-981-97-6722-9

Coupling generation algorithm, 188, 189, 197

D
DAG, 186, 189, 196, 197
d-dimensional unitary operator, 103, 105–107
Decay effect, 185, 186
Decoherence, 67, 70, 199
Decoherence noise, 67
Decrement gate, 227
Decrypting party, 104, 105, 107, 109, 118, 119, 121–123
Density operator, 71, 95, 236, 246
Dependent variable, 23, 24
Deterministic polynomial-time algorithm, 70
Diffusion and confusion property, 219, 223, 224
Direct attack, 163
Discrete logarithm problem, 4, 247
Discrete-time Quantum Walk (DQW), 211, 213, 220, 221, 224, 226
Dynamic Full Quantum One-way Function (DF-QOWF), 183, 184, 187–190, 192–196, 198, 199, 229
Dynamic mapping, 183

E
Eavesdropping attack, 163, 182, 210
Eigenspace, 17
Eigenvalue, 16, 17
Einstein-Podolsky-Rosen (EPR), 18, 135, 248
Encrypting party, 91, 104, 105, 108, 109, 117, 119, 122, 123, 126, 127, 132, 133
Enhanced quantum superdense coding, 59, 63, 67
Entangled quantum state, 204
Entangled state, 19, 64, 67, 160, 191, 201, 202, 205
Entanglement lost, 67
Evaluated circuit, 135, 138, 142, 143, 148, 149, 151
Exponential quantum states, 52, 54, 55, 130
Extractable obfuscation, 3

F
$\mathcal{F}$-homomorphic, 141, 148
Fidelity, 67, 83, 97, 98
Floyd-Warshall algorithm, 189, 194
Force search attack resistance, 218
Forgery attack, 182, 183, 201, 210, 217, 218
Forgery attack resistance, 218
Full Quantum One-way Function (F-QOWF), 159–162, 164–167, 172, 176, 177, 181, 183–189, 192–195, 200–208, 210, 229
Full quantum trapdoor one-way function, 183, 184, 195, 229
Fully Homomorphic Encryption (FHE), 110, 111, 135
Functional equivalence, 8, 22, 25, 32, 44, 46, 55, 56, 62, 66, 73, 75, 81, 88, 124, 125, 174, 180, 236, 251
Functionality encryption, 1

G
Generalized quantum power function, 7, 24, 51, 56, 59, 67
Generalized quantum power function with coefficient, 67
GHZ state, 64, 162, 194, 195, 249
GHZ-Computational-Hadamard Basis (GCH), 162, 164, 166
Graph-based access control problem, 235, 237, 238
Grouped Coarse-Grained Boson Sampling (GCGBS), 211, 212
Grover's algorithm, 4
Grover search, 150, 151, 154
Grover-type matrices, 214, 215

H
Hadamard gate, 18, 53, 55, 64, 144, 150, 153
Hash function, 41, 42, 45, 47, 48, 83, 159, 160, 204, 211, 212, 216–224, 227–229, 250
Heisenberg's uncertainty principle, 210
Hermitian conjugate, 15
Hermitian operator, 16, 17
Hilbert space, 15, 20, 38, 42, 71, 89, 102, 111, 113, 115, 162, 213, 236, 246
Homomorphic operators, 102, 103, 111
Honest-Verifier Quantum Zero-Knowledge proof (HVQZK), 247
HVQPZK, 247
HVQSZK, 247

Hypergraph-FQOWF, 205–208, 210

I
Image verification algorithm, 190–192, 200
Image-overlap verification algorithm, 192
Increment gate, 227
IND-CCA1, 69
IND-CCA2, 70
IND-CPA, 69, 70, 72, 77, 92, 95, 127, 128
IND-CPA security, 70, 77, 95
Independent variable, 23, 24
IND-secure, 70, 72, 74, 75, 78, 83, 87, 89, 93, 98
IND security, 74, 77, 83, 91, 93, 95, 97
Indistinguishability, 6, 41, 69, 70, 72, 82, 87, 88, 92, 93, 127, 247
Indistinguishability-secure quantum symmetric encryption scheme, 74
Indistinguishable Obfuscation (iO), 3, 7, 70
Indistinguishable security, 2, 80, 82, 134
Information-theoretically indistinguishable, 71
Information theory, 6, 87, 185
Injective function, 42
Inner product, 15, 16, 42, 43, 46, 47, 166, 170
Input-cell, 176–179, 182, 195, 203–206, 210
Interchangeability, 101, 103, 105, 107, 119, 121, 122
Inverse algorithm, 195
Inverse function, 90

K
Key update, 135–137, 140, 142, 145–148, 150, 153, 154
KO operation, 26

L
Leading Coefficient (LC), 56, 57, 59–63, 65, 66, 190, 192–194, 196, 200, 201
Leakage resilience, 70, 78
Learnable, 11
Learnable quantum circuit family, 11
Learning-with-errors, 66
Length-preserving permutation oracle, 32, 250
Lively quantum walk, 159, 211–217, 219, 221, 224–229
Logical quantum circuits, 4, 183, 184

M
Matrix decomposition, 143, 145, 146
Measurement operators, 17
Measurement result, 16, 19, 38, 53, 60, 74, 80, 83, 95, 116, 131, 139, 152, 154, 166, 182, 190, 191, 197, 198, 210
Minting algorithm, 187, 200
Mixed quantum state, 108, 126
Multi-bit output point function, 2, 40
Multi-parameter quantum state, 53, 130
Multi-participant quantum cryptographic, 205
Multi-valued quantum multi-point function, 39, 117, 125
Multi-valued quantum point obfuscation, 36, 47, 110, 111, 113, 117, 124, 155
Multi-valued quantum random Oracle model, 36–38, 113, 114
Multi-valued quantum single-point function, 39, 40, 46, 116, 117, 124, 125
Multi-valued quantum single-point obfuscation, 39, 116, 117, 119, 122, 127, 128
Multi-valued quantum state, 36, 38, 111–113, 115, 119, 122, 125
Multi-valued unitary operator, 38, 115, 119–122
Multipartite entanglement, 201

N
National Institute of Standards and Technology (NIST), 4
Nearly orthogonal, 37, 43, 113, 114
Noiseless amplifier, 67
Noisy Intermediate-scale Quantum (NISQ), 4, 183, 185
Non-Clifford gates, 102, 135, 138, 141, 145, 151
Non-cloning theorem, 37, 210
Non-interactive quantum homomorphic encryption, 101, 135, 155
Non-interactive Zero-knowledge Proof on Quantum State (NIZKoQS), 248, 249
Nonlinear function, 7, 15, 23–27, 29, 31, 51–56, 67, 129–132
Non-reusable, 243
Norm, 170
Normal operator, 16
NP, 247, 252

O
Obfuscatable, 8, 11, 12, 25, 26, 32–35, 43, 44, 46, 47, 55, 56, 62, 66, 124, 125, 239–242, 250–252
Obfuscated parameter, 53, 62, 66, 131
Obfuscation, 1–3, 6–12, 21–23, 25, 26, 31, 32, 34–37, 40, 41, 43–46, 48, 51–55, 59, 60, 62–64, 66–70, 73, 77, 79, 83, 88–90, 92, 93, 95, 98, 102, 104, 105, 107–109, 114, 115, 117, 122, 125, 127–131, 134, 155, 172, 174, 179, 180, 205–208, 235–243, 247, 250–253
Obfuscation-based full quantum one-way function, 176, 177, 181, 203, 204, 208
Oblivious Transfer (OT), 160, 249, 250, 253
One-way function, 7, 20, 21, 23, 78, 88, 129, 134, 159–162, 164, 165, 172, 173, 183, 185–187, 195, 203, 212
One-wayness, 41–43, 46, 161, 162, 164, 165, 181, 184, 187, 192–195, 201, 203, 207, 210, 218, 222, 229
One-way trapdoor function, 90, 92, 95
Oracle implementable, 8
Orthogonal, 37, 43, 46, 47, 112–114, 214, 215

P
Pauli matrix, 16, 24, 25, 28, 52, 53, 56, 70, 131
PC, 189–194, 196, 201
Periodic quantum walk on a cycle, 214, 218
Polynomial expansion, 22, 25, 44, 46, 55, 56, 62, 66, 73, 124, 125, 174, 236
Polynomial function, 25, 27, 31, 55–57, 68
Polynomial-sized pseudo-deterministic quantum circuit, 67
Polynomial slowdown, 2, 8, 33, 88, 172, 241, 251
Polynomial-Time (PT), 70
Positive operator, 16
Positive Operator-valued Measure (POVM), 17, 18
Post-quantum indistinguishable obfuscation, 7
Postulate of the measurement, 17
Postulate of the evolution, 17
Preimage resistance, 212, 213, 218
Privacy-preserving database query, 101
Private key, 54, 89–91, 102, 111, 131–133, 166, 187, 204, 209
Probabilistic Polynomial-Time (PPT), 70, 161, 184
Program obfuscation, 2
Projective measurement, 17, 168
Public key, 4, 21, 54, 89–91, 93, 95, 131–134, 161, 187, 204, 209
Public-key quantum money, 7, 186
Pure quantum one-way function, 177

Q
QASIG, 208, 209
QHFL, 216, 217, 219, 221–224, 226–229
QLib, 83, 97
QPZK, 246, 247, 250, 251
QSZK, 246, 247
Quantum access control, 235, 236, 238, 240–243
Quantum-accessible Random Oracle model, 19, 20, 29, 32, 33, 35, 41, 239, 243, 250, 251
Quantum adversary, 20, 160, 167
Quantum aggregate signature, 201, 202, 208–210
Quantum asymmetric encryption, 7, 87, 89, 91–93, 95, 97, 98
Quantum bit commitment, 6
Quantum Black-box obfuscator, 7, 73, 174, 242
Quantum blockchain, 201, 202, 204, 229
Quantum Circuit (QC), 1, 3–12, 21, 22, 25, 28, 29, 32–35, 37, 39, 40, 44, 51, 52, 56, 60, 61, 63–65, 67, 68, 70, 73, 80, 81, 83, 84, 87, 94, 97, 102, 106, 110, 115–117, 120, 123, 135, 136, 138–143, 145, 146, 148, 151, 152, 154, 155, 159, 161, 164, 172–174, 176–190, 192–198, 201, 202, 205–208, 210, 224, 226–229, 235, 236, 240, 241, 246, 247, 250–252
Quantum circuit family, 8, 11, 34, 35, 37, 115, 236, 240, 252
Quantum circuit optimization, 4, 184–188, 192
Quantum collision attack, 42–47
Quantum communication system, 53, 131
Quantum composite function, 68
Quantum cryptography, 1, 4–6, 12, 15, 20, 31, 87, 159, 161, 186, 187, 200, 235, 243, 245
Quantum currency, 6, 7, 186, 187, 200, 201
Quantum delegation computation, 247
Quantum digital signature, 113, 160, 172, 201
Quantum error correction, 87, 171

Quantum Fully Homomorphic Encryption (QFHE), 102, 110, 111, 113, 117, 119–125, 127–129, 135, 155
Quantum hash function, 41, 42, 45, 47, 48, 83, 159, 160, 211, 212, 216, 217, 221, 227–229
Quantum-hash random oracle, 113
Quantum Homomorphic Encryption (QHE), 6, 7, 69, 101–111, 124, 129, 131–143, 146–151, 154, 155
Quantum hypergraph states, 201–207, 209, 229
Quantum identity authentication, 143, 160, 161, 165–167, 170–172
Quantum IND-CCA2, 69
Quantum interpreter, 22, 52–56, 59, 61, 65, 68, 97, 130, 131, 236
Quantum iO, 7, 70
Quantum Key Distribution (QKD), 69, 160, 204, 235, 248
Quantum measurement, 16, 17, 20, 38, 53, 55, 62, 65, 112, 115, 116, 118, 130, 131, 134, 135, 173, 188, 193, 197, 218
Quantum measurement bases, 38, 112, 113, 115
Quantum mechanics, 5, 6, 17, 67, 87, 102, 110, 173, 186, 211, 229, 242
Quantum Message Authentication (QMA), 6, 172, 181, 182, 201, 252
Quantum money protocols, 160
Quantum multi-party computation, 6, 143
Quantum NAND relationship, 54, 55, 131
Quantum non-malleability, 69
Quantum nonlinear function, 7, 15, 23–27, 29, 31, 52–56, 67
Quantum n-th power function, 56–59, 63–66
Quantum obfuscated adversary-challenger game, 37, 114
Quantum obfuscation, 1, 6–8, 11, 12, 15, 21–27, 29, 35–37, 46, 48, 51, 52, 54–56, 59, 62, 63, 66, 67, 69, 70, 83, 87–90, 93, 95, 97, 98, 101, 102, 104, 105, 109, 113, 114, 125, 129–132, 134, 155, 159, 172–174, 176–181, 195, 201, 203, 204, 208, 229, 235–237, 242, 243, 245, 252–254
Quantum obfuscator, 7, 8, 21–23, 25, 26, 35, 38, 43–47, 52, 54–56, 59, 63, 66, 67, 70, 73, 74, 79, 115, 124, 130, 134, 174, 176, 177, 180, 236, 237, 242
Quantum oblivious transfer, 160, 249, 253
Quantum One-Time Pad (QOTP), 6, 69–71, 76, 79, 82, 87, 102, 111, 136–142, 146–150
Quantum one-way function, 20, 21, 23, 129, 134, 159–162, 164–167, 172, 173, 176, 177, 181, 183–190, 192–196, 198, 200–205, 208, 211, 229
Quantum operator, 15, 16
Quantum OR operation, 54, 131
Quantum point function, 2, 7, 23, 26–28, 31–33, 35, 36, 41, 45, 47, 73, 74, 79–81, 87–91, 98, 114, 124, 174, 181, 187, 188, 193–195, 197, 198, 235, 239, 245, 250, 251, 253
Quantum point function with general output, 251, 253
Quantum point obfuscation, 7, 23, 31, 35, 36, 40–48, 69, 73, 74, 79–81, 83, 87--89, 91, 98, 101, 103, 105, 110, 111, 117, 124, 129, 155, 172, 174, 181, 182, 247, 250, 252
Quantum polynomial function, 25, 27, 31, 55, 57, 68
Quantum Polynomial Time (QPT), 4, 9, 11, 21, 22, 33, 34, 44, 70–74, 76, 80, 82, 88, 92, 95, 96, 125, 131, 132, 134, 236, 251, 252
Quantum polynomial time algorithm, 37
Quantum power function, 7, 23, 24, 26–28, 31, 51–57, 59–62, 67, 93, 95–97, 130, 131, 155
Quantum power function interpreter, 28, 53, 54, 130, 131
Quantum power obfuscation, 24, 51, 54, 66, 67, 93, 95, 97, 98, 129–132, 134, 155
Quantum-qubit mapping, 187
Quantum query, 21
Quantum Random Oracle Model (QRO), 20
Quantum secret sharing, 6
Quantum secure direct communication, 6, 235
Quantum-secure obfuscator with auxiliary inputs, 35
Quantum-secure One-Way Function (qOWF), 7, 78, 160, 172, 173, 176–181, 183, 185, 187, 194, 201, 211, 212, 229
Quantum signature, 6
Quantum simulator, 22, 143
Quantum standard model, 46
Quantum state, 3, 6, 8, 15–29, 33, 35, 37–40, 42, 43, 46, 47, 52–57, 59–61, 63, 70, 71, 89–91, 95, 97, 98, 102–105, 107–109, 111–117, 119, 121–126, 128, 130–132, 134, 136–142, 145, 146, 148–150, 159, 160, 162, 165–167,

172, 174, 176–183, 187–190, 192–198, 200–206, 209–213, 216–218, 225, 226, 228, 229, 236, 238, 242, 243, 246–249, 252
Quantum state vector, 57
Quantum symmetric encryption, 7, 41, 69–72, 74, 75, 77–81, 83, 87, 182, 209
Quantum teleportation, 6, 7, 18, 19, 24–29, 52, 53, 55, 59, 60, 62, 63, 66, 67, 130, 248
Quantum Turing machine, 19
Quantum VBB obfuscation, 70
Quantum XOR operation, 53, 55, 131
Quantum Zero-Knowledge (QZK), 245–249, 252–254
Qubit rotation, 89–91, 98

R
Random Oracle (RO) model, 7, 19, 20, 29, 32, 33, 35–38, 40–42, 47, 56, 69, 96, 113–115, 124, 125, 239, 243, 250, 251
Restored leading coefficient, 62, 65
Restored parameter, 52, 53, 130
Reusable-black-box quantum obfuscation, 35
Reverse operation, 45, 80, 199
Reverse traversal technique, 185
Rotation operator, 47, 58, 135, 137–139, 141, 155, 163, 164
RS, 237

S
Secure Multiparty Quantum Computation (SMQC), 253
Secure quantum network coding, 6
Secure quantum one-way trapdoor function, 92, 95
Security analysis, 15, 19, 20, 29, 77, 81, 91, 95, 104, 108, 124, 131, 134, 142, 149, 166, 171, 182, 210, 217
Security reduction, 41, 211
Self-adjoint, 71
Semantic security, 69
Sensitivity, 219, 221–223, 228
Shor's algorithm, 4, 67, 201
Simple obfuscation, 2, 11
SP, 237
SQMC, 253
Standard model, 41, 42, 46
Strong Church-Turing thesis, 70
Strong one-way function, 161, 185, 212
Superposition state, 19, 20, 28, 89, 90, 150, 151, 164, 197, 243
SWAP-based BidiREctional Heuristic Search Algorithm (SABRE), 185–187, 189, 193, 194, 197–199
SWAP-test, 166, 167, 182, 190–192, 200, 211
Symmetric encryption, 2, 6, 7, 41, 69–72, 74, 75, 77–81, 83, 87, 182, 209

T
Tensor product, 54, 60, 128, 162
Toffoli Gate (TG), 36, 45, 61, 62, 66, 79, 80, 237
Trapdoor DF-QOWF, 195
Trivial quantum obfuscatable family, 11
Trivial quantum obfuscation, 11
$T/T^{\dagger}$ gate, 135, 139, 141, 142

U
Unforgeability, 70
Uniform distribution, 219, 224, 228
Unitary matrix, 3, 39, 40, 43, 96, 116, 117, 143–145, 155
Unitary operator, 16, 38, 101, 103, 105–107, 115, 119–122, 137, 167, 168, 212, 213, 216, 225
Unitary transformation, 17, 53, 56, 104, 124, 130
Universal Quantum Circuits (UQCs), 102, 110, 138, 145, 151

V
Vectors, 16, 38, 57, 112, 115, 116, 118, 168
Verifier impersonation attack, 163, 170
Virtual Black-box Obfuscator (VBB), 2, 41, 69, 70, 74, 76, 81, 93
Virtual Grey-box Obfuscation (VGB), 2, 3, 41

W
Witness Hiding (WH), 247, 253

X
X gate, 79
XOR operation, 53, 55, 79, 131, 153

Z
Zero-knowledge proof, 3, 245–249, 252, 254
Z gate, 201–203, 206, 207, 209

SPRINGER NATURE

GPSR Compliance

The European Union's (EU) General Product Safety Regulation (GPSR) is a set of rules that requires consumer products to be safe and our obligations to ensure this.

If you have any concerns about our products, you can contact us on ProductSafety@springernature.com

In case Publisher is established outside the EU, the EU authorized representative is:

Springer Nature Customer Service Center GmbH
Europaplatz 3
69115 Heidelberg, Germany

The manufacturer's authorised representative in the EU is Springer Nature Customer Service Centre GmbH, Europaplatz 3, 69115 Heidelberg, Germany. If you have any concerns regarding our products, please contact ProductSafety@springernature.com

Printed and bound by CPI Group (UK) Ltd, Croydon, CR0 4YY
01/10/2026
02225857-0004